THE ROADS FROM RIO

At the 1992 United Nations Conference on Environment and Development, popularly known as the Rio Earth Summit, the world's leaders constructed a new "sustainable development" paradigm that promised to enhance environmentally sound economic and social development. Twenty years later, the proliferation of multilateral environmental agreements points to an unprecedented achievement, but these agreements are worth examining for their shortcomings as well as their successes.

This book provides a review of twenty years of multilateral environmental negotiations (1992–2012). The authors have participated in most of these negotiating processes and use their first-hand knowledge as writers for the International Institute for Sustainable Development's *Earth Negotiations Bulletin* as they illustrate the changes that have taken place over the past twenty years. The chapters examine the proliferation of meetings, the changes in the actors and their roles (governments, non-governmental organizations, secretariats), the interlinkages of issues, the impact of scientific advice, and the challenges of implementation across negotiating processes, including the Framework Convention on Climate Change, the Convention to Combat Desertification, the Convention on Biological Diversity, the Commission on Sustainable Development, the UN Forum on Forests, the chemicals conventions (Stockholm, Basel, and Rotterdam), the Montreal Protocol on Substances that Deplete the Ozone Layer, the Convention on International Trade in Endangered Species, the Convention on Migratory Species, and the International Treaty on Plant Genetic Resources for Food and Agriculture.

Pamela S. Chasek is a professor of political science and director of the International Studies Program at Manhattan College in New York.

Lynn M. Wagner is the manager/editor of knowledge management projects for IISD Reporting Services.

THE ROADS FROM RIO

Lessons Learned from
Twenty Years of Multilateral
Environmental Negotiations

Edited by

Pamela S. Chasek
and
Lynn M. Wagner

Routledge
Taylor & Francis Group

NEW YORK AND LONDON

First published 2012
by RFF Press
711 Third Avenue, New York, NY 10017

Simultaneously published in the UK
by RFF Press
2 Park Square, Milton Park, Abingdon, Oxon OX14 4RN

RFF Press is an imprint of the Taylor & Francis Group, an informa business

© 2012 Taylor & Francis

Library of Congress Cataloging-in-Publication Data
The roads from Rio : lessons learned from twenty years of
multilateral environmental negotiations / edited by Pamela S. Chasek,
Lynn M. Wagner.
    p. cm.
Includes bibliographical references and index.
1. Environmental policy. 2. Global environmental change.
3. Environmental protection–International cooperation. 4. Environmental
impact analysis. I. Chasek, Pamela S., 1961- II. Wagner, Lynn M.
GE170.R56 2012
304.2–dc23   2011043322

ISBN13: 978–0–415–80975–7 (hbk)
ISBN13: 978–0–415–80977–1 (pbk)
ISBN13: 9780–203–12556–4 (ebk)

Typeset in Bembo
by Cenveo Publisher Services

About Resources for the Future *and* RFF Press

Resources for the Future (RFF) improves environmental and natural resource policymaking worldwide through independent social science research of the highest caliber. Founded in 1952, RFF pioneered the application of economics as a tool for developing more effective policy about the use and conservation of natural resources. Its scholars continue to employ social science methods to analyze critical issues concerning pollution control, energy policy, land and water use, hazardous waste, climate change, biodiversity, and the environmental challenges of developing countries.

RFF Press supports the mission of RFF by publishing book-length works that present a broad range of approaches to the study of natural resources and the environment. Its authors and editors include RFF staff, researchers from the larger academic and policy communities, and journalists. Audiences for publications by RFF Press include all of the participants in the policymaking process—scholars, the media, advocacy groups, NGOs, professionals in business and government, and the public.

CONTENTS

List of Illustrations   *ix*
Acknowledgments   *xii*
Foreword by Raúl A. Estrada-Oyuela   *xiv*
Foreword by Langston Goree   *xviii*
Acronyms   *xxi*

1   An Insider's Guide to Multilateral Environmental
    Negotiations since the Earth Summit   1
    Pamela S. Chasek and Lynn M. Wagner

PART I
Evolution of Process   **17**

2   Raising the Tempo: The Escalating Pace and
    Intensity of Environmental Negotiations   19
    Joanna Depledge and Pamela S. Chasek

3   Earth Negotiations on a Comfy Couch: Building
    Negotiator Trust through Innovative Processes   39
    Deborah Davenport, Lynn M. Wagner, and Chris Spence

4   Informing Policy: Science and Knowledge in Global
    Environmental Agreements   59
    Pia M. Kohler, Alexandra Conliffe, Stefan Jungcurt,
    Maria Gutierrez, and Yulia Yamineva

PART II
Evolution of Actors 83

5 Global Alliances to Strange Bedfellows:
The Ebb and Flow of Negotiating Coalitions 85
Lynn M. Wagner, Reem Hajjar, and Asheline Appleton

6 Singing the Unsung: Secretariats in
Global Environmental Politics 107
Sikina Jinnah

7 Witness, Architect, Detractor: The Evolving Role
of NGOs in International Environmental Negotiations 127
Stanley W. Burgiel and Peter Wood

PART III
Evolution of Issues 149

8 What's in a Name? 151
Pamela S. Chasek, Maria Gutierrez, and Reem Hajjar

9 Trade and Environment: Old Wine in New Bottles? 174
Kati Kulovesi, Sabrina Shaw, and Stanley W. Burgiel

10 Climate Change Bandwagoning: Climate Change
Impacts on Global Environmental Governance 199
Sikina Jinnah and Alexandra Conliffe

11 Implementation Challenges and Compliance
in MEA Negotiations 222
*Elisa Morgera, Elsa Tsioumani, Soledad Aguilar,
and Hugh S. Wilkins*

Conclusions 251

12 Lessons Learned on the Roads from Rio 253
Pamela S. Chasek, Lynn M. Wagner, and Peter Doran

*Appendix: Summaries of Selected Multilateral
Environmental Agreements* 273
List of Contributors 291
Index 296

ILLUSTRATIONS

Figures

2.1 Negotiation by exhaustion at the seventh session of the
United Nations Forum on Forests in 2007   28

2.2 The first process to "go paperless" was the Montreal Protocol
at its MOP 20 in Qatar in 2008   32

2.3 When secretariats project negotiating text on a big screen in
the front of the room, all delegations know whether or not
their proposals have been incorporated into the draft   33

2.4 South African President Jacob Zuma, Chinese Premier
Wen Jiabao, Indian Prime Minister Manmohan Singh, and
Brazilian President Luiz Inacio Lula da Silva at the 2009
Copenhagen Climate Change Conference   35

3.1 The "Vienna Setting," pioneered by Juan Mayr in the Biosafety
Negotiations, has been used in multiple negotiations since 2000   44

3.2 During the final negotiation session on the Biosafety
Protocol, delegates chose colored teddy bears from a
bag to determine the sequence of speakers   46

3.3 Using "comfy chairs" at a UNFCCC seminar   51

4.1 IPCC Secretary Renata Christ and IPCC chairman
Rajendra K. Pachauri   63

4.2 The POPs Review Committee   71

4.3 Indigenous and local communities at the CBD COP   76

5.1 European delegates confer during the third meeting of
the Conference of the Parties to the Rotterdam Convention
in October 2006   88

5.2 G-77 delegates consult on the penultimate day of UNFF 8   96
5.3 Ministers from China, Brazil, India, and South Africa at the
     2009 Copenhagen Climate Change Conference   100
6.1 Ahmed Djoghlaf, CBD Executive-Secretary   115
6.2 CMS Executive-Secretary Robert Hepworth shakes hands with
     Minister Makhtumkuli Akmuradov of Turkmenistan, following
     the signing of a Memorandum of Understanding (MOU) on the
     Saiga Antelope in November 2005   118
7.1 NGOs and groups such as the International Indigenous Forum
     on Biodiversity increased their involvement in CBD discussions   135
7.2 At ITTC 42, Greenpeace rappelled from the roof of the hotel
     in which the session was being held to suspend a banner
     protesting forest destruction   138
8.1 In 2007, the UNCCD COP adopted a ten-year strategic
     plan for the period 2008–2018   157
8.2 NGOs rallied through the final hours of the development
     of the Biosafety Protocol in January 2000   161
8.3 NGOs at the United Nations Climate Change Conference in
     Bali in 2007 expressed concern about the status of the
     REDD negotiations   165
8.4 Jan McAlpine, director of the UNFF Secretariat, stated in
     2009 that without some sort of input from forestry experts,
     forests under the UNFCCC would be seen as nothing but
     "sticks of carbon"   166
9.1 During the negotiations on the CBD's Guiding Principles
     on Invasive Alien Species, the Australian delegation
     objected to the final text because of the impact on trade   181
9.2 Negotiations on the Nagoya Protocol raised a suite of
     trade-related issues that continue after its adoption at
     COP 10 in October 2010   183
9.3 Bolivian President Evo Morales at UNFCCC COP 16 in
     Cancún in December 2010   186
9.4 Gerald Nelson, International Food Policy Research
     Institute, during the Cancún Climate Change Conference
     in 2010   190
10.1 Ahmed Djoghlaf, Executive-Secretary, Convention on
     Biological Diversity, and Luc Gnacadja, Executive-Secretary,
     UN Convention to Combat Desertification, at the Cancún
     Climate Change Conference in 2010   204
10.2 At the fourteenth meeting of the CBD's Subsidiary
     Body on Scientific, Technical and Technological Advice,
     a side-event looked at geo-engineering and the challenges
     faced by the CBD   206

10.3 NGOs at UNFCCC COP 15 calling for an end to
     deforestation   209
11.1 The CITES Secretariat proposed at COP 12 in 2002 to
     eliminate from the Convention's title the term "endangered
     species" to give account of its widened scope in addressing
     species that may not be in danger of extinction but nevertheless
     require regulation   224
11.2 During CBD COP 10, developing countries dramatically
     backed up their long-standing demands for sufficient
     financing for CBD implementation   227
11.3 Co-Chairs Jimena Nieto and René Lefeber celebrated the
     adoption of the Nagoya-Kuala Lumpur Supplementary
     Protocol on Liability and Redress to the Cartagena
     Protocol on Biosafety in October 2010   230
11.4 NGOs protesting Canada's position opposing a reference
     to the need to reduce GHG emissions by 25–40% at
     UNFCCC COP 13 in Bali, Indonesia   235

Tables

1.1 MEAs and International Environmental Processes
    Addressed in Each Chapter   11
5.1 Coalitions and Discussion Groups in Four Issue Processes   103
6.1 Sample of Biodiversity Treaties (1935–2004)   112
6.2 Global Chemicals and Toxics Agreements (1954–2006)   121
7.1 CBD Program of Work on Protected Areas   134
8.1 UNCCD Strategic Objectives and Expected Impacts: 2008–2018   158

Boxes

1.1 Multilateral Environmental Agreements Concluded: 1992–2012   4
1.2 Protocols and Amendments to Existing Treaties: 1992–2012   5
6.1 Biodiversity Liaison Group   116
6.2 Chief Executives Board on Coordination   120

ACKNOWLEDGMENTS

This book has been made possible by the inspiration, encouragement, and assistance of our colleagues at the *Earth Negotiations Bulletin*. We also thank those governments that have supported our work over the last two decades and those colleagues in UN bodies and treaty secretariats who have trusted us with the access that has allowed us to both contribute to and participate in these processes from the inside. We would also like to thank the delegates and others who have shared their insights with us "in the corridors" at the negotiations from which our ideas for this book grew. On the twentieth anniversary of the *Earth Negotiations Bulletin*, this book is our effort to give back to our sources and colleagues in the hope that it will provide even a small return on the inspiration and insights that they have given to us.

Art Hanson, President of the International Institute for Sustainable Development (IISD) from 1992 to 1998, brought the *Earth Negotiations Bulletin* to IISD and allowed us to run budget deficits for our first few years while we established ourselves and built up an external donor base, and we are grateful for his early support and confidence in what we were doing.

This project benefited from comments we received on drafts presented at the 2011 annual meeting of the International Studies Association, with special thanks to our discussant, Steinar Andresen. In addition, the authors of this volume thank the following people for their contributions to, reviews, and critiques of the various chapters: Steinar Andresen, Melanie Ashton, Douglas Bushey, Florence Daviet, Kelly Levin, Wagaki Mwangi, Uriel Safriel, Micaela Samodelov, Matt Sommerville, Andrey Vavilov, and Heather Wright. The authors of this volume contributed very useful reviews of other chapters in this collection as well as the introduction and the conclusion, and we greatly appreciate their enthusiasm and insights as we moved from concept to completion on this project. We also thank

Don Reisman, who first approached us with the idea for this book, and the anonymous peer reviewers, who gave us great feedback along the way.

Thanks are also due to the digital editors and photographers for the *Earth Negotiations Bulletin,* whose photographs appear throughout the book: Dan Birchall, Franz Dejon, Angeles Estrada, David Fernau, Anders Gonçalves da Silva, Tallash Kantai, Leila Mead, Diego Noguera, Markus Staas, and Ken Tong.

Last, but certainly not least, Pamela Chasek thanks her family—Kimo, Sam, and Kai Goree—for putting up with "another book" and providing patience, support, and love. Lynn Wagner thanks her family—Matt, Lydia, and Siri Grund—for their patience, humor, and understanding when she has excused herself to attend negotiations and to work on this book. It is for you that we have watched the direction taken on the roads from Rio, and for you that we hold hope for the direction that the future paths will take.

Pamela S. Chasek
Lynn M. Wagner

FOREWORD

Raúl Estrada

It is with great pleasure that I write this foreword for "The Roads from Rio". As one of many who walked those roads for years doing my best to contribute, I very much appreciate the efforts of the *Earth Negotiations Bulletin* over the last two decades, and I particularly appreciate the value of this book: it will help to remember, to learn, and to advance.

A team of scholars, lecturers, and experts has produced a methodologically well organized product. I have run most of those roads from Rio as a negotiator. Protecting the environment on behalf of my country is a must, because we are proud of our habitat and grateful for our territory's natural resources.

At the same time, in order to reach agreements, it is always necessary to take into account political and economic limitations, your own limitations and also those of others. We work on the land of the possible, which in many cases is far from the heaven of the best.

This book contains descriptions of basic facts and outcomes. It also has interpretations of the processes. By the late 1980s, the impact of the agreement reached in the Montreal Protocol on Substances that Deplete the Ozone Layer—differentiating for the first time commitments for developed and developing countries—and the inspiration and challenges that emerged from the report of the Brundtland Commission in *Our Common Future*, plus the fall of the Berlin Wall, created the circumstances to hope for a substantive change in the organized international community. We truly believed that material and human resources, until then devoted to the political confrontation of the Cold War, might constitute a peace dividend, devoted to fulfill mankind's needs, including environmental protection.

International concern with anthropogenic deterioration of the environment emerged earlier in the twentieth century with emphasis either on health protection, such as the International Labor Organization's Convention Concerning the Use of White Lead in Painting (1921), or on the preservation of species, such as the Convention Relative to the Preservation of Fauna and Flora in Their Natural State, adopted in London in 1933, to promote the creation of national parks and reserves, particularly in Africa. The trend grew in the 1940s and 1950s with a number of international agreements, but the holistic concept of environment only became visible for the international community in the 1960s.

Preparation for the 1972 Stockholm Conference was a hard diplomatic task, developed in ECOSOC, the Second Committee of the UN General Assembly and, of course, the PrepCom meetings. The name, UN Conference on the Human Environment, shows where the accent was placed. Global items were softly reflected in the agenda and the conclusions. We, developing countries, were very much concerned by the conflict between ecological protection and economic growth. Socialist countries didn't participate at the conference, with the exception of China, Cuba, and Yugoslavia.

UNEP and Habitat were established following recommendations of the conference. Their projects and numerous initiatives, including international instruments for the protection of the ozone layer and the Basel Convention on the Control of Transboundary Movements of Hazardous Wastes, paved the way to the 1992 Rio Conference.

Fifteen years after Stockholm, the international interest, in a progressive mood, was focusing on environmental needs. Decisions were adopted to prepare for the Rio Summit. Important political principles were enshrined in 1972 as, among others, the mandate to safeguard the natural resources of the earth for the benefit of present and future generations, and the recognition that states have the sovereign right to exploit their own resources pursuant to their own environmental policies, and the responsibility to ensure that activities within their jurisdiction or control do not cause damage to the environment of other states or of areas beyond the limits of national jurisdiction. But a number of new ideas were advanced in the international approach, starting with the name of the Rio summit: UN Conference on Environment and Development.

In Stockholm, all countries were considered on an equal footing: arriving at Rio, the principle of common but differentiated responsibilities was already consecrated. These, and other axioms included in the Rio Declaration such as the precautionary approach and the definition that environmental issues are best handled with participation of all concerned citizens at the relevant level, have since guided the work of negotiators on the roads from Rio de Janeiro.

The Rio Declaration also says that unilateral actions to deal with environmental challenges outside the jurisdiction of the importing country should be avoided. Following the language of Article XX of the 1947 General Agreement on Tariffs and Trade (GATT), the document adds that trade policy measures for environmental purposes should not constitute a means of arbitrary or unjustifiable discrimination or a disguised restriction on international trade. Trade limitations to protect natural resources have been applied since the beginning of the adoption of environmental agreements. Unilateral trade measures have caused disputes among governments, but no legal controversy has risen because of the content of an environmental agreement.

As can be seen in the chapters of this book, the roads were not perfectly paved but they allowed valuable progress for more than a decade. The situation is somehow less promising today. A landmark event marking the negative change of mood in international environmental policy is, in my view, the letter sent by U.S. President George W. Bush on March 11, 2001, informing senators that he would not look for the consent of the Senate to ratify the Kyoto Protocol that the United States had signed.

There was progress after that, but the shadow of limited participation of states in global efforts started growing. Readers will be able to form their own opinion out of the information and assessment of different negotiating processes described in this book. Naturally, I do not agree with each and every point made by the authors, but they clearly provide a wise approach to the facts.

The recent financial crisis and the serious difficulties of the world economy nowadays are weakening the international focus on environmental needs. The shy references to green economy in the G20 documents of 2009 are not yet driving efforts toward an ecologically inspired global economic model. The process looks like a loop, starting up softly in the late 1960s, growing slowly but consistently toward the 1992 Rio Summit, departing with new strength from there, but declining by the middle of the first decade of the twenty-first century.

The decision-making process for environmental matters is subject to comments in this book. Since international law and, consequently, international environmental law are decentralized systems, states are sovereign and there is no global authority over them. Ergo, the consent of each negotiating government is required to establish a legally binding regimen. A classic example is the 1982 UN Convention on the Law of the Sea, finally adopted by a majority of states but still excluding a major power from its constituency. For that reason, consensus has become the basic decision-making process on the roads from Rio.

In my experience, consensus is difficult to achieve but possible to obtain. It needs to be married with leadership. This book cites the case of Ambassador Tommy Koh dealing with the draft Rio Declaration. That is not the only case. Many others may be presented as examples. On the other hand, in my view, lack of leadership is a risk. The climate negotiating process was not adequately driven from 2005 to 2010, and this lack of leadership has been at the root of many failures, including the 2009 Copenhagen Conference.

The absence of organic international environmental governance is also part of the observations and conclusions in this book. Again, to improve the system, consensus is needed. In the UN system, in addition to the multilateral environmental agreements, the UN Environment Programme, the Commission on Sustainable Development (CSD), which was created after Rio, and the UN

Development Programme also contribute in this arena. But in spite of the efforts of the UN Secretary-General, they work without the necessary coordination. Global environmental governance could be enhanced in a top-down kind of process suggested by France a few years ago, or in a bottom-up approach such as enhanced coordination among clusters of conventions with a similar focus, such as atmosphere, biological processes, or chemical protection. The World Intellectual Property Organization (WIPO) could be a model to follow if the bottom-up approach is the preferred option. In such a case, international bureaucracies need to be carefully aligned.

There is a long way to go on the roads from Rio. As in any other travel, economic possibilities and friendliness among participants are conditions for success. The information and judgments contained in this book can help to select the itinerary and advise participants on the journey.

Ambassador Raúl A. Estrada-Oyuela
Buenos Aires, Argentina

FOREWORD

Langston Goree

It was during the third meeting of the Preparatory Committee (PrepCom) for the United Nations Conference on Environment and Development (UNCED), back in August 1991, that I convinced a small group of colleagues to join me at a hotel in Ferney-Voltaire, across the French border from the meeting in Geneva, to write a summary of the first week of negotiations. As one of the co-chairs of the daily NGO Strategy Sessions, I thought that having a summary of progress on issues would be a useful tool for civil society as we prepared to do our lobbying each morning. However, after we uploaded our first "issue" to the NGO computer networks such as Econet and Greennet and made some photocopies in Yolanda Kakabadse's office in the Palais des Nations, a strange thing occurred. Somehow, bootleg versions of our report began circulating among government delegates and we began getting requests from governments for copies. One delegate actually said, "I need to fax this back to my capital to let them know what is going on here." A delegate from the Soviet Union waved a faxed copy at me and demanded that I give him the next issue when it was ready, "so that I can send to Moscow and not have Moscow send to me." At that point I realized that, while what we were doing was useful for NGOs, we were doing something that would also benefit many other actors in the negotiation process.

During the interim period, between the end of the third PrepCom and the beginning of the final, five-week meeting of the Preparatory Committee in March 1992, Johannah Bernstein, Pamela Chasek, and I decided to publish daily issues of our reports at PrepCom IV. No one had told us that following thirty-four negotiating streams and publishing each day for five weeks with only three writers would be impossible, so on March 2, 1992 we published the first issue of the *Earth Summit Bulletin,* with the assistance of Island Press and with funding from the Ford Foundation, The Compton Foundation, and the W. Alton Jones Foundation.

As the weeks passed, many of the delegates came to rely on our daily reports and appreciated the transparency that we brought to the process, often contributing bits of text to our work from closed meetings. Even in those early days, diplomats would slip us copies of draft texts and whisper to us what was really going on in the meeting. It was in our third issue that we began the "In the Corridors" section, which has proven to be a favorite part of the "ENB" (*Earth Negotiations Bulletin*) for our readers over the last twenty years.

Following the success of the *Earth Summit Bulletin* in New York, we were convinced that we had to try to raise the money and publish in Rio during the Earth Summit in June 1992. Johannah Bernstein undertook the job of fundraising, convincing several governments and a new Canadian organization called the International Institute for Sustainable Development (IISD) to support us. We raised enough to pay for our travel to Rio, room, board, a small office in the Rio Center, and 10,000 photocopies per day. Somehow, the three of us survived, but not without the help of Maurice Strong's assistant, Lucas Assunção, who presented us with "All Areas Special Guest" passes, which guaranteed us unprecedented access throughout the meeting. Since that meeting in 1992, we have never participated in a meeting as NGOs or media, but always as guests of the Secretariat. Both this distinction that we were part of the conference process, and our decision to remain politically neutral in our reports, have contributed greatly to our success over the years.

Following UNCED, Johannah, Pam, and I returned to our professional and academic pursuits and thought we were leaving the *Earth Summit Bulletin* behind. However, the director of communications at IISD, Nick Sonntag, approached us to ask if we would like to continue publishing, but as part of IISD. As a result, during the last quarter of 1992, we were acquired by IISD, changed the name of the publication to the *Earth Negotiations Bulletin* (ENB) and continued to follow the work of the UN General Assembly's Second Committee as it dealt with the Rio follow-up issues, including the creation of: the Commission on Sustainable Development, the United Nations Convention to Combat Desertification, the Conference on Straddling Fish Stocks and Highly Migratory Fish Stocks, and the Conference on the Sustainable Development of Small Island Developing States. Since then, the ENB has grown and thrived under the tent of IISD, becoming a flagship publication of the organization.

Knowledge-based organizations, such as IISD's Reporting Services, are essentially worth no more than their accumulated intellectual capital. Our value as an institution cannot be measured in equipment, patents, buildings, or land. Instead, our value lies in the contribution that our team members make, based on their knowledge, to the reports and information that we produce. We succeed or fail as a conference reporting service and knowledge broker on the accuracy, reliability, and timeliness of our work, and for this we rely on our writers, editors, and thematic experts to be the best of the best.

Today, with more than sixty writers and editors with one foot in academia and the other in real-time policymaking, the ENB provides a grounded and "insider" perspective on environmental governance and multilateral agreement processes that is unique among researchers. The long hours spent by ENB writers sitting inside the conference rooms during informal–informal negotiations, contact groups, working groups and high-level segments, shoulder to shoulder with policymakers at work, have resulted in a perspective on these events that is extraordinary. Over the past twenty years, we have provided coverage of more than 525 meetings of thirty different environment and development-related negotiation processes, in addition to coverage of nearly 200 other meetings as part of our *Your Meeting Bulletin* publication. This book, in addition to the archives of all of our coverage, which is available at www.iisd.ca, is the culmination of twenty years of sitting in the back of the room. As many have commented over the years, the *Earth Negotiations Bulletin* and the transparency it provides to multilateral environmental negotiations represent one of the most important "unofficial" outputs of the Earth Summit.

Langston James "Kimo" Goree
Director, IISD Reporting Services

ACRONYMS

ABS	access and benefit sharing
ACIA	Arctic Climate Impact Assessment
AHEG PARAM	Ad Hoc Expert Group on Consideration with a View to Recommending Parameters of a Mandate for Developing a Legal Framework on All Types of Forests
AIA	advance informed agreement
ALBA	Bolivarian Alliance for the Peoples of Our America
AOSIS	Alliance of Small Island States
APEC	Asia-Pacific Economic Cooperation
BASIC	Brazil, South Africa, India, and China
BCH	Biosafety Clearing-House
BINGO	Big International Non-Governmental Organization
BLG	Biodiversity Liaison Group
C&I	criteria and indicators
CANZ	Canada, Australia, and New Zealand
CBD	Convention on Biological Diversity
CCS	carbon capture and storage
CDM	Clean Development Mechanism
CEB	Chief Executives Board
CFCs	chlorofluorocarbons
CITES	Convention on International Trade in Endangered Species of Wild Fauna and Flora
CLI	country-led initiative
CMS	Convention on Migratory Species
CO$_2$	carbon dioxide
COFO	Committee on Forestry (FAO)

COP	Conference of the Parties
CPF	Collaborative Partnership on Forests
CSD	UN Commission on Sustainable Development
CST	Committee on Science and Technology
ECOSOC	United Nations Economic and Social Council
EIG	Environmental Integrity Group
ENB	*Earth Negotiations Bulletin*
EU	European Union
ExCOP	Extraordinary Meeting of the Conference of the Parties
FAO	Food and Agriculture Organization of the United Nations
FSC	Forest Stewardship Council
G-77	Group of 77 (developing country negotiating bloc)
GATT	General Agreement on Tariffs and Trade
GC/GMEF	UNEP Governing Council/Global Ministerial Environment Forum
GEF	Global Environment Facility
GHGs	greenhouse gases
GM	genetically modified
GMOs	genetically modified organisms
GNP	gross national product
GURTs	genetic use-restriction technologies
GWP	global warming potential
HCFCs	hydrochlorofluorocarbons
HFCs	hydrofluorocarbons
IAF	international arrangement on forests
IFF	Intergovernmental Forum on Forests
IGOs	intergovernmental organizations
IISD	International Institute for Sustainable Development
ILCs	indigenous and local communities
INCD	Intergovernmental Negotiating Committee on the International Convention to Combat Desertification
IPCC	Intergovernmental Panel on Climate Change
IPF	Intergovernmental Panel on Forests
IPRs	intellectual property rights
ITPGR	International Treaty on Plant Genetic Resources for Food and Agriculture
ITTA	International Tropical Timber Agreement
ITTC	International Tropical Timber Council
ITTO	International Tropical Timber Organization
IUCN	International Union for the Conservation of Nature and Natural Resources/World Conservation Union
JI	Joint Implementation

JUSSCANNZ	Japan, United States, Switzerland, Canada, Australia, Norway, New Zealand (coalition)
LBI	legally binding instrument
LDCs	least developed countries
LMOs	living modified organisms
LULUCF	Land Use, Land-Use Change and Forestry
MA	Millennium Ecosystem Assessment
MDGs	Millennium Development Goals
MEAs	multilateral environmental agreements
MLS	Multilateral System
MOP	Meeting of the Parties
NBSAP	National Biodiversity Strategy and Action Plan
NGOs	non-governmental organizations
NLBI	non-legally binding instrument
ODA	official development assistance
ODS	Ozone Depleting Substance(s)
OECD	Organization for Economic Cooperation and Development
OPEC	Organization of Petroleum Exporting Countries
PGRFA	plant genetic resources for food and agriculture
PIC	prior informed consent
POPs	persistent organic pollutants
POPRC	Persistent Organic Pollutants Review Committee
REDD	reducing emissions from deforestation and forest degradation
REDD+	reducing emissions from deforestation and forest degradation and the role of conservation, sustainable management of forests and enhancement of forest carbon stocks in developing countries
RST	Review of Significant Trade
SBI	Subsidiary Body for Implementation
SBSTA	Subsidiary Body for Scientific and Technological Advice
SBSTTA	Subsidiary Body on Scientific, Technical and Technological Advice
SFM	sustainable forest management
SICA	Central American Integration System
SIDS	small island developing states
SMTA	standard material transfer agreement
TEEB	The Economics of Ecosystem Services and Biodiversity Study
TRAFFIC	Trade Records Analysis of Flora and Fauna in Commerce
TRIPS	WTO Agreement on Trade-related Aspects of Intellectual Property Rights
UNCCD	United Nations Convention to Combat Desertification

UNCED	United Nations Conference on Environment and Development
UNCHE	United Nations Conference on the Human Environment
UNCSD	United Nations Conference on Sustainable Development (Rio+20)
UNCTAD	United Nations Conference on Trade and Development
UNEP	United Nations Environment Programme
UNFCCC	United Nations Framework Convention on Climate Change
UNFF	United Nations Forum on Forests
UNGA	United Nations General Assembly
WCED	World Commission on Environment and Development
WCMC	World Conservation Monitoring Center
WMO	World Meteorological Organization
WSSD	World Summit on Sustainable Development
WTO	World Trade Organization
WWF	World Wildlife Fund/Worldwide Fund for Nature

1

AN INSIDER'S GUIDE TO MULTILATERAL ENVIRONMENTAL NEGOTIATIONS SINCE THE EARTH SUMMIT

Pamela S. Chasek and Lynn M. Wagner

The year 1992 was a time of phenomenal flux and fluidity in the international community. The Soviet Union disintegrated, taking with it the Communist alternative to the market economy and ending the Cold War, which had dominated international politics for four decades. Yugoslavia fragmented into five new states and war erupted. Twelve European countries signed the Maastricht Treaty creating the European Union, a milestone in political and economic integration. China signed the Nuclear Non-Proliferation Treaty. There were earthquakes in Turkey, Nicaragua, and Indonesia, and devastating hurricanes in Florida and Hawaii. An oil tanker, the *Aegean Sea*, went aground near Spain, spilling 80,000 tonnes of crude oil. Rigoberta Menchú, an indigenous Guatemalan woman, won the Nobel Peace Prize. Egypt's Boutros Boutros-Ghali was elected as the first UN Secretary-General from Africa. As the Soviet Union and Yugoslavia collapsed, their territories splintered into new states and between 1990 and 1992 UN membership had grown by twenty to reach 179. Amidst all of this turmoil and change, the United Nations Conference on Environment and Development (UNCED) convened in Rio de Janeiro in June 1992, marking the largest ever gathering of heads of state and government to promote economic development, reduce poverty, and preserve and protect the earth's ecological systems.

The Earth Summit, as the conference became known, presented the first post-Cold War test of whether the international community possessed the will and the wisdom to create a new system based on cooperation to develop sustainably and improve the human condition. As UNCED Secretary-General Maurice Strong pointed out in 1992, "This is the first time in history that the leaders of all countries of the earth will assemble to make decisions that will literally shape the future of the world" (Shabecoff 1996, 129). It was a chance for the United Nations to prove that it could be an effective force in defining a new form of global peace. And it was the first significant opportunity for the North (industrialized countries) and the South (developing countries) to elaborate on how they might combine economic and social development concerns with those of environmental protection as governments struggled to operationalize the concept of sustainable development. Despite the euphoria immediately following the Earth Summit that a new "partnership" had been struck between North and South, Maurice Strong acknowledged that only time would tell whether it would produce historic changes in the way the human community ordered its affairs; the conference itself, he said, was only a beginning (Strong 1992).

Indeed, the Earth Summit marked a number of beginnings: the creation of new institutions for sustainable development, including the United Nations Commission on Sustainable Development; the signing of two new environmental treaties—the United Nations Framework Convention on Climate Change and the Convention on Biological Diversity; and the adoption of the Rio Declaration on Environment and Development, Agenda 21, and the Forest Principles.[1] The Earth Summit was also the first UN conference to firmly embrace the participation of representatives from non-governmental organizations (NGOs), business, and industry. Agenda 21 created the concept of "Major Groups"—Business and Industry, Children and Youth, Farmers, Indigenous Peoples, Local Authorities, NGOs, the Scientific and Technological Community, Women, and Workers and Trade Unions—whose participation was recognized as necessary to achieve sustainable development.

The Earth Summit also launched a new era in the creation of international environmental treaty regimes, which redefined the nature of global environmental governance and multilateral environmental negotiations. Leading into the June 1972 United Nations Conference on the Human Environment (UNCHE), also known as the Stockholm Conference, many of the approximately 200 global or regional environmental treaties that had been registered with the United Nations and other international organizations at that point were bilateral or did not establish governing bodies or requirements for regular meetings. The United Nations Environment Programme (UNEP) was created as a result of the decisions taken at the Stockholm Conference and stimulated new activities in the international environmental arena, but twenty years later, leading into the June 1992 United Nations Conference on Environment and Development, multilateral environmental accords remained focused on preservation or conservation, usually of a specific media, such as oceans, or specific fauna (UNEP 2007).

The organization of UNCED stemmed from two United Nations General Assembly (UNGA) resolutions. In 1983, UNGA passed a resolution (38/161) on the "Process of Preparation of the Environmental Perspective to the Year 2000 and Beyond." This resolution established the World Commission on Environment and Development (WCED). Chaired by Gro Harlem Brundtland, former Prime Minister of Norway, the WCED came to be known as the

"Brundtland Commission" and delivered in its 1987 report, *Our Common Future*, the most cited definition of sustainable development: development that meets the needs of the present without compromising the ability of future generations to meet their own needs (WCED 1987). Subsequently, UN member states adopted UNGA resolution 44/228 in December 1989, calling for a global meeting to devise integrated strategies that would halt and reverse the negative impact of human activities on the physical environment and promote environmentally long-term sustainable economic development in all countries. Under the masterful leadership of its chair, Singapore Ambassador Tommy Koh, the UNCED preparatory committee undertook two years of intensive preparations and negotiations, in which the international community acknowledged the interaction between society and bio-physical problems as well as the global nature of environmental problems and their solutions.

Together, the agreements launched at the Earth Summit constituted a blueprint of a global partnership for achieving sustainable development. Among its many recommendations for the promotion of a new global sustainable development paradigm was a call for the development of additional international environmental law through the process of multilateral negotiations. In Chapter 39 of Agenda 21 (International Legal Instruments and Mechanisms), the participating states agreed that there was a need for "further development of international law on sustainable development, giving special attention to the delicate balance between environmental and developmental concerns" (United Nations 1992, 281). With this in mind, Agenda 21 recommended the negotiation of a number of new international conventions and protocols that would further the integration of environment and development in the international system. This recommendation triggered what could be referred to as an explosion of interest in multilateral environmental negotiations. Following UNCED, the number of multilateral environmental agreements and organization of meetings to discuss global efforts to redress these problems has expanded, with the total number of environmental agreements now reaching over 1,000 (data from Mitchell 2002–2011).

The negotiation of multilateral environmental agreements, and follow-up negotiations to further their development and to assist in their implementation, has become a prominent characteristic of the twenty years since the Earth Summit. Since 1992, seventeen new global environmental agreements have been adopted (see Box 1.1), in addition to twenty-one new protocols or amendments to existing global treaties (see Box 1.2). Under the 1979 Bonn Convention on Migratory Species, fifteen new memoranda of understanding on the conservation of specific species have been concluded. In addition, nearly one hundred regional treaties, protocols, and amendments to existing regional treaties or protocols have been concluded in the twenty years since 1992. And these numbers do not even include agreements to establish regional environmental or conservation institutions or commissions, to manage shared watercourses, or to address nuclear waste, transport or safety issues. Furthermore, many of these and other conventions and protocols adopted before 1992 convene regularly scheduled meetings of their governing bodies, which negotiate resolutions and decisions related to the implementation of the agreements, creating an ever increasing number of days that are scheduled annually to negotiate sustainable development issues.[2]

BOX 1.1 MULTILATERAL ENVIRONMENTAL AGREEMENTS CONCLUDED: 1992–2012

1992   United Nations Framework Convention on Climate Change

1992   Convention on Biological Diversity

1994   International Tropical Timber Agreement

1994   United Nations Convention to Combat Desertification in those Countries Experiencing Serious Drought and/or Desertification, particularly in Africa

1995   Agreement for the Implementation of the Provisions of the United Nations Convention on the Law of the Sea of December, 10 1982 relating to the Conservation and Management of Straddling Fish Stocks and Highly Migratory Fish Stocks

1996   International Convention on Liability and Compensation for Damage in Connection with the Carriage of Hazardous and Noxious Substances by Sea

1998   Rotterdam Convention on the Prior Informed Consent Procedure for Certain Hazardous Chemicals and Pesticides in International Trade

2001   International Convention on Civil Liability for Bunker Oil Pollution Damage

2001   Stockholm Convention on Persistent Organic Pollutants

2001   Agreement on the Conservation of Albatrosses and Petrels

2001   International Convention on the Control of Harmful Anti-Fouling Systems on Ships

2001   International Treaty on Plant Genetic Resources for Food and Agriculture

2004   International Convention for the Control and Management of Ships' Ballast Water and Sediments

2006   International Tropical Timber Agreement

2009   Hong Kong International Convention for the Safe and Environmentally Sound Recycling of Ships

2009   Agreement on Port State Measures to Prevent, Deter and Eliminate Illegal, Unreported and Unregulated Fishing

2009   Statute of the International Renewable Energy Agency

BOX 1.2 PROTOCOLS AND AMENDMENTS TO EXISTING TREATIES: 1992–2012

1992   Copenhagen Amendments to the 1987 Montreal Protocol on Substances that Deplete the Ozone Layer

1992   Protocol to amend the 1969 International Convention on Civil Liability for Oil Pollution Damage

1992   Protocol to amend the 1971 International Convention on the Establishment of an International Fund for Compensation for Oil Pollution Damage

1993   Amendment to Annex I and II to the 1972 Convention on the Prevention of Marine Pollution by Dumping of Wastes and Other Matter

1993   Agreement to Promote Compliance with International Conservation and Management Measures by Fishing Vessels on the High Seas

1994   Agreement relating to the Implementation of Part XI of the United Nations Convention on the Law of the Sea of 10 December 1982

1996   Protocol to the 1972 Convention on the Prevention of Marine Pollution by Dumping of Wastes and Other Matter

1995   Amendment to the 1989 Basel Convention on the Control of Transboundary Movements of Hazardous Wastes and their Disposal

1997   Montreal Amendment to the 1987 Montreal Protocol on Substances that Deplete the Ozone Layer

1997   Kyoto Protocol to the 1992 United Nations Framework Convention on Climate Change

1999   Beijing Amendment to the 1987 Montreal Protocol on Substances that Deplete the Ozone Layer

1999   Basel Protocol on Liability and Compensation for Damage Resulting from Transboundary Movements of Hazardous Wastes and their Disposal

2000   Cartagena Protocol on Biosafety to the Convention on Biological Diversity

2000   Protocol on Preparedness, Response and Cooperation to Pollution Incidents by Hazardous and Noxious Substances

2003   Protocol to the 1992 International Convention on the Establishment of an International Fund for Compensation for Oil Pollution Damage

2003   Protocol on Civil Liability and Compensation for Damage Caused by the Transboundary Effects of Industrial Accidents on Transboundary Waters to the 1992 Convention on the Protection and Use of Transboundary Watercourses and International Lakes and to the 1992 Convention on the Transboundary Effects of Industrial Accidents

2003	Protocol on Strategic Environmental Assessment to the Convention on Environmental Impact Assessment in a Transboundary Context
2003	Protocol on Pollutant Release and Transfer Registers to the Convention on Access to Information, Public Participation in Decision-Making and Access to Justice in Environmental Matters
2003	Amendments to the Annex of the Protocol of 1978 relating to the 1973 International Convention for the Prevention of Pollution by Ships
2010	Nagoya–Kuala Lumpur Supplementary Protocol on Liability and Redress to the Cartagena Protocol on Biosafety
2010	Nagoya Protocol on Access to Genetic Resources and their Fair and Equitable Sharing of Benefits Arising from their Utilization to the Convention on Biological Diversity

The expanding number of meetings and agreements has followed an organic path, with the negotiation of one treaty leading to follow-up meetings to address implementation efforts, and new understandings of the requirements of sustainable development leading to additional meetings and mechanisms to address it and to incorporate the relevant actors. Each conference and event has been organized as an independent instrument, based on the global priorities at that time, but a review of the progression of events reveals an evolutionary path, the understanding of which contributes to a better understanding of the process and outcome at each point on the policymaking road. For example, UNCHE, in 1972, stimulated the development of environmental institutions, including UNEP and national environment ministries. These new actors triggered the ability to assess and identify further issues to be addressed. UNCED, in 1992, initiated global efforts to address sustainable development in a holistic way. Ten years after UNCED, the World Summit on Sustainable Development (WSSD) convened in Johannesburg, South Africa, and focused on bringing the three pillars of sustainable development (economic, social, and environmental) together again, and sought to reinvigorate implementation efforts on the UNCED outcomes in part through encouraging partnerships between public (government) and private (businesses and non-governmental groups) actors (Churie Kallhauge et al. 2005).

And now, on the eve of the twentieth anniversary of the 1992 Earth Summit, the international community is preparing for another global event, the United Nations Conference on Sustainable Development (UNCSD, also referred to as Rio+20), which seeks to build on past events and redirect efforts where the international community has found shortcomings with existing approaches. The twenty years since the Earth Summit, punctuated by the WSSD and UNCSD, reveal a story of different interpretations of sustainable development that have reflected the different priorities of the "North" and "South". The themes selected for UNCSD—a green economy in the context of sustainable development and poverty eradication, and the institutional framework for sustainable development—reflect the continuing struggle to bring the three pillars of sustainable development together.

While these international efforts, and this book, focus on the international environmental negotiations and agreements coming out of the 1992 Earth Summit, it is useful to keep in mind that the events at UNCED and during the past twenty years have had impacts beyond the multilateral environmental agreements and the UN system, including in the World Trade Organization, international financial institutions, regional and subregional organizations, national governments, and civil society. There are many lessons learned from analyzing the past twenty years of MEA negotiations and we have come a long way, but negotiating agreements can only go so far. Once an agreement is reached, it must be ratified and implemented nationally, and many factors influence the success of these efforts, including other elements of the international system. Nonetheless, the negotiation experience of the past twenty years remains a valid area of inquiry, as it can demonstrate the challenges, power relationships, and competing interests that the international community has faced.

Negotiations as an International Environmental Policymaking Tool

Although various types of public–private partnerships and other voluntary approaches are becoming increasingly important, the traditional "hard law" multilateral environmental agreement (MEA) is still the dominant form of international environmental governance, although it is interesting to note that the nature of an instrument (whether it will be a treaty or some other type of agreement) is often one of the most difficult issues to reach agreement on. And these processes are no easy feat. The task of achieving international agreement on any issue is extremely challenging, and environmental issues are no exception, with the combination of scientific uncertainty, politics, economics, citizen activism, and lobbying by industry and special interest groups. The negotiations themselves are complex and involve multiple, interlinked issues and actors. They are usually preceded by extensive scientific fact-finding. The debate then centers on various response strategies, although political and economic rivalries and sovereignty or national interest concerns often get in the way. Any solution is constrained by the costs of deploying new technologies and concerns about the fair allocation of the costs involved (Chasek 2001a, 2).

Negotiations represent the process through which states create these collective arrangements for environmental management. International negotiation is the process by which representatives from two or more states seek to combine divergent values in an agreed decision (Zartman and Berman 1982, 1). Multilateral negotiation can be defined as the process of simultaneous negotiation by three or more parties over one or more issues that aims at agreement acceptable to all participants (Touval 1991, 351). Multilateral negotiations are multi-party, multi-issue and multi-role. Within this context, multilateral environmental negotiations have their own set of distinguishing attributes.[3] Although not unique to multilateral environmental negotiations, the multi-party character of these talks introduces certain challenges. Although any party may agree with any other party, and eventually all parties presumably reach agreement, the multi-party assumption implies the existence of autonomous entities, each with interests and interest groups of their own that underpin their positions (Chasek 2001a; Zartman 1994). As a result, group dynamics and networks play an important role in the process, especially with regard to coalition formation, the role of interpersonal relationships, the development of leadership, and the institutional context within which many multilateral negotiations take place (Chasek 2001a, 25).

While states play the primary roles in determining the outcomes, they are not the only actors in multilateral environmental negotiations. There is a multiplicity of different types of participants, including the scientific community, NGOs, business and industry, the media, intergovernmental organizations (IGOs), and secretariats who influence the positions of individual state actors, the international negotiation process, and the outcomes. Thus, the conclusion of a successful agreement requires interdisciplinary approaches to define the national interest of a party or interest group, with input collected from policymakers, scientists, states, and a variety of other stakeholders who will be involved in implementing any agreement reached (Faure and Rubin 1993, 21).

Environmental negotiations involve multiple, interconnected issues. What may at first appear to be a relatively straightforward environmental issue, such as protecting the ozone layer, soon turns out to have important economic, social, and political implications. And when these negotiations take place in the international arena, the various implications multiply in importance and assume the form of additional issues on the table (Faure and Rubin 1993, 21). Furthermore, the technicality of many environmental issues often requires the diplomats to deploy technical expertise in addition to diplomatic experience (Scott 1985, 45).

Furthermore, environmental issues are sufficiently complex that a variety of negotiating, decision-making and advisory roles are necessary. For example, Sjöstedt, Spector, and Zartman (1994, 11) claim negotiators are found to either Drive, Conduct, Defend, Brake, or Cruise. Drivers try to organize the participants to produce an agreement that is consonant with their own interests. Conductors also seek to produce an agreement but from a neutral position, with no interest axe of their own to grind. Defenders focus on a limited number of the issues on the table, concerned more with a specific issue than with the overall success of the negotiations. Brakers oppose or modify proposals, either related to the broad treaty regime or on specific issue items. Cruisers are filler, with no strong interests of their own and, thus, are available to act as followers.

Depending on the roles that participating states play in a negotiation, the role diversity can allow the issue and party complexities to be combined in an agreeable outcome, or to delay or prevent an outcome.

Another characteristic of multilateral environmental negotiations is the need for cooperation to underpin collective progress on tackling an environmental problem through an MEA, given free rider concerns. Delegates to multilateral negotiations usually find themselves confronted with a procedural trade-off between efficiency, fairness, and legitimacy (Hopmann 1996, 247). Therefore, majority rule or the "one state, one vote" voting procedure does not always work. Although a consensus-based model would never work, or be expected, within an individual country's domestic government decision making (such as in parliament), it is the process that the international community must rely upon. The most common decision rule in environmental treaties since 1992 has been the attainment of consensus—a decision rule in which, essentially, abstention is an affirmative rather than a negative vote (Zartman 1994, 5). Consensus involves the continuation of negotiations in an endeavor to reach a compromise that will be reasonably acceptable to all, so that even states with some objections will not press them by insisting on a vote, but will content themselves with making statements on their position before or after the adoption of the agreement. In this way, although the resultant agreement will generally, in order to generate consensus, be expressed in more general or "constructively" ambiguous terms (sometimes referred to as "least common denominator agreement"), the expectation is that it is more likely to be put into practice by all states affected than if it were adopted by a divisive vote (Birnie and Boyle 1992, 19; Chasek 2001a, 32). Nonetheless, pressure to accept consensus language is often so high that parties may agree to the text at the eleventh hour so as not to be blamed for the failure of the negotiations.

To effectively address global environmental issues, there is a need for democratic negotiation processes that facilitate engagement and bring together the agreement of the international community. Although the system that we have can be cumbersome and difficult, it has resulted in unparalleled achievements over time. Yet the system has become more and more complex since 1992, as environmental issues have become more and more integrated into economic policies and the various MEAs have created their own policy interlinkages. Increasingly, international policymakers have tried to rationalize the existing negotiation processes and reform the system of international environmental governance, but the identification of, let alone agreement on, a comprehensive and effective overhaul of the system has been difficult to achieve.

Our View of the Post-UNCED Negotiation Process

This book provides a comprehensive view of multilateral environmental negotiations since 1992, focusing on the evolution of process, actors, and issues.

The authors of this volume present a unique perspective on the evolution of environmental negotiations. We have participated in most of these negotiating processes and have used our first-hand knowledge as writers for the *Earth Negotiations Bulletin* (ENB) to describe the changes we have seen over this twenty-year period.

Since 1992, delegates, NGOs, the media, and academics that follow UN environment and development negotiations have relied on the *Earth Negotiations Bulletin* (ENB) as an indispensable record of a number of negotiating processes (Chasek 2001b). The ENB, which is published by the Winnipeg, Canada-based International Institute for Sustainable Development (IISD), provides objective and balanced daily and summary reports of UN negotiations on environment and development issues. Beginning with coverage of the UNCED preparatory process in 1992 (under the name *Earth Summit Bulletin*), the ENB has provided coverage of more than 525 meetings of thirty different environment- and development-related negotiation processes.

ENB writers and editors come from over forty countries on six continents. Over the past two decades, more than 200 people have worked on the ENB from various academic and professional backgrounds. They include former diplomats and United Nations officials, academics, lawyers, students, and journalists. The authors of this volume represent a cross-section of this group and, with one foot in academia and the other in real-time policymaking, ENB writers provide a grounded and insider perspective on multilateral environmental negotiations that is unique among researchers in this field. As a result, the chapters in this book represent the culmination of years of attendance, observation, and analysis of formal and informal negotiations, contact groups, working groups, and plenary sessions, shoulder to shoulder with policymakers, UN officials, Ambassadors, ministers, and heads of state and government.

This book is divided into three sections that examine the evolution of process, actors, and issues of multilateral environmental negotiations since 1992. Using a cross-section of multilateral environmental negotiating processes as examples, we use our unique vantage point to illustrate key trends and changes that we have witnessed over the past twenty years across different fora (see Table 1.1).

Evolution of the Process of Multilateral Environmental Negotiations: How Are the Negotiations Conducted?

The way in which negotiations are conducted, impasses are brokered, and scientific advice is integrated into the negotiations has evolved since 1992. As Depledge and Chasek emphasize in Chapter 2, there has been a proliferation of agenda items, documents, and informal groups and late nights, along with an escalation in the level at which many negotiations are conducted, coupled with advances in information technology, which have dramatically accelerated the speed and extent of communications. This chapter documents this intensification, finding

TABLE 1.1 MEAs and International Environmental Processes Addressed in Each Chapter

MEAs and Bodies in Case Studies	Ch. 2	Ch. 3	Ch. 4	Ch. 5	Ch. 6	Ch. 7	Ch. 8	Ch. 9	Ch. 10	Ch. 11
UN Conference on Environment and Development (UNCED)						X				
UN Commission on Sustainable Development (CSD)				X					X	
UN Convention to Combat Desertification (UNCCD)	X		X			X				
United Nations Framework Convention on Climate Change (UNFCCC)	X	X	X	X		X	X			X
Forests	X	X		X		X		X	X	
Montreal Protocol on Substances that Deplete Ozone	X		X		X					
Convention on Biological Diversity (CBD) and/or its Protocols	X	X	X	X		X		X	X	X
Convention on International Trade in Endangered Species (CITES)			X	X		X	X		X	X
International Treaty on Plant Genetic Resources for Food and Agriculture (ITPGR)										X
Agriculture								X		
Convention on Migratory Species (CMS)	X			X						
Ramsar Convention on Wetlands of International Importance	X									
Rotterdam, Stockholm, and Basel Conventions	X			X						

that it reflects the rising profile of environmental issues and the maturity of many regimes.

Chapter 3, by Davenport, Wagner, and Spence, reviews activities in biosafety, forests, and climate change negotiations in attempts to build trust among actors. The chapter suggests that, in cases where there is the potential for compromise, a well-formulated approach may help generate the trust and "space" needed for negotiators to find common ground. It also notes that the proliferation of "Track II-type" trust-building techniques in various multilateral environmental processes indicates that the value of building trust among negotiators has not been lost on meeting organizers.

The final chapter in the first section examines the provision and integration of scientific advice into negotiations. Kohler, Conliffe, Jungcurt, Gutierrez, and Yamineva examine the ongoing institutionalization of scientific advice in a variety of regimes. While scientific advice is an important feature of environmental policymaking, the authors note that "Science advice has been shown to be unable to overcome fundamental differences in economic interest, limited in its ability to resolve value conflicts and issues of international equity, and has not improved decision making in negotiations reigned by mistrust where delegates have engaged in legal trench wars." Science has not provided the panacea to environmental decision making that some hoped it would.

Evolution of Actors: Who *is at the Table?*

The next section reviews the evolution of the actors involved in the negotiations during the two decades following the Earth Summit, examining coalitions, secretariats, and non-governmental organizations.

Chapter 5 presents the evolution of state coalitions since 1992. Wagner, Hajjar, and Appleton identify the coalitions that states have used to present their interests and how they have evolved from political groupings formed primarily around North (developed countries) and South (developing countries) allegiances to more specific interest-based alignments.

Chapter 6 reviews the role that secretariats play in advancing an MEA-based regime. Jinnah presents an examination of what she labels "a defining feature" of post-Earth Summit global environmental politics: "overlap management." In undertaking this role, she notes that "secretariats have capitalized on their unique characteristics to emerge as key actors in ameliorating a central cause of stagnant global environmental problem solving in the post-1992 period: too many organizations with too few resources."

NGOs, the third category of actors examined in this section, have experienced the greatest change since 1992. Burgiel and Wood review the diversity of groups within the NGO category in the CBD and forests regimes, which they find differ by issue focus, political orientation, strategic approach, geographical representation and spread, size, and resources. They categorize the roles or strategic orientation of NGOs as witness, architect and/or detractor, and suggest that this division provides a way to understand strategic differences among various NGOs as well as within a single NGO over time.

Evolution of Issues: What *is* Under Discussion?

The final section of this book contains four chapters that examine different aspects related to *what* is under discussion. As Chasek, Gutierrez, and Hajjar note in Chapter 8, on issue definition within different environmental and sustainable development negotiation processes, "Half the battle of multilateral negotiations is reaching agreement on what issues will actually be negotiated." What states have agreed to negotiate confines the realm of solutions that they can discuss. The examples of issue definition presented in this chapter demonstrate the challenge of defining the issues as well as the increased linkages between economics, trade, development, and environmental issues that have characterized environmental negotiations since 1992.

Chapter 9 examines how controversies relating to trade and environment have surfaced in multilateral negotiations, both under MEAs and under the World Trade Organization (WTO). Kulovesi, Shaw, and Burgiel elaborate on how trade concerns have infiltrated multilateral environmental negotiations both as high-profile, contentious issues of debate and as a general subtext to ongoing discussions. With reference to agriculture, biodiversity, and climate change, the authors illustrate the broadening of the trade and environment debate, precisely because environmental policy has become increasingly inseparable from economic and trade policy.

We then move from examining the implications of how issue definition and substantive priorities within individual sustainable development regimes and vis-à-vis regimes outside the sustainable development realm to examining how issues are defined in a situation of what Jinnah and Conliffe explore as "bandwagoning" onto the climate change regime. In Chapter 10, Jinnah and Conliffe find that defining an issue area in relation to other environmental issue areas can involve positive and negative results. They suggest that "bandwagoning allows for other environmental issues to benefit from the contemporary political/financial attention on climate politics," building momentum for the other regimes' climate-related aspects as well as helping to define issue linkages among sustainable development regimes. However, this examination indicates that it can also "involve political maneuvering that dilutes climate or linking regimes' policy."

Chapter 11, by Morgera, Tsioumani, Aguilar, and Wilkins, examines the evolution of implementation challenges under four MEAs, in light of how parties have defined and redefined MEAs' mandates over time. This chapter offers a study in how negotiators' definitions of implementation challenges and compliance systems have facilitated or stalled the conclusion of negotiations of MEAs or broader agenda items under MEAs.

Still a Long Way to Go

This book illustrates that much has changed in the twenty years since the Earth Summit and, from this perspective, the road ahead will also be characterized by a continuous evolution of process, actors, and issues. As environmental issues and our understanding of them become more complex and increasingly integrated with local, regional, and global economic issues and interests, the international community may have to consider new ways of doing business. However, change is not always easy. For decades, in spite of the difficulties and frustrations inherent in the current environmental governance system within the UN system, multi-lateral negotiation has remained a key approach to international policy approaches. As long as governments are not ready and willing to surrender global environmental decision making and their own sovereignty to a supranational body with legislative and enforcement powers, multilateral negotiation will continue to be an important means of managing global and transboundary environmental problems. We have written this volume in an effort to provide insights into this ever-evolving process of international environmental governance, based on our view of the negotiations as participant observers. In the concluding chapter, we draw on the chapters and our two decades of observations to put these negotiations into the global context and set forth a number of lessons learned for the next twenty years.

Notes

1 The Forest Principles are officially named "Non-Legally Binding Authoritative Statement of Principles for a Global Consensus on the Management, Conservation and Sustainable Development of All Types of Forests."
2 A good source of information about environmental law is ECOLEX, a database operated jointly by FAO, IUCN, and UNEP. See www.ecolex.org.
3 This is not a complete list of attributes. For more details, see Chasek 2001a, and Sjöstedt 1993.

Works Cited

Birnie, Patricia W. and Alan E. Boyle. 1992. *International Law and the Environment.* New York: Oxford University Press.

Chasek, Pamela S. 2001a. *Earth Negotiations: Analyzing Thirty Years of Environmental Diplomacy.* Tokyo: UNU Press.

Chasek, Pamela S. 2001b. NGOs and State Capacity in International Environmental Negotiations: The Experience of the Earth Negotiations Bulletin. *Review of European Community and International Environmental Law* 10(2):168–176.

Churie Kallhauge, Angela, Gunnar Sjöstedt, and Elisabeth Corell. 2005. *Global Challenges: Furthering the Multilateral Process for Sustainable Development.* Sheffield, UK: Greenleaf Publishing.

Faure, Guy-Olivier and Jeffrey Z. Rubin. 1993. Organizing Concepts and Questions. In *International Environmental Negotiation,* edited by Gunnar Sjöstedt. Newbury Park, CA: Sage Publications.

Hopmann, P. Terrence. 1996. *The Negotiation Process and the Resolution of International Conflicts*. Columbia, SC: University of South Carolina Press.

Mitchell, Ronald B. 2002–2011. *International Environmental Agreements Database Project (Version 2010.3)*. http://iea.uoregon.edu/ (accessed June 22, 2011).

Shabecoff, Philip. 1996. *A New Name for Peace*. Hanover, NH: University Press of New England.

Scott, Norman. 1985. The Evolution of Conference Diplomacy. In *International Geneva, 1985*, edited by L. Dembinski. Lausanne: Payot Lausanne.

Sjöstedt, Gunnar. 1993. *International Environmental Negotiation*. Newbury Park: Sage Publications.

Sjöstedt, Gunnar, Bertram I. Spector and I. William Zartman. 1994. The Dynamics of Regime-building Negotiations. In *Negotiating International Regimes: Lessons Learned from the United Nations Conference on Environment and Development*, edited by Gunnar Sjöstedt, Bertram I. Spector and I. William Zartman. London: Graham and Trotman, 3–20.

Strong, Maurice. 1992. Opening Statement to the Rio Summit (3 June 1992). http://www.mauricestrong.net/20081004165/rio/rio/rio2.html (accessed June 12, 2011).

Touval, Saadia. 1991. Multilateral Negotiation: An Analytic Approach. In *Negotiation Theory and Practice*, edited by J. William Breslin and Jeffrey, Z. Rubin. Cambridge, MA: The Program on Negotiation at Harvard Law School.

UNEP (United Nations Environment Programme). 2007. *Negotiating and Implementing Multilateral Environmental Agreements (MEAs): A Manual for NGOs*. Nairobi: UNON. http://www.unep.org/dec/docs/MEAs%20Final.pdf (accessed June 19, 2011).

United Nations. 1992. *Agenda 21*. New York: United Nations.

WCED (World Commission on Environment and Development). 1987. *Our Common Future*. New York: Oxford University Press.

Zartman, I. William. 1994. Two's Company and More's a Crowd: The Complexities of Multilateral Negotiation. In *International Multilateral Negotiation*, edited by I. William Zartman. San Francisco: Jossey Bass Publishers, 1–12.

Zartman, I. William and Berman, Maureen R. 1982. *The Practical Negotiator*. New Haven: Yale University Press.

PART I
Evolution of Process

2

RAISING THE TEMPO

The Escalating Pace and Intensity of Environmental Negotiations

Joanna Depledge and Pamela S. Chasek

The Earth Summit in Rio de Janeiro in 1992 launched a new era of global environmental negotiations. Only the most far-sighted, however, could have predicted that, over the next twenty years, the global environmental agenda would grow in scope and intensity to compete with the "hard" issues of security, disarmament, and trade. Two decades later, the calendar of global environmental meetings consists of a near continuous round of negotiations, including regular issue-specific talks on climate change, biodiversity, desertification, chemicals, fisheries, forestry, ozone depletion, hazardous waste, and endangered and migratory species, among others. Factoring in the various ministerial and summit-level gatherings regularly convened by the UN Environment Programme (UNEP), the UN General Assembly (UNGA) and the UN Commission on Sustainable Development (CSD), not to mention numerous national, subregional, and regional workshops and discussions, barely a fortnight goes by without an environmental meeting somewhere on the planet.

And at stake is not just the number of negotiating sessions, but also their pace and complexity, characterized by a proliferation of agenda items, documents, informal groups, late nights, and, of course, political controversies. At the same time, there has been an escalation in the level at which many negotiations are conducted, with ministers and even heads of state now becoming involved in day-to-day talks that used to be the preserve of diplomats and other functionaries. These trends in the evolution of global environmental negotiations have also coincided with extraordinary advances in information technology, which have dramatically accelerated the speed and extent of communications. All this amounts to a clear *intensification* of negotiations across the global environmental arena. This chapter examines this phenomenon, and the impact it has had on global environmental policymaking.

A Crowded Schedule

More Treaties

The annual calendar of global environmental negotiations has become ever more crowded over the past twenty years, primarily because the total number of environmental treaties in force or under negotiation, and environmental processes underway, has mushroomed. Prior to the 1970s, there were already nearly 200 global or regional environmental treaties registered with the United Nations and other international organizations. However, many of these were bilateral, did not establish governing bodies or separate secretariats, and their parties did not meet on a regular basis. Thus, when heads of state gathered in Rio de Janeiro in 1992, there were only a handful of international environmental treaties that held regularly scheduled conferences or meetings of the parties, including:

- 1971 Ramsar Convention on Wetlands of International Importance;
- 1973 Convention on International Trade in Endangered Species of Wild Fauna and Flora (CITES);
- 1983 International Tropical Timber Agreement; and
- 1985 Vienna Convention for the Protection of the Ozone Layer and its 1987 Montreal Protocol on Substances that Deplete the Ozone Layer.

However, following the Earth Summit, a series of new global environmental treaties entered into force, all of which convened regular negotiating sessions. These include:

- 1989 Basel Convention on the Control of Transboundary Movement of Hazardous Wastes and their Disposal;
- 1992 UN Framework Convention on Climate Change (UNFCCC) and its 1997 Kyoto Protocol;
- 1992 Convention on Biological Diversity (CBD) and its 2000 Cartagena Biosafety Protocol;
- 1994 UN Convention to Combat Desertification (UNCCD);
- 1998 Rotterdam Convention on the Prior Informed Consent Procedure for Certain Hazardous Chemicals and Pesticides in International Trade;
- 2001 Stockholm Convention on Persistent Organic Pollutants (POPs); and
- 2001 International Treaty on Plant Genetic Resources for Food and Agriculture.

In addition to these global treaties, numerous regional agreements on watercourses, fisheries, and air pollution, as well as annual meetings of the UNEP Governing Council/Global Ministerial Environment Forum (UNEP GC/GMEF) and the CSD, also compete for time on the international "to do" list.

More Meetings

For many global environmental treaties, the typical meeting cycle consists of two main negotiating sessions—a conference of the parties (COP) or meeting of the parties (MOP), plus at least one meeting of a subsidiary body or bodies—each lasting one or two weeks. Some environmental conventions have kept to this cycle annually, such as the ozone regime. Others have cut back on their annual COPs; the biodiversity and desertification COPs, for example, meet only every two years, even though they initially met annually. The Basel, Rotterdam, and Stockholm Conventions hold COPs every two to three years. In some cases, notably the climate change and biodiversity regimes, there has been what might be termed "session creep." In the run-up to key conferences, where protocols are to be adopted or other important decisions taken, additional negotiating sessions have been organized to provide more time for parties to reach a consensus. In 2009, for example, in the run-up to the Copenhagen Climate Change Conference that was due to define the future of the climate change regime post-2012, delegates attended six negotiating sessions, covering ten weeks, instead of the usual annual cycle of two fortnight-long sessions. When the Copenhagen Climate Change Conference failed to reach a comprehensive outcome, the pace continued almost unabated in 2010 and 2011. As part of the negotiations on the Cartagena Biosafety Protocol, several informal sessions and two extraordinary sessions of the COP were also convened in 2000 and 2001. Similarly, the CBD added additional negotiating sessions onto the calendar in 2010 to ensure completion at its COP 10 in Nagoya, Japan, of the Nagoya-Kuala Lumpur Supplementary Protocol on Liability and Redress, and the Nagoya Protocol on Access and Benefit Sharing (ABS).[1] The concern is that the tendency to add such sessions—especially in the climate change regime—appears to be edging the expanded annual cycle toward the norm, rather than the exception, draining negotiators as well as donor budgets for MEA-related activities, including implementation of the agreements under discussion.

Over the past decade in particular, regular negotiating sessions in many environmental regimes have been increasingly supplemented by additional gatherings *in between* sessions, including workshops, expert and committee meetings, and political consultations. The climate change calendar on the UNFCCC website, for example, reveals that some kind of meeting organized by the secretariat was scheduled for nearly 140 days during 2009. The joint calendar of the Basel, Rotterdam, and Stockholm Convention Secretariats also points to a crowded agenda on chemicals management and hazardous waste. In yet another treaty regime, in 2010 alone the CBD Secretariat convened over fifty meetings and workshops.

This busy schedule reflects the maturity of many environmental regimes, which have developed a sophisticated institutional architecture to support and monitor negotiations and implementation. A particularly important source of intersessional work lies in the many technical and regional events taking place to boost on-the-ground action. The CBD and UNCCD, for example, hold regular capacity-building and technical workshops aimed at treaty implementation. Many of these smaller meetings and workshops are now scheduled back to back with full negotiating sessions, or are held in clusters. While this reduces the number of journeys and travel costs, it often means that a standard two-week negotiating session can stretch out much longer.

The demands on the time of environmental delegates do not end with the official meetings organized by the regimes themselves. Delegates regularly receive invitations to additional "unmissable" events, convened by other organizations. These include thematic summits organized by the UNGA (such as those on climate change in 2009, biodiversity in 2010, and desertification in 2011), along with smaller, more select get-togethers such as the Major Economies Forum convened by the United States, or regional parleys, for example, under the auspices of the African Union or the Asia-Pacific Economic Cooperation group (APEC). All this is in addition to the private bilateral and multilateral talks that are critical to ensuring progress in the negotiations. Delegates from "major" countries, as well as secretariat staff, may find themselves almost permanently on the road—or at the airport—as major conferences loom. Of course, all these meetings require preparation beforehand, and debriefing on return. It goes without saying that the life of an environmental negotiator is a busy one.

The proliferation of meetings impacts disproportionately on poorer countries. Sending delegates to an ever-increasing number of environmental meetings has resource implications, which many countries simply cannot afford. The result is that many smaller developing countries are not represented at some intersessional gatherings, thereby losing potential influence. It is important to recognize, however, the efforts of the international community to address this problem: most regimes within the UN system cover the travel and subsistence expenses of one or two delegates from developing countries, including for many official intersessional meetings. Nonetheless, the point remains that a greater number of meetings spreads resources more thinly, which is felt far more keenly by smaller and poorer countries. Furthermore, the more time officials spend on the road, the less time they spend actually working on treaty implementation on the ground. In a large developed country this may not be a big issue, but in a small developing country it could have a serious impact on implementation activities, as the same small office is often responsible for both negotiation and implementation.

Another repercussion is the human cost, which is not confined to poor delegations. The quasi-nomadic lifestyle of environmental negotiators, with long periods away from home, inevitably takes its personal toll. Complaints of "meeting fatigue" or "negotiation fatigue" are now rife, with participants expressing weariness of such frequent travel. Delegates to climate change conferences routinely joke that they should purchase an apartment in Bonn (the seat of the

Secretariat) since they spend so much time there. In the run-up to the Copenhagen Climate Change Conference, the *Earth Negotiations Bulletin* (2008) reported that "previously unheard comments about 'family friendly' scheduling and meeting facilities are coming to the fore in a process where delegates previously took pride in their 'stamina' in handling the long hours. As one delegate joked, 'immunity discussions should include the many divorces this Convention will cause over the next two years.'" This experience is shared in other regimes. During the final stages of the CBD negotiations on ABS in Nagoya, a delegate confided to the *Earth Negotiations Bulletin* (2010b) that as "most ABS negotiators have been travelling non-stop for two years to negotiate this Protocol, they want to get this done and get their lives back."

In addition, there can be no ignoring the carbon footprint of the growing environmental "travelling circus." In 2005, researchers estimated that fifteen years of climate policy negotiations had, so far, caused CO_2 emissions of about 150,000 tonnes, mostly through air transportation (Michaelowa and Lehmkuhl 2005). This is roughly equivalent to the annual emissions of a small island state, such as Samoa; that is, tiny, but a contribution nonetheless. Multiplied across all the environmental treaties and processes, the figures become significant. There is growing awareness of the need to tackle this carbon footprint—lest meeting organizers and negotiators be accused of hypocrisy—and many host countries now take steps to limit the environmental impact of conferences held on their soil. The Danish Presidency of the Copenhagen Climate Change Conference, for example, declared that it would be carbon neutral, and the Mexican hosts of the subsequent Cancún Conference engaged in similar initiatives. In 2009, the climate change COP itself formally requested the Secretariat "within available resources ... to offset the greenhouse gas emissions of [its] operations and activities" (decision 12/CP.15, UNFCCC 2010).

More Issues

A clear sign of rising intensity is the growing number of agenda items and sub-items under consideration at any one COP. In the case of the climate change regime, the big jump in items took place after the adoption of the 1997 Kyoto Protocol, and to a lesser extent since the launch of negotiations under the Bali Action Plan in 2007. In 1996, for example, its Subsidiary Body for Scientific and Technological Advice (SBSTA) had to consider seven substantive issues on its agenda, and the Subsidiary Body for Implementation (SBI), just two. By 2010, the SBSTA was addressing fifteen items, and the SBI, twenty-four. Other regimes have also experienced inexorably expanding agendas. The CBD COP in Nagoya, for example, had twenty-seven substantive items on its agenda, compared with eighteen substantive items ten years before.

This again reflects the maturity of the Rio Conventions, whereby issues evolve and institutional learning uncovers ever more topics of relevance to the negotiations. Moreover, at the beginning of a process, governments may have only a general understanding of their national interests relative to the topic at hand. Over time, national positions tend to become much more sophisticated, generating demand for new agenda items. Examples of new items added to the climate change agenda over the past few years include the implications of hydrofluorocarbon (HFC) projects under the Clean Development Mechanism (CDM), more detailed consideration of forestry and soil-carbon issues, and carbon capture and storage (CCS). The CBD has added agenda items on biodiversity and climate change (including a sub-item on geo-engineering), and biofuels, to name a few. The Montreal Protocol and the Stockholm Convention continue to add new chemicals to their agendas. The Basel Convention has added electronic waste and ship-breaking. As well as tackling emerging issues, negotiators must also review progress on their previous decisions at subsequent meetings, thus clocking up yet more items requiring consideration. At the same time, it is notoriously difficult to ever declare an issue "closed," so few older items are retired.

Another problem is that parties will often seek to place their "pet" issues on as many agendas as possible, to ensure maximum attention. The *Earth Negotiations Bulletin* (2008), for example, reported that, at a climate session in 2008, "many issues, such as technology, mitigation, bunker fuels, CCS and the Kyoto mechanisms, [were] addressed in two or more subsidiary bodies under two or more agenda items." As well as eating up time and generating more work, this can lead to confusion and poor decision making. Although some regimes have tried to organize the issues on the table more rationally—such as the CBD, which has adopted seven thematic areas of work, with not all items taken up at each session—this has rarely reduced the complexity and length of the agenda.

Ever-expanding agendas have led to the growing specialization of environmental negotiations. Nowadays, most delegations have specialists who focus on specific issues within the broader negotiations, such as forestry, the CDM, or adaptation in the case of the climate change regime. Given the proliferation of issues, such specialization is a prerequisite for effective participation in the negotiations. Resource-strapped developing countries, however, will often lack specialists for certain topics and a small handful of individuals will need to cover a large number of agenda items. As a result, these poorer delegations tend to get left in the dust as the discussions get more technical and go beyond the level of expertise of their negotiators. This may provoke them to seek refuge in familiar issues—such as demands for new and additional financial resources, technology transfer, and capacity building—that enable them to actively engage in the negotiations. While this may allow the participation of more delegates, it often does little to advance the substantive discussions or move beyond existing deadlocks.

Specialization also leads to significant implementation challenges. As negotiations become more complex, they not only become more exclusionary, but their outcomes also become more difficult to implement without trained and experienced specialists. Once again, this poses greater challenges for the poorer developing countries. The fact that, at the time of writing, less than 2 percent of CDM projects were located in Africa pays testimony to the difficulties faced by some in keeping up with the complexities of implementation.

More Participants

The number of participants attending negotiating sessions has ballooned over the past decade, particularly at meetings of the Rio Conventions. While attendance at the Kyoto Climate Change Conference in 1997 was considered massive at the time, with over 9,000 participants, this was dwarfed by the 40,000 people who descended upon the Copenhagen Climate Change Conference in 2009. Likewise, the Nagoya CBD COP in 2010 attracted 7,000 participants, compared with 4,000 at the previous CBD COP in Bonn in 2008. A longer participants list inevitably means more invitations to a greater number of meetings, side events and social gatherings, placing additional strain on over-taxed delegates. This circus of distractions can also cause logistical challenges as a result of increased security and delays in accessing meetings. This was certainly the case at both the Copenhagen and the Cancún Climate Change Conferences. The delicate balance between creating a transparent and participatory process, and meeting the desire for expediency in bringing the talks to a smooth conclusion, increasingly challenges meeting organizers and pushes these processes to the limits of what they can be expected to produce (see Chapter 3 for some ways that organizers have responded).

More and Longer Documents

The multiplication of agenda items translates into a mounting volume of documentation, which delegates must read if they are to meaningfully participate in the negotiations. In 2010, the climate change SBSTA and SBI each had at least twenty-three documents to consider for their mid-year negotiating session; the equivalent figure in 1996 was ten for the SBSTA and just two for the SBI. The CBD averages a massive 100 documents for each COP. The UNCCD had fifty-seven documents for its parallel meetings of the COP, the Committee on Science and Technology and the Committee for the Review of the Implementation of the Convention in 1999, and over eighty documents in 2011. In many cases, these negotiating documents are supplemented by a plethora of country reports and technical papers. Secretariats have taken to publishing many of these only on the internet in order to reduce the volume of paper documentation. This may save trees, but delegations still have to read them if they are to remain fully abreast of the issues at hand. For some smaller delegations, this is simply impossible. The volume of documentation produced in-session raises specific challenges, since it is almost always in English only and is typically published just hours or even minutes before being tabled for discussion. This puts non–native English speakers at a disadvantage, as they must often consider, sometimes even adopt, documents that have not yet been translated.

More Informal Groups

More substantive issues on the agenda mean more informal groups. Negotiations in an open, formal plenary with all delegates present are difficult and cumbersome enough at the best of times, but become unmanageable when there are so many complex and detailed issues on the agenda. Informal groups streamline the decision-making process by allowing texts to be discussed by smaller, more specialized groups of negotiators, who then present their work to the wider body of states in plenary for final decision making.[2] Depending on the stage of negotiation and the specific topic, informal groups may be known as contact groups, drafting groups, working groups, informal consultations, or other terms. The common characteristic of these settings is that they are conducted in English only, and often exclude NGOs. There is an unwritten rule in many environmental regimes that no more than two meetings (including informal groups) should be held at any one time. This practice is usually respected at the beginning of a session, but is invariably abandoned when deadlines approach.

In the final days of landmark sessions, there may be many meetings of informal groups taking place simultaneously. This was the case during the final stages of the Cartagena Biosafety negotiations (both the first round in Cartagena, Colombia, in 1999, and the resumed session in Montreal in 2000), the final stages of the CBD ABS negotiations in Nagoya, as well as all of the key climate change meetings: Kyoto, The Hague, Bonn, Marrakesh, Bali, Copenhagen, Cancún and Durban. Even some of the older conventions, such as the Montreal Protocol, which rarely used contact groups before 2000, now convene small groups to negotiate decisions on numerous agenda items.

Secretariats and chairpersons will go to considerable lengths to inform delegates of progress in the negotiations and the time/venue of informal group meetings. Inevitably, however, as informal meetings proliferate, it becomes more and more difficult for delegations, especially small ones, to keep track of the numerous strands in the negotiations. During the Cartagena Biosafety negotiations, for example, the Jamaican delegate recalled "it was extremely difficult for us, a small delegation, as there were so many groups meeting at the same time … The time of these meetings often changed from one hour to the next. Working out how to be available … became too much of a challenge, and eventually one simply gave up" (Fisher 2002). Scheduling so many meetings can also leave little time for delegates to think, let alone craft a creative tradeoff among various interest groups' positions and secure approval for new options from their capitals. Reminiscing on the many simultaneous meetings in Cartagena, the US delegate reflected that "while negotiators were indeed fully employed during these negotiating sessions, they had little or no opportunity to actually identify common ground" (Enright 2002).

The multiplication of informal groups can also complicate the substance of negotiations. Issues under discussion are often linked, at least politically if not in technical terms, and need to be considered together if a package deal is to be agreed. Having so many informal groups can lead to confusion and inconsistency, as similar issues are discussed in different groups, generating varied results.

At major conferences, and especially in the final stages, action is rarely confined to open plenaries and official informal groups. When talks stall—as they often do—the chairperson may resort to convening more select groups to try to broker an overall political deal. These may include a "Friends of the Chair" group, an "expanded Bureau," or other political consultations. Such a group can also be useful in trying to bring together the various strands of work and forge a coherent package. What the negotiations gain in efficiency, however, they often lose in transparency (see Chapter 3). Added to these political consultations will be myriad private talks, huddles, and hard bargaining at the bilateral, regional, and constituency levels, not to mention press conferences, interviews, and NGO briefings. In the final few days of major conferences, no one will really know what meetings are taking place, where, and at what time. During the Bali Climate Change Conference in 2007, for example, the Chinese delegation openly berated the Secretariat for organizing a plenary meeting at the same time as a crucial ministerial consultation, suspecting some kind of conspiracy to dupe the plenary into adopting something while the ministers were huddled in a back room. The truth, however, was more prosaic: neither the Secretariat nor the Indonesian presidency was able to keep track of all the multiple meetings taking place throughout the conference center, leading to the unfortunate clash.

The Compression of Time

With all the ongoing activity, it is not surprising if time takes on new meaning during environmental negotiations, especially during major conferences. The rules of procedure of most environmental treaties in the UN system state that meetings should run from 10:00 a.m. to 1:00 p.m. and from 3:00 to 6:00 p.m. This schedule allows time for regional and constituency group meetings, and accommodates the working practices of interpreters, since plenary meetings are conducted in all six of the UN's official languages. As with the "two-meeting rule," these hours are respected where possible, but then abandoned as negotiations go to the wire. Informal groups routinely run late into the night, and round-the-clock meetings, spilling out beyond the scheduled end of the session, have become almost *de rigueur* before agreement is eventually reached (or abandoned) on a new treaty or key set of decisions. The climate change regime has experienced perhaps the most extreme cases of "negotiation by exhaustion," a term that was apparently coined by the Tanzanian Chair of the Group of 77 on the last night of the Kyoto Protocol negotiations in 1997. Each one of the UNFCCC's landmark decisions since 1995 has been taken after an all-night meeting, with the conference eventually closing more than eighteen hours after its scheduled end and negotiators complaining of working twenty-four to seventy-two hours with little to no sleep. This is not the sole province of the climate change regime. Both the extraordinary session of the CBD COP in Cartagena in 1999, which was supposed to adopt the Cartagena Protocol, and the resumed session in Montreal in 2000, which did adopt the Protocol, ended at 6:00 a.m.—twelve hours after the scheduled close of the meetings. The gavel came down relatively early, at around 3:00 a.m., on the 2010 CBD Nagoya Conference that adopted the Nagoya Protocol on ABS, but not without "intense, late-night sessions marked by numerous parallel deliberations, and down-to-the wire negotiations" (ENB 2010c). The United Nations Forum on Forests was only able to adopt the non-legally binding instrument on all types of forests in 2007 after an all-night negotiating session that concluded at 6:00 a.m. (Figure 2.1). Even back in 1994, the UNCCD treaty text was adopted at 8:00 a.m. on a Saturday, after the clock was "stopped" at 6:00 p.m. the day before to allow negotiations to continue.

The tendency for "negotiation by exhaustion" reflects the brinkmanship that characterizes highly controversial negotiations, whereby delegations are unwilling to reach agreement until the very last moment, in the hope of extracting extra concessions from others. It also reflects the maxim that operates throughout the environmental arena, and indeed elsewhere, whereby "nothing is agreed until

FIGURE 2.1 Negotiation by exhaustion at the seventh session of the United Nations Forum on Forests in 2007. Photo courtesy of IISD/*Earth Negotiations Bulletin*

everything is agreed." This adversarial approach means that even the slightly easier decisions cannot be approved until the most difficult issues have been resolved, thus "backloading" the final, decisive negotiations into the last few hours of a conference—and beyond.

The round-the-clock nature of environmental negotiations has significant repercussions. For a start, negotiation by exhaustion means that momentous decisions on global environmental policy are taken by delegates who are massively sleep deprived. At best, this leads to poor drafting. At worst, serious mistakes or problems in the text are overlooked. Several mistakes slipped into the Kyoto Protocol presented for adoption to the COP plenary, for example, which had to be corrected weeks later through a "technical review." The adoption of the Bonn Agreements on climate change in 2001, sealing a political deal on the implementation details of the Kyoto Protocol, suffered from confusion and controversy over which version of the text was correct. The Copenhagen Accord, partly because it evolved so late in the negotiations, is full of concepts and terms that do not fit with the existing legal framework of the climate regime.

Adversarial negotiation by exhaustion, coupled with the general intensity of proceedings over many days, means that tempers and emotions can run high, so that conference "finales" often descend into highly dramatic events. This situation causes significant problems for the consensus-based decision-making processes envisioned under many of these treaties. While providing fodder for waiting news crews, undiplomatic exchanges can have long-lasting ramifications for the future negotiating atmosphere. The final hours at the Copenhagen Climate Change Conference—involving insulting outbursts, bloodied hands (accidentally self-inflicted), and personal accusations thrown at the COP President—provide extreme examples (ENB 2009).

The Technological Revolution

The proliferation of global environmental negotiations over the past twenty years has unfolded at the same time as revolutionary advances in information and communication technology. When delegates arrived in Rio de Janeiro for the Earth Summit in June 1992, they were greeted with something new—the ability to rent mobile telephones at the airport. Thus, for the first time at a global environmental meeting, the more technologically adventurous diplomats were able to stay in contact with their delegations and their capitals while sitting in the conference rooms. The technology was so new that delegates had not yet mastered the "silence" mode. As the *Earth Summit Bulletin* reported on June 4, 1992, "Amidst the chirping of cellular phones, the UN Conference on Environment and Development officially opened" (*Earth Summit Bulletin* 1992).

The internet and email were also in their infancy in 1992. NGOs had just started to communicate through email using the Institute for Global Communications' "Econet" email and bulletin board system. The Earth Summit

Secretariat became the first UN body to actually post documents on "Econet" in 1991. In June 1994, at the final session of the UNCCD negotiations in Paris, when the *Earth Negotiations Bulletin* launched its website, www.iisd.ca, most negotiators had never even heard of the World Wide Web. Today, the wide-spread use of the internet, reliable mobile phones, and powerful handheld computer devices have profoundly impacted the conduct of negotiations.

The expansion of the internet and the ability to send information electroni-cally has made the submission and exchange of proposals and ideas infinitely easier. During negotiations throughout most of the 1990s, most proposals from parties were submitted to the Secretariat in hard copy and had to be re-typed before they could be published in an official compilation document. Those official compilations were then sent in hard copy to national focal points, often leading to a considerable delay before their receipt by the negotiators themselves. Nowadays, almost all documents are posted on the internet, making them available to any interested stakeholder, not just government delegates.

A remarkable development has been the use of the internet to transmit live "webcasts" of negotiations. Anyone unable to attend the historic climate nego-tiations in Bali, Copenhagen, or Cancún, for example, could watch the webcast of plenary sessions live in the comfort of their own home or office. The UNFCCC website, among others, now boasts several means of ensuring "virtual participa-tion" at its sessions, including through the social-networking site Facebook, the video-sharing site YouTube, and the information network Twitter.

It is difficult now to imagine a time when mobile phones were not common currency. During the early stages of the Kyoto Protocol negotiations in 1995, NGOs were banned from the negotiating floor and confined to the galleries during meetings to ensure that they could not unduly influence delegates. By the time of the Kyoto Conference in December 1997, such a ruling was redundant, as anyone with the right database could contact key delegations, at least from well-resourced countries, by mobile phone. Sebastian Oberthür and Hermann Ott report how "the telephone increasingly became the medium for diplomacy" during the last tense hours of negotiations on the Kyoto Protocol (Oberthür and Ott 1999, 88).

Today, mobile phones are an integral part of the negotiation process, speeding up and expanding the scope of communications. To some extent, they help com-pensate for the multiplication of forums and the potential for confusion and inconsistency. Colleagues in different contact groups can call or send text mes-sages to one another to check on relevant developments and coordinate their positions. Officials can confirm possible compromises or emerging text with superiors back in their capitals, perhaps sending sections of text on their "smart phones." NGOs banned from closed informal groups may use their mobile phones to try to put their views forward, through text messages and emails to friendly delegations. During tense moments in a plenary meeting, delegates—who must sit behind their country placards, often a long way from negotiating partners—may frantically send text messages to allies to consult on how to move forward. Even secretariat staff on the podium may receive text messages urging them to advise the meeting chairperson one way or another. This is, apparently, what happened during the dramatic final plenary of the Copenhagen Climate Change Conference, when it looked like the COP President, Danish Prime Minister Lars Løkke Rasmussen, was losing the confidence of delegates and the conference might end without even "noting" the Copenhagen Accord.

The mushrooming use in negotiating rooms of, first, laptop computers, followed by handheld devices a decade or so later, have also transformed the conduct of negotiations in many subtle ways. In the early 1990s, the only laptops in negotiating rooms were typically those belonging to the *Earth Negotiations Bulletin* team, who sat in the back of the room close to one of the few power outlets in the entire conference room. In 1994, the Secretariat for the desertification negotiations became one of the first to use laptops during sessions to keep track of amendments to the text of the draft convention. Nowadays, laptops are almost as ubiquitous—at least among the best-resourced delegations—as pens and paper. According to one commentator, the most profound technological revolution was the installation at UN Headquarters of electric sockets at delegate tables, enabling participants to use their laptops during plenary sessions.[3] Most major conference centers now also enjoy this facility. Laptops or handheld devices allow delegates to refer to documents, consult websites, email colleagues, type up impressions of the meeting, transcribe key exchanges, or just get on with other work (or watch sporting events) while the negotiations are actually taking place. No major conference site is complete without a large delegate computer center, with free internet access, invariably packed full of delegates typing away frantically almost round the clock.

The media has been a particular beneficiary of the revolution in information technology. Gone are the days when reporters had to scramble around the basement of UN Headquarters, or other conference centers, trying to find a telephone or internet connection of sufficient quality to file a report for an evening news broadcast. Handheld wireless devices enable on-the-spot reporting to twenty-four-hour news channels. And the media no longer provides the only "window" on the negotiations to the outside world. Dozens of bloggers now supply a running commentary on their view of the negotiations, instantaneously available to anyone in the world with an internet connection or a Twitter feed. The media and other internet broadcasters are often far speedier than official UN channels in releasing news: at the Copenhagen Climate Change Conference, the *Earth Negotiations Bulletin* (2009) reported that "many delegates first learned about the Copenhagen Accord on the internet … long before the official UNFCCC document was produced." Clearly, technological advances are exposing environmental regimes to greater outside scrutiny than ever before.

Technological advances have had some positive environmental impacts. Hard copies of documents are no longer routinely sent out to all parties in the run-up to conferences, the expectation being that delegations will read them on their computers, and print out only those they really need. The mass of paper that still abounds at large environmental conferences, however, demonstrates that old habits die hard.

Nonetheless, the terrible sight of tons of paper being dumped at the close of environmental meetings may soon be a thing of the past. Some environmental processes are pioneering "paperless" UN conferences, whereby computer networks, combined with the distribution of laptops to delegations without their own, eliminate the need for paper copies of documents. The first process to "go paperless" was the Montreal Protocol at its MOP 20 (Qatar, 2008) (Figure 2.2), with others following suit, including the Chemicals Conventions meetings, the ongoing negotiations on mercury,[4] and the UNEP GC/GMEF. In a post by the Global Environmental Governance Project on Twitter,[5] UNEP executive director Achim Steiner claimed that the initiative had saved 400,000 sheets of paper at UNEP GC-26 (February 2011). The *Earth Negotiations Bulletin* (2011) reported an overall positive reaction by delegates to that paperless meeting, the largest to date, despite teething problems, notably power failures and lost internet connections.

As in all walks of life, however, technology is a double-edged sword. Technological advances mean that more can be done in less time, and this has heightened, rather than alleviated, the intensity and stress of the negotiations. The ease with which proposals can be submitted seems to have discouraged

FIGURE 2.2 The first process to "go paperless" was the Montreal Protocol at its MOP 20 in Qatar in 2008. Photo courtesy of IISD/*Earth Negotiations Bulletin*

FIGURE 2.3 When secretariats project negotiating text on a big screen in the front of the room, all delegations know whether or not their proposals have been incorporated into the draft. Photo courtesy of IISD/*Earth Negotiations Bulletin*

restraint among delegates, with an ever-greater volume of proposed text reaching secretariats, as demonstrated in recent climate change and CSD negotiations. Furthermore, when secretariats project negotiating text on a big screen in the front of the room, all delegations know whether or not their proposals have been incorporated exactly into the draft, and feel more honor-bound to defend their precise formulation (Figure 2.3). This reduces the chairperson's crucial room for maneuvering, in the privacy of his/her office, to "tweak" submitted proposals in the interests of producing a more consensual draft. Managing the huge amount of words and data that must be read and digested is also proving to be a difficult task, especially for smaller delegations. The problem is no longer insufficient information, but too much. Data management systems and techniques take on a new urgency in this era of copious information sources.

Technological know-how and devices do not come cheap and, as ever, it is the rich who are best able to seize the opportunities presented by the technological revolution. This is opening up yet another capacity gap compared with less well-resourced delegations, for which sophisticated devices such as smart phones and powerful laptops are often unaffordable. Internet connections also remain slow or unreliable in many poorer developing countries.

The relentless glare of the media has its drawbacks, as news reports can ricochet back to impact on the negotiations themselves. At the Copenhagen Climate Change Conference, for example, US President Barack Obama's announcement to the waiting media that a "deal" had been struck in a closed meeting was broadcast live, including on TV screens within the conference center. This incensed many delegates who had not yet seen or heard about the "deal" through official channels. In addition, information technology has facilitated a disturbing trend in "leaks." Not only were several texts "leaked" during Copenhagen and made widely available on the internet, but recordings of private meetings, taken by indiscreet delegates on their mobile phones, were released after the conference (*Environmental Policy and Law* 2010). This poses worrying questions for the privacy of the negotiation process, and the extent to which delegates can speak freely without fearing that their inevitably difficult exchanges will not remain confidential.

Raising the Stakes: Ministers and Heads of State

Another facet of the intensification of negotiations is the way in which ministers are becoming more involved, and often at an earlier stage in the process. COPs and MOPs have traditionally included a "high-level segment," usually on the last two days of the session, where ministers (sometimes joined by a few heads of state) are invited to deliver a statement to plenary. The expectation is, then, that ministers from "key" countries will provide input to the negotiations, usually as part of a "Friends of the Chair" group, helping to resolve a handful of intractable issues. The reasoning is that there comes a point when officials reach the limits of their mandates, but ministers have the authority to make far-reaching decisions. Certainly, ministers have played a very important role in the development of international environmental regimes over the past twenty years. Without ministers to instruct delegates to change their positions, or to meet with their counterparts from other countries, the landmark environmental treaties now in force, and associated decisions such as the Marrakesh Accords on climate change, would never have come into being.

Over time, there has been a tendency to try to involve ministers more deeply in the negotiation process. In the climate context, this trend can be dated back to COP 6 in The Hague in 2000, where the Dutch COP President, Jan Pronk, sought to involve his ministerial colleagues more closely and at an earlier stage, in the hope of overcoming profound political divisions among parties. Unfortunately, the talks eventually collapsed, but the tendency to engage ministers in day-to-day negotiations has continued. At a number of environmental negotiations, including the UNFCCC, the UNCCD, the CSD, and the Stockholm Convention on POPs, among others, the formal high-level segment, where ministers used to deliver prepared monologues often late into the night to almost empty plenary rooms, has been replaced or supplemented by thematic "roundtables," where speeches are interspersed with efforts to encourage more interactive exchanges. Ministers are now also routinely expected to co-chair, and participate in, informal groups. During the 2002 World Summit on Sustainable Development, for example, ministers spent many days and late nights throughout the meeting negotiating the Johannesburg Plan of Implementation, on which lower-level officials had been unable agree. At the 2010 Cancún Climate Change Conference, the COP President paired ministers from developed and developing countries and assigned them key issues on which to facilitate negotiations (see Chapter 3 for more on this technique).

The Copenhagen Climate Change Conference took a dramatic step up in further raising the level of negotiations with 119 heads of state and government attending the session at the invitation of the COP President (Figure 2.4). Several of these heads of state ended up participating actively in the final negotiation process. Even the position of COP President, previously only ever held at the ministerial level, was taken over by the Prime Minister of Denmark. This is certainly not typical of environmental negotiations. Usually, heads of state attending an environmental COP or MOP confine their activities to delivering statements, social occasions, and discussions within their own delegations.

The participation of ministers, however, let alone heads of state, has never been straightforward in environmental negotiations. Diplomats and other government officials will typically have been working full time on the issue at hand for many years, and have attended a succession of negotiating meetings. Most ministers, however, tend to be responsible for a much wider portfolio, and may only be able to devote a portion of their time to the environmental issue under negotiation. In many cases, ministers have little experience of UN meetings

FIGURE 2.4 South African President Jacob Zuma, Chinese Premier Wen Jiabao, Indian Prime Minister Manmohan Singh, and Brazilian President Luiz Inacio Lula da Silva during informal consultations during the 2009 Copenhagen Climate Change Conference. Photo courtesy of IISD/*Earth Negotiations Bulletin*

and may not be fluent in English. Moreover, ministers and heads of state are political animals who like to work at the political level rather than wordsmithing with commas, "shoulds," "shalls," and "to the extent possibles." These problems can help to explain why the arrival of ministers or heads of state has not always served as the desired magic wand at negotiations.

Implications for Global Environmental Policymaking

Taken as a whole, global environmental negotiations over the past twenty years have undoubtedly intensified. To some extent, this is a positive trend, reflecting the greater time, resources, and political attention lavished on environmental issues by the international community. Technological breakthroughs have certainly brought greater transparency to the negotiations and, in many ways, facilitated the work of negotiators.

Intensification, however, has a dark side. For a start, it disproportionately affects the smaller and poorer delegations, which are unable to scale up the available resources to participate in negotiations in line with the increasing demands they face. For some, intensification has generated just too many meetings happening in too many different places, often with duplicative mandates. This, combined with the trend toward the greater specialization of delegates in order to cope with intensification, has led to fragmentation, and with it conflicting agendas and inconsistency in rules and norms (Najam et al. 2006, 14). This trend is ironic, given that the interconnections between global environmental problems are becoming increasingly apparent. In the ozone regime, for example, connections with the response to climate change are coming to the fore, notably in dealing with hydrofluorocarbons. The CBD and forestry regimes are also major stakeholders in the evolving commitments under the climate change regime on land-use change and forestry. Just as the need for synergistic implementation is becoming more urgent, responsibility for negotiating and implementing solutions to global environmental problems is becoming more dispersed.

Overall, intensity should not be confused with achievement. More agenda items, meetings, ministers, and computers do not always correlate with more substantive and useful decisions. Bombarded with documents, exhausted by long nights and non-stop travel, juggling high-level instructions, and dazed by never-ending input from "improved" technology, it is easy to imagine how even the best-resourced diplomats may, ironically, produce weaker outcomes and lose sight of the real problems they are supposed to address. Some environmental negotiations may be engaged in frenzied activity, but they have little to show for it. To this point, the *Earth Negotiations Bulletin* (2010a) questioned whether the climate change process more closely resembles the tortoise, making slow but inexorable progress, or the hamster, spinning on a wheel—constantly active, but never actually getting anywhere. While the "tempo" of international environmental negotiations has quickened, the pace of actual progress on many environmental issues has slackened since the first few heady years following the Earth Summit.

Perhaps the greatest danger is that intensive activity provides an *illusion* of real progress, a convenient focus of political attention and energy that masks continuing environmental deterioration. Without wishing to, the global environmental governance system may have become more preoccupied with perpetuating a cycle of continuous negotiations rather than securing real change through the effective implementation of those agreements that have been reached.

Unsurprisingly, intensification has led many to question the current system of global environmental governance, both within individual processes (notably the climate change regime) and the UN system more broadly (see Chapter 12). The reform of global environmental governance has been the subject of much debate in the UNGA and UNEP, as well as in numerous governments, expert seminars, and conferences. However, just as in the environmental negotiations taking place around the world, consensus is elusive. Twenty years after the Earth Summit, negotiators have finessed the art of all-night meetings, creative wordsmithing, use of new and emerging technologies, and negotiation by exhaustion. The question that remains is this: how long can some of these unsustainable practices continue? Is the world merely negotiating while the planet burns?

Notes

1 The full title is the Nagoya Protocol on Access to Genetic Resources and the Fair and Equitable Sharing of Benefits Arising from their Utilization.
2 For an analysis of different negotiating forums, see Depledge 2005. This work also includes further analysis of other issues discussed in this chapter, including the role of ministers, time management, and documents.
3 The authors are grateful to an anonymous reviewer for this point.
4 The full name of the process is the Intergovernmental Negotiating Committee to prepare a global legally binding instrument on mercury.
5 See http://twitter.com/#!/GEGproject/status/40793437347385344.

Works Cited

Depledge, Joanna. 2005. *The Organization of Global Negotiations: Constructing the Climate Change Regime*. London: Earthscan.

ENB (*Earth Negotiations Bulletin*). 2008. Twenty-eighth Session of the UNFCCC Subsidiary bodies, Second Session of the Ad Hoc Working Group under the Convention, and Fifth Session of the Ad Hoc Working Group under the Kyoto Protocol: 2–13 June 2008. *Earth Negotiations Bulletin* 12(375). http://www.iisd.ca/download/pdf/enb12375e.pdf. (accessed December 6, 2010).

ENB. 2009. Summary of the Copenhagen Climate Change Conference: 7–19 December 2009. *Earth Negotiations Bulletin* 12(459). http://www.iisd.ca/download/pdf/enb 12459e.pdf (accessed December 6, 2010).

ENB. 2010a. Summary of the Bonn Climate Talks: 2–6 August 2010. *Earth Negotiations Bulletin* 12(478). http://www.iisd.ca/download/pdf/enb12478e.pdf (accessed December 6, 2010).

ENB. 2010b. CBD COP 10 Highlights: Wednesday, 27 October 2010. *Earth Negotiations Bulletin* 9(542). http://www.iisd.ca/download/pdf/enb09542e.pdf (accessed December 6, 2010).

ENB. 2010c. Summary of the Tenth Conference of the Parties to the Convention on Biological Diversity: 18–29 October 2010. *Earth Negotiations Bulletin* 9(544). http://www.iisd.ca/download/pdf/enb09544e.pdf (accessed December 5, 2010).

ENB. 2011. GC-26 GMEF Highlights: Monday, 21 February 2011. *Earth Negotiations Bulletin* 16(86). http://www.iisd.ca/download/pdf/enb1686e.pdf (accessed May 18, 2011).

Earth Summit Bulletin. 1992. UNCED Highlights: Wednesday, 3 June 1992. *Earth Summit Bulletin* 2(4). http://www.iisd.ca/vol02/0204000e.html (accessed May 31, 2011).

Enright, Cathleen A. 2002. Miami Group: United States. In *The Cartagena Protocol on Biosafety: Reconciling Trade in Biotechnology with Environment and Development.* Edited by Christoph Bail, Robert Falkner, and Helen Marquard. London: Earthscan/RIIA.

Environmental Policy and Law. 2010. Final Stages of the Copenhagen Conference "No Longer Secret." *Environmental Policy and Law* 40(4): 134.

Fisher, Elaine. 2002. Like-Minded Group: Jamaica. In *The Cartagena Protocol on Biosafety: Reconciling Trade in Biotechnology with Environment and Development.* Edited by Christoph Bail, Robert Falkner, and Helen Marquard. London: Earthscan/RIIA.

Michaelowa, Axel and David Lehmkuhl. 2005. Greenhouse Gas Emissions Caused by the International Climate Negotiations. *Climate Policy* 4(3): 337–340.

Najam, Adil, Mihaela Papa and Nadaa Taiyab. 2006. *Global Environmental Governance: A Reform Agenda.* Winnipeg, Canada: International Institute for Sustainable Development.

Oberthür, Sebastian and Hermann Ott. 1999. *The Kyoto Protocol: International Climate Policy for the 21st Century.* Berlin: Springer Verlag.

UNFCCC 2010. Report of the Conference of the Parties on its Fifteenth Session, Held in Copenhagen from 7 to 19 December 2009. FCCC/CP/2010/11/Add.1.

3

EARTH NEGOTIATIONS ON A COMFY COUCH

Building Negotiator Trust through Innovative Processes

Deborah Davenport, Lynn M. Wagner, and Chris Spence

Picture, if you will, those individuals charged with protecting the environment—representatives of their countries' best interests who have been sent to collectively identify actions to protect living species, save the forest, stop climate change, or any other of the myriad problems our planet faces—sitting not in a plenary hall in a UN conference center, but on comfy couches, in tropical resorts, drawing toy objects from a bag to determine their speaking order. These approaches have already been used individually in negotiations on these issues, and there is reason to think that they might help negotiators to reach a consensus decision. The assumption underlying these approaches is that they help to foster trust among negotiators, and this theory has been put to the test across a range of international environmental policymaking processes. As negotiations become more complex—due to the number of negotiating coalitions, the obligations under discussion, and the transparency of decision-making processes that the international community requires—these innovative approaches become ever more important.

This chapter dovetails with the cases discussed in Chapter 5 on coalitions. The discussion in Chapter 5 presents the post-1992 country coalitions at work and in flux, through case studies from the sustainable development regimes created twenty years ago to address biodiversity, forests, and climate change. While the interactions examined in that chapter primarily focus on the relationships among state representatives *within* each coalition, this chapter examines issues related to the relationship *between and among* representatives from the coalitions in these same regimes. It focuses in particular on innovative processes and techniques that have been used to help move coalitions toward a negotiated conclusion at points when the talks have stalemated.

As many chapters in this book note, the complexity of issues under negotiation and the number of stakeholders involved in global environmental negotiation processes have increased since the 1992 Rio Earth Summit. With these changes has come the need for creative processes to resolve impasses. Back in 1992, Tommy Koh, chairing the PrepCom IV negotiations leading to the UNCED conference, took what today might sound like an unbelievably heavy-handed approach to push delegates to reach an agreement on the Rio Principles:

> Koh took over negotiations during the final days of the session after reaching an agreement that the process would continue with the group limited to eight G-77 countries and eight OECD countries. He rightly judged that the time had finally come for reaching an agreement in this difficult matter, but that the necessary concessions could only be obtained in a smaller configuration. After 24 hours, he produced a clean text with 27 principles. Using his personal authority to the maximum, he later managed to have the text adopted by the Committee in the early morning hours without changes. This became the only unbracketed text to go forward to Rio, where he again managed to have it adopted without any changes.
>
> (Gören-Engfeldt 2009)

Of course, the Rio Principles were simply that: principles, not actual commitments to behavior changes and certainly not binding. In 1992, the biggest obstacles to achieving negotiated outcomes at UNCED emanated from the North–South character of the negotiations. Twenty years later, however, as growing knowledge of the scientific complexity of the issues in question has been matched by the complexity of commitments under negotiation, there are myriad possibilities for stalemate. In instances where trends have contributed to stalemates in negotiations, a number of innovative processes have been attempted within the negotiating fora. These processes seek to enhance the likelihood of consensus and the effectiveness of outcomes. The innovative processes under consideration in this chapter are all efforts to develop trust among negotiating partners in order to foster consensus agreements on significant global environmental problems.

As the negotiations over issues first addressed in Rio in 1992 have incorporated agenda items on more stringent obligations and higher costs, the cost of agreement is higher to each negotiating state, and thus agreement has become more difficult for government representatives. The specter of higher costs for one's own country can also be exacerbated by mistrust over whether one's negotiating counterparts will actually comply with agreements. Trust among negotiators therefore becomes all the more important. This chapter considers specific cases of negotiations on biosafety, forests, and climate change in which methods similar to the so-called "Track II" approach to conflict resolution were used to break down barriers and build trust between representatives of entrenched coalitions, to explore the role of trust. The cases are selected based on our observation of Track II-type methods in post-UNCED environmental negotiations; while it is not possible to claim that they have been effective without rigorous testing, this review of the use of these approaches seeks to point out areas where they have been tried, to consider their potential effectiveness and encourage further examination.

Trust as the Aim?

Is building trust among diplomats important for achieving effective cooperative outcomes in international negotiations? Scholars of international politics aim to identify methods for enhancing cooperation at the state level to achieve common aims such as preserving or restoring aspects of the global environment that are under threat. Cooperation is vital, but is difficult to attain in large multilateral talks among states focused on their own interests, especially when self-interest conflicts with larger common goals. Over twenty years ago, scholarship on international cooperation focused on the question of how to increase cooperation despite the hindrances posed by competition among states, taking that competition as a given (see, e.g., Axelrod 1984; Downs et al. 1996; Olson 1965). Much research therefore centered on how institutions might monitor and improve enforcement of agreements or how powerful states can foster or coerce agreement, although many of these ideas were developed through the study of economic cooperation, which can encompass different incentive structures than efforts to achieve cooperation on addressing environmental issues.

There is now growing evidence of a shift in attitude within some environmental policymaking fora toward addressing what was formerly considered innate competition between states in a different way, by shifting the incentives of actors. This, it is hypothesized, can be done by shifting the ways in which people understand their interests. The theory of social constructivism does just this. Coincidentally sharing the Earth Summit's anniversary when it was first used to explain one aspect of international interactions (Wendt 1992), social constructivist theory has over twenty years become one of the four major schools of international relations theory. According to the theory, interests are the product of identity, and human identity is the product of the multiple and possibly overlapping, even conflicting, groups of which we consider ourselves members. This theory holds that identity can influence one's interests far more than any other single factor, such as desire for wealth or power, as has been assumed by theorists of other schools such as liberal economics and the "realist" school of international relations (see, e.g., Gilpin 1987; Morgenthau 1956; Oye 1986; Smith 1776/1977). Identity formation is also more fluid than has been supposed, which leaves the door open for creative negotiation techniques to have more influence than realist and neoliberal theorists have considered.

For negotiations, focusing on diplomats' identity is particularly valuable, as it expands the potential range of possibilities for fostering cooperative and effective outcomes in two related ways. First, research confirms the intuitive assumption that mutual identification with a group is associated with trust between the members of that group. Levels of trust vary, and trust may of course be misplaced or abused and so is fragile to some extent, but trust levels usually vary most strongly with the degree to which an individual (the "trustor") identifies with the "trustee" as a member of the same identity group. The closer the identity group— usually inversely related to size of the group—the greater the trust. Second, identity evolves over time, and new or different identities can be fostered. In some ways, fostering such group identification is perhaps easier than it would at first seem, because humans crave to "belong" and seek out like-minded others with whom we form attachments.

In international environmental negotiations over the last twenty years, increasing efforts have been made to reduce barriers between participants from countries with very divergent interests, reduce competitive behaviors and concerns, and develop areas of trust through building unity and empathy among the negotiators as members of a common group with shared interests. This is critically important as negotiations over environmental issues have deepened over time to entail prospects of more stringent obligations and higher costs. As trust among negotiators and in the negotiation process itself becomes more important, innovative mechanisms may assist in building the common identities that foster trust to help negotiators reach agreement on those issues, particularly where there may be overlapping underlying, and perhaps unexpressed, state interests.

Through case studies involving negotiations on biosafety, forests, and climate change, we identify examples in which Track II-type methods were used in attempts to break down barriers and build trust between representatives of entrenched coalitions. Track II methods involves the expansion of traditional boundaries of diplomacy in negotiation processes and are viewed in comparison to the official negotiations (referred to as Track I) (Montville and Davidson 1981; also see Fisher 1989, 208). This approach usually involves informal, unofficial, or non-governmental initiatives that take place outside the official negotiating modes, many times with the constituents but not the individuals who are in the negotiating rooms. Track II efforts are intended to help parties overcome barriers to reaching agreement by shifting the parties' perceptions of each other and the issues under discussion. Track II methods were originally identified as such from conflict resolution approaches employed in the Middle East, such as meetings of civil society representatives that took place outside official negotiation processes in an effort to change the landscape in the impasses between Israelis and Palestinians.

The current examination takes these methods as a starting point, but considers instances in which they have been integrated into the negotiating track (see Chasek 2011 and Fisher 2005, 2006 for other such examinations). The methods employed in the cases we examine are related to Track II conflict resolution methods, yet they take place in the context of and are integrated into ongoing global negotiations over environmental issues. Unlike a typical Track II situation, the negotiating agenda was already adopted in the cases examined, but negotiation impasses led some actors to pursue alternative discussion structures, thus these Track II methods have been integrated into Track I (official) negotiations. In the following three cases, we explore the potential for such approaches to help generate the trust and "space" needed for negotiators to find common ground in cases where there is the possibility for compromise.

Teddy Bears for Biosafety

The first case focuses on impasse resolution techniques used during the final year of negotiations on the Cartagena Protocol on Biosafety, whose adoption was originally planned for 1999 but on which agreement was not achieved until almost a full year later. The negotiating body—the Open-ended Ad Hoc Working Group on Biosafety—was established by the Conference of the Parties to the Convention on Biological Diversity at its second session in 1995. This group held its first meeting in July 1996 and was to have completed its deliberations in time for a ceremonial adoption session in February 1999. However, these talks on the cross-border movement of genetically modified organisms (relabeled "living modified organisms" (LMOs) in the context of these negotiations) raised interconnected concerns related to environment, trade, and agriculture and were relatively contentious.

Instead of concluding as planned, the negotiations continued into the period set aside for the ceremonial adoption, and two extra week-long sessions ultimately were added to the negotiating schedule, with agreement finally reached in January 2000. During the two extra sessions, the chairperson employed a number of creative techniques to help negotiators resolve the impasse. These techniques centered on the use of a unique negotiating arrangement that sought to create a representative, transparent, and fair format.

Juan Mayr, the Colombian Minister of Environment, served as President of the Extraordinary Conference of the Parties (ExCOP), which took place in Cartagena, Colombia, in February 1999 and had been written into the calendar as a ceremonial session to adopt the Biosafety Protocol. Negotiators had not concluded their talks when the ExCOP was to commence, however, and Mayr suggested that the negotiations should continue in a small working group consisting of ten spokespersons representing the country groupings that had emerged during the talks. This originally named "Group of 10" contained one spokesperson from Central and Eastern Europe, one from the European Union, one from Central America and the Caribbean, two from the "Miami Group" (Argentina, Australia, Canada, Chile, the United States, and Uruguay), four from the "Like-minded Group" (the majority of developing countries), and one from the "Compromise Group" (Japan, Mexico, Norway,

South Korea, and Switzerland[1]) (Falkner 2002, 17–18; Mayr 2002, 223; Nobs 2002, 187).

Several of these coalitions had formed, based on the discovery of shared interests among their members, during the biosafety talks. Recognizing that the traditional ways of seating and calling on groups—usually centered around the Group of 77 developing countries, the European Union, and the other advanced Western economies—were not facilitating the discussion of all interests, Mayr realized that the organization would need to change if there was to be agreement on the Protocol (Mayr 2002, 222). During the first additional week of talks, in September 1999, in Vienna, Austria, the "Group of 10" was slightly transformed, with each major group (the Miami Group, Like-minded Group, Compromise Group, European Union, and Central and Eastern Europe) having two spokespersons sitting at a roundtable in what came to be called the "Vienna Setting" for the remainder of the Biosafety Protocol talks (Figure 3.1).

Mayr developed additional procedural controls that sought to balance the need to focus the discussions on reaching resolution while ensuring that the groups felt sufficient involvement with and ownership of the outcome—unlike the Tommy Koh example in 1992 discussed in the introduction to this chapter. Each spokesperson was permitted to have two advisors (representatives from other countries within the spokesperson's coalition), which increased the representation of countries at the table while still controlling the number of

FIGURE 3.1 The "Vienna Setting," pioneered by Juan Mayr in the Biosafety Negotiations, has been used in multiple negotiations since 2000, including the World Summit on Sustainable Development and the ABS negotiations under the Convention on Biological Diversity, shown here. Photo courtesy of IISD/*Earth Negotiations Bulletin*

participants seeking to offer input to the talks. At the same time, although only ten spokespeople sat at the table, flanked by their advisors, the room was open to observers, leading to some standing-room-only situations.

Such transparency is often lost in such small working groups, where for various reasons, from space constraints to the desire to limit the number of possible voices in a session, small "chair's groups" often disappear to a back room to hammer out critical portions of an agreement. In its final analysis of the incomplete February 1999 ExCOP, the *Earth Negotiations Bulletin* suggests that this procedural arrangement positively influenced the talks. It notes that the mood at the "all but stalled" talks changed when Mayr "injected renewed optimism into the process by forming the 'Group of 10.' Delegates applauded the representative nature of the Group and the fact that it also included advisors" (ENB 1999, 13). While the final trade-offs were negotiated in private, the openness of the process leading to the final, all-night talks left many participants complimenting its fairness and transparency, as well as its efficiency (Nobs 2002, 192; Samper 2002, 73).

Mayr's organization of the negotiating coalitions and procedural controls should be given most of the credit for reinvigorating the talks as they built negotiators' trust in the process, but two gimmicks that he employed during the final week of negotiations in 2000 demonstrate a creative approach that worked the empathy angle among negotiators. The first involved a bag full of colorful teddy bears, to which he had assigned various names based on positive virtues, such as justice. Mayr had each coalition draw a bear out of this bag each day, to determine the order in which coalitions would be called[2] (Mayr 2002, 227; Samper 2002, 73) (Figure 3.2). On the penultimate day, he further "requested all in attendance [in the Vienna Setting] to stand, clasp hands, and to ponder how to move the process forward" (ENB 2000b, 1). Mayr describes the event as follows: "Getting all the participants—more than 1000 of them—to hold hands was another symbol of unity that helped to relax the atmosphere and to reaffirm the common purpose of all present to complete the Protocol" (2002, 227). The *Earth Negotiations Bulletin* analysis of these techniques emphasizes the role they played in moving the talks to a conclusion:

> In the final hour, many credited the mien and bearing of ExCOP President Juan Mayr for instilling delegates with a sense of levity and hope, along with a distinct imperative to conclude the Protocol. His grab-bag of colored stuffed animals used to randomly select the speaking order within the *feng shui*-structured "Vienna Setting" provided both comic relief, as well as a sense of equity and transparency.
>
> *(ENB 2000a, 11)*

An additional Track II-type technique that built empathy among negotiators, and was also identified by participants as having contributed to the success

FIGURE 3.2 During the final negotiation session on the Biosafety Protocol, delegates chose colored teddy bears from a bag to determine the sequence of speakers, with the negotiator who drew the green "Protocol Bear," called "Testaverde," being called on first. At the end of the negotiations, Testaverde was given to the representative of the European Community and accompanied several negotiators as they signed the Protocol. Here, Danish negotiator and former chair of the negotiations, Veit Kester, holds Testaverde during the signing ceremony on the sidelines of the fifth meeting of the Conference of the Parties to the CBD, in May 2005.
Photo courtesy of IISD/*Earth Negotiations Bulletin*

of the negotiations, involved a visit to Ethiopia by members of the Miami Group, at the invitation of the Ethiopian lead speaker for the Like-Minded Group, Tewolde Berhan Gebre Egziabher (Ballhorn 2002; Enright 2002). Australian, US, Argentine, and Canadian negotiators met with several African Group negotiators and toured Ethiopian facilities, markets, and farms "to improve our mutual understanding of one another's basic concerns and positions" (Ballhorn 2002, 110). During the final negotiation session in Montreal, the relationships that had been developed during this trip allowed the Miami and Like-Minded Groups "to forge ahead toward agreement through the last hours, without politics or posturing" (Enright 2002, 102). The discussions in Ethiopia did not immediately change the negotiating groups' positions, but they did develop a better understanding of the concerns each brought to the table and greater willingness to work with each other's positions and to explore whether they could identify overlapping options.

Retreats on Forests

The forests issue differs from climate change and biodiversity in that there is no global legally binding agreement on forests. Policymaking related to forests is taken up in multiple negotiating processes, notably within the United Nations Forum on Forests (UNFF), the International Tropical Timber Organization (ITTO), and the FAO Committee on Forestry (COFO), as well as under the Convention on Biological Diversity and what is today the most significant source of funding for forest work, the United Nations Framework Convention on Climate Change (UNFCCC). In at least two of these processes, attempts have been made to "informalize" deliberations through holding meetings in formats that could be described as "retreats." In the past fifteen years, these have taken place in resorts and vacation spots such as Guadalajara, Mexico, Baden-Baden, Germany, Cartagena, Colombia, and Bali, Indonesia. In some circumstances, they have been smaller meetings and included the use of luxury or resort hotels.

The UNFF, like the bodies discussed under the climate change and biosafety cases, evolved out of the results of the 1992 Earth Summit. Unlike climate change and biodiversity or biosafety, however, forests are not covered under a global convention. As a result, discussions of global forest policy have moved from venue to venue. In 2000, these discussions ended up at the UNFF, which was created as a subsidiary body of the UN Economic and Social Council (ECOSOC). The UNFF was scheduled to complete a review of the international arrangement on forests (IAF) at its fifth meeting (UNFF 5) in 2005, five years after its inception. Even as early as 2000, when language calling for such a review was originally agreed, some envisioned that the primary aim of the review would be to decide whether or not to finally initiate negotiations toward a legally binding instrument on global forest policy, some thirteen years after the original effort to negotiate a global forest convention was abandoned (Davenport 2005). The evolution of the UNFF as a body that was acknowledged by many participants and observers to be stagnating (Davenport and Wood 2006; Mankin 2007) caused the scheduled review to take on an element of urgency in the minds of many. By 2005, the question for everyone was how to find a way forward given that no one saw the status quo as providing adequate protection for forests. However, views on the future of institutionalized global forest policymaking varied significantly, from those wanting a binding convention to those who still vehemently opposed this idea.

In an effort to resolve this long-enduring conflict and reach agreement on how to improve upon the status quo, two intersessional meetings took place between UNFF 4, in May 2004, and UNFF 5. First, an Ad Hoc Expert Group on Consideration with a View to Recommending the Parameters of a Mandate for Developing a Legal Framework on All Types of Forests (AHEG PARAM) met in September 2004. This meeting took place at UN Headquarters in New York, following normal UNFF practice. According to the report of the meeting, "many experts said that they had been impressed by the positive mood and atmosphere at the meeting and the constructive discussions" (ECOSOC 2004, 6) of numerous options for the future structure of the IAF. However, the primary question of whether to pursue a legally binding agreement still remained. Most of the options formulated for the future IAF could fit into one of two mutually exclusive categories of either developing the existing structure or using a convention or Protocol approach.

Many participants expressed interest in continuing the discussion, so the AHEG PARAM meeting was followed by a "country-led initiative" (CLI) in Guadalajara, Mexico, the following January. One of the two goals for the meeting was that

> [p]articipants ..., while acting in their personal capacities, [would] deepen and expand their understanding of the expectations, goals and ambitions held by others for a future IAF; providing an informal contribution that [would] help to provide a basis for their consideration of the decision to be made at UNFF 5, thus contributing to an atmosphere of mutual respect and harmony in these important deliberations
>
> *(Country-Led Initiative in Support of UNFF 2005, 3)*

In other words, the goals set out by the conveners were similar to those of the empathy and trust-building exercises discussed in the conflict resolution literature on Track II. Locating the discussions in the sunny warmth of Mexico rather than at UN Headquarters during a cold, gray New York winter was also intended to help move the discussion forward, and this aim was achieved. Whereas the AHEG PARAM in New York had identified fourteen overarching objectives for the future IAF—as either a stronger UNFF or as a legally binding instrument (ECOSOC 2004)—the Guadalajara CLI meeting reduced this number to five overarching objectives, including:

1. protecting and maintaining global forest cover for the long-term economic, social, and environmental wellbeing of all people that depend on forests;
2. promoting the management, conservation, and sustainable development of all types of forest and their contribution to the achievement of the Millennium Development Goals (MDGs);
3. facilitating, catalyzing, and accelerating implementation of sustainable forest management, especially through the Collaborative Partnership on Forests members;
4. reversing the rate of deforestation and forest degradation as well as rehabilitating and restoring the degraded forestland to productive state; and
5. securing high-level political attention and commitment to forests, especially to mobilize financial and technical resources to implement the forest agenda.

This outcome was then reflected in four "global objectives" that were incorporated into the final decision on moving the IAF forward, which was ultimately agreed—not in 2005 as planned, but at the following UNFF meeting in 2006:

1. reversing the loss of forest cover worldwide through sustainable forest management, including protection, restoration, afforestation and reforestation, and increasing efforts to prevent forest degradation (from #4 above);
2. enhancing forest-based economic, social and environmental benefits, including by improving the livelihoods of forest-dependent people (from #1 and #2 above);
3. increasing significantly the area of protected forests worldwide and other areas of sustainably managed forests, as well as the proportion of forest products from sustainably managed forests (from #3 above); and
4. reversing the decline in official development assistance for sustainable forest management and mobilizing significantly increased new and additional financial resources from all sources for the implementation of sustainable forest management (from #5 above).

These objectives were incorporated almost without change into the final outcome of this process, the so-called Non-Legally Binding Instrument on Forests (NLBI), ultimately agreed at UNFF 7. Thus the AHEG PARAM/CLI process as a whole, and particularly the Guadalajara meeting, contributed to the final decision. Informal comments by delegates at various times during the multi-year UNFF forest process suggest that the "retreat" helped to shape the outcome, based on concerns over the political polarization of permanent delegations at UN Headquarters in New York on the international forest policy process[3] and a desire to engage in efforts to make progress in delicate negotiations in more congenial surroundings when opportunities for this exist.

Neither the AHEG PARAM nor the Guadalajara meeting reached any conclusion as to a future institutional modality for the international arrangement on forests, but the purpose of such workshops is not to reach a final conclusion. Rather, they serve to "produce creative ideas, [and] options or recommendations that can enrich and redirect policy making" (Fisher 2005), words that are echoed in the work of the AHEG PARAM process.

It is difficult to assess whether the informal process could have been improved or whether experimentation with further empathy- and trust-building techniques could have produced a better outcome. However, one possible area of weakness is worth consideration. The chairs of AHEG PARAM were not invited to participate in the group that ultimately drafted the negotiating text for UNFF 5's consideration after the intersessional meetings had taken place. Whether or not this indicated simply a lack of official interest in the possibility of "transfer" from the informal to the formal negotiating tracks, there were complaints that the ideas produced in the intersessionals could not have had as much influence on the official negotiations within the UNFF itself as they might have if the intersessional chairs had been invited to participate in the drafting group.[4]

On the other hand, the substance of the discussions on objectives at both of these intersessionals appears to have contributed to the NLBI global objectives that were ultimately agreed in 2007. Negotiators did eventually reach agreement on very politically charged issues, and the fact that further intersessionals were held after UNFF 5 to help further the process suggests a perception that these efforts were worthwhile.

Can Pairs Trump a Full House? How to Win at the High-Stakes Climate Game

As the regime has evolved during the past twenty years, negotiations held under the UNFCCC have been become increasingly complex and challenging. Many UNFCCC insiders observe that the issue naturally lends itself to complexity: because climate change poses such a massive global threat and the greenhouse gases responsible are integral to almost every human economic activity, the implications of any global agreement are immense. Whether a deal is reached or not, the climate "game" is one with trillions of dollars at play (McKibben 2010).

In such a high-stakes game, governments can perhaps be forgiven for exercising great care and caution, and even appearing to put narrow interests before the greater global good. Given the high economic, social, and environmental stakes, UNFCCC negotiations are often characterized by mistrust and suspicion among negotiators. It is therefore no surprise that the organizers of key negotiating sessions have been willing to experiment with various tactics to help build trust and confidence in an effort to reduce the tension and mutual mistrust.

These innovations first came to the fore in 2005, when preliminary negotiations began on a future agreement to cover the period after 2012—the year when the Kyoto Protocol's first "commitment period" expires. The Protocol includes clear targets for industrialized countries and members of the former Soviet bloc for the years 2008–2012. However, it does not establish specific targets beyond that point, which poses a major challenge for negotiators. In particular, it had become clear by 2005 that climate science demanded action on a scale that dwarfed the agreements enshrined in the Kyoto Protocol. This would probably require serious actions from all countries, not just those from the industrialized countries, particularly as developing countries' share of global emissions continues to grow. However, such logic had the potential to conflict with developing countries' legitimate desire to pull their people out of poverty—a task made doubly difficult if they were forced to take on burdensome new duties for a problem not of their making. Reconciling the twin aims of development and combating climate change in a way that would be agreeable to all 194 parties to the UNFCCC was never going to be simple (Spence 2005).

Take a Seat ... a Very Comfy Seat

In this context, anything that might help improve trust and remove suspicions among key players was taken into consideration by meeting organizers. The first efforts were characterized by the *Earth Negotiations Bulletin* as the "Comfy Armchair Theory" (ENB 2005, 7) (Figure 3.3). In this manifestation, meeting organizers promoted a:

> laid-back approach that seemed to put participants at ease. In addition, many delegates commented on the comfortable red armchairs placed on the stage for the government experts. The podium was lowered to make it more on a level with participants—again to lessen the formality of the occasion. Some compared it to a "television talk show" setting, while others likened the use of "comfy chairs"[5] and the informal approach to a "nice fireside chat."

FIGURE 3.3 Using "comfy chairs" at a UNFCCC seminar in 2005: Jürgen Trittin, Federal Minister for the Environment, Nature Conservation and Nuclear Safety, Germany, and Ginés González García, Minister of Health and Environment of Argentina and COP-10 President, who said that the seminar was an opportunity to rebuild trust and confidence. Photo courtesy of IISD/ *Earth Negotiations Bulletin*

Such techniques may have helped generate what was certainly a positive atmosphere and an "open, frank and broad-ranging ... exchange of information" (ENB 2005, 7). The initial success of this tactic subsequently resulted in several other in-session seminars and other efforts to reduce formality and encourage open exchanges and mutual understanding. The underlying assumption is that such exercises can help build openness to and appreciation of others' positions, and that "win–win" compromises can emerge from a positive environment conducive to agreement. This approach rejects notions of negotiations as a zero-sum game of winners and losers. The in-session seminars and other informal discussions, commencing with the comfy chair format, helped delegates gain a greater appreciation of each other's views and positions on their weighty agenda leading up to the thirteenth meeting of the Conference of the Parties (COP 13) and the third session of the Conference of the Parties serving as the Meeting of the Parties (COP/MOP 3) in Bali in 2007, where they finalized the "Bali roadmap," which set out a clear framework and a deadline for reaching a much bigger agreement in Copenhagen in 2009. The Bali success can be attributed to many factors, including painstaking preparations and "unprecedented high-level political, media and public attention to climate change science and policy" (ENB 2007, 18). However, concerted,[6] ongoing trust-building exercises, including the informal dialogues held over the previous two years, played a part in transforming the negotiating paradigm from one of uncertainty into a clear roadmap for securing a post-2012 agreement. For instance, Müller refers to a "raised level of trust" that resulted in agreement on the Adaptation Fund and was brought about, at least in part, by informal discussions that helped the EU and developing countries reach an understanding (Müller 2008). The Bali talks, however, only needed to develop a "road map" for further negotiations.

The Copenhagen Casino: Losing with a Royal Flush and Full House

Such ongoing efforts at building trust and empathy fell flat at Copenhagen in December 2009. Expectations for this meeting were high, with many hoping for a legally binding treaty that would chart a clear path forward in the post-2012 period. Instead, the meeting ended acrimoniously, resulting in only a non-binding agreement, the Copenhagen Accords, which was "noted" (rather than adopted) by parties (ENB 2009).

On the surface, the organizers were holding a strong hand at the start of the meeting. They had succeeded in persuading over 120 world leaders to attend, thus raising the stakes and the pressure for a strong outcome. In poker language, such a stellar cast might equate to a "royal flush"—an unbeatable hand.

Another noteworthy feature of the Copenhagen event was the massive attendance. By the end of the meeting, over 40,000 individuals from eligible organizations had registered to participate (ENB 2009). While the venue's capacity was less than 20,000, the organizers had not placed a limit on registrations, perhaps in the belief that participation from all stakeholders should be encouraged.

Ultimately, neither of these noteworthy features helped. Negotiators were unable to bring talks to a point that would allow their leaders to put their signatures to a strong outcome. Instead, Prime Ministers and Presidents arrived in the final days of the meeting faced with a wide array of outstanding and immensely complex issues left on the table. In addition, other stakeholders were literally left out in the cold due to space limitations at the venue, while organizers mistimed the release of documents they hoped would help build consensus, and further compounded the situation by not distributing them to all players, making them appear to be "secret" texts. Furthermore, the sheer number of participants meant that it was impossible to achieve the sense of inclusiveness and openness to all stakeholders that had characterized some of the negotiations in previous years. Trust building is a difficult exercise at the best of times, but it is not helped when thousands of participants end up locked out of the building. These missteps left a sense of exclusion and back-room horse-trading that was in opposition to the transparency and trust-building organizers had sought to generate in the early stages, prior to the adoption of the Bali Road Map (ENB 2009).

A Cancún Comeback: Winning with "Two of Kind"

The UNFCCC process redeemed itself somewhat in December 2010, when a more satisfactory outcome was gained with the help of the new UNFCCC Executive-Secretary, Christiana Figueres, working in close alliance with the Mexican hosts of the Cancún Climate Change Conference. From the outset, the organizers of this conference were at pains to avoid some of the errors from Copenhagen. Müller speaks of the "cathartic" experience of the Cancún negotiations (2011, 1) and lists numerous innovations. This time there were no "secret" texts. There were periodic "stock-taking" briefings in the plenary hall for all participants, thus greatly increasing the real transparency of the process. The objective was clearly to heal some of the wounds from Copenhagen.

One new feature at Cancún was the decision to pair up key ministers to work together on some of the thornier issues. For each key topic, one developing country minister and one developed country minister were tasked with convening talks among negotiators and finding a way forward. This approach seemed to find favor with many, and perhaps the sense of ownership it generated among ministers and other senior officials helped move things forward. At the meeting's end, there was a far greater sense of agreement and achievement than had existed in Copenhagen, with only one delegation, Bolivia, standing against the consensus (ENB 2010).

Lessons for Future Negotiations

Why did Cancún and other meetings examined in this paper succeed where Copenhagen did not? Some of the trust-building techniques examined here appear to have helped move talks forward. Useful efforts included informal dialogues, generating a sense of inclusiveness and participation, and building a sense of ownership. Equally, it is clear that some missteps in Copenhagen hurt the prospects for an outcome, beyond the scope of repair by any comfy couch conversation.

While innovative techniques appear to be promising for some situations, they can only go so far. The lessons of Chapter 5 of this volume, on coalitions, must also be understood. Some seismic geopolitical shifts have intruded on the climate change talks and a post-2012 agreement will need all countries to be involved. Unlike the Kyoto talks in 1997, which essentially involved arguments among industrialized countries about their individual levels of commitment, the game has changed and developing countries are now much more important players. The "BASIC" Group (Brazil, South Africa, India, and China) demonstrated this in Copenhagen when they refused to accept a draft text put forward by the Danish host government, and essentially rewrote the terms of the deal along with the United States (ENB 2009). It was these major developing economies who played the key role in determining the Copenhagen outcome, upstaging the Europeans and other major players—something almost unimaginable in Kyoto twelve years earlier, when the industrialized countries still dominated both politically and economically.

The stakes of the issue under negotiation represent another major factor in how far innovative techniques can go in facilitating an outcome. Politicians fear that taking a wrong step—playing their cards poorly—could in turn have enormous social and economic consequences domestically. At a meeting such as Copenhagen, where the stakes were highest, such fears and complexity may create challenges that no comfy couch can solve. It is unquestionably easier to reach a deal at a meeting such as Cancún or Bali, which were essentially "staging post" meetings toward a bigger moment, with bigger commitments. Quite simply, there was less at stake for negotiators in Bali or even Cancún than in Copenhagen. Similarly, the ultimate agreement reached in the forest negotiations discussed here retreated from the deepest potential commitment, a legally binding instrument on forests. Of the cases presented here, the Biosafety Protocol perhaps represented the greatest level of additional commitment to which negotiators agreed.

Another variation in the cases, and influence on the outcomes, is the urgency for a cooperative outcome. The deadlines for negotiations within the global forest regime have been less rigid than they have been for the other two cases, no doubt linked to the fact that there is no consensus on even beginning negotiations toward a legally binding agreement in the first place. Thus, there have been numerous meetings where no agreement is reached on starting a full negotiating process toward a convention but where the possibility of doing so in the future is held in reserve through decision language, in order to appease those who have pushed most strongly for a legally binding instrument. Second, the labels of "forest," "climate change," and "biosafety" themselves demonstrate a fundamental difference in these cases given that, in the latter two, the problem to be addressed is much more visible and the measures to be taken thus potentially more easily envisaged as a whole (see Chapter 8).

On the other hand, as shown in Copenhagen, innovative negotiating techniques may only produce substantial outcomes if parties come to the negotiating table with something genuine and tangible to offer in a mutually beneficial exchange. In the case of Copenhagen, there is still an argument that some key players were unable to do this, and still saw the negotiations as a zero-sum outcome that would inevitably result in "winners" and "losers." This arguably differed from the situation in Cancún, where strenuous efforts had been made in the preceding year to identify benefits for almost every negotiating group. The change of attitude among many countries is undoubtedly linked to the fact that tangible benefits being offered post-Cancún, through the promise of funding for REDD+ (reducing emissions from deforestation and forest degradation in developing countries, as well as conservation, sustainable management of forests, and enhancement of carbon stocks) and other funds, seem to hold the potential to be great enough to sway hearts and minds toward effective cooperation to combat climate change. Additionally, the Mexican organizers in Cancún had clearly learned from the Copenhagen experience and made a concerted effort to build greater transparency and inclusiveness in their event.

While the case studies here show that Track II techniques cannot guarantee success in a negotiation, in some cases a well-formulated approach may help generate the trust and "space" needed for negotiators to find common ground, in cases where there is the potential for compromise. Innovative approaches such as those described here can help to build a sense of inclusion, participation, and, ultimately, ownership. The proliferation of these Track II techniques in various multilateral environmental processes suggests that their value has not been lost on meeting organizers. What the next innovation may be is open to question. However, if precedent is any indicator, it is not inconceivable that one day we may see delegates negotiating from comfy lounge chairs under swaying palms, teddy bears in hand.

Notes

1 New Zealand and Singapore also participated in the Compromise Group in Montreal in January 2000 (Galvez 2002, 208).
2 Mayr first introduced this method of determining speaking order during the Vienna meeting, when colored balls were used to accomplish this task (Mayr 2002, 227).

3 Private communications from delegates at CSD 1995, IPF 1997, IFF 1998, and UNFF 2005, 2008, 2009.
4 Interview with member of British delegation to UNFF 5, January 2007.
5 The title of the chapter draws from this case, with editorial liberties taken in preference of the alliterative "comfy couch" referenced in the title.
6 Private communications with delegates at UNFCCC COPs 12, 13, and 14.

Works Cited

Axelrod, Robert. 1984. *The Evolution of Cooperation*. New York, NY: Basic Books.

Ballhorn, Richard. 2002. Miami Group: Canada. In *The Cartagena Protocol on Biosafety: Reconciling Trade in Biotechnology with Environment and Development?* Edited by Christoph Bail, Robert Falkner, and Helen Marquard. London: Earthscan/RIIA.

Chasek, Pamela S. 2011. Creating Space for Consensus: High-Level Globe Trotting into the Bali Climate Change Conference. *International Negotiation* 16(1): 87–108.

Country-Led Initiative in Support of UNFF on the Future of the International Arrangement on Forests. 2005. The Guadalajara Report: Co-Chairs' Report, 25–28 January 2005, Guadalajara, Mexico (The Guadalajara Report).

Davenport, Deborah S. 2005. An Alternative Explanation for the Failure of the UNCED Forest Negotiations. *Global Environmental Politics* 5(1):105–130.

Davenport, Deborah S. and Peter Wood. 2006. UNFF-5, -6 and -7: Finding the Way Forward for the International Arrangement on Forests. *Review of European Community and International Environmental Law (RECIEL)* 15(3): 316–326.

Downs, George, David M. Rocke, and Peter N. Barsoom. 1996. "Is the Good News about Compliance Good News about Cooperation?" *International Organization* 50(3): 379–406.

ENB (*Earth Negotiations Bulletin*). 1999. Summary of the Sixth Session of the Open-Ended Ad Hoc Working Group on Biosafety and the First Extraordinary Session of the CBD Conference of the Parties: 14–23 February 1999. *Earth Negotiations Bulletin* 9(117). http://www.iisd.ca/download/pdf/ENB09117e.pdf (accessed January 4, 2011).

ENB. 2000a. Summary of the Resumed Session of the Extraordinary Meeting of the Conference of the Parties for the Adoption of the Protocol on Biosafety to the Convention on Biological Diversity: 24–28 January 2000. *Earth Negotiations Bulletin* 9(137). http://www.iisd.ca/download/pdf/ENB09137e.pdf (accessed March 8, 2011).

ENB. 2000b. ExCOP Highlights: Thursday, 27 January 2000. *Earth Negotiations Bulletin* 9(136). http://www.iisd.ca/download/pdf/ENB09136e.pdf (accessed January 5, 2011).

ENB. 2005. Summary of the UNFCCC Seminar of Governmental Experts: 16–17 May 2005. *Earth Negotiations Bulletin* 12(261). http://www.iisd.ca/download/pdf/enb12261e.pdf (accessed June 22, 2011).

ENB. 2007. Summary of the Thirteenth Conference of the Parties (COP 13) to the UNFCCC and the Third Meeting of the Parties to the Kyoto Protocol: 3–15 December 2007. *Earth Negotiations Bulletin* 12(354). http://www.iisd.ca/download/pdf/ENB12354e.pdf (accessed March 8, 2011).

ENB. 2009. Summary of Copenhagen Climate Change Conference: 7–19 December 2009. *Earth Negotiations Bulletin* 12(459). http://www.iisd.ca/download/pdf/ENB12459e.pdf (accessed March 8, 2011).

ENB. 2010. Summary of the Cancún Climate Change Conference: 29 November–11 December 2010. *Earth Negotiations Bulletin* 12(498). http://www.iisd.ca/download/pdf/ENB12498e.pdf (accessed March 8, 2011).

Enright, Cathleen A. 2002. Miami Group: United States. In *The Cartagena Protocol on Biosafety: Reconciling Trade in Biotechnology with Environment and Development?* Edited by Christoph Bail, Robert Falkner, and Helen Marquard. London: Earthscan/RIIA.

Falkner, Robert. 2002. Negotiating the Biosafety Protocol: The International Process. In *The Cartagena Protocol on Biosafety: Reconciling Trade in Biotechnology with Environment and Development?* Edited by Christoph Bail, Robert Falkner, and Helen Marquard. London: Earthscan/RIIA.

Fisher, Ronald J. 1989. Prenegotiation Problem-Solving Discussions Enhancing the Potential for Successful Negotiation. In *Getting to the Table: The Processes of International Prenegotiation.* Edited by Janice Gross Stein. Baltimore, MD: Johns Hopkins University Press.

Fisher, Ronald J. 2005. *Paving the Way: Contributions of Interactive Conflict Resolution to Peacemaking.* Lanham, MD: Lexington Books.

Fisher, Ronald J. 2006. Coordination Between Track Two and Track One Diplomacy in Successful Cases of Prenegotiation. *International Negotiation* 11(1): 65–89.

Galvez, Amanda. 2002. Compromise Group: Mexico. In *The Cartagena Protocol on Biosafety: Reconciling Trade in Biotechnology with Environment and Development?* Edited by Christoph Bail, Robert Falkner, and Helen Marquard. London: Earthscan/RIIA.

Gilpin, Robert. 1987. *The Political Economy of International Relations.* Princeton, NJ: Princeton University Press.

Gören-Engfeldt, Lars. 2009. *From Stockholm to Johannesburg and Beyond.* Stockholm: The Government Offices of Sweden.

Mankin, Bill. 2007. MY POW or Yours? Choosing a Leadership Agenda for the UNFF. Unpublished discussion paper.

Mayr, Juan. 2002. Environment Ministers: Political Perspectives on the Final Negotiations: Colombia. In *The Cartagena Protocol on Biosafety: Reconciling Trade in Biotechnology with Environment and Development?* Edited by Christoph Bail, Robert Falkner, and Helen Marquard. London: Earthscan/RIIA.

McKibben, Bill. 2010. *EAARTH.* New York, NY: Henry Holt and Co.

Montville, Joseph, and William Davidson. 1981. Foreign Policy According to Freud. *Foreign Policy* 45(Winter): 145–157.

Morgenthau, Hans. 1956. *Politics Among Nations.* New York, NY: Alfred A. Knopf.

Müller, Benito. 2008. On the Road Again! Impressions from the Thirteenth UN Climate Change Conference. http://www.oxfordclimatepolicy.org/publications/documents/comment_0208–2.pdf (accessed June 22, 2011).

Müller, Benito. 2011. UNFCCC–The Future of the Process: Remedial Action on Process Ownership and Political Guidance. http://www.climatestrategies.org/component/reports/category/55/302.html (accessed June 22, 2011).

Nobs, Beat. 2002. Compromise Group: Switzerland. In *The Cartagena Protocol on Biosafety: Reconciling Trade in Biotechnology with Environment and Development?* Edited by Christoph Bail, Robert Falkner, and Helen Marquard. London: Earthscan/RIIA.

Olson, Mançur. 1965. *The Logic of Collective Action: Public Goods and the Theory of Groups.* Cambridge, MA: Harvard University Press.

Oye, Kenneth, ed. 1986. *Cooperation under Anarchy.* Princeton, NJ: Princeton University Press.

Samper, Christian. 2002. The Extraordinary Meeting of the Conference of the Parties (ExCOP). In *The Cartagena Protocol on Biosafety: Reconciling Trade in Biotechnology with Environment and Development?* Edited by Christoph Bail, Robert Falkner, and Helen Marquard. London: Earthscan/RIIA.

Smith, Adam. 1776/1977. *An Inquiry into the Nature and Causes of the Wealth of Nations.* Chicago, IL: University of Chicago Press.

Spence, Chris. 2005. *Global Warming: Personal Solutions for a Healthy Planet.* New York, NY: Palgrave MacMillan.

ECOSOC (United Nations Economic and Social Council). 2004. Report of the Ad Hoc Expert Group on Consideration with a View to Recommending the Parameters of a Mandate for Developing a Legal Framework on All Types of Forests (E.CN.18/2005/2) (AHEG PARAM Report 2004).

Wendt, Alexander. 1992. Anarchy is What States Make of It: The Social Construction of Power Politics. *International Organization* 46, 2(Spring): 391–426.

4

INFORMING POLICY

Science and Knowledge in Global Environmental Agreements

*Pia M. Kohler, Alexandra Conliffe, Stefan Jungcurt,
Maria Gutierrez, and Yulia Yamineva*

In *The Day After Tomorrow*, a 2004 disaster movie about accelerated climate change, a lone American climatologist is called to a United Nations-like meeting of world leaders to report on the latest scientific information relating to the impending catastrophe facing the planet. While the image of a single scientist speaking truth to the assembly of global decision makers presents powerful imagery for Hollywood, it could not be further from the way in which countries turn to the science community for guidance on environmental challenges.

The global environmental problems we face today, ranging from acid rain and climate change to chemical pollution and ecosystems management, to name only a few issue areas, require decision makers to have a strong understanding of the scientific processes and trends at play to guide their policymaking. Consequently, over time a broad array of mechanisms has been put in place to provide expert guidance as global environmental agreements are negotiated and implemented.

While the institutional arrangements developed to enable science to inform policy are diverse, so too is the success that these arrangements have achieved. Evidence since 1992 suggests that informing policy, no matter how convincing or solid the science, is not a straightforward process. Besides, science and policy are not completely separate worlds, and boundaries between them are often difficult to define. The question of who produces science, and for what purpose, matters.

In this chapter, we first provide an overview of the types of institutional arrangement put in place for science to inform global environmental policy-making. We then explore the track record of expertise across several regimes, notably climate, ozone, biodiversity, desertification, wetlands, chemicals management, sustainable development, and endangered species protection, to examine who mandates these scientific advisory efforts, who provides the advice, and who legitimizes it. Finally, we use these examples to suggest how science might best inform policy in the future, while discussing what we should *not* expect from science in the sustainable development policymaking process.

The Landscape of Expert Advice in Global Environmental Politics

Prior to the 1992 Earth Summit, international environmental agreements paid little attention to the means through which scientific knowledge was to inform decision making. While several internationally negotiated agreements stated the need to make decisions on the basis of sound scientific information, they did not as a rule specify the source of such advice or a specific procedure or institution for delivering the advice to the parties to the agreement. For example, the 1971 Ramsar Convention on Wetlands of International Importance especially as Waterfowl Habitat calls on parties to "encourage research and the exchange of data and publications regarding wetlands and their flora and fauna" (Ramsar Convention 1971, Article 4.3) and notes that the Conference of the Contracting Parties (COP) can "request relevant international bodies to prepare reports and statistics on matters which are essentially international in character affecting wetlands" (Ramsar Convention 1971, Article 6.2). The convention also provides for party representatives at COP meetings to include "persons who are experts on wetlands or waterfowl by reason of knowledge and experience gained in scientific, administrative and other appropriate capacities" (Ramsar Convention 1971, Article 7.1). Yet there are no references as to what constitutes a relevant international body, nor consideration to the need for representativeness, whether geographic, gender or other, in the advice provided. Furthermore, the Ramsar Conference of the Contracting Parties did not have a dedicated science advisory body until 1993, when parties established the Scientific and Technical Review Panel.

Similarly, the 1973 Convention on International Trade in Endangered Species of Wild Fauna and Flora (CITES) underscores the role of science and looks to parties to designate national scientific authorities to aid in implementing the Convention. In contrast to the Ramsar Convention, CITES did entrust a body—the Secretariat—to "undertake scientific and technical studies" (CITES 1973, Article XII). As such, there were no guidelines on who, beyond the Secretariat staff, was to provide scientific advice until specific Committees on Plants and on Animals were established in 1986 (Gehring and Ruffing 2008).

In the post-Earth Summit period, parties to multilateral environmental agreements (MEAs) recognize even more the need for science to inform policymaking in a deliberate manner, and have experimented with an array of institutional arrangements to meet this need. These experiments have taken place at the same time that scholars have increasingly scrutinized the role of science and science advisers in policymaking. In particular, the common understanding of science and policy as two separate realms, with science "speaking truth to power," has been questioned. In her 1990 book, *The Fifth Branch: Science Advisers as Policymakers*, Sheila Jasanoff argues for a richer understanding of the role of expertise in public decision making. She critiques two prevailing views, namely that of scientists entrusted as validators of science-intensive policies, and that of participation as the "antidote to abuse of expert authority" (Jasanoff 1990, vii).

When looking to the ways in which scientific knowledge is brought to bear in policymaking, it is useful to apply a framework developed through the study of global environmental assessments (Cash et al. 2003; Social Learning Group 2001a, 2001b). Credibility, legitimacy, and salience are identified as key elements contributing to the success of an assessment. As Cash et al. (2003, 8086) explain:

> *Credibility* involves the scientific adequacy of the technical evidence and arguments. *Salience* deals with the relevance of the assessment to the needs of decision makers. *Legitimacy* reflects the perception that the production of information and technology has been respectful of stakeholders' divergent values and beliefs, unbiased in its conduct, and fair in its treatment of opposing views and interests. Our work shows these attributes are tightly coupled, such that efforts to enhance any one normally incur a cost to the others.

When looking to the evolution of efforts to institutionalize science advice, we can witness challenges faced in designing scientific advisory bodies that produce scientifically credible outputs, while also ensuring that these outputs meet the needs of the decision makers (most often the COP overseeing the scientific body), while following procedures that will confer the necessary legitimacy on any scientific output produced by the body. Several of the cases discussed in this chapter illustrate instances where parties have achieved greater success along one of these metrics, yet achieving success across all three has proven more elusive.

Importantly, within the context of MEAs, scientific bodies are often expected to act not only as providers of scientific advice, but also as hybrid science-policy institutions that serve as a mediation point between the broader science community and the parties (Miller 2001). More recent work has scrutinized these institutions as sites of knowledge co-production, where the science and policy realms come together to co-produce new knowledge (Jasanoff 2004). We examine scientific bodies with both roles in mind.

Structural Variety

As we analyze the range of outcomes in informing global environmental policy-making, it is important to understand the landscape of expert advice, notably the variety both in structure and in function. Over time, various actors—ranging from scientists to politicians to parties to MEAs—have put in place several broad typologies of institutions for facilitating the production of expert advice for policymakers. We briefly outline some of the key institutions that today comprise the landscape of sources of expert advice for MEAs, and underscore how these structural choices affect who is providing advice and how, and the ensuing consequences for credibility, legitimacy, and salience.

State-of-the-Art Assessments

State-of-the-art assessments provide comprehensive overviews of available evidence and understanding around a particular environmental challenge. They have often been driven by members of the expert and scientific community who have recognized the need to take stock of science and knowledge around a given environmental concern in order to inform policymaking. The preparation of one-off, state-of-the-art assessments has rarely led to enduring institutional structures to deliver continuous expert analyses, and is more generally, but not always, driven by the scientific community as a short-term effort. The large-scale involvement of the scientific community in such assessments can enhance the output's credibility, but such assessments can also be vulnerable to weaknesses in salience, especially as the output may not be geared at a particular treaty framework and may not be produced in a format suitable for policy uptake.

One of the best-known stand-alone assessments is the 2005 Millennium Ecosystem Assessment (MA), which assessed the consequences of ecosystem change for human wellbeing (MA 2005). The MA was spurred by a group of leading scientists, and was later coordinated through the UN Environment Programme (UNEP), the World Bank, the UN Development Programme, and the World Resources Institute, and eventually called for by the UN Secretary-General in 2000.

Another example is the Arctic Climate Impact Assessment (ACIA), conducted by the International Arctic Science Committee and the Arctic Council science working groups on the Arctic Monitoring and Assessment Program and on the Conservation of Arctic Flora and Fauna. This effort, led by the United States and bringing in participation from the seven other Arctic countries, was prepared over five years by "an international team of over 300 scientists, other experts, and knowledgeable members of the indigenous communities" (ACIA 2005, preface). It has been highlighted for its unique means of including indigenous knowledge in such an assessment (Long Martello 2008). The ACIA's close relationship with the Arctic Council provided it enhanced salience because there was a built-in political forum for addressing its result. Yet its solid grounding in academic research—as evidenced by the hosting of its Secretariat at the International Arctic Research Center at the University of Alaska Fairbanks—and its broad participation of stakeholders and academics as contributors enhanced its legitimacy and credibility.

Stand-alone Panels

In contrast to one-off assessments, there has been a push to establish stand-alone panels that can provide many of the advantages of one-off assessments while also providing the continuity and reactivity that can increase the salience of advice for policymaking. Such stand-alone panels are sometimes advocated by the scientific community, as in the case of the recently established International Panel on Chemical Pollution (IPCP), or by a government, as in the French government's effort, launched in 2005, to establish a stand-alone panel for biodiversity (ENB 2005a, 2009a).

Among these structures, the Intergovernmental Panel on Climate Change (IPCC) has emerged as a unique institution that provides similar input to policy-making as stand-alone assessments, but with a continuing infrastructure and insti-tutional footprint (Figure 4.1). The IPCC was established in 1988 by the United Nations World Meteorological Organization (WMO) and UNEP. Although a significant amount of scientific evidence on climate change had built up at that time, its founding was triggered by a number of factors, including: the activism of Mostafa Tolba, then executive director of UNEP; the insufficient links with

FIGURE 4.1 IPCC Secretary Renata Christ and IPCC Chairman Rajendra K. Pachauri. The IPCC won the Nobel Peace Prize in 2007. Photo courtesy of IISD/*Earth Negotiations Bulletin*

policy of the Advisory Group on Greenhouse Gases, a small group of experts charged with the matter; and lack of consensus among US agencies on climate change (the Department of Energy and the Environmental Protection Agency had each conducted assessments with very different results) (Agrawala 1998a). Consequently, the US suggested a new body to engage governments and involve official experts and "reassert governmental control and supervision over what was becoming an increasingly prominent political issue" (Bodansky 1993).

The IPCC does not undertake research of its own; rather, it evaluates existing peer-reviewed published research to provide policy-relevant yet neutral and non-prescriptive consensus views (IPCC 1998). Thus, the IPCC occupies an intermediary position in the science–policy relationship, in which it sits outside both the realm of scientific inquiry and the actual decision making. Research on the IPCC highlights its unique and somewhat ambiguous nature as a science-policy institution (see Agrawala 1998a; Skodvin 2000).

The IPCC's design and complex assessment procedures represent attempts to enable both scientific credibility and international political legitimacy (Agrawala 1999). Its credibility is established by thousands of scientists from around the world, nominated by governments, who work for free as authors, contributors, and reviewers. The scientists are organized in three different working groups dealing with all aspects of climate change. These groups undertake assessments in cycles that last approximately six years. Once finished, the reports go through a review process by experts who have developed expertise and have publications in areas of the assessment. Legitimacy is enhanced through the review of the IPCC's reports by 194 countries. This review process includes approval of a Summary for Policymakers (SPM) for each of the working group reports, line-by-line, in a plenary session. Thus the expert advice in the SPMs is intensely debated by policymakers who represent the political interests of their countries. These attempts to bring legitimacy to the process, however, have also been criticized for diluting expert advice to wording that all can agree, leading to what some refer to as the "lowest common denominator."

Despite its shortcomings, the IPCC is generally agreed to be "the most extensive and carefully constructed intergovernmental advisory process ever known in international relations" (Grubb et al. 1999, 4). For close to two decades, the IPCC has represented the only full-fledged example of a stand-alone panel, and its overall success has long prompted policymakers and experts in other spheres to demand similar institutional arrangements, as discussed in the conclusions.

Subsidiary Bodies under a Specific Treaty

Subsidiary bodies represent another typology for institutionalizing expert advice for global environmental decision making. Subsidiary bodies are established by and report to the COP of a particular treaty while also benefiting from the institutional and organizational support of the treaty's Secretariat. Their main purpose is to provide their respective COPs with advice on scientific and technical matters. Because their agendas are set by the COP, in principle the advice they provide responds directly to the needs of the COP, and should thus be salient. There are two large classes of subsidiary bodies worthy of examination here: broad membership bodies, where any party to the treaty in question can send representatives, and limited membership committees, where parties delegate the provision of advice to a smaller group of experts.

Broad Membership Subsidiary Bodies

All three Rio Conventions were designed to include broad membership subsidiary bodies: the United Nations Framework Convention on Climate Change (UNFCCC) established a Subsidiary Body for Scientific and Technological Advice (SBSTA); the Convention on Biological Diversity (CBD) established a Subsidiary Body on Scientific, Technical and Technological Advice (SBSTTA); and the UN Convention to Combat Desertification (UNCCD) established a Committee on Science and Technology (CST). Participation in each of these subsidiary bodies is open to government representatives competent in the relevant fields of expertise from all member country parties. NGOs and representatives of universities and other scientific institutions can attend as observers. In theory, then, broad membership facilitates legitimacy through broad geographic representation. In practice, however, attention to political representation has often trumped quality of expertise, leaving these bodies to operate as what some observers have called a "mini-COP," with limited input of actual scientific and technical expertise (e.g. ENB 1999b).

Limited Membership Subsidiary Bodies or Committees

Several treaties have opted for limited membership subsidiary committees as a means of delegating the responsibility for advice to a smaller group of experts than would be called upon if each party could send an expert of their choosing. Such limited membership bodies are often designed to have specific expertise/qualification requirements in addition to arrangements for delegation, and often include specific guidelines on rules of procedure for producing advice. Relative to broad membership bodies, limited membership specialized committees have the potential to deliver more credible science as membership is often scrutinized to ensure the appropriate scientific fields of expertise are present, although the latter is dependent on parties having a sufficient knowledge of the underlying science to identify the range of expertise necessary for such scientific credibility. Further, the extent to which designated experts act in their individual capacity rather than acting as agents of their governments or employers can also impact the scientific credibility of the advice they generate.

Numerous treaties have adopted limited membership specialized committees to provide specific operational advice—a function discussed in the following section. For instance, under the Stockholm and Rotterdam Conventions, review committees are tasked with recommending whether new substances should be subject to the treaties' provisions. The size and membership of these committees were the focus of extensive negotiations by parties, with discussions centering largely on the committee's size and its geographic make-up (see ENB 1999a, for example). Indeed, the limited size of these bodies, often underscored as necessary for efficient deliberations, comes at the expense of the legitimacy that broad membership affords. This trade-off requires parties to provide greater oversight over which criteria to prioritize in setting membership.

Parties to MEAs often opt for a combination of broad and limited membership bodies to provide expert advice. Under the ozone regime, an open-ended working group, carried out according to the same rules as a COP (where parties and observers can send delegates, and where proceedings are carried out with simultaneous translation in the six official UN languages), meets annually to prepare decisions for the COP on the basis of reports from the Protocol's panels, namely the Technology and Economic Assessment Panel, the Scientific Assessment Panel, and the Environmental Effects Panel. These three panels have been described as "the pillars of the ozone protection regime since the very beginning of the implementation of the Montreal Protocol" (Ozone Secretariat 2004). They draw on experts nominated both by parties and by an international scientific advisory group—thus shoring up the output's legitimacy and credibility. Another example of the delegation of specific issues to smaller groups is the Ad hoc Technical Expert Groups under the CBD, which report back to SBSTTA.

Functional Variety

The diversity of arrangements for providing expert advice in global environmental decision making is not limited to the institutional structures in place. Notably, the function of the expertise being called on plays an important role in the extent to which it retains credibility, legitimacy, and salience. In examining the existing landscape, we identify three key functions that expert advice is called on to provide: framing issues and raising awareness, providing operational advice, and creating momentum for a policy shift.

Issue Framing and Awareness Raising

An important role played by expert advice, and by the bodies established to produce such advice, is issue framing, which can often lead to awareness raising. For example, early international assessments on the connection between CFC use and ozone layer depletion catalyzed global, coordinated action on the topic (i.e., through the adoption of the Vienna Convention and its Montreal Protocol).

Similarly, the Arctic Monitoring and Assessment Programme (AMAP) put in place in 1991 by Arctic countries to monitor the levels of pollutants and to assess their effects in the Arctic environment, helped frame efforts to negotiate a Protocol on Persistent Organic Pollutants (POPs) under the Convention on Long-Range Transboundary Air Pollution. AMAP also informed negotiations that led to the adoption of the Stockholm Convention on POPs (ENB 2005b).

The IPCC could be considered an extreme version of this: shortly after its inauguration, the IPCC was formally tasked by the UN General Assembly not only with conducting assessments of science, impacts, and responses, but also with identifying "elements for inclusion in a possible future international convention on climate" (IPCC 2004), thereby shaping what would eventually be the UNFCCC. Thus, in its initial years, the IPCC fulfilled the dual role of assessing knowledge to advise policy, and at the same time directly helping shape policy itself.

Such awareness-raising efforts usually pre-date the negotiation of a treaty and are often stand-alone or one-off assessment efforts. However, the way the issue is framed at the early stages of expert review can shape policy options in the longer term. For instance, some have argued that the very identification of environmental issues as global problems is a result of the efforts of large-scale assessments. The concept of "global climate" was coined by the IPCC. Similarly, the idea of "biological diversity" and the construction of a global rate of biodiversity loss were developed only in the context of the negotiation of the CBD. Among biologists and ecologists, it is still highly contested whether these constructs are a useful representation of the global aspects of the problems of ecosystem resilience (Miller and Edwards 2001).

Operational Advice

Perhaps the most visible contribution of expert advice in the day-to-day operation of MEAs are the tasks that parties entrust to subsidiary bodies and expert groups to inform decision making that in turn facilitates the implementation of treaty requirements. In this regard, some expert bodies have achieved a greater level of credibility, legitimacy, and salience in their output than others. Our experiences across a wide range of MEAs suggest that limited membership expert bodies provided by parties with clear frameworks for decision making have often been most successful in delivering broadly accepted and credible advice to their COPs. These deliberations, however, are not always without controversy, and the production of such operational advice can sometimes fall prey to concerns relating to the legitimacy or credibility of the output that are not related to the quality of the science as such.

While broad membership subsidiary bodies lend well to legitimacy in providing the expert advice required for achieving a treaty's governance goals, in practice they have often failed to deliver salient and timely advice to parties.

For example, parties to the UNCCD have complained that the CST is inefficient and ineffective in part because of its large size and composition (ENB 2001). Even at the first meeting of the COP, participants to the UNCCD process worried that the CST would be dominated by "politically oriented members and never get down to 'scientific business'" (ENB 1997), a problem they felt also existed in the UNFCCC and CBD subsidiary bodies. Indeed, the CST did not agree to impact indicators until 2009 and it will take more time to develop the accompanying methodology and data collection strategy. Many believe, however, that in addition to its size, the politicization and lack of necessary expertise within the CST is at least in part to blame.

Some restricted membership expert groups have had better success at providing operational advice than many of the broad membership subsidiary committees, but under specific conditions only. For example, under the Montreal Protocol, parties have established technical options committees with clearly defined mandates, such as reviewing nominations for critical use exemptions from parties that wish to continue using specific amounts of chemicals scheduled for phase out. One such expert group, the Methyl Bromide Technical Options Committee (MBTOC), presents its recommendations for critical use exemptions for final approval by the Protocol's Meeting of the Parties (i.e., by policymakers, not by experts). The Meeting of the Parties has not always accepted in full the MBTOC's recommendations. Notably, in 2004 and 2005, parties had to hold extraordinary Meetings of the Parties as they could not reach agreement on the MBTOC's recommendations at their ordinary meetings (ENB 2004, 2005c).

Why did this occur? In discussing the recommendations forwarded to them, many parties—especially from developing countries—raised concerns as to the legitimacy of the MBTOC process, in particular relating to the lack of participation by experts from developing countries. Subsequently, parties have revised the membership and transparency provisions for the Technical Options Committees, which have thus proven more successful in applying decision-making guidelines and generating recommendations that are accepted by parties with limited discussion.

Building Momentum

Large-scale global assessments have proven particularly useful in garnering momentum and changing the framing of a problem to engage specific groups in the search for the solutions to global problems. The most well-known example of late is the Stern Review on the Economics of Climate Change (Stern 2006), which shifted attention to the long-term costs of inaction on climate change, thereby leading to a stronger engagement of business and other private actors in the climate change discussion. The 2005 Millennium Ecosystem Assessment (MA), which shifted the common perception of biodiversity loss as an issue concerned primarily with conservation to one concerned primarily with the sustainable flow of ecosystem services for human wellbeing, is another example. The success of the Stern Review and the MA prepared the ground for the 2010 stand-alone assessment on biodiversity, The Economics of Ecosystem Services and Biodiversity (TEEB) Study (TEEB 2010). The TEEB Study centers on an economic analysis of the value of biodiversity. Its primary focus was not on the development of new knowledge, but on the comprehensive translation of existing knowledge into a language more accessible to those actors concerned, with the aim of making the case for their engagement.

Interestingly, neither the MA nor TEEB has had much of a direct impact on the negotiations in the respective for a (there are very few direct references to the MA in decisions of the CBD, for example). Rather, most of the influence has been of an indirect nature by changing public perceptions of the problem and thereby changing the discourse in the relevant scientific bodies and the negotiations.

Reviewing the Track Record: Successes, Failures, and Limitations to the Delivery of Expert Advice

The experiences of delivering advice to decision makers across a wide range of MEAs reveal varying degrees of success. Our goal is not to identify clear causal mechanisms between success level and the institutional make-up or type of advice being produced. Rather, we can identify several factors that have often had an impact on not only the credibility, legitimacy, and salience of advice, but have also shaped the way in which advice is taken up by the relevant policymaking body. Of the many trends we could discuss, we highlight three lessons learned since 1992: (1) the identity of the experts delivering advice matters; (2) experts cannot answer all of the questions that decision makers pose, nor can they make moral, ethical, or value-related judgments; and (3) expert advice must be understood within the broader political scope of the negotiations that it is intended to inform. Our examples demonstrate that there is no single best approach, and that flexibility and adaptability are key.

Expert Identity

An underlying theme in our discussion of the form and function of expert advice thus far is that, for policymakers, it matters *who* produces expert advice to help inform decision making. This is exemplified by the often lengthy deliberations between parties when establishing membership guidelines for an expert body. The existence of a wide array of types of expert body demonstrates the variety of interpretations of balance, depending on the attributes of experts that parties judge to most affect the credibility, legitimacy, and salience of the advice being produced. Among those attributes are: prescriptions on the diversity of disciplines to be represented; guidelines for the institutional affiliation of those designated as eligible to be experts; criteria to achieve geographic balance and/or balance between developed and developing countries; and personal diversity, including gender (Kohler 2006). Importantly, even though membership and procedures for expert groups are often carefully negotiated, agreed-upon balance may not always play out in practice, especially as parties may only be entitled to put forward one nomination, a selection in which they may struggle to achieve all of the criteria they have agreed upon.

Expert bodies, while often meant to be carefully crafted institutions held up to apolitical ideals, are often a locus where developed/developing country dynamics can spill over from the policy arena. Concerns relating notably to geographic diversity in the membership of experts producing advice can affect both the credibility and the legitimacy of the output. The interpretation of what geographic representation means, however, varies and can be the subject of great debate. Take, for example, the negotiations between 2002 and 2004 over the establishment of the POPs Review Committee (POPRC) under the Stockholm Convention. While the Convention text calls for geographic balance, including between developed and developing country parties, some countries interpreted this to mean that experts on the committee should be designated by parties from each of the UN's five regions, with membership numbers proportional to the number of parties in each region. A contrasting position instead preferred the ozone regime model which, in its expert committees, strives for a 50/50 balance between experts from developed and developing country parties. While advocates for the latter underscored that reducing the proportion of experts from developed country parties would undermine the credibility of the output, parties were also struggling with other constraints on membership, including, for example, size and the number of experts from parties that would necessitate financial assistance to take part in the committee's work. In the end, parties opted for geographical distribution proportional to party membership in each of the UN's five regions,[1] a compromise made possible by an agreement to facilitate full participation by all nominated experts by providing for simultaneous translation at POPRC meetings (ENB 2005b).

In 2009 and 2011, parties to the Stockholm Convention considered nominations to list an additional ten substances as POPs under the Convention (Figure 4.2). In what is largely attributed as a testament to the credibility and legitimacy of the POPRC process, parties adopted the committee's recommendations (ENB 2009b, 2011). The geographic diversity on the committee also played a role in how the committee's advice was relayed to parties, as experts from all five geographic regions attended the COP and were able to play into the skillful "stage management" as the POPRC's procedures were validated and defended.[2]

In the case of climate, the IPCC aspired for broad geographical representation from its establishment in 1988. By that time, developed countries had accumulated considerable scientific expertise on climate issues, but many other nations were not convinced by research findings generated in developed countries.

FIGURE 4.2 The POPs Review Committee nominated an additional ten substances to be listed as POPs under the Convention in 2009 and 2011. Photo courtesy of IISD/*Earth Negotiations Bulletin*

Climate change was often viewed by developing countries as an attempt by the developed world to hamper economic growth in the South. Hence, establishing an intergovernmental scientific assessment panel in such context was meant to help engage governments worldwide in climate change negotiations (Agrawala 1998a; Hecht and Tirpak 1995). The important part of that task was to gain trust and acceptance of scientific findings by developing country governments through the broad involvement of developing country scientists. It was the first chair of the panel, Bert Bolin, who noted: "don't you think credibility demands global representation?" (Schneider 1991, quoted in Agrawala 1998b).

The panel has several arrangements in place to assist developing country researchers participate in the assessment, such as financial support to attend meetings, and has conducted many capacity-building activities in developing countries. The panel's decision in 2008 to use the Nobel Peace Prize money for creating a scholarship fund for young scholars specifically from least developed countries and small island developing states represents another step toward a more active capacity-building role of the IPCC and an attempt to redress the pervasive imbalance (ENB 2008a).

Nevertheless, maintaining broader participation of scientists from developing countries remains a challenge for the IPCC. Despite the considerable efforts by the panel, the authorship of the IPCC reports consists mainly of developed country scientists, especially in Working Group I, which addresses the physical basis of climate change (Yamineva 2010). The reasons are varied, with some reflecting practical obstacles to participation of developing country scientists in the assessment, for example, lack of access to peer-reviewed articles, language barriers and visa difficulties, and the lack of remuneration for the demanding job of authors. A more fundamental problem relates to the uneven distribution of scientific expertise between North and South, which displays itself in the imbalanced distribution of scientists and peer-reviewed research among developed and developing countries.

The implications for policymaking can be significant. Some scholars have claimed that because developed country scientists dominate in the IPCC, issue framing has been unjust to the global South (Biermann 2006). For example, assessments do not distinguish between "survival" emissions in the South and "luxury" emissions in the North (Agarwal and Narain 1991; Parikh 1994). Greater geographic balance among scientists in the IPCC might have helped to frame this issue differently.

Geographic representation, of course, is only one of many ways to conceive of legitimate representation. The Ramsar Convention on Wetlands may present one of the more complex models. In their most recent revision to the *modus operandi* of the Convention's Scientific and Technical Review Panel, parties provided not just for experts from across the Convention's seven regions, but also identified issue-specific expertise needs, as well as providing for institutional diversity by ensuring participation by NGOs (ENB 2008b).

While parties to the Ramsar Convention identified issue expertise and NGO representation as critical to increasing the credibility, legitimacy, and salience of the advice their expert groups deliver, parties to other conventions have valued other metrics. For example, the CBD's Working Group on Article 8(j) and related issues[3] provides a forum for the active participation of indigenous and local communities (ILCs) on issues relating to the conservation and use of "the knowledge, innovations and practices of indigenous and local communities embodying traditional lifestyles relevant for the conservation and sustainable use of biological diversity and promote their wider application" (CBD 1992). In the Article 8(j) Working Group, ILCs have the same standing as delegates of parties. Within the mandate set by Article 8(j), the working group develops draft decisions, work programs, and guidelines with significant input from ILCs and their traditional knowledge, codes of conduct, and *sui generis* systems for the protection of traditional knowledge, such as, for example the voluntary Akwe: Kon Guidelines on Cultural, Environmental and Social Impact Assessments (ENB 2007, 2009c).

The Limits of Expert Advice: What Advice Cannot Do

Although policymakers expect a great deal from expert advice, experience demonstrates that there are some things it cannot (and perhaps should not) do.

For example, sometimes expert advice simply cannot answer the questions that policymakers pose. An example from the UNFCCC is the problem of distinguishing between natural and direct and indirect effects when accounting for carbon in Land Use, Land-Use Change and Forestry (LULUCF) activities. The Kyoto Protocol makes clear that for LULUCF activities to count as carbon sinks and generate credits, any change in land use has to be the result of a "direct human-induced" action (UNFCCC 1998). However, distinguishing what is a natural or an indirect effect from a human-induced one is far from easy. Forest fires, for example, which are a cause of sink reversal, can result from a natural event such as lightning, or a direct or indirect human act, such as accidental fire or inadequate forest management. Much more complex is discounting for indirect nitrogen deposition, elevated carbon dioxide concentrations above their pre-industrial level (i.e., current greenhouse gases accumulated in the atmosphere), and activities and practices before the reference year (Gutierrez 2011). When the UNFCCC asked the IPCC in 2003 to develop practicable methodologies to "factor out" direct human-induced changes in carbon stocks from those due to indirect human-induced and natural effects, the IPCC responded that "the scientific community cannot currently provide a practicable methodology" that would do so (IPCC 2003). The problem—known as "factoring out"—had to be brought back to the negotiating table to be addressed with a political decision.

While there are some questions that are simply too complex for science to answer in a manner that satisfies decision makers, others involve moral or ethical questions that are perhaps better answered directly by policymakers. For example, when IPCC Working Group III attempted an economic valuation of the social costs of climate change impacts, including human life, for the Second Assessment Report, the writing team used controversial assumptions based on the available literature on the "value of statistical life." These assumptions were based on economists' calculation that human life is valued differently in developed and developing countries, since risk of death is not valued equally between countries (i.e., based on a "willingness to pay" approach). Developing country delegates reacted with indignation at the suggestion that human lives in their countries were somehow worth less than in rich countries (a cash value of US$1.5 million was assigned to a human life in the OECD, for example, while one in a developing country was assigned a mere US$150,000). The disagreement between the economists who had written the report and the policymakers was such that the Working Group III report failed to get plenary approval in July 1995, and although governments eventually accepted the chapter, they changed the Summary for Policymakers in such a way that it implicitly criticized the underlying chapter. In angry response, the IPCC authors dissociated themselves from the summary (Brack and Grubb 1996).

Similarly, the CBD SBSTTA has been unable to provide advice on the use of genetic use-restriction technologies (GURTs) in agriculture. These technologies were presented as a solution to concerns regarding cross-breeding between genetically modified variants and variants in the wild, opposed by civil society groups who raised ethical concerns and suspected the technology would be used to control the use of seed. In view of the complexity of the issue, SBSTTA established an Ad hoc Technical Expert Group (AHTEG) to prepare a report on the potential social impacts of GURTs for small farmers. The chair of the group drafted a report, which was rejected several times at SBSTTA meetings and was never forwarded to the CBD COP to inform a decision on GURTs. Several developed country parties rejected the report as biased, while others insisted on using the report as a "sound" basis for decision making. Eventually a COP decision was taken without making reference to the AHTEG report or any guidance provided by SBSTTA. As the debate around GURTs became more and more politicized and value-laden, SBSTTA discussions reached a deadlock that could not be solved within the scientific realm (ENB 2003, 2005a, 2006). Interestingly, the experience with discussions on GURTs and other similarly politicized issues have led to institutional learning in terms of both the development of formal procedures for addressing new and emerging issues and the informal behavior of SBSTTA delegates and chairs (ENB 2007).

Expert Advice in Broader Negotiation Dynamics

Experience demonstrates that science does not inform policy in a vacuum; it does so within the broader context in which negotiations unfold. Many factors, ranging from politics to financing and timing, influence the uptake of expert advice by policymakers.

On the surface, the Montreal Protocol seems to provide an example of science directly informing policy; scientific advancements have led parties to the Protocol to amend and/or adjust phase-out schedules at least nine times. As summarized by Executive-Secretary Marco González (2009, 6), "Parties have consistently followed scientific advice and promoted technology innovation in a virtuous cycle: new findings leading a swift political response which further promoted new technologies options." Yet to suggest that science feeds directly into policy without intermediary steps is misleading. As González concedes, in the case of the Montreal Protocol, the establishment of a financial mechanism to support developing countries' phase-out schedules facilitated the uptake of science by policymakers. The more recent debacle surrounding the phase-out of HFCs (see Chapter 10) suggests that politics may increasingly trump science within the Montreal Protocol.

Timing also plays a critical role in the uptake of science by policymakers. As Agrawala (1997, 25) notes, "The appropriateness of an assessment activity is a function of where the issue is in the policy cycle." For example, the negotiations for the Nagoya Protocol on Access and Benefit-sharing show that timing definitely matters for effective uptake of scientific as well as technical and legal advice. Faced with increasing complexity and confusion during the negotiations (Chapter 2 elaborates on this topic), CBD parties decided at COP 9 to convene a series of legal and technical expert groups on specific issues to be addressed in the regime, including consultations on the concept and definition of "utilization of genetic resources," which is core to the international regime. After the convening of the expert group, the scientific community repeatedly raised—without success—concerns about including emerging methods of biotechnological use of genetic resources, such as in silico techniques and synthetic biology in the concept of utilization. The definition of concepts turned out to be one of the most controversial issues in the debate. Mistrust among parties and difficulties in capturing complex scientific activities in legal terms made it nearly impossible to go beyond the definition of genetic resources already embodied in the CBD (ENB 2010a, 2010b). Many delegates and observers of the scientific community noted after the conclusions of the negotiation that such issues relating to the definition would have needed to be raised in advance of the text-based legal negotiations. Once the legal experts in the delegations had wrapped their minds around a certain set of legal terms and lines of conflict, the process became resistant to new insights from the scientific community.

Further, in several instances, the delegation of issues to expert bodies has become a significant component of broader negotiation dynamics. In some instances, expert bodies have provided a forum for discussion of certain policy or value questions for which there is no time to develop party positions at what are often over-scheduled COP meetings (see Chapter 2). Yet, such an approach can be a double-edged outcome. The expert body can create a forum where the expertise available can help parties refine their position in light of greater understanding of the question at hand. In other contexts, however, deliberations within the expert body of a question best suited to a political forum can entrench the divide among parties. For example, under the CBD, while the special status of ILC representatives is limited to the Article 8(j) Working Group, it has raised their profile in other bodies of the CBD, including the COP. Over time, the standing of ILCs has improved to the point that they can force greater attention to their concerns and their contributions as knowledge holders by threatening to "walk out" of negotiations (Figure 4.3). This strategy threatens to undermine the legitimacy of decisions taken in the absence of ILC representatives (see Chapter 7 for more on this and other strategies NGOs have employed to further their goals). Furthermore, some parties have made it a matter of principle to endorse proposals made by ILC representatives. These strategies were especially successful for ILCs in the negotiation of the Nagoya Protocol on access and benefit sharing. The main effect was to improve legitimacy of the negotiations. The uptake in salient scientific advice, however, was limited in this case since ILCs' main concerns were to safeguard their interests with regard to ABS (ENB 2010a).

FIGURE 4.3 Under the CBD, the standing of indigenous and local communities has improved to the point that they can force greater attention to their concerns and their contributions as knowledge holders. Photo courtesy of IISD/ *Earth Negotiations Bulletin*

Informing Politics: Lessons Learned

Science acquires a new and powerful role with the expectation that it is to inform policy. This expectation affects the way the questions are framed, and how the problem is presented: certain matters are attended to at the expense of others; some questions are identified as political and removed from inquiry, while others are addressed as if they were merely technical and had no political implications. Because science is not neutral and free floating but is very much located in a context of competing domestic interests and institutions, its work and its influence tend to reflect this context. These problems are intensified when the discussion moves to the international level. Clearly, the questions that are interesting to developed countries are not the same as those interesting to developing countries, yet the latter often depend on the science done in the former for the articulation of legitimate solutions. The framing and basic assumptions are also determined in this way. Besides, some aspects of science do not even translate well into policy-making. The most obvious case is how scientific "uncertainties" in climate change science have been used politically to downplay the severity of the problem and the role of humans in changing the climate. Yet uncertainty is the engine of science; it is what keeps scientific inquiry alive.

In any case, the role of science in coaching environmental policy has greatly reinforced the independent status of science, and its credibility depends on how neutral it is perceived to be. The public is sensitive about being influenced by special interests. Conversely, given the influence of science, the government is sensitive to the opinion of scientists and may attempt to control them. The concern with science standing for special interests is well founded, and breaches in sovereignty are often newsworthy, as business and industry may in effect form alternative "epistemic communities" by paying scientists and funding research organizations. These cases have sparked the creation of a number of NGOs whose mission is to disclose scientists' connections and links as a way to assure transparency in information. There is now SinksWatch, CDMWatch and CarbonTradeWatch, in addition to ExxonSecrets and others. Environmental groups also gain legitimacy from employing established academics to prepare reports on specific issues. These trends are expected to continue.

As we enter the post-2012 era of global environmental politics, one can also expect new and emerging technologies to substantially alter the way in which expert advice is co-produced and brought to bear in policy negotiations. Some of these efforts are already under way. For example, in the context of the POPs Review Committee, the Stockholm Convention Secretariat is working to develop an in-house social-networking interface to facilitate the committee's intersessional work. Similarly, the Ramsar Convention Secretariat has established the Scientific and Technical Review Panel Support Service, which also provides an online interface to facilitate the panel's work.

On the institutional side, there is a trend to emulate the structure of the IPCC for other issue areas such as biodiversity and desertification, often described as "IPCC-envy," suggesting that such attempts see the IPCC model as a panacea to the science deficit in decision making. The consultations for an Intergovernmental Platform on Biodiversity and Ecosystem Services (IPBES) show, however, that delegates and scientists are attempting to learn from the IPCC experience and the MA and other assessments by establishing a process that will service several biodiversity-related conventions and be more responsive to the needs of these various processes. It remains to be seen to what extent it is feasible for several parallel institutions to provide the necessary expertise and the extent to which experts can, on a largely pro bono basis, continually prepare state-of-the-art assessments of knowledge relating to every overarching environmental challenge. Yet, even if it is unrealistic that expert communities will be able to organize several IPCC-style expert bodies operating in parallel, the visibility of the IPCC, and the emerging scrutiny on expert advice in other MEAs, likely means that representation/diversity as a means of achieving the legitimacy of expert advice may now be considered a given. Indeed, we may now be in an era where it would be considered illegitimate to draw expertise from a body that does not have a minimum of geographic, economic, institutional, and personal diversity among those providing expertise.

Transparency is likewise increasingly recognized as an essential component of successful negotiations, and there is a potential for transparency to transform the way in which expert advice is produced in these settings. Indeed, it will be interesting to see how the scientific community's long-standing tradition of maintaining credibility through "blindness" rather than through transparency is transformed as it reconciles the expectation of transparency to achieve political legitimacy.

Notes

1   The UN's five geographic regions are Latin America and the Caribbean, Africa, Asia, Eastern Europe, and Western Europe and Others.
2   For a more extensive discussion of how science advice can be performed, especially in relation to managing what happens on front stage and behind the curtain, see Hilgartner (2000).
3   CBD Article 8 addresses *in situ* conservation of biodiversity.

Works Cited

ACIA. 2005. *Arctic Climate Impact Assessment.* Cambridge, UK: Cambridge University Press.

Agarwal, Anil and Sunita Narain. 1991. *Global Warming in an Unequal World: A Case of Environmental Colonialism.* New Delhi: Centre for Science and Environment.

Agrawala, Shardul. 1997. Explaining the Evolution of the IPCC Structure and Process. ENRP Discussion Paper E-97–05. Boston: Kennedy School of Government, Harvard University.

Agrawala, Shardul. 1998a. Context and Early Origins of the Intergovernmental Panel on Climate Change. *Climatic Change* 39(4): 605–620.

Agrawla, Shardul. 1998b. Structural and Process History of the Intergovernmental Panel on Climate Change. *Climatic Change* 39(4): 621–642.

Agrawala, Shardul. 1999. Early Science-Policy Interactions in Climate Change: Lessons from the Advisory Group on Greenhouse Gases. *Global Environmental Change* 9(2): 157–169.

Biermann, Frank. 2006. Whose Experts? The Role of Geographic Representation in Global Environmental Assessments. In *Global Environmental Assessments: Information and Influence.* Edited by Ronald Mitchell, William Clark, David Cash, and Nancy M. Dickson et al. Cambridge, MA: MIT Press.

Bodansky, Dan. 1993. The United Nations Framework Convention on Climate: A Commentary. *Yale Journal of International Law* 18: 451–558.

Brack, Duncan and Michael Grubb. 1996. Climate Change: A Summary of the Second Assessment Report of the IPCC. Briefing Paper No. 32. London: The Royal Institute of International Affairs.

Cash, D., W. Clark, F. Alcock, N. Dickson, N. Eckley, D. Guston, J. Jäger, and R. Mitchell. 2003. Knowledge Systems for Sustainable Development. *Proceedings of the National Academy of Sciences of the United States of America* 100(4): 8086–8091.

CBD. 1992. *Convention on Biological Diversity.* New York: UN.

CITES. 1973. *Convention on International Trade in Endangered Species of Wild Fauna and Flora.* Washington, DC: UN.

ENB. 1997. Summary of the First Conference of the Parties to the Convention to Combat Desertification: 29 September–10 October 1997. *Earth Negotiations Bulletin* 4(116). http://www.iisd.ca/download/pdf/enb04116e.pdf (accessed May 27, 2011).

ENB. 1999a. Report of the Sixth Session of the INC for an International Legally Binding Instrument for the Application of the Prior Informed Consent Procedure for Certain Hazardous Chemicals and Pesticides in International Trade: 12–16 July 1999. *Earth Negotiations Bulletin* 15(20). http://www.iisd.ca/download/pdf/enb1520e.pdf (accessed June 19, 2011).

ENB. 1999b. Summary of the Fourth Session of the Subsidiary Body for Scientific, Technical and Technological Advice and the Intersessional Meeting on the Operations of the Convention on Biological Diversity: 21–30 June 1999. *Earth Negotiations Bulletin* 9(126). http://www.iisd.ca/download/pdf/enb09126e.pdf (accessed May 27, 2011).

ENB. 2001. Summary of the Fifth Conference of the Parties to the Convention to Combat Desertification: 1–13 October 2001. *Earth Negotiations Bulletin* 4(160). http://www.iisd.ca/download/pdf/enb04160e.pdf (accessed May 27, 2011).

ENB. 2003. Summary of the Ninth Meeting of the Subsidiary Body on Scientific, Technical and Technological Advice of the Convention on Biological Diversity: 10–14 November 2003. *Earth Negotiations Bulletin* 9(262). http://www.iisd.ca/download/pdf/enb09262e.pdf (accessed 2 April 2011).

ENB. 2004. Summary of the Extraordinary Meeting of the Parties to the Montreal Protocol: 24–26 March 2004. *Earth Negotiations Bulletin* 19(34). http://www.iisd.ca/download/pdf/enb1934e.pdf (accessed April 30, 2011).

ENB. 2005a. Summary of the International Conference "Biodiversity Science and Governance": 24–28 January 2006. *Biodiversity: Science and Governance Bulletin* 100(5). http://www.iisd.ca/download/pdf/sd/sdvol100num5e.pdf (accessed April 30, 2011).

ENB. 2005b. Summary of the First Conference of the Parties to the Stockholm Convention: 2–6 May 2005. *Earth Negotiations Bulletin* 15(117). http://www.iisd.ca/download/pdf/enb15117e.pdf (accessed April 30 2011).

ENB. 2005c. Summary of the Twenty-Fifth Meeting of the Open-Ended Working Group of the Parties to the Montreal Protocol on Substances that Deplete the Ozone Layer and the Second Extraordinary Meeting of the Parties to the Montreal Protocol: 27 June–1 July 2005. *Earth Negotiations Bulletin* 19(41). http://www.iisd.ca/download/pdf/enb1941e.pdf (accessed April 30, 2011).

ENB. 2006. Summary of the Eighth Meeting of the Conference of the Parties to the Convention on Biological Diversity: 20–31 March 2006. *Earth Negotiations Bulletin* 9(363). http://www.iisd.ca/download/pdf/enb09363e.pdf (accessed April 2, 2011).

ENB. 2007. Summary of the Fifth Meeting of the Working Group on Access and Benefit-sharing and the Fifth Meeting of the Working Group on Article 8(j) and Related Provisions of the Convention on Biological Diversity: 8–19 October 2007. *Earth Negotiations Bulletin* 9(398). http://www.iisd.ca/download/pdf/enb09398e.pdf (accessed April 2, 2011).

ENB. 2008a. Summary of the Twenty-Ninth Session of the Intergovernmental Panel on Climate Change: 31 August–4 September 2008. *Earth Negotiations Bulletin*. 12(384). http://www.iisd.ca/download/pdf/enb12384e.pdf (accessed May 26, 2011).

ENB. 2008b. Summary of the Tenth Conference of the Parties to the Ramsar Convention on Wetlands: 28 October–4 November 2008. *Earth Negotiations Bulletin* 17(32). http://www.iisd.ca/download/pdf/enb1732e.pdf (accessed April 30, 2011).

ENB. 2009a. Summary of the Second Session of the International Conference on Chemicals Management: 11–15 May 2009. *Earth Negotiations Bulletin* 15(175). http://www.iisd.ca/download/pdf/enb15175e.pdf (accessed April 2, 2011).

ENB. 2009b. Summary of the Fourth Conference of the Parties to the Stockholm Convention on Persistent Organic Pollutants: 4–8 May 2009. *Earth Negotiations Bulletin* 15(174). http://www.iisd.ca/download/pdf/enb15174e.pdf (accessed May 26, 2011).

ENB. 2009c. Summary of the Sixth Meeting of the Working Group on Article 8(j) and Related Provisions of the Convention on Biological Diversity: 2–6 November 2009.

Earth Negotiations Bulletin 9(482). http://www.iisd.ca/download/pdf/enb09482e.pdf (accessed April 2, 2011).

ENB. 2010a. Summary of the Ninth Meeting of the Working Group on Access and Benefit-sharing of the Convention on Biological Diversity: 22–28 March 2010. *Earth Negotiations Bulletin* 9(503). http://www.iisd.ca/download/pdf/enb09503e.pdf (accessed April 2, 2011).

ENB. 2010b. Resumed ABS 9 Highlights: Sunday, 11 July 2010. *Earth Negotiations Bulletin* 9(522). http://www.iisd.ca/download/pdf/enb09522e.pdf (accessed April 2, 2011).

ENB. 2011. Summary of the Fifth Conference of the Parties to the Stockholm Convention on Persistent Organic Pollutants: 25–29 April 2011. *Earth Negotiations Bulletin* 15(182). http://www.iisd.ca/download/pdf/enb15182e.pdf (accessed May 26, 2011).

Gehring, Thomas and Eva Ruffing. 2008. When Arguments Prevail over Power: The CITES Procedure for the Listing of Endangered Species. *Global Environmental Politics* 8(2): 123–148.

González, Marco. 2009. Statement from the Executive-Secretary for the Vienna Convention and the Montreal Protocol. In *Twenty Years of Ozone Decline: Proceedings of the Symposium for the 20th Anniversary of the Montreal Protocol*. Edited by Christos Zerefos, Georgios Contopoulos, and Gregory Skalkeas. Dordrecht, the Netherlands: Springer.

Grubb, Michael, Christiaan Vrolijk, and Duncan Brack. 1999. *The Kyoto Protocol: A Guide and Assessment*. London: Earthscan.

Gutierrez, Maria. 2011. Making Markets out of Thin Air: A Case of Capital Involution. *Antipode* 43(3): 639–661.

Hecht, Alan D. and Dennis Tirpak. 1995. Framework Agreement on Climate Change: A Scientific and Policy History. *Climatic Change* 29(4): 371–402.

Hilgartner, Stephen. 2000. *Science on Stage: Expert Advice as Public Drama*. Stanford, CA: Stanford University Press.

IPCC. 1998. Principles Governing IPCC Work. http://www.ipcc.ch/pdf/ipcc-principles/ipcc-principles.pdf (accessed June 10, 2011).

IPCC. 2003. IPCC Statement on its Response to Decision 11/CP.7 Paragraph 3 (d)–LULUCF Task 3. Milan, 2 December.

IPCC. 2004. *16 Years of Scientific Assessment in Support of the Climate Convention*. Geneva: Intergovernmental Panel on Climate Change. http://www.ipcc.ch/pdf/10th-anniversary/anniversary-brochure.pdf (accessed May 27, 2011).

Jasanoff, Sheila. 1990. *The Fifth Branch: Science Advisers as Policymakers*. Cambridge, MA: Harvard University Press.

Jasanoff, Sheila. 2004. *States of Knowledge: The Co-Production of Science and Social Order*. London: Routledge.

Kohler, Pia M. 2006. Science, PIC and POPs: Negotiating the Membership of Chemical Review Committees under the Stockholm and Rotterdam Conventions. *Review of European Community & International Environmental Law* 15(3): 293–303.

Long Martello, Marybeth. 2008. Arctic Indigenous Peoples as Representations and Representatives of Climate Change. *Social Studies of Science* 38(3): 351–376.

MA. 2005. Overview of the Millennium Ecosystem Assessment. http://www.maweb.org/en/About.aspx (accessed May 26, 2011).

Miller, Clark A. 2001. Hybrid Management: Boundary Organizations, Science Policy, and Environmental Governance in the Climate Regime. *Science, Technology & Human Values* 26(4): 478.

Miller, Clark A. and P.N. Edwards (eds.). 2001. *Changing the Atmosphere: Expert Knowledge and Environmental Governance*. Cambridge, MA: MIT Press.

Ozone Secretariat. 2004. Assessment Panels. http://www.unep.ch/ozone/Assessment_Panels/index.shtml (accessed May 26, 2011).

Parikh, Jyoti. 1994. North-South Issues for Climate Change. *Economic and Political Weekly* 29(45/46): 2940–2943.

Ramsar Convention. 1971. *Convention on Wetlands of International Importance especially as Waterfowl Habitat*. Ramsar, Iran: UN.

Skodvin, Tora. 2000. *Structure and Agent in the Scientific Diplomacy of Climate Change: An Empirical Case Study of Science-Policy Interaction in the Intergovernmental Panel on Climate Change*. Dodrecht, Boston, and London: Kluwer Academic Publishers.

Social Learning Group. 2001a. *Learning to Manage Global Environmental Risks; Volume 1: A Comparative History of Social Response to Climate Change, Ozone Depletion and Acid Rain*. Cambridge, MA: The MIT Press.

Social Learning Group. 2001b. *Learning to Manage Global Environmental Risks; Volume 2: A Functional Analysis of Social Response to Climate Change, Ozone Depletion, and Acid Rain*. Cambridge, MA: The MIT Press.

Stern, Nicholas. 2006. *Stern Review on the Economics of Climate Change*. London: UK Treasury.

TEEB. 2010. *The Economics of Ecosystem Services and Biodiversity Study*. http://www.teebweb.org/AboutTEEB/Background/AimsObjectives/tabid/1040/Default.aspx (accessed May 26, 2011).

UNFCCC. 1998. *Kyoto Protocol to the United Nations Framework Convention on Climate Change*. New York: UN.

Yamineva, Yulia. 2010. The Assessment Process of the Intergovernmental Panel on Climate Change: A Post-Normal Science Perspective. Unpublished PhD dissertation. Cambridge, UK: University of Cambridge.

PART II
Evolution of Actors

5

GLOBAL ALLIANCES TO STRANGE BEDFELLOWS

The Ebb and Flow of Negotiating Coalitions

Lynn M. Wagner, Reem Hajjar, and Asheline Appleton

The geopolitical landscape of 1992 differed greatly from what exists today and the coalitions that states use to achieve their goals in environmental negotiations have reflected these changes. For a number of years after the Earth Summit, alliances at sustainable development negotiations assumed a predictable pattern. The chairperson would first call on the spokesperson of the Group of 77 and China, a coalition of developing countries; following which the chair would call on the country holding the six-month Presidency for the European Community (which started to co-exist with the European Union in 1993); following which representatives who were speaking on behalf of their own country would offer statements. A few other countries would offer their positions at subsequent points in the negotiations, but the broad outlines of the range of positions and actors likely to move the outcome one direction or another was fairly clear following this initial *tour de table*.

In the intervening twenty years, however, existing country coalitions have grown or fragmented and new coalitions have emerged, with many reflecting their members' particular interests in a specific negotiating process as well as changes in broader geo-political arrangements. For example, the Group of 77 developing countries, with members ranging from oil-producing Middle Eastern countries to climate change-vulnerable small island states, has not presented a common position on all issues during climate change negotiations. Furthermore, at the 2009 Copenhagen Climate Change Conference, four developing countries with relatively strong economies and high greenhouse gas emission levels—Brazil, South Africa, India, and China—began openly caucusing as the BASIC Group. The European coalition has evolved, as the European Union (EU) membership has grown to incorporate formerly communist Eastern European countries and successive European treaties have affected the authority that the coalition's spokesperson wields. A non–consensus-based coalition has become a frequent caucusing body for non-European industrialized countries: JUSSCANNZ brings representatives from several developed countries (identified below) together to discuss positions prior to negotiating sessions, although each member speaks individually during the negotiations and participation in this group is relatively fluid.

These primary coalitions essentially divide the talks into developed versus developing country groups (or North versus South), but lines of division exist within each of these designations and new interest-based coalitions have occasionally crossed the North–South boundaries. The creation and evolution of each group introduces the need to adjust the pattern of interaction among negotiating groups.

This chapter examines these lines of division and their fluidity. We review the organization and general conduct involved with the primary coalitions, and then explore case studies of the evolution of coalitions in the biodiversity, forests, and climate change regimes, to examine the role and changing nature of coalitions. The biodiversity case study reviews efforts to move the Biosafety Protocol nego-tiations toward agreement in the face of newly formed coalitions, focusing on how the organization of coalitions within a meeting room can facilitate a nego-tiation's progress. The forest case study reviews the changing interests of various actors within the negotiations over a period of several years, and how these changing interests affected coalition formation and, as a result, the ability to reach an agreement. The climate change case study reviews the wide variety of coali-tions that have emerged, particularly among the developing countries, within the negotiations for the future of the climate change regime. Together, these cases suggest how coalitions emerge, splinter, and can be organized to facilitate efforts to bring representatives from more than 190 countries to agreement.

Coalitions in the Post-Earth Summit Period

With approximately 190 countries having ratified many of the multilateral envi-ronmental agreements (MEAs) negotiated under UN auspices (see Appendix), coalitions offer diplomats in large multilateral negotiations a way to increase the "strength" of their position—a position presented on behalf of multiple countries often is given more weight than a position presented by a single country (espe-cially a "small" single country). In addition, coalitions create a necessary structure to reduce the number of speakers who will take the floor during negotiations to present specific positions. While most of the MEAs examined in this book operate on a consensus basis, which gives veto power to every party to a negotiation, a country's ability to contribute constructively to the outcome relies on negotiator skill, influence, and presence in a negotiation, all of which can be enhanced when countries enter into coalitions with like-minded countries (Gupta 2000; UNEP and FIELD 2007; University of Joensuu 2007).

We begin this examination with a review of the coalitions used within the United Nations Commission on Sustainable Development (CSD), which was established by the 1992 Earth Summit to follow up on the decisions taken at that meeting. Negotiators at the CSD have generally relied on a small number of coalitions—the Group of 77 and China, the European Union, JUSSCANNZ and the Countries with Economies in Transition/Eastern and Central European countries (Wagner 1999). An introduction to these coalitions sets the stage for the consideration of how states have organized and reorganized themselves in environment and sustainable development negotiations since 1992.

At the 1994 meeting of the second session of the CSD, as had been the case at the inaugural session of the CSD in 1993, many discussions began with the Chairperson, German Minister for the Environment, Nature Conservation and Nuclear Safety Klaus Töpfer, calling first on the representative for the Group of 77 and China, followed by the representative for the European Union. After these two coalition spokespersons presented their group's positions, a number of individual countries took the floor, often beginning with the United States, but these subsequent speakers rarely identified themselves as presenting the position of additional countries (ENB 1994). Several years later, four coalitions generally dominated CSD discussions: the Group of 77 and China, the European Union, the Countries with Economies in Transition, and JUSSCANNZ. The latter group consisted of (J) Japan, the (US) United States, (C) Canada, (A) Australia, (NZ) New Zealand, and at various times also incorporated (S) Switzerland, (N) Norway, and other non-EU members of the Organization for Economic Cooperation and Development (OECD).

The Group of 77 and China includes almost all countries in the African, Asian, and Latin America and Caribbean regional groups, which at times serve as negotiating coalitions themselves. The group's coordinating country rotates between each region on an annual basis and generally provides its negotiating spokesperson. The group does not always inherently share the same interests, but its strength relies on cohesion, particularly on agenda items related to economic issues. Disparities between member states based on stage of development—for example, Brazil versus the least developed countries—and resource interests—for example, oil-producing states versus small island states—can lead to a tenuous group position or even no group position at times (Gupta 2000, 10.2).

In 1993, the European Community of twelve countries started to co-exist with the European Union, following the adoption of the Maastricht Treaty. By 2007, a further fifteen countries had joined this coalition, bringing the total number of countries to twenty-seven. The new accessions have added complexity to the process of developing an internal EU negotiating position, especially given that the economic interests of the newly acceding states (primarily from formerly communist Eastern Europe) were generally different from those of the original European Economic Community. Nonetheless, compared with the Group of 77 and China, this coalition consists of a comparatively small group of states and benefits from its centralized bureaucracy in Belgium, where representatives often meet to develop common positions prior to UN negotiations (UNEP and FIELD 2007).

Although the EU's internal decision-making process faces the same influences and pressures involved with all negotiations (Marsh 2005, 157)—representatives of "small" countries, for example, have a limited ability to push their preferences compared with "big" countries—the EU usually projects the outward appearance of a highly cohesive group during UN negotiations. During policy negotiations, it is rare for EU member states to take the floor to present their individual position. Until recently, the country holding the rotating, six-month EU Presidency served as the spokesperson for negotiations on most sustainable development issues, and the European Commission has supplied the spokesperson for the EU on topics for which the member states have ceded authority to the EU, including on fisheries, agriculture, and trade (Figure 5.1).

However, the Lisbon Treaty, adopted in 2009, introduced a new structure to the delivery of the European position. The European Commission, rather than the government holding the six-month EU Presidency, now speaks in the name of the "European Union," although the modalities for this switch have not been smooth. For example, at the first meeting of the Intergovernmental Negotiating Committee to Prepare a Global Legally Binding Instrument on Mercury,

FIGURE 5.1 European delegates confer during the third meeting of the Conference of the Parties to the Rotterdam Convention on the Prior Informed Consent Procedure for Certain Hazardous Chemicals and Pesticides in International Trade, in October 2006. Photo courtesy of IISD/*Earth Negotiations Bulletin*

in June 2010, the EU member states had not reached agreement to give the European Commission formal authorization to negotiate, and so the coalition was not able to enter a formal position during the week-long session (ENB 2010b). And while the European Commission spoke in the name of the European Union the month prior to the merrcury meeting, at CSD 18 in May 2010, during negotiations the following week during the first session of the Preparatory Committee for the United Nations Conference on Sustainable Development, the Group of 77 and China challenged whether the European "Community" had been considered an observer at the UN until then, and not the European "Union" (ENB 2010a). To that point, it had been the "European Community" that had become party to multilateral environmental agreements. To resolve the issue, the EU notified the UN about a "change in name" from the European Community to European Union and, on May 3, 2011, the United Nations General Assembly passed Resolution 65/276 on "Strengthening of the United Nations System: Participation of the European Union in the work of the UN" (UN General Assembly 2011).

A third country grouping was formed when Japan and the United States began consulting with the CANZ group (Canada, Australia, and New Zealand) in 1995, creating JUSCANZ (Newell 1997). Switzerland, Norway and several other non-EU OECD countries (including Iceland, Andorra, Republic of Korea, Liechtenstein, Mexico, San Marino, Turkey, and Israel), (UNEP and FIELD 2007, 26) also occasionally consult with this relatively unstructured group (often referred to as JUSSCANNZ to reflect participation beyond the original five countries). Depending on the negotiating session, the JUSSCANNZ members may hold pre-conference phone calls or informal discussions during a negotiation, but they do not develop consensus positions and each speaks individually during intergovernmental negotiations.

The final primary coalition in the CSD negotiations is that of the Russian Federation, the former Soviet republics and the Central and Eastern European countries. These countries have worked together in a coalition that at times has been referred to as the "countries with economies in transition." This group has sought to establish its post-communist era identity at the same time that several members have worked to join another coalition—the European Union. Compared with the other three coalitions discussed above, this coalition offers relatively few statements. It is represented by an internally selected country and, when this spokesperson does take the floor, it is often to propose adding references to the resource needs of its member states in addition to the needs of developing countries. The countries with economies in transition are not eligible for certain funds that are designated for developing countries, even though some of their economies are on a par with other developing countries' economies.

These four coalitions—the Group of 77 and China, the EU, JUSSCANNZ, and the Central and Eastern European countries (countries with economies in transition)—have, for the most part, dominated the CSD negotiations, which address sustainable development topics at a fairly general level and do not result in legally binding decisions. However, as a sign of the increasing differentiation of group interests, by 2010 the CSD Chairperson called on no fewer than ten representatives of groups to offer opening statements. The Group of 77 and China and the EU continued as most prominent coalition groups with a single spokesperson, but their opening statements were joined by statements from representatives of the Least Developed Countries, the Group of Landlocked Developing Countries, the Rio Group, the Arab Group, the African Group, the Alliance of Small Island States, the Pacific Small Island Developing States, and the Caribbean Community (ENB 2010c). These other groups coordinated in some cases only to develop an opening statement and did not appear to present a united front during the negotiations or to break with the larger Group of 77 position, but the contrast with the coalition framework from sixteen years earlier remains: coalitions are differentiating and organizing around specific interests. Only time (and the subject under negotiation) will tell what the next country-based arrangement of coalitions will be.

From this introduction of the basic country alignments within the CSD, this chapter now turns its focus to case studies of the coalitions used within the biodiversity, forests, and climate regimes to illustrate how countries have organized themselves in interest-based coalitions as the obligations under negotiation have increased.

Biodiversity: Readjusting the Process for Issue-Specific Coalitions

In the Biosafety Protocol negotiations, as previously discussed in Chapter 3, Juan Mayr, Colombian Minister of Environment, was expected to step in only at the end of the negotiations to preside over the ceremonial session to adopt the Protocol to the Convention on Biological Diversity. Mayr was to serve as President of the Extraordinary Conference of the Parties, which was to take place in Cartagena, Colombia, in February 1999. Instead, as the talks reached a stalemate, Mayr took the helm and used what turned into an approximately one-year period of extended negotiations to organize the delegates and facilitate a resolution.

As he stepped into his role in February 1999, he quickly recognized that an impediment to reaching agreement stemmed from the fact that country positions were not falling in line with the traditional coalitions. In particular, the grain-exporting countries of Argentina, Australia, Canada, Chile, the United States, and Uruguay had created an issue-specific "Miami Group." This new group brought together countries from the Group of 77 and China and JUSSCANNZ coalitions, and supported an agreement that would enhance the potential of biotechnology and ensure protections against trade restrictions on agricultural exports. The European position, however, more closely aligned with that of the majority of developing countries, preferring to follow the precautionary principle and guard against possible negative effects of biotechnology (see also Chapters 8 and 9). Given the differences in position among delegations from the North and South, as well as overlapping positions of delegations from developing and developed countries, the traditional ways of organizing the seating and speaking order for negotiators were hampering the process of identifying all positions, ensuring that all negotiators felt their position had received an equal chance to be "heard," and searching for acceptable alternatives.

To address these challenges, Mayr proposed that the negotiations should continue in a small working group consisting of ten spokespersons representing the country groupings that had emerged during the talks. He also made special provisions to ensure that each of the issue-specific coalitions would have an equal chance to raise their concerns. This originally named "Group of 10" contained one spokesperson from Central and Eastern Europe, one from the European Union, one from Central America and the Caribbean, two from the Miami Group, four from the "Like-minded Group" (the majority of developing countries), and one from the "Compromise Group" (Japan, Mexico, Norway, South Korea, and Switzerland[1]) (Falkner 2002, 17–18; Mayr 2002, 223; Nobs 2002, 187).

Several of these coalitions had formed during the biosafety negotiations and Mayr recognized that the next phase of negotiations would need to move away from traditional ways of seating and calling on groups—usually centered around the Group of 77, the European Union, and the other advanced Western economies—if there were to be agreement on the Protocol (Mayr 2002, 222). During the first additional week of talks, in September 1999 in Vienna, Austria, the "Group of 10" was slightly transformed, with each major group (the Miami Group, Like-minded Group, Compromise Group, European Union, and Central and Eastern European group) having two spokespersons sitting at a roundtable in what came to be called the "Vienna Setting" for the remainder of the Biosafety Protocol negotiations.

Mayr developed additional procedural controls that sought to balance the need to focus the discussions on reaching resolution while ensuring that the groups felt sufficient involvement with and ownership for the outcome. In particular, each spokesperson was limited to two advisors, which would increase the representation of countries at the table while still controlling the number of participants seeking to offer input to the talks. (See Chapter 3, which identifies additional factors related to this organizational structure that facilitated the ultimate agreement on the Protocol.) As this case study demonstrates, the recognition of new coalitions and efforts to ensure they all have a voice in the talks can play an important role in facilitating an outcome. But it is not always so easy, as was the case of the splintering and emergence of new coalitions and their impact on negotiations within the United Nations Forum on Forests.

Forests: Issue-Driven Dismantling and Reassembling of Coalitions

The opening statement of Jamaica, on behalf of the Group of 77 and China, at the fifth session of the United Nations Forum on Forests (UNFF 5) in 2005, focused on the importance of identifying appropriate financial mechanisms and predictable funds for sustainable forest management (SFM), technology transfer, capacity building, and linking SFM and socioeconomic development (ENB 2005). This was a predictable statement from this coalition, which had held firm on forests issues since the 1992 Earth Summit, throughout the successive Intergovernmental Panel on Forests (IPF), Intergovernmental Forum on Forests (IFF), and UNFF processes. This negotiating bloc shared many principal interests relating to international forestry, and as was its custom, began the UNFF 5 negotiations with a single spokesperson. But as more specific issues were put on the table, the coalition weakened due to its members' diverging interests regarding the possibility of negotiating a legally binding instrument on forests and quantifiable, time-bound goals.

Eventually, the Group of 77 (G-77) and China stopped speaking as one. By the closing plenary, the collapse of the G-77 within the UNFF talks was apparent, and negotiations were stalled while new groups began to emerge. For the next three years, new coalitions were formed from within and outside the G-77, united by common interests on specific issues, as delegates negotiated the details of the new forest instrument. However, once the Non-Legally Binding Instrument on All Types of Forests was successfully negotiated at UNFF 7, the G-77 re-emerged as a coalition at UNFF 8, to negotiate a financing mechanism. In this section, we review the dismantling and reassembly of coalitions between UNFF 5 and UNFF 8, and outline the issues and interests that brought about these transformations.

The origins

Forest issues at UNCED in 1992 were among the most contentious, with positions polarized along a North–South divide. Much of the North argued that forests are of global importance and thus there should be strong supranational agreements to govern them. Meanwhile, the South maintained that forests are a matter of national sovereignty; countries have the sovereign right to exploit their forests for development, and if some supranational agreement were to limit this right, then they should be duly compensated for lost development opportunities (Poore 2003). This division contributed to a collapse of the idea of a forests convention even prior to UNCED. Instead, delegates devoted their time to difficult negotiations that resulted in the Non-legally Binding Authoritative Statement of Principles for a Global Consensus on the Management, Conservation and Development of All Types of Forests (Forest Principles), which was adopted along with Agenda 21 in Rio.

It took another three years before sufficient trust was re-established between North and South to allow the forest dialogue to continue at the Commission on Sustainable Development in 1995.[2] This meeting resulted in the establishment of the Intergovernmental Panel on Forests, which began a period of international forest dialogue in various formats (Intergovernmental Panel on Forests, Intergovernmental Forum on Forests, and finally the creation of the UN Forum on Forests in 2000) that sought to advance global action based on the Forest Principles. In 2005, delegates arrived at the fifth and, what many thought was supposed to be, final session of the UNFF prior to coming to a decision on the next steps in international forestry. UNFF 5 negotiators had assigned themselves the task to review the effectiveness of the international arrangement on forests (IAF) and redesign the arrangement, if necessary. Therefore, it was time for them to revisit the issue of whether to negotiate a forests convention.

To Legally Bind or Not to Legally Bind?

Many negotiators believed that the purpose of an IAF would be to raise the profile of forests and forestry on the international agenda and garner more political commitment toward sustainable forest management. But countries had opposing views as to how this would be best accomplished. Options on the table included: a legally binding convention; a Protocol as part of an existing convention; or some sort of voluntary code or instrument.

In the global North, Canada, the EU, Norway, Switzerland, and others were at that time still firm believers in a legally binding instrument (LBI) as the way forward. The United States was the only country from the North that had vocally opposed a convention, preferring instead a code. Japan and Switzerland eventually believed this option had merit as a compromise (ENB 2005).

However, the divisions between proponents of the LBI and non-LBI options were more disruptive within the G-77. Argentina, Chile, Mexico, Guatemala, Costa Rica, Cuba, China, and several African countries, among others, were willing to agree to negotiate an LBI. Other countries, however, would not even consider tabling the option (Brazil, Venezuela, and India being the most vocal). Early at UNFF 5, the Brazilian delegates did not even want to consider a voluntary code, but they eventually warmed to the idea of negotiating a non-legally binding instrument (NLBI). As it became clear that delegates were nowhere near a consensus on this issue, a compromise was reluctantly reached by agreeing to the idea of revisiting the "possibility of negotiating an LBI" in 2015, when once again a review of the IAF would be tabled. The G-77 went along with this, but added that not all of its members agreed. In the end, no text was adopted at UNFF 5, and the issue was put on hold until the forum's subsequent session.

But this was not the only reason why the G-77 was struggling to speak with one voice at UNFF 5. On a related theme of securing political commitment on forests, delegates were negotiating global goals/strategic objectives. Whether to call them goals or objectives, and whether they should be time-bound and/or quantifiable, led to further rifts within the G-77. Mexico, Argentina, and other non-Amazon Latin American countries sided with the EU, Canada, Switzerland, New Zealand, and others who strongly advocated that they should be time-bound and quantifiable, stating that this was necessary to move from the status quo and increase political commitment. Meanwhile, Brazil and Colombia were adamant that the strategic objectives were not to be time-bound or quantifiable. By the end of UNFF 5, the goals/objectives were agreed *ad referendum*, with no timelines or targets, and all text was forwarded to UNFF 6.

Coalitions within the G-77 that were quietly emerging at UNFF 5 based around the LBI and goals/objectives issues were fully formed at UNFF 6, with several intractable issues deepening divisions. Newly represented at UNFF 6 were the "Amazon Group" (with India more often than not supporting their position), the African Group, and SICA (Central American Integration System, often supported by other Latin American non-Amazonian countries). SICA sided with many positions taken by countries in the North, which were more or less united (apart from the United States) in pushing for time-bound quantifiable targets, inserting language on promoting payments for ecosystem services and non-timber forest products, and in general trying to insert stronger language in the session's draft decision. The North was also united on wanting better use of existing funds, and inserting language referring to illegal logging and land tenure. The Amazon Group and India continued to be adamantly against time-bound or quantifiable targets, and strongly pushed against including any language on illegal logging (ENB 2006).

LBI supporters for the most part dropped their cause and focused on strengthening language in the NLBI, perhaps as a precursor to tackling the subject of an LBI again in 2015. Canada, however, stood out among the group by blatantly stating that, if UNFF did not seek to negotiate an LBI, they would pursue other options for negotiating one.[3] And that is what they did—they began discussing an LBI with several like-minded countries from the North and the South, meeting on the sidelines of UNFF meetings. However, all members of this new group, except Canada, continued to actively participate in UNFF and the NLBI negotiations. Canada remained mostly silent at subsequent UNFF meetings.

All the same sticking points discussed at past UNFF sessions re-surfaced at UNFF 7, as delegates negotiated the details of the NLBI. The new coalitions within the G-77 remained more or less intact, although the Amazon Group was no longer speaking as one. Instead, Brazil, Venezuela, and Colombia spoke individually, mostly supporting one another's position. The one exception was Venezuela's strong opposition to referring to payments for ecosystem services, which the other two did not comment on, but the Central American countries, the African Group, the EU, and Switzerland strongly supported their inclusion.

This was similar to the arrangement with the Central American countries, who were no longer speaking as SICA yet still supported the statements of each other and Mexico. The African Group remained united with a distinct opinion—they sided with the Amazon countries on not having time-bound targets, but were more willing to consider an LBI in the future. In the end, no language on quantifiable time-bound targets was included in the NLBI. Instead, a compromise was reached by settling on a reference to developing national programs that include specific goals. No language on illegal logging, tenure, or procurement policies was included in the NLBI—countries such as Switzerland and the EU fought hard for such terms, but had to give them up if there was any hope of acceptance by Brazil, Venezuela, and India. With the United States unrelenting on the need for a reference to illegal logging, Brazil compromised with reference to illegal "practices." Another issue that divided delegations along the lines of the new coalitions was whether or not, and how, to define SFM in the NLBI. The EU, Australia, New Zealand, Japan, and Mexico wanted to include a definition of SFM in the NLBI, while the African Group and Indonesia preferred referring to the seven thematic elements of SFM,[4] and Brazil and Colombia preferred no definition at all (ENB 2007).

In fact, the only issue that the new coalitions within the G-77 could agree on during UNFF 6 and UNFF 7 was the need to establish a global forest fund. After the NLBI had been successfully concluded at UNFF 7, only one issue remained on the table: financing. UNFF 8 was primarily focused on negotiating a financing mechanism for the implementation of SFM, for which the North–South divide dutifully returned. The G-77 spoke with one voice during the opening of UNFF 8 in 2009, for the first time since the disaggregation of the bloc at UNFF 5 in 2005 (Figure 5.2). As one developing country delegate explained, now that the only remaining issue was money, they all put their other differences behind them and joined together to push for a global forest fund. Meanwhile, the North favored better use of existing funds, and pushed for a facilitative process to enhance country implementation. At UNFF 7, when the EU first presented the option of a facilitative process, Brazil, Colombia, and Venezuela would not consider it, while the African Group and Mexico were more open to discussions. Yet at UNFF 8, the G-77 remained united throughout. Despite rumors in the hallways that some African countries were warming to the idea of a facilitative process, the G-77 firmly and jointly stood its ground on a forest fund. Negotiators from Brazil and Argentina, who in the previous UNFF sessions had been in complete opposition on several issues, sat side by side at UNFF 8, both advising the spokesperson for the bloc, Sudan. During an all-night negotiating session on the final day of UNFF 8, it looked like the only way to bridge the North–South divide was to set up an intersessional process to review the facilitative process, which delegates had envisioned would start right after UNFF 8, and consider establishing a fund at a later session, based on this review. However, at the very last minute, the US delegate could

FIGURE 5.2 Nadia Osman, Sudan, for the G-77 and China (with veil), with Fernando Coimbra, Brazil, seated on her right and other G-77 delegates around her, consult on the penultimate day of UNFF 8. Photo courtesy of IISD/*Earth Negotiations Bulletin*

not agree to the language, and the negotiations ended without agreement[5] (ENB 2009a).

Coalitions in the forest arena changed substantially over these five years of UNFF negotiations. The initial North–South divide gave way to new alliances as issue-specific interests, emerging during negotiations of a forest instrument, brought to light divergences within traditional groupings. This pattern of changing coalitions based on issue specificity was made all the more clear when the North–South alignments were reassembled after the details had been negotiated, and the broader, overarching issue was put back on the table—financing. We now turn to another case study in which traditional coalitions have exhibited divisions: climate change.

Climate Change: Group Unity and Division

The international community's efforts to adopt a comprehensive approach for integrating environmental considerations into economic development under the umbrella of the United Nations Framework Convention on Climate Change (UNFCCC) strikes at the very heart of each country's economic interests. The current UNFCCC process has been described as the most ambitious and complicated multilateral environmental negotiations ever. As deliberations toward an agreement on the post–2012 period continue, more and more human economic activities have been brought under the realm of the climate change regime. The complexity of the process in terms of reaching agreement on institutions, procedures, and processes for mitigation, financing, adaptation, technology, and REDD+ (reducing emissions from deforestation and forest degradation, and the role of conservation, sustainable use of forests and enhancement of carbon stocks in developing countries), for example, has increased. It could be suggested that the emergence of coalitions is simply a reflection of this convolution as various country groups strive to ensure that their economic and developmental interests are protected under any eventual outcome. This notwithstanding, the UNFCCC process has always been characterized by different interest groups brought about by both the OECD and the Group of 77 and China failing to reach common negotiating positions (Sands 1995, 273) during the negotiation of the Convention.

UNFCCC coalitions, as is the case in other multilateral environmental negotiations, predictably tend to follow a North–South divide. However, the division between North and South is sometimes grey. Some countries in the G-77, such as Singapore, Kuwait, Qatar, Saudi Arabia, and the United Arab Emirates, are relatively wealthy. In the North, less affluent countries such as the Czech Republic, Estonia, Poland, Bulgaria, Latvia, Lithuania, and Romania have now been absorbed into the EU.

Developed countries have been represented by three major coalitions: the European Union, the Umbrella Group and the Environmental Integrity Group (EIG). The EU is a party to the Convention and its members meet regularly to agree on a common negotiating position. Complications in the coordination of the EU position are evidenced by their problems in agreeing on climate and burden sharing, or even how to implement this group's internally adopted 30 percent emission reduction target. This difficulty is due in part to the differing economic circumstances, and therefore priorities, of the EU member states.

The Umbrella Group was formed following the adoption of the Kyoto Protocol in 1997 and consists of a loose coalition of non-EU developed countries. The group emerged from the JUSSCANNZ group, which had been active during the Kyoto Protocol negotiations, although without a single spokesperson. The Umbrella Group usually consists of Australia, Canada, Iceland, Japan, New Zealand, Norway, the Russian Federation, Ukraine, and the United States. The Environmental Integrity Group, formed in 2000, comprises Mexico, the Republic of Korea, and Switzerland—the OECD countries that do not coordinate with the EU or Umbrella Group.

The G-77, the largest coalition, has a membership that reflects varying interests and priorities on climate change. The group consists of the least developed countries (LDCs), small island developing states (SIDS), countries with significant forest reserves, African states, countries that also belong to the Organization of Petroleum Exporting Countries (OPEC), and major developing economies such as Brazil, China, India, and South Africa. The G-77 also represents sub-coalitions comprising the Alliance of Small Island States (AOSIS), the African Group, and LDCs. While these three sub-coalitions prioritize adaptation to the effects of climate change and the corresponding financing required for implementation, the emphasis for oil-producing developing countries is on the need to *adapt* to the impact of response measures resulting from the loss of revenue as countries reduce their consumption of fossil fuels and turn to more renewable clean forms of energy. The position of oil producers on response measures is generally at odds with the G-77 position as a whole, especially from AOSIS and other developing countries vulnerable to climate change. Furthermore, many developing countries have taken a very keen interest in pushing for compensation for avoided deforestation under the REDD+ negotiations. The emerging economies in the group are also interested in technology transfer. Given the increasingly divergent, disparate interests and concerns within this group, some developed country commentators have questioned the relevance of the G-77 in the climate process. To put it mildly, coordination is complicated, compounded by the fact that this group does not meet intersessionally to establish common negotiating positions prior to negotiating sessions. Individual countries and sub-groups within this group therefore intervene on issues of interest to them, in addition to the efforts of the coordinators of the group to present group-wide positions.

Since the negotiation of the Convention, which was opened for signature at the 1992 Earth Summit, the economic landscape for many of the group's members has changed dramatically, with countries such as China and India having undergone considerable economic transformation. China is now the leading emitter of carbon dioxide, a key greenhouse gas addressed in the Convention, and has overtaken Japan as the second largest economy after the United States. Developed countries, particularly the United States, have said they will not agree to any future obligations under the Convention unless high carbon dioxide-emitting emerging economies also take on measurable, reportable, and verifiable commitments.

The G-77 has consistently opposed the introduction[6] of terms such as "advanced developing," "emerging economies," and "major developing economies" by developed countries, which would divide the G-77 based on economic level. At the other end of the spectrum, the group has also objected to efforts to introduce the concept of "poor" developing countries, based on the level of economic development (ENB 2009b). The Bali Action Plan, which was adopted in 2007 as a two-year process aimed at finalizing a binding agreement in 2009 in Copenhagen, opened up this Pandora's box by introducing the terms "developed" and "developing country" parties, in departure from references to "Annex I" and "non-Annex I" countries, the terms used in the Convention text itself to distinguish countries based on their level of development as listed in the annexes to the UNFCCC. The G-77 opposes any distinction based on economic development, emissions, and mitigation potential, citing the right of its members to develop along with the notion of the obligation of developed countries to repay an historic climate debt. China, however, appeared to soften its position during the 2010 Geneva Dialogue on Climate Finance,[7] and pointed to the need for consideration of the special concerns and aspirations of SIDS, LDCs, land-locked, and African countries. There are, of course, developing countries that would like to see differentiation of countries in terms of vulnerability, taking into account the special interests of LDCs, SIDS, landlocked, and African countries, while there are other developing countries that oppose differentiation based on vulnerability criteria. This issue is particularly important to LDCs, who would like a "fairer" share of climate funds to be allocated to them. Annex I parties, meanwhile, would like advanced developing countries and other developing countries to contribute money to the finance mechanism, which presents an additional dynamic within the group.

Division Lines

When one considers the structure of the G-77 and the different layers of interests, it becomes easy to see why, with so many competing economic and development interests, new coalitions have emerged as the negotiations have evolved. For example, the BASIC Group, consisting of (B) Brazil, (S) South Africa, (I) India and (C) China, was formed when these four countries reached an agreement just before the Copenhagen Climate Change Summit in November 2009 (Olsson et al. 2010) (Figure 5.3). These countries were instrumental in brokering the Copenhagen Accord. There remain, however, big differences in many of the positions among these countries, and this alternate forum flies in the face of the internal G-77 objection to differentiation in treatment among developing countries. These countries, however, did not negotiate under the UNFCCC as BASIC. The BASIC Group has pushed the concept of evolution to a BASIC+ configuration, and has invited a number of key countries to their meetings, including the spokespersons for the G-77 and for other interest groups within the G-77. The BASIC Group has also reported back to the Group of 77 and China regarding their periodic meetings, as a measure of transparency and accuracy regarding the BASIC Group.

The Bolivarian Alliance for the Peoples of Our America (ALBA) was held responsible by many for scuppering a deal at the 2009 Copenhagen Climate Change Conference. ALBA is an organization based on social, political, and economic integration between the countries of Latin America and the Caribbean and is associated with the socialist and social democratic countries of Bolivia, Venezuela, Ecuador, Nicaragua, and Cuba. ALBA consistently takes a very a hard line on a number of issues during negotiations, including its opposition to the use of market mechanisms to control carbon emissions and calling for 7 percent of developed countries' gross domestic product (GDP) to be designated for climate change finance (ENB 2010d). Bolivia cut a lonely figure during the Cancún

FIGURE 5.3 Ministers from China, Brazil, India, and South Africa at the 2009 Copenhagen Climate Change Conference, on their way to meet with the COP President for consultations. Photo courtesy of IISD/*Earth Negotiations Bulletin*

climate change talks, in December 2010, as the only dissenting voice expressing opposition to the adoption of the Cancún Agreements. This country listed a number of substantive concerns and argued that lack of consensus prevented the proposed COP and COP/MOP decisions from being adopted.[8] However, this position did not win any significant support from parties or observers, and the Cancún Agreements were adopted (ENB 2010e).

Additional coalitions consist of the newly formed group that is lobbying for special recognition of the circumstances and vulnerabilities of mountainous developing countries. Armenia, Kyrgyzstan, and Tajikistan have agreed to establish the Group of Mountain Landlocked Developing Countries, while Nepal has been invited to join this group but prefers to establish a "Mountain Alliance Initiative." An informal relationship between Arabic-speaking countries has also emerged and they speak on issues as the Arab Group.

Discussion Groups as the Way Forward?

Two additional groups worthy of consideration do not operate as negotiating coalitions, but rather as discussion groups that seek to explore the issues outside the negotiating halls and to build consensus on the organizers' agenda. In this regard, many commentators heralded the emergence in Copenhagen of the Cartagena Dialogue for Progressive Action as a positive step toward breaking the stand-off between developing and developed countries that has punctuated the UNFCCC process (Australian Government 2010, 104). The group spans both North and South, including: Antigua and Barbuda, Australia, Bangladesh, Belgium, Colombia, Costa Rica, Ethiopia, France, Germany, Ghana, Indonesia, Malawi, Maldives, Marshall Islands, Mexico, Netherlands, New Zealand, Norway, Peru, Samoa, Spain, Tanzania, Thailand, Timor-Leste, Uruguay, the United Kingdom, and the European Commission. The Cartagena Dialogue for Progressive Action is described as:

> an informal space, open to countries working toward an ambitious, comprehensive and legally binding regime in the UNFCCC and committed, domestically, to becoming or remaining low carbon economies. The aim of the Dialogue is to discuss openly and constructively the reasoning behind each other's positions, exploring areas of convergence and potential areas of joint action.
>
> *(Costa Rica 2010)*

The creation of this coalition recognizes that, in order for a comprehensive climate deal to be brokered, some of the traditional coalitions may need to break down and countries will need to reach across their traditional divides.

A second such discussion group is the Major Economies Forum, which was originally created as the Major Economies Meeting by former U.S. President George W. Bush. The membership in this group also straddles the North–South divide, with invited members including: Australia, Brazil, Canada, China, the European Union, France, Germany, India, Indonesia, Italy, Japan, Mexico, the Republic of Korea, the Russian Federation, South Africa, the United Kingdom, and the United States.

While the Cartagena Dialogue for Progressive Action seeks to draw on the issue power of the ethics of protecting vulnerable countries, with the Maldives—a country that is expecting serious impacts from climate change—as the convener, the Major Economies Forum draws on the issue power that comes from involving the major emitters of greenhouse gases whose action is required if climate change is to be addressed in any meaningful way. An agreement has to take everyone's interests into account in order for it to be acceptable to all, but the traditional coalitions have not yet demonstrated their ability to deliver such an outcome. Whether one of these approaches will contribute to changes in the coalition dynamics, and have the power to persuade all UNFCCC parties, or give rise to further splintering of coalitions and action on a smaller multilateral basis, remains to be seen.

Evolution of Issue-based Coalitions

From a division of countries into four main coalitions—the Group of 77 and China developing countries, the European Union, the JUSSCANNZ coalition of non-EU industrialized countries, and the countries with economies in transition—to more issue-specific arrangements, countries have coordinated their participation in post-1992 environmental negotiations through evolving alignments. An understanding of the membership and organization of these coalitions contributes to a better understanding of the negotiated outcomes. The case studies presented in this chapter suggest that instances of coalitional instability result in difficulties for negotiators to achieve consensus, and efforts to recognize and adjust to the instability may contribute to moving toward agreement.

As the issues addressed in the post-1992 regimes have moved from the initial framework, agreements for cooperation to stronger obligations, such as documentation requirements on trade in living modified organisms through the Biosafety Protocol and the negotiation of legal obligations for forests management or for greenhouse gas emission reductions to address climate change, the traditional coalitions have not served as well. Country interests crossed coalition lines in the Biosafety Protocol and forests negotiations. Country interests have also varied within coalitions, particularly in the climate change negotiations. And the case studies presented here suggest that negotiations in which coalitions are not stable or well defined will experience challenges in reaching an agreement. The fact that negotiations are addressing increasing obligations is the primary reason for the difficulties, but until the negotiators are able to identify their own and other countries' preferences, and subsequently align and organize themselves accordingly, the process of discussing options for an agreement will be impeded.

Table 5.1 depicts the coalitions reviewed in this chapter. While coalitions in multilateral environmental negotiations are often described as divided along North–South lines, we find in the cases examined here that there are many divisions even within these categories. The EU and JUSSCANNZ countries do not always agree on a preferred outcome. In the biosafety case, for example, the EU's position was closer to that of developing countries than that of many JUSSCANNZ countries. The countries that often coordinate as JUSSCANNZ have been especially fluid in their coalition formation, from the United States and Canada taking individual positions in the forests talks and joining with fellow grain exporters (including developing countries) in the biosafety talks (and in the latter case, participating in a coalition with positions opposed to the Compromise Group, which included other members of JUSSCANNZ), and creating a slightly different "umbrella" group in the climate change negotiations.

Divisions within the Group of 77 and China coalition have been the most fluid. The uniting issue for this group is financing, but on many other agenda items different issue-based groups have been active. The forests and climate change negotiations demonstrate ways in which the developing countries have expressed their interests in the talks by the company that they keep. Of particular note, the Amazon countries stood together in forests talks, and the largest, most rapidly industrializing developing countries have come together in the climate change negotiations.

TABLE 5.1 Coalitions and Discussion Groups in Four Negotiation Processes

CSD Coalitions	Biodiversity Coalitions	Forests Coalitions	Climate Coalitions	Climate Discussion Groups
European Union JUSSCANNZ	**European Union Compromise Group:** Japan, Norway, Switzerland, Republic of Korea, Mexico	**European Union** Norway Japan, Switzerland Canada US	**European Union Environmental Integrity Group:** Mexico, Republic of Korea, Switzerland	**Cartagena Dialogue:** Australia, Belgium, France, Germany, the Netherlands, New Zealand, Mexico, Norway, Spain, the UK, and European Commission
	Miami Group: US, Australia, Canada		**Umbrella Group:** Australia, Canada, Iceland, Japan, New Zealand, Norway, Russian Federation, Ukraine, US	**Major Economies:** US, Canada, Italy, Japan, Republic of Korea, Russian Federation, the EU, Australia, France, Germany, Mexico, the UK, with Denmark, New Zealand, and Spain also invited at times
Group of 77 and China	Argentina, Chile, Uruguay	**SICA (Central American Integration System)**	**AOSIS**	Brazil, China, India, Indonesia, South Africa with Barbados, Colombia, Democratic Republic of the Congo, Singapore also invited at times
	Like-Minded Group	**African Group**	**BASIC:** Brazil, South Africa, India, China	
		Non-Amazon Latin American and others: Argentina, Chile, Mexico, Guatemala, Costa Rica, Cuba, China	**ALBA:** Bolivia, Venezuela, Ecuador, Nicaragua, Cuba	
			Mountain Coalition Group	
			Arab Group	
		Amazon Group: Brazil, Venezuela, Colombia plus India	**LDCs**	
			African Group	
Central and Eastern European	**Central and Eastern European**			

In these and other examples presented in this chapter, for negotiations on specific obligations we find that countries have organized themselves to flex their issue-specific power. Geopolitical alliances form a background influence on countries' alliances and the overall state of international relations can be viewed from these talks. The expansion of the European Union and its efforts to present a single voice on the world stage, the efforts of the United States to find its voice in the unipolar-drifting-to-multipolar world, and the developing countries' desire to play a role on the world stage are all evident in these negotiations. But, more importantly, we see the use of issue-based coalitions, through which countries have attempted to influence the outcome based on their power vis-à-vis the specific issue under discussion. Efforts to understand international environmental negotiations, or to facilitate their progress (if you are in a position similar to Juan Mayr's in the biosafety case study), should consider where the issue-specific power for an agenda item lies, and evaluate the dynamics among the company that those countries are keeping.

Notes

1 New Zealand and Singapore also participated in the Compromise Group in Montreal in January 2000 (Galvez 2002, 208).
2 For more details on this, see ENB 1995.
3 Argentina made a similar statement at UNFF 6.
4 These elements were previously agreed as key components of SFM.
5 The decision on financing was forwarded to UNFF 9. A special session of UNFF 9 convened late in 2009. After seventeen years of debate on this issue, this special session ended with the adoption of a decision on financing. The Forum established an intergovernmental process to conduct in-depth analysis of all aspects of forest financing over the following four years, and a "Facilitative Process" on forest financing, to assist countries to mobilize funding from all sources. The intergovernmental ad hoc expert group will analyze existing financing strategies for sustainable forest management, and explore ways to improve access to funds, including the option of establishing a voluntary global forest fund.
6 This objection has been raised in the context of the negotiations in the Ad Hoc Working Group on Long-term Cooperative Action under the UNFCCC.
7 The Geneva Dialogue on Climate Finance was held from 2–3 September, 2010 (IISD RS 2010).
8 Bolivia argued that "the text replaces binding mechanisms for reducing greenhouse gas emissions with voluntary pledges that are wholly insufficient. These pledges contradict the stated goal of capping the rise in temperature at 2°C, instead guiding us to 4°C or more. The text is full of loopholes for polluters, opportunities for expanding carbon markets and similar mechanisms—like the forestry scheme REDD—that reduce the obligation of developed countries to act" (Solon 2010).

Works Cited

Australian Government. 2010. 2009–10 Annual Report: Department of Climate Change and Energy Efficiency. http://www.climatechange.gov.au/en/about/accountability/annual-reports/~/media/publications/annual-report/dcc-annual-report-200910.ashx (accessed June 8, 2011).

Costa Rica. 2010. Chair's Summary of the Third Meeting of the Cartagena Dialogue for
    Progressive Action: 31 October–2 November 2010. http://www.minae.go.cr/ejes_
    estrategicos/ambiente/Cambio%20Climatico/Tercera%20reunion%20del%20Dialogo
    %20de%20Cartagena/Chairman%20s%20Statement%20COSTA%20RICA.pdf
    (accessed January 20, 2011).
ENB (*Earth Negotiations Bulletin*). 1994. CSD Highlights: Monday, 16 May 1994.
    Earth Negotiations Bulletin 5(16). http://www.iisd.ca/vol05/0516000e.html (accessed
    February 20, 2011).
ENB. 1995. A Review of Selected International Forest Policy Meetings. 13(1). http://
    www.iisd.ca/download/pdf/enb1301e.pdf (accessed June 23, 2011).
ENB. 2005. Summary of the Fifth Session of the UN Forum on Forests: 16–27 May 2005.
    Earth Negotiations Bulletin 13(133). http://www.iisd.ca/download/pdf/enb13133e.pdf
    (accessed February 20, 2011).
ENB. 2006. Summary of the Sixth Session of the UN Forum on Forests: 13–24 February
    2006. *Earth Negotiations Bulletin* 13(144). http://www.iisd.ca/download/pdf/
    enb13144e.pdf (accessed February 20, 2011).
ENB. 2007. Summary of the Seventh Session of the UN Forum on Forests: 16–27 April
    2007. *Earth Negotiations Bulletin* 13(162). http://www.iisd.ca/download/pdf/
    enb13162e.pdf (accessed February 20, 2011).
ENB. 2009a. Summary of the Eighth Session of the UN Forum on Forests: 20 April–1
    May 2009. *Earth Negotiations Bulletin* 13(174). http://www.iisd.ca/download/pdf/
    enb13174e.pdf (accessed February 20, 2011).
ENB. 2009b. SB30 and AWG Highlights: 2 June 2009. *Earth Negotiations Bulletin* 12(412).
    http://www.iisd.ca/download/pdf/enb12412e.pdf (accessed March 15, 2011).
ENB. 2010a. Summary of the First Prepcom of the UN Conference on Sustainable
    Development: 17–19 May 2010. *Earth Negotiations Bulletin* 27(1). http://www.iisd.ca/
    download/pdf/enb2701e.pdf (accessed February 20, 2011).
ENB. 2010b. First Meeting of the Intergovernmental Negotiating Committee to Prepare
    a Global Legally Binding Instrument on Mercury: 7–11 June 2010. *Earth Negotiations
    Bulletin* 28(6). http://www.iisd.ca/download/pdf/enb2806e.pdf (accessed February
    20, 2011).
ENB. 2010c. Summary of the Eighteenth Session of the Commission on Sustainable
    Development: 3–14 May 2010. *Earth Negotiations Bulletin* 5(292). http://www.iisd.ca/
    download/pdf/enb05292e.pdf (accessed February 20, 2011).
ENB. 2010d. SB32 and AWG Highlights: 3 June 2010. *Earth Negotiations Bulletin* 12(465).
    http://www.iisd.ca/download/pdf/enb12465e.pdf (accessed March 16, 2011).
ENB. 2010e. Summary of the Cancún Climate Change Conference: 29 November–11
    December 2010. *Earth Negotiations Bulletin* 12(498). http://www.iisd.ca/download/
    pdf/enb12498e.pdf (accessed March 14, 2011).
Falkner, Robert. 2002. Negotiating the Biosafety Protocol: The International Process. In
    *The Cartagena Protocol on Biosafety: Reconciling Trade in Biotechnology with Environment and
    Development?* Edited by Christoph Bail, Robert Falkner, and Helen Marquard. London:
    Earthscan/RIIA.
Galvez, Amanda. 2002. Compromise Group: Mexico. In *The Cartagena Protocol on Biosafety:
    Reconciling Trade in Biotechnology with Environment and Development?* Edited by Christoph
    Bail, Robert Falkner, and Helen Marquard. London: Earthscan/RIIA.
Gupta, Joyeeta. 2000. *On Behalf of My Delegation, … : A Survival Guide for Developing
    Country Climate Negotiators.* Center for Sustainable Development in the Americas
    (CSDA) and the International Institute for Sustainable Development (IISD). http://
    www.cckn.net/www/completeindex.html (accessed February 13, 2011).
IISD RS (International Institute for Sustainable Development Reporting Services). 2010.
    Summary of the Geneva Dialogue on Climate Finance: 2–3 September 2010. *Geneva
    Dialogue on Climate Finance Bulletin* 179(1). http://www.iisd.ca/download/pdf/sd/
    ymbvol179num1e.pdf (accessed February 20, 2011).

Marsh, Duncan R. 2005. Friends and Foes: Industrialised Countries in Multilateral Environmental Negotiations. In *Global Challenges: Furthering the Multilateral Process for Sustainable Development*. Edited by Angela Churie Kallhauge, Gunnar Sjöstedt, and Elisabeth Corell. Sheffield, UK: Greenleaf Publishing.

Mayr, Juan. 2002. Environment Ministers: Political Perspectives on the Final Negotiations: Colombia. In *The Cartagena Protocol on Biosafety: Reconciling Trade in Biotechnology with Environment and Development?* Edited by Christoph Bail, Robert Falkner, and Helen Marquard. London: Earthscan/RIIA.

Newell, Peter. 1997. A Changing Landscape of Diplomatic Conflict: The Politics of Climate Change Post-Rio. In *The Way Forward: Beyond Agenda 21*. Edited by Felix Dodds. London: Earthscan.

Nobs, Beat. 2002. Compromise Group: Switzerland. In *The Cartagena Protocol on Biosafety: Reconciling Trade in Biotechnology with Environment and Development?* Edited by Christoph Bail, Robert Falkner, and Helen Marquard. London: Earthscan/RIIA.

Olsson, Marie, Aaron Atteridge, Karl Hallding, and Joakim Hellberg. 2010. Together Alone? Brazil, South Africa, India, China (BASIC) and the Climate Change Conundrum. Stockholm Environment Institute Policy Brief. http://sei-international. org/mediamanager/documents/Publications/SEI-PolicyBrief-Olsson-BASIC-ClimateChangeConundrum.pdf (accessed June 19, 2011).

Poore, Duncan. 2003. *Changing Landscapes: The Development of the International Tropical Timber Organization and Its Influence on Tropical Forest Management*. London: Earthscan.

Sands, Philippe. 1995. *Principles of International Environmental Law*. New York, NY: Cambridge University Press.

Solon, Pablo. 2010. Why Bolivia Stood Alone in Opposing the Cancún Climate Agreement, guardian.co.uk (21 December). http://www.guardian.co.uk/environment/cif-green/2010/dec/21/bolivia-oppose-cancun-climate-agreement (accessed June 24, 2011).

UNEP (UN Environment Programme) and Foundation for International Environmental Law Development (FIELD). 2007. *Guide for Negotiators of Multilateral Environmental Agreements*. United Nations: Earthprint.

UN General Assembly. 2011. Sixty-fifth General Assembly Plenary: 88th Meeting (AM). UN Department of Public Information. http://www.un.org/News/Press/docs/2011/ga11079.doc.htm (accessed June 8, 2011).

University of Joensuu. 2007. *Multilateral Environmental Agreement Negotiator's Handbook*, 2nd edition. Joensuu, Finland: UNEP and University of Joensuu. http://unfccc.int/resource/docs/publications/negotiators_handbook.pdf (accessed February 20, 2011).

Wagner, Lynn M. 1999. Negotiations in the UN Commission on Sustainable Development: Coalitions, Processes and Outcomes. *International Negotiation* 4(2): 107–131.

6

SINGING THE UNSUNG

Secretariats in Global Environmental Politics

Sikina Jinnah

Secretariats are often dismissed as merely administrative support organs for inter-governmental organizations. They perform mundane tasks such as organizing meetings, distributing documents, and maintaining websites, but are assumed to have little impact on governance outcomes. Although these administrative tasks are indeed part of the secretariat repertoire, they by no means complete it. Secretariats are much more than administrative lackeys. Specifically, the pages that follow illuminate some important ways that secretariats fit into a post-1992 global environmental governance system. This chapter focuses on how, to varying degrees, secretariats have capitalized on their unique characteristics to emerge as key actors in ameliorating a central cause of stagnant global environmental problem solving in the post-1992 period: too many organizations with too few resources.

As this volume demonstrates, the post-1992 environmental governance landscape is characterized by a proliferation of environmental agreements (see Chapter 2.) Although one might expect that an increase in environmental agreements would result in an increase in global environmental problem solving, in fact problem solving has been limited. There are many reasons for this, including a lack of political will, capacity, and/or reputational concerns (Chasek 2001; Najam 2005; Weiss and Jacobson 1998). Critically, as multilateral environmental agreements (MEAs) have proliferated, the negotiation burden has increased dramatically, particularly on developing states (Muñoz et al. 2009). Against this backdrop, there has been a push at multiple levels in recent years to "manage overlap" between these proliferating international environmental agreements (Jinnah 2010). As this chapter demonstrates, secretariats have emerged as central actors in this process.[1]

Although specific approaches vary significantly, overlap management efforts are policies and practices aimed at two things: (1) decreasing duplication of efforts across international agreements; and/or (2) increasing synergies and cooperation between them. This chapter illuminates the variety of ways in which secretariats have played a key role in working toward these objectives by moving beyond their administrative functions to substantively engage and, indeed, to oversee many aspects of treaty governance. Further, the chapter argues that not only are secretariats uniquely able to play this role in overlap management, but also their ability to do so is a valuable arrow in our quiver when thinking about how to overcome the "too many organizations with too few resources" barrier that plagues post-1992 global environmental problem solving.

In order to fully understand how secretariats have grown into this overlap management role in the post-1992 Earth Summit era, we must first understand what secretariats are. The subsequent section therefore begins with a discussion of this topic, arguing that their constellation of characteristics uniquely position secretariats to manage regime overlap more efficiently and effectively than other actors. The chapter then turns to a discussion of overlap management in practice by focusing on global biodiversity governance, arguing that the biodiversity secretariats have played an important role in building and framing the contemporary architecture of overlap management. The subsequent section discusses some emerging overlap management strategies in the chemicals issue area, which has begun to redefine overlap management in recent years. The concluding section summarizes the major arguments and reflects on the future trajectory of overlap management and secretariats' role therein.

What is a Secretariat?

A Secretariat is most simply an international bureaucracy. MEA secretariats vary somewhat in terms of size, budgets, and operational structure. For example, many operate from within UNEP (e.g., the Convention on Biological Diversity (CBD), Basel Convention, Montreal Protocol), others are institutionally linked to the United Nations (e.g., the UNFCCC, UNCCD), while still others function outside the UN structure entirely (e.g., the Ramsar Convention). The Rio Conventions' (UNFCCC, UNCCD, and CBD) budgets tend to be larger than those of most other MEAs (Muñoz et al. 2009).

Despite these differences, MEA secretariats share some fundamental characteristics. In essence, contemporary Secretariat functions and identity are consistent with our classic understanding of bureaucracies as full-time salaried professionals who support state actors in carrying out official business through a hierarchical rule-based organization (Weber 1922). Classic understandings of secretariats, however, also overlook some defining features of these actors that position them to manage overlap between international regimes. Specifically, secretariats' international character, permanence, authority, and "veil of legitimacy" (Depledge 2005) are key attributes that allow them to play this role.[2]

Despite national quota systems for staff representation within the UN system, Secretariat staff members are not meant to represent national positions. Rather, they are expected to act in an impartial capacity with a view to supporting the rules and norms of the regimes they service. In other words, Secretariat staff members are explicitly *international* in character in that they do not represent their home governments but are nationally impartial international civil servants.[3] We often take this assumption for granted in their contemporary form; however, this was a point of much contention within discussions of the world's first Secretariat: the League of Nations (Ranshofen-Wertheimer 1945). Although the international, and as such impartial, character of Secretariat staff is imperfect, akin to a scientist's relationship to objectivity, it is the bedrock of trust between member states and secretariats. This trust, based on a perception of impartiality, is a necessary condition for secretariats to substantively participate in global governance, overlap management, or otherwise.

In addition, most regime secretariats are *permanent* bodies of their organizations. Staff members are typically career international civil servants who are responsible for making a range of day-to-day operational decisions. As noted by Ranshofen-Wertheimer (1945, 345) in reference to the League of Nations: "Between sessions of the policymaking organs and its numerous committees, the Secretariat was the only concrete evidence of the League's existence." While this is an overstatement with respect to many contemporary secretariats, it highlights the special permanent position of the Secretariat in international politics. Namely, whereas member states manage treaty negotiations and implementation as part of a much larger docket of their activities, secretariats are full-time managers of the treaties they service. As such, secretariats are the operational hubs of these regimes. When it comes to coordination of daily, weekly, or even monthly activities between large numbers of actors across two or more international regimes, there is nobody better suited to manage the process than Secretariat staff.

Secretariat management of regime overlap is not merely a function of convenience however. Secretariats are also *authoritative* actors, deserving of responsibility for regime operation. As full-time managers they know better than anyone else: what is operationally possible; what is functionally realistic; and how to best achieve coordination goals on the ground. Recognizing this potential, states often explicitly endow secretariats with rational–legal authority (Barnett and Finnemore 2004; Weber 1922) in mandating them to identify options for synergy building between global environmental regimes. In turn, secretariats draw from their regime-specific expertise (Barnett and Finnemore 2004; Biermann and Siebenhüner 2009), social networks, and institutional memory (Jinnah 2008, 2010, 2011) to carry out and indeed extend these tasks by not only identifying options, but also by influencing how the process of overlap management itself unfolds within the regimes they support.

Finally, in operating behind a "veil of legitimacy," secretariats have found regime-specific mechanisms to comfortably interpret their mandates, notably as they relate to overlap management. Unlike other governance actors, Secretariats do not often seek acknowledgment for their ideas. Rather, they tend to downplay their influence over governance processes; for example, by channeling their ideas through chairpersons or member states, and clearly framing ideas as proposals for review, rather than recommendations for action. In short, secretariats are generally happy to allow others to take credit for their ideas in order to maintain their impartiality and achieve relevant regime objectives.

Secretariats since 1992

Anecdotal field observations from contributors to this volume coupled with pre-liminary analyses of Secretariat budget growth (Muñoz et al. 2009) suggest that secretariats have increased in size and complexity since 1992. However, their core structural attributes have remained fairly constant. Indeed, contemporary secretariats mirror many of the attributes of the first international Secretariat created to administer the League of Nations. They remain international and largely anonymous in character, trained experts in their area of governance, and the life blood of the treaties they service between meetings of the member states. In short, they remain international civil servants on whom smooth regime operation increasingly depends.

Secretariat functions have, however, evolved in response to their surrounding governance architecture; the post-1992 period is no exception. As highlighted by Sandford (1994, 2), between the 1972 Stockholm and 1992 Rio Conferences Secretariat functions evolved in response to the increased use of the Convention–Protocol framework, the inclusion of financial mechanisms into many treaties, and the increased focus on regional initiatives. Similarly, Secretariat evolution in the post-1992 era has evolved in response to parallel contemporary changes in global environmental governance. In short, Secretariat function evolves in a way that seizes on capacity vacuums, and results in increasing state reliance on secretariats. One critical post-1992 evolution is the increased number of overlapping environmental treaty regimes.

In the post-1992 era, secretariats have seized on the need to manage a crowded overlapping governance space against the backdrop of limited state capacity. As discussed above and throughout this volume, global environmental governance has expanded dramatically since 1992 with new treaties and protocols emerging to address environmental problems in areas ranging from climate change to trade in genetically modified organisms. Fragmenting global environmental govern-ance into discrete, highly specialized agreements facilitates consensus building and, as such, "progress." However, state capacity and/or will to keep pace with this increasingly complex structure have not kept pace with its evolution.

Overlap in the form of duplication and uncoordinated problem solving abounds between international environmental treaties.

Taken together, the key attributes of secretariats, coupled with the increasingly complex governance architecture that surrounds them, position secretariats to move beyond the mere administrative role that generally characterizes their activities. Specifically, these variables have uniquely positioned secretariats to substantively engage in global governance by managing overlap between international regimes. Indeed, recent research suggests that secretariats are playing a particularly important role in managing inter-regime cooperation, or "overlap management" (Jinnah 2010, 2011; Oberthür 2009). This emerging role for secretariats is a defining feature of the post-1992 era in global environmental politics. It is the secretariats' role in managing this narrow but increasingly important slice of governance that is the focus of the remainder of this chapter.

Overlap Management in Practice

As noted above, secretariats tend to operate behind a "veil of legitimacy." That is, they are constantly in a balancing act between using their expertise to ensure smooth operation of their treaty regimes, while simultaneously not overstepping their mandate and member states' expectations—at least publically. For example, one Secretariat staff member explained how, rather than suggesting outright to her Conference of the Parties (COP) that it would make sense to protect a particular species (in part) due to complementary protection measures under an overlapping treaty, she seeded the idea with a sympathetic party, who subsequently successfully proposed the measure in plenary. This behind-the-scenes maneuvering is common among secretariats, although not always successful in achieving the desired outcome.

As such, it is difficult to "observe" much of secretariats' most interesting and potentially influential work in the plenary hall itself. Secretariats go to great lengths to obscure evidence of their influence in order to maintain their legitimacy and the trust of their member states.

Biodiversity

Global biodiversity governance has evolved in a stepwise and fragmented manner. Rather than addressing the problem comprehensively under a single treaty, countries have focused on narrow slices of the broader biodiversity loss problem. There are well over 150 international treaties addressing global biodiversity loss. Together, these agreements attempt to govern global biodiversity loss via a "collective of partially overlapping and nonhierarchical regimes," or what we might call the biodiversity "regime complex" (Raustiala and Victor 2004, 277). Table 6.1 highlights some of the regimes that make up the biodiversity regime

TABLE 6.1 Sample of Biodiversity Treaties (1948–2004)

MEA	Entry into Force (year)	Biodiversity Objective
Convention for the Regulation of Whaling	1948	Evolved over time from ensuring sustainability of whaling industry to protection of whales for conservation
Convention on International Trade in Endangered Species (CITES)	1975	Prevent species extinction resulting from international trade
Ramsar Convention	1975	Protection of wetlands especially for water fowl habitat
Convention for the Protection of the World Cultural and Natural Heritage	1975	Protection of biological formations that are of outstanding universal value from the aesthetic or scientific point of view
Convention on Biological Diversity (CBD)	1993	Conservation and sustainable use of biodiversity and equitable sharing of benefits arising from such use
Convention on Migratory Species (CMS)	1983	Conserve migratory species and their habitats
Cartagena Protocol on Biosafety	2003	Ensure the safe transfer, handling, and use of living modified organisms that may have adverse effects on the conservation and sustainable use of biological diversity
International Treaty on Protection of Genetic Resources for Food and Agriculture (ITPGR)	2004	Ensure the conservation and sustainable use of plant genetic resources for food and agriculture and the fair and equitable sharing of the benefits arising out of their use

complex, highlighting the diversity of topics addressed and the long time span along which they have emerged.

This large number of generally uncoordinated treaties, each addressing a narrow slice of the larger conservation pie, has resulted in a highly fragmented biodiversity regime complex and necessarily results in areas of overlap between the various agreements. Secretariats within the biodiversity regime complex have emerged as key players in managing this overlap. In short, they have taken on the task of fusing fragmentation in global biodiversity governance. They have done this by drawing from their expertise, social networks, and institutional memory to identify legal, political, and scientific points of overlap between the various biodiversity regimes, and used this knowledge to define and drive the rules and practices for managing that overlap. The CBD case highlights the experience of a key Secretariat in this process; however, many aspects of the CBD experience are also reflected across other biodiversity treaties.

Convention on Biological Diversity

The CBD treaty text (1992) provides the original mandate for inter-regime cooperation (i.e., overlap management), and identifies the Secretariat as a key participant in fulfilling this mandate (see Appendix). Specifically, Article 23 paragraph 4(h) mandates the COP to "contact, through the Secretariat, the executive bodies of Conventions dealing with matters covered by this Convention with a view to establishing appropriate forms of cooperation with them." Similarly, Article 24.1(d) mandates the Secretariat to "coordinate with other relevant bodies, and in particular to enter into such administrative and contractual arrangements as may be required for the effective discharge of its functions." Although these mandates identify cooperative activities as an important goal of the Convention, they provide little direction as to *how* overlap management should be pursued. In short, cooperation-related mandates tend to be vague, leaving much flexibility in the Secretariat's hands. As noted by one staff member during an interview, "we can always find a mandate to justify what we want to do." The CBD Secretariat has seized this as an opportunity to define and drive the overlap management process in important ways.

Defining Governance Architecture

First, the CBD Secretariat has been a pivotal actor in defining and constituting the architecture of overlap management itself. Prior to the Secretariat's action in this area, overlap management was all but absent in this realm of international politics. Now, the CBD Secretariat's thumb print is visible on overlap management activities not just within the CBD but also across the entire biodiversity regime complex.

An analysis of CBD COP decisions on "cooperation with other conventions" (i.e., overlap management) from 1992 to 2010 reveals that nearly all tools used by the COP to mandate overlap management activities can be traced back to one document produced by the Secretariat in 1995 (UNEP/CBD/COP/2/Inf.2). This document was produced in response to a COP request to outline possible modes of cooperation with other conventions. This document is the source of many later decisions related to overlap management within the CBD. Its most important contributions are its identification of areas where cooperation might be pursued, and specific "recommendations for action."

On the former, the Secretariat suggests: coordinated implementation across conventions (i.e., development of mutually reinforcing policies aimed at conservation); coordination between institutional bodies (i.e., COPs, scientific bodies, etc.); coordination of COP agendas (i.e., making "Cooperation with other Conventions" a regular agenda item); harmonization of national reporting between biodiversity conventions (i.e., rather than stretching capacity through multiple overlapping reporting requirements); partnerships between secretariats; development of joint work programs; and the supportive role of UNEP (i.e., as a coordinating entity). Aside from harmonization of reporting, which has not materialized, despite significant interest, *all* of these options have been adopted and institutionalized by CBD parties.[4]

On the latter, three of the four recommendations (on harmonized reporting, joint work programs between the biodiversity conventions, and, critically, Secretariat leadership in these activities) were included in the COP's final decision on this matter (COP II/13). Analysis of subsequent COP decisions on "cooperation with other conventions" further reveals that many, if not most, of these decisions over the years were in fact drafted by the Secretariat and adopted with minor (if any) amendments (Jinnah 2008). Through drafting decisions, which subsequently mandate the Secretariat to undertake certain activities, the Secretariat in effect defines its own mandate, in particular vis-à-vis cooperative activities. This has resulted in the Secretariat positioning itself to take the lead on overlap management governance. Although this role for secretariats is hardly surprising to those working directly on these issues on the ground, it is one that has not been adequately considered in evaluating the influence or importance of these actors.

The overlap management tools identified by the CBD Secretariat in this document continue to serve as the backbone of overlap management within the CBD and beyond. While seemingly unimaginative and commonplace now, these ideas were new and cutting-edge tools for global environmental governance when originally articulated by the CBD Secretariat in 1995.

Framing Political Linkages

Climate change issues have gained an increasingly central role in CBD discussions over the past few years. Climate-related discussions permeated various discussions at COP 10 in Nagoya, Japan, with key decisions on the matter, most notably a de facto ban on climate-related geo-engineering activities (ENB 2010b). Now seemingly commonplace in CBD discussions, the entrée of climate change-related issues has actually been evolving steadily since the first decision on coral bleaching at COP 4 in 1998, to the infusion of climate-related issues across the CBD agenda at COP 10 in 2010. These discussions really began to pick up steam in 2007, when the CBD's then new Executive-Secretary Ahmed Djoghlaf took a leadership role in folding climate change issues into the biodiversity agenda (see also Chapter 10). This change was most notable at SBSTTA 12 in 2007, when Djoghlaf focused his opening remarks almost exclusively on the linkages between biodiversity and climate change (Figure 6.1), some might argue ignoring the more pressing issues under consideration at that meeting (ENB 2007).

FIGURE 6.1 Ahmed Djoghlaf, CBD Executive-Secretary, urged delegates to prepare the scientific basis for addressing the links between biodiversity conservation and climate change in his opening statement at SBSTTA 12 in July 2007. Photo courtesy of IISD/*Earth Negotiations Bulletin*

As such, in addition to defining governance structures and drafting decisions on overlap management, the CBD Secretariat has also influenced overlap management in a second very different, and important, way. Led by its Executive-Secretary, Djoghlaf, between 2007 and 2010 the CBD Secretariat attempted to change the way CBD actors (parties and beyond) understand the overlap between climate change and biodiversity. The CBD Secretariat acted as a "norm entrepreneur" in trying to shape the way actors who traditionally influence biodiversity governance understand how biodiversity and climate change should relate to one another and how this interface should be managed.[5] In short, the Secretariat reframed biodiversity from a passive victim of climate impacts, to an active player in climate response measures (i.e., adaptation).[6]

Specifically, the Secretariat filtered, framed, and reiterated strategic frames of the biodiversity–climate change linkage that positioned biodiversity as a tool for climate adaptation and ensuring human security. This reframing is significant in that a major hurdle to selling the benefits of biodiversity conservation to countries with more pressing development concerns has been the perceived limited relevance of conservation to human wellbeing. This reframing helped to overcome a key "priorities barrier" to conservation. That is, in framing conservation as a tool for human adaption and for ensuring human security, the Secretariat helped to shape the way in which CBD parties think about, value, and channel resources for conservation.

The mechanism by which the Secretariat did this is indicative of the emerging domain of Secretariat politics as norm entrepreneurs. In 2006–2007, the Secretariat launched an aggressive marketing campaign through over 100 public statements aimed at reframing the biodiversity–climate change linkage in a way that emphasized biodiversity's active role in climate solutions. The Secretariat introduced new frames (e.g., climate change leads to biodiversity loss, which in turn creates human security concerns) to the CBD discourse, and strategically emphasized existing frames (e.g., biodiversity can help humans adapt to climate change) that foreground aspects of the linkage that make conservation objectives more attractive to developing countries.

In summary, the CBD Secretariat has emerged as a central actor in overlap management in at least three ways. First, and critically, the Secretariat defined the prevailing governance tools of overlap management through a key document in 1995. These tools are now commonplace across not only the CBD's work but also throughout biodiversity governance, and beyond. Second, the CBD Secretariat has played an important role in drafting COP decisions. This practice, also common in global biodiversity governance (and in some cases beyond this realm), is worth noting because it often results in the Secretariat defining its own mandates. In the CBD case, this is the primary mechanism the Secretariat uses to position itself as a central node in overlap management. Finally, the CBD Secretariat has played an important role as a norm entrepreneur. It has gone to great lengths to strategically frame the overlap between biodiversity and climate change in a way that helped to overcome "priorities barriers" to conservation by constructing biodiversity as a tool for adaptation and human security (Jinnah 2011)[7] (see also Box 6.1).

BOX 6.1 BIODIVERSITY LIAISON GROUP

Another key mechanism by which biodiversity secretariats manage overlap is the Biodiversity Liaison Group (BLG). Established in 2004, the BLG serves as a forum for the heads of the core biodiversity secretariats (CBD, CMS, CITES, Ramsar Convention on Wetlands, and World Heritage Convention) to manage overlap between them. The BLG has officially met seven times and has held one retreat from 2004 to 2010. These meetings have resulted in a variety of recommendations about how to maximize synergies in the implementation of these conventions, and have produced a CD-ROM on the common elements of implementation of the Addis Ababa Principles and Guidelines. More information about the BLG, including meeting reports and the CD-ROM can be found here: http://www.cbd.int/cooperation/related-conventions/blg.shtml.

Convention on Migratory Species

Among the old guard in global biodiversity protection, the Convention on Migratory Species (CMS) came into existence before the Earth Summit, entering into force in 1983. It aims to protect migratory species throughout their ranges by providing a forum in which member governments can negotiate ways to protect migratory species through, for example, species-specific conservation agreements. CMS goals and objectives overlap substantially with other biodiversity conventions. Areas of overlap with the CBD are obvious, given the CBD's broad conservation objectives, which include conservation of migratory species. However, there are also areas of overlap between CMS and the Convention on International Trade in Endangered Species (CITES).

The CMS Secretariat initiated an overlap management strategy with the CITES Secretariat to enhance conservation of a species that is both migratory and threatened due to international trade: the Saiga Antelope. Cooperation between CMS and CITES formally began in September 2002 when the two Secretariats signed a Memorandum of Understanding (MOU) highlighting their overlapping goals. In an annex to the MOU, various specific options for overlap management were identified, including joint activities related to species of common concern. However, the two Secretariats initiated cooperation on the Saiga Antelope before the MOU was agreed by their member governments. This overlap management initiative was largely driven by the CMS Secretariat and began despite the absence of a specific mandate for the CMS Secretariat to cooperate on this issue. This case is interesting because, when the CMS Secretariat initiated overlap management activities on this issue, the Saiga Antelope was not listed under CMS, and three of the five range states (a country in which a particular species lives) were not parties to CMS. Despite these obstacles, the CMS Secretariat strategically used normative, functional, and membership overlap[8] with CITES to catalyze the listing of this previously unprotected and highly threatened migratory species in the CMS Appendices, and lured a new party (Kazakhstan) to the Convention.

The Saiga Antelope was listed in CITES Appendix II in 1995, thereby restricting its trade through use of export permits. However, the preponderance of scientific data both within and external to the two conventions suggest that the Saiga Antelope's eminent extinction warranted the most stringent level of protection afforded only to those species listed in CITES Appendix I[9] (Bekenov et al. 1998; Milner-Gulland et al. 2001). Despite this preponderance of scientific evidence, the Saiga Antelope was not protected *at all* under CMS until COP 7 in September 2002,[10] following a Secretariat-led overlap management initiative to catalyze conservation of the species.

In May 2002, the CMS and CITES Secretariats jointly sponsored the Elista International Workshop on the Saiga Antelope in Elista, Kalmykia Republic, Russian Federation (CMS Secretariat 2002). Largely spearheaded by the CMS Secretariat, the Elista workshop marked the entrée of Saiga conservation under CMS. The workshop, and the IUCN-chaired technical workshop immediately preceding it, were attended by all five Saiga range states (Kazakhstan, Mongolia, Russian Federation, Turkmenistan, and Uzbekistan), the CMS and CITES Secretariats and a number of interested NGOs. It achieved "unprecedented cooperation" (United States quoted in CITES 2003) on Saiga issues, and produced a CMS MOU on Saiga conservation between four of the five range states, and a draft Action Plan for conservation, restoration, and sustainable use of the Saiga Antelope.

These achievements are remarkable because, as noted above, Saiga was not listed in the CMS Appendices at that time and two of these range state signatories were not yet parties to CMS (Kazakhstan and the Russian Federation). Both states were parties to CITES, suggesting that their participation in the Elista workshop was strategically facilitated by holding the workshop jointly with CITES. Further, shortly following the Elista workshop, the Saiga Antelope was listed in CMS Appendix II at COP 7 in September 2002. In addition, one year after the Saiga MOU was opened for signature in 2005, Kazakhstan officially acceded to CMS (Figure 6.2).[11]

FIGURE 6.2 CMS Executive-Secretary Robert Hepworth shakes hands with Minister Makhtumkuli Akmuradov of Turkmenistan, following the signing of a Memorandum of Understanding (MOU) on the Saiga Antelope in November 2005. Behind them are delegates of Uzbekistan, Mongolia, the Council for Game and Wildlife Conservation, IUCN and WWF International, which also signed the MOU. Photo courtesy of IISD/*Earth Negotiations Bulletin*

Lacking a specific mandate to work on the Saiga Antelope, this case highlights the CMS Secretariat's unique ability to act autonomously in the realm of overlap management, identifying a species that should be of concern to the Convention and creating strategic partnerships for conservation of that species. The Secretariat was able to leverage staff time and financial resources to a particular overlap management activity prior to any COP consideration of the matter. Why was this so?

The CMS Secretariat strategically leveraged various aspects of its highly flexible mandate, which is unique among the biodiversity conventions in that it explicitly grants the Secretariat a great deal of autonomy. Whereas many Secretariats' mandates vis-à-vis overlap management require some creativity to influence the process, the CMS Secretariat enjoys an unusual amount of direct autonomy. Most importantly, the CMS Secretariat is mandated to: maintain liaison with and promote liaisons between the parties and other international organizations concerned with migratory species; obtain from any appropriate source reports and other information that will further the objectives and implementation of this Convention; and invite the attention of the Conference of the Parties to any matter pertaining to the objectives of this Convention (CMS Article 9).

Together these functions allow the CMS Secretariat to do exactly what it did in the Saiga case: identify species of concern, cooperate with other international organizations to collect information on the species, and bring the issue to the COP for consideration. The CMS Secretariat also has a unique relationship with its parties that facilitated this process. Whereas in many other forums the Secretariat is seen as a "servant," the CMS Secretariat has a more horizontal relationship with its parties. In contrast, at CITES COP 14 in The Hague in 2008, a delegate took the floor in plenary to say that the "Secretariat is our servant!" This delegate's sentiment appears to be widespread and is consistent with the majority of the scholarly literature's characterization of secretariat participation in international relations.

The 2006–2011 CMS Strategic Plan lends insight into how this relationship positions the Secretariat to take a leadership role in overlap management. The plan notes that "the Secretariat has the function of a *driving and coordinating force*" (CMS Article 5.2 emphasis added) that the "Parties, the Secretariat and the Scientific Council are the *main actors* for achieving most of [the Strategic Plan's] targets," (CMS Article 5.3, emphasis added) and that "the indicators for the [Strategic Plan's] Objectives and Targets … will *mainly require actions by the Secretariat* and the Scientific Council, but some inputs will also be needed from Contracting Parties" (CMS Article 5.3, emphasis added). This suggests that the CMS Secretariat's role in implementation of the Convention is reflective of an advisory partnership between the CMS Secretariat and parties, allowing the CMS Secretariat to operate further outside of its veil of legitimacy than many of its contemporaries can, including the CBD.

This case illuminates an additional way that secretariats have influenced global environmental politics in the post-1992 era. Namely, against the backdrop of an increasingly dense policy space, the CMS Secretariat was able to increase parties' ability to achieve the Convention's objectives through strategic management of overlap between closely related treaties. It was able to draw non-parties into discussions about an issue of concern to CMS by cooperating with another treaty (CITES) to which those countries were party. Further, this case highlights the CMS Secretariat's entrepreneurial character, which: catalyzed the listing of Saiga Antelope in the CMS Appendices; facilitated the development of a conservation agreement (the Saiga MOU) for this highly threatened migratory species before it was listed; and even brought a new party (Kazakhstan) to the Convention through that process. As overlap between global environmental treaties continues to increase in the post-1992 era, secretariats are in a unique position to capitalize on these connections to harness synergies and influence policy outcomes (see Box 6.2). The CMS Secretariat has proven to be one of the more proactive in this regard, largely due to the unusual level of authority endowed to it by its mandate.

Chemicals

Like biodiversity governance, chemicals governance is also fragmented across over 279 international agreements and modifications.[12] Also like biodiversity governance, governance of chemicals and other toxics is old, dating back to at least 1904 with the convention between Alsace-Lorraine, Baden, Bavaria, Hesse, the Netherlands and Prussia Relative to the Carriage of Inflammable Substances on the Rhine (see Table 6.2).

BOX 6.2 CHIEF EXECUTIVES BOARD ON COORDINATION

The CEB is the oldest and most high-level body that addresses overlap management within the UN system. It is composed of the heads of twenty-eight UN organizations, which meet twice a year, and it is chaired by the UN Secretary-General. Renamed the CEB in 2001, the CEB dates back to 1948 when the Secretary-General established the Administrative Committee on Coordination (ACC). The ACC was created to ensure the full and effective implementation of UN agreements by coordinating operation between the decentralized UN bodies and specialized agencies. The CEB covers a variety of thematic areas, including climate change, system-wide coherence, and science and technology. More information on the CEB and its work can be found here: http://www.unsceb.org/ceb/home.

TABLE 6.2 Global Chemicals and Toxics Agreements (1954–2006)

MEA	Entry into Force (Year)	Objective
International Convention for the Prevention of Pollution of the Sea by Oil (MARPOL)	1954	Prevention of pollution of marine environments by ships from operational or accidental causes
Montreal Protocol on Substances that Deplete the Ozone Layer	1987	Protection of the ozone layer by phasing out use of ozone depleting substances
Protocol on Persistent Organic Pollutants to the Convention on Long-Range Transboundary Air Pollution (LRTAP)	2003	Protects against long-range air emissions of chemical substances that persist in the environment and can bioaccumulate in the food web
Basel Convention on the Control of Transboundary Movements of Hazardous Wastes and Their Disposal	1992	Controls the international movement of hazardous wastes with the goals of environmentally sound management and protecting human health
Stockholm Convention on Persistent Organic Pollutants	2004	Creates a framework to eliminate, restrict, or reduce unintentional production and use of listed chemicals
Rotterdam Convention on the Prior Informed Consent Procedure for Certain Hazardous Chemicals and Pesticides in International Trade	2004	Establishes a mechanism to obtain consent before importing certain hazardous pesticides and industrial chemicals

In recent years, creative new initiatives to managing overlap between the global chemicals agreements have emerged. These initiatives have gone deeper into overlap management than the MOUs, joint work programs, and co-hosted workshops that dominate synergy-building between the biodiversity-related MEAs. Rather, chemicals governance has taken creative strides toward institutionalizing synergistic work (Selin 2010). One of these initiatives was the Ad Hoc Joint Working Group (AHJWG) on Enhancing Cooperation and Coordination between the Rotterdam Convention on the Prior Informed Consent Procedure for Certain Hazardous Chemicals and Pesticides in International Trade, the Stockholm Convention on Persistent Organic Pollutants, and the Basel Convention on the Control of Transboundary Movements of Hazardous Wastes and Their Disposal.

Ad Hoc Joint Working Group on Enhancing Cooperation and Coordination

The AHJWG represents an important example of a body to manage overlap between MEAs. Originally proposed for establishment by the Stockholm

Convention in 2006 (decision SC-2/15 para 3), the AHJWG proposal was also sent to the Rotterdam and Basel COPs for consideration and subsequent adoption.[13] Composed of representatives from fifteen country parties to each of the three conventions, the AHJWG was established to prepare joint recommendations on overlap management for submission to the COPs of the three conventions.

Through its three meetings between April 2007 and March 2008, the AHJWG was instrumental in generating ideas and proposals for how to manage overlap within the global chemicals regime. Some of these ideas built on experience within the biodiversity regime, such as the AHJWG's consideration of back-to-back meetings, its suggestion that parties share experiences, and perhaps even the Synergies Oversight Team, made up of the heads of the three Convention Secretariats, that mirrors the Biodiversity Liaison Group described in Box 6.1. However, many of the ideas emerging from the AHJWG's work have been novel and hold potential to re-shape the dominant overlap management architecture that was developed by the CBD in 1995, as discussed above.

Most interestingly, responding to the AHJWG suggestion, the three chemicals COPs held a three-day simultaneous extraordinary meeting (ExCOP) in February 2010. What could have easily been a merely symbolic meeting of these three bodies actually resulted in major substantive changes to overlap management in the chemicals regime. The omnibus decisions resulting from the ExCOP and subsequently adopted by all three individual COPs mandated key activities to facilitate implementation, such as joint audits and synchronization of budget cycles (ENB 2010a).[14] The decisions also mandated the establishment of joint services, for a trial period of three years, in such areas as legal, financial, administrative, and information technology services. Most visibly, parties agreed to appoint a joint head of the three Secretariats for a trial period of two years and, critical to on-the-ground implementation, they agreed to jointly use the Basel and Stockholm Conventions' regional centers.[15]

These initiatives are still in their infancy, with the joint head, Jim Willis, only appointed in 2011. As a possible fulcrum of the evolving overlap management architecture, the influence of the Secretariats will in large part depend on how the joint head envisions, interprets, and fulfills the vague mandate set out before him/her. If the joint head is an entrepreneurial leader who is keen to play the role of a norm entrepreneur, it is likely that the Secretariat may play a very visible and important role in the continued evolution of overlap management strategies. However, because the joint head position is only approved for a trial period of two years, after which time the position will be reviewed, it is likely that the joint head will tread carefully in those first couple of years. This leader will be engaged in a delicate balance of demonstrating value added in terms of improved implementation, while simultaneously maintaining his/her "veil of legitimacy" so as not to upset those parties that see the Secretariat as their "servant."

Conclusions

In some respects, secretariats have not changed much since 1992. Their basic structure and core functions remain the same. However, the proliferation of multilateral environmental agreements in the post-1992 era has created a crowded governance system in which states increasingly rely on secretariats to carry out core regime tasks (e.g., verification missions, drafting decisions, and capacity-building workshops) and emerging governance objectives (i.e., overlap management). This is because many states, particularly many developing ones, lack the capacity to effectively juggle the continually growing and often overlapping set of obligations laid out in these agreements. Secretariats are in a unique position to drive this governance process due to their expertise, social networks, and "veils of legitimacy." In short, secretariats have emerged as key actors in managing the mismatch between the large number of obligations states have taken on and their limited capacity to effectively implement those obligations.

The biodiversity cases (CBD and CMS) discussed in this chapter explore the realm of largely informal Secretariat-initiated overlap management in the absence of direct instruction from member states. These cases highlight four ways that secretariats influence overlap management: defining governance tools; drafting secretariat mandates; framing linkages in ways that further regime objectives; and facilitating treaty implementation through strategic cooperative relationships. These overlap management tools, largely defined by the CBD and used throughout biodiversity governance, formed the foundation of overlap management in the post-1992 era.

Although still quite new, recent movements in the chemicals regime indicate that overlap management may be changing. First, overlap management in the chemicals regime appears to be evolving through more formal, institutionalized structures, such as the joint Secretariat head. This suggests that states have recognized Secretariat capacity to manage overlap, and have accordingly endowed them with important, formalized overlap management functions. Further, whereas pre-existing overlap management is largely defined by international-level collaborations (i.e., between secretariats), the recent developments in chemicals governance appear to be moving toward national-level initiatives that are focused on concrete implementation activities, such as the shared use of the Basel and Stockholm regional centers. This move toward more implementation-oriented objectives is likely to yield greater results for problem solving than previous overlap management initiatives.

Although the treaties explored in this chapter address closely related issues, and are governed by similar state actors, Secretariat tactics and goals differ significantly across cases. These differences illuminate both the wide breadth and potential for Secretariat participation in global affairs, and that overlap management is evolving as states increasingly recognize this potential. Nevertheless, secretariats face a number of challenges in realizing this potential. For example, many secretariats are grappling with decreasing budgets and increasing workloads, and all secretariats must constantly tread the fine line between promoting the aims of their MEAs, and maintaining the trust of their parties. Indeed, secretariats have been slapped on the hand for crossing this boundary on some occasions (note the example above from CITES COP 14).

As bureaucratic entities, uncontrolled Secretariat governance certainly raises questions about governance legitimacy. Aside from politically appointed directors, Secretariat staff are after all hired through internal, non-transparent, and undemocratic processes. Further, as suggested here and elsewhere in related literature, the interests and motivations of Secretariat staff tend to reflect successful implementation of the agreements they service. Albeit somewhat counterintuitive, this does not always reflect the interest of the member states. For example, some countries may participate in a treaty process solely to obstruct or weaken the ability of a treaty to achieve its outcomes. In these cases, objections to Secretariat participation are expected. These concerns, however, must not preclude our willingness to harvest the potential that Secretariat expertise and networks bring to overlap management. If harnessed carefully and effectively, this potential can play an important role in overcoming at least one key governance challenge in the post-Earth Summit era, that of too many organizations with too few resources.

Notes

1 Other actors of course participate in overlap management as well. For example, chairs and member states clearly play an important role. This chapter focuses on secretariats because their role is understudied in the academic literature to date.
2 For a general overview of Secretariat functions see Sandford 1994.
3 Secretariats are also international in the sense that they are composed of representatives from various countries. This characteristic of secretariats is not relevant to their impartiality however.
4 There is, however, a joint initiative between UNEP, GEF, and UNEP-WCMC to create a joint reporting system for the Rio Conventions called the GEF Project on Integrated Reporting to Rio Conventions. See http://rioconventionsreporting.net/.
5 On norm entrepreneurs, see Finnemore and Sikkink 1998 and Ingebritsen 2002.
6 This discussion summarizes Jinnah 2011. Please refer to this article for a more detailed discussion of this case.
7 Although it should be noted that this influence has not permeated the climate regime, indicating that the secretariat's influence in this respect is limited to CBD discussions. See also Chapter 10 for a related discussion on this topic.
8 For more detail on the difference between these types of regime overlap, see Selin and VanDeveer 2003, and Young 2002.
9 CITES Appendix I prohibits trade in listed species.
10 The CMS-CITES MOU was also adopted at this meeting.
11 All range states have now ratified the MOU except Turkmenistan, which is not a party to either CITES or CMS.
12 Data from Mitchell. 2002–2011.

13 The AHJWG was adopted by COP decisions: SC-2/15 (Stockholm Convention), RC-3/8 (Rotterdam Convention), and VIII/8 (Basel Convention).
14 The content of the omnibus decisions from the ExCOP was adopted by each of the three Conventions through Decisions SC-4/34 (2009), IX/10 (2008), and RC-4/11 (2008).
15 Some of these ideas can be preliminarily traced back to a document produced by the Stockholm Convention Secretariat for its second COP in 2006. However, a more thorough document analysis would be necessary to ascertain if this was the original source of these ideas as we saw in the CBD case described above.

Works Cited

Barnett, Michael and Martha Finnemore. 2004. *Rules for the World: International Organizations in Global Politics*. Ithaca and London: Cornell University Press.
Bekenov, A.B., I.A. Grachev, and E.J. Milner-Gulland. 1998. The Ecology and Management of the Saiga Antelope in Kazakhstan. *Mammal Review* 28(1): 1–52.
Biermann, Frank and Bernd Siebenhüner (eds.). 2009. *Managers of Global Change: The Influence of International Environmental Bureaucracies*. Cambridge, MA: MIT Press.
CITES. 2003. Review of Significant Trade in Specimens of Appendix II Species: Conservation of Saiga Tatarica. AC19 Doc.8.6. http://www.cites.org/eng/com/AC/19/E19–08–6.pdf (accessed June 15, 2011).
Chasek, Pamela S. 2001. NGOs and State Capacity in International Environmental Negotiations: The Experience of the Earth Negotiations Bulletin. *Review of European Community and International Environmental Law* 10(2): 168–176.
CMS Secretariat. 2002. CMS Statement to the 12th Meeting of the Conference of the Parties to CITES. November 3–15, 2002, Santiago, Chile. http://www.cms.int/news/PRESS/nwPR2002/cms_cites12cop_statement.htm (accessed June 15, 2011).
Depledge, Joanna. 2005. *The Organization of Global Negotiations: Constructing the Climate Change Regime*. London: Earthscan.
ENB (*Earth Negotiations Bulletin*). 2007. Summary and Analysis of the 12th Session of the Subsidiary Body on Scientific Technical and Technological Advice of the Convention on Biological Diversity: 2–13 July 2007. *Earth Negotiations Bulletin* 9(382). http://www.iisd.ca/download/pdf/enb09382e.pdf (accessed February 23, 2011).
ENB. 2010a. Simultaneous Extraordinary Meetings of the Conferences of the Parties to the Basel, Rotterdam, and Stockholm Conventions (ExCOPs), *and* Eleventh Special Session of the UN Environment Programme Governing Council/Global Ministerial Environment Forum: 22–26 February 2010. *Earth Negotiations Bulletin* 16(84). http://www.iisd.ca/download/pdf/enb09373e.pdf (accessed February 23, 2011).
ENB. 2010b. Summary of the 10th Conference of the Parties to the Convention on Biological Diversity: 18–29 October 2010. *Earth Negotiations Bulletin* 9(544). http://www.iisd.ca/download/pdf/enb09544e.pdf (accessed February 23, 2011).
Finnemore, Martha and Kathryn Sikkink. 1998. International Norm Dynamics and Political Change. *International Organization* 52(4): 887–917.
Ingebritsen, Christine. 2002. Norm Entrepreneurs. *Cooperation and Conflict* 37(1): 11–23.
Jinnah, Sikina. 2008. Who's in Charge? International Bureaucracies and the Management of Global Governance. Dissertation. Berkeley: Environmental Science, Policy, and Management, UC Berkeley.
Jinnah, Sikina. 2010. Overlap Management in the World Trade Organization: Secretariat Influence on Trade-Environment Politics. *Global Environmental Politics* 10(2): 54–79.
Jinnah, Sikina. 2011. Marketing Linkages: Secretariat Governance of the Climate-Biodiversity Interface. *Global Environmental Politics* 11(3): 23–43.

Milner-Gulland, E.J., M.V. Kholodova, A. Bekenov, O.M. Bukreeva, I.A. Grachev, L. Amgalan, and A.A. Lushchekina. 2001. Dramatic Declines in Saiga Antelope Populations. *Oryx* 35(4): 340–345.

Mitchell, Ronald B. 2002–2011. International Environmental Agreements Database Project (Version 2010.3). http://iea.uoregon.edu/ (accessed January 10, 2011).

Muñoz, Miquel, Rachel Thrasher, and Adil Najam. 2009. Measuring the Negotiation Burden of Multilateral Environmental Agreements. *Global Environmental Politics* 9(4): 1–13.

Najam, Adil. 2005. Developing Countries and Global Environmental Governance: From Contestation to Participation to Engagement. *International Environmental Agreements* 5: 303–321.

Oberthür, Sebastian. 2009. Interplay Management: Enhancing Environmental Policy Integration Among International Institutions. *International Environmental Agreements: Law, Policy, and Economics* 9(4): 371–391.

Ranshofen-Wertheimer, Egon F. 1945. *The International Secretariat: A Great Experiment in International Administration*. Washington, DC: Carnegie Endowment for International Peace.

Raustiala, Kal and David G. Victor. 2004. The Regime Complex for Plant Genetic Resources. *International Organization* 58: 277–309.

Sandford, Rosemary. 1994. International Environmental Treaty Secretariats: Stage-Hands or Actors? In *Green Globe Yearbook of International Co-operation on Environment and Development 1994*. Edited by Helge Ole Bergesen and Georg Parmann. Oxford: Oxford University Press.

Selin, Henrik. 2010. *Global Governance of Hazardous Chemicals: Challenges of Multilevel Governance*. Cambridge, MA, and London: MIT Press.

Selin, Henrick, and Stacy D. VanDeveer. 2003. Mapping Institutional Linkages in European Air Politics. *Global Environmental Politics* 3(3): 14–46.

Weber, Max. 1922. *Economy and Society*, translated by G. Roth and C. Wittich (1978). Berkeley, Los Angeles, London: University of California Press.

Weiss, Edith Brown and Harold K. Jacobson. 1998. *Engaging Countries: Strengthening Compliance with International Environmental Accords*. Cambridge, MA: MIT Press.

Young, Oran. 2002. *The Institutional Dimensions of Global Change: Fit Interplay and Scale*. Cambridge, MA, and London: MIT Press.

7

WITNESS, ARCHITECT, DETRACTOR

The Evolving Role of NGOs in International Environmental Negotiations

Stanley W. Burgiel and Peter Wood

Since the Earth Summit in 1992, civil society and, more specifically, non-governmental organizations (NGOs) have been critical players in the negotiation of multilateral environmental agreements. The Earth Summit signaled a watershed moment in NGO engagement in international environmental policy discussions, with 2,400 NGO representatives attending the summit itself, and an additional 17,000 attending the parallel NGO Forum (UN 1997). Prior to UNCED, NGO involvement in UN meetings and conferences was primarily restricted to large organizations with accreditation to the Economic and Social Council (ECOSOC). However, UNCED Secretary-General Maurice Strong held a clear vision for the integration of civil society into the discourse (and action) on sustainability, alongside formal governmental involvement (Kjellén 2008). Strong believed that greater NGO participation would result in greater legitimacy of the Earth Summit and its outcomes.

The large increase in NGO participation at UNCED gave rise to a range of different activities, as some NGOs were clearly interested in influencing governmental positions and the negotiating process itself, whereas others took more interest in parallel negotiations on climate and biodiversity and others were more interested in the Global Forum that took place alongside the Earth Summit (Engfeldt 2009). As a result of the UNCED process, NGOs were able to receive consultative status with the Commission on Sustainable Development (CSD), which helped shift their role in UN fora from being solely mute observers and information providers to being political players (Mucke 1997).[1] A key symbol of this new status was the change in their physical access to the negotiators within UN Headquarters conference rooms. The "observer galleries" they once sat in were elevated and completely separated by a wall from the "floor" where the negotiators sat, but after the Earth Summit these galleries were often unoccupied because NGOs were allowed onto the floor of the conference rooms and hallways during post-UNCED-related meetings, where they could interact more freely with government delegates.

If UNCED was the breakthrough in NGO involvement, signifying a movement from a passive observer to a more engaged actor in negotiations, a closer examination of the post-1992 era reveals significant diversity of groups within this category that differ by issue focus, political orientation, strategic approach, geographical representation and spread, size, and resources. Thus there is a wide spectrum of NGOs (along many axes), which en masse cannot be easily painted with one brush. This diversity, and even conflict over issues within the NGO community, arguably adds additional vibrancy to multilateral environmental negotiations. This chapter examines the "NGO community" using a rough categorization of the roles (or strategic orientation) that they play within environmental negotiations as witness, architect, and/or detractor. While these are not mutually exclusive categories, they do allow a first cut at the issue using the utilitarian perspective of how NGOs engage with a process.

This categorization will also entail a closer look at the nature of influence and action, resources and changes over time, and negotiating fora within each type of role. This perspective reveals both a diversity of roles among NGOs as well as potentially within the same NGO over time, thereby allowing for a more dynamic analysis. Substantively, these issues will be examined within case studies on the Convention on Biological Diversity (CBD) and its treatment of protected areas, and international forest policy negotiations. Since UNCED, both the CBD and forest negotiations have been focal points for NGO engagement on environmental and natural resource issues, which allow for an extended analysis of NGO interaction over two decades.

Witness, Architect, Detractor

The roles of NGOs in multilateral negotiations have been analyzed across a number of fora and issues (Betsill and Corell 2008; Mwangi 2005; Wapner 1996; Willetts 2000). This analysis will examine these roles in terms of strategic orientation in the post-UNCED era. Given the limiting conditions around NGO participation in environmental negotiations prior to UNCED, one can argue that overall they played a more passive role. The shift in NGO status during and post-UNCED has broadened that dynamic across a spectrum ranging from passive to more active engagement. Within this frame, three rough categorizations for NGO roles can be discerned: witness, architect, and/or detractor.

Witness: in this role, NGOs observe negotiating processes with a primary objective of monitoring and documenting overall progress and/or the positions of particular countries. NGOs can play a role in raising public awareness particularly related to progress on key issues or the performance of their national delegation. Other groups may possess technical or scientific expertise relevant to the discussions that are provided as information for consideration, yet without a broader political agenda or emphasis on how it gets integrated into policy outcomes.

Architect: as architects, NGOs engage constructively in the negotiating process by working with governments in country, lobbying at intergovernmental meetings, and providing input to secretariats. These NGOs may be focused on introducing new issues into the debate, influencing the framework for how specific issues are addressed, or lobbying for text in a particular decision. Pending available resources and influence, some NGOs may work across all of these scales. In some cases, NGOs may be invited to form part of a national delegation, blurring the distinction between government and non-governmental actors. NGOs may also provide technical and financial resources to further bolster their influence and credibility.

Detractor: in this role, NGOs may be involved in the negotiating process, but primarily from a critical perspective. Additionally, they may question the process's credibility and legitimacy, pursue the issue within another process, or seek to establish a new forum in which to move their agenda forward. They may exclude particular concepts under a multilateral environmental agreement's (MEA) outcomes, due to objections over the issue itself or potentially a preference to support alternatives under another process. These NGOs may also seek to deter governments from taking particular positions, and frequently use the media and other outreach efforts to rally the public.

Strategic Dynamism: NGO Roles over Time and between Processes

On any given issue there may be NGOs that fall into each of these categories: there may be some that "witness," some who act as "architects," and some who try to "detract" from the process. This may change depending on the MEA or process in question. For example, while most NGOs boycott forest discussions under the International Tropical Timber Organization (ITTO), the ITTO still has a Civil Society Advisory Group with a representative attending each meeting. An NGO playing the detractor under one negotiating process, such as the ITTO, may in turn be an architect on the same issue under another MEA, such as the CBD or the United Nations Framework Convention on Climate Change (UNFCCC). Similarly, an NGO may play different roles on an issue over the course of time. For example, an NGO may initially begin as a witness or architect if they see a process as legitimate and worthy of their efforts, but may switch to detractor if they feel it has lost legitimacy. The threat of "walking out" on a process (moving to "detractor") can also be used as a strategy to increase influence, where NGO buy-in is seen as desirable (for purposes of public relations, etc.). Thus, the roles that NGOs play as witness, architect, and detractor will depend on their overall strategic plan and objectives, and the progress they achieve by using a given approach.

The ultimate purpose of NGO involvement in multilateral environmental agreements is to exert influence, whether in the negotiations themselves, at the point of implementation or in some other manner. The nature and success of such influence also relates to the type of role that they play, as well as the resources that they can bring to bear. An NGO "witness" may report on positions taken by governments, thereby raising its accountability domestically. An architect might be influential in crafting the language of a decision or, more broadly, elements of a work program, and if endowed with additional financial or personnel resources might play a role in implementation, thereby realizing decision language at the site level. Finally, a detractor may shame a government in the media or raise significant questions about the legitimacy of a process that ultimately shifts the way in which the discussions continue, or may establish an alternative process.

In sum, one hypothesis is that the nature of NGO influence and action varies across roles, resources, and opportunities. The second hypothesis is that the role of an NGO (or NGO coalition) may shift over time and/or across negotiating fora. The objective of an NGO is not ultimately to play any of the roles listed above, but instead to use those strategies to achieve its aims. Decisions on what role to play depend on factors such as:

*   openness of a process to NGO participation;
*   potential for a process to deliver positive vs. negative results (as defined by the NGO);
*   potential for the NGO to influence the process;
*   available political, economic, and informational/knowledge resources; and
*   reputational risks or benefits of being involved in a particular process.

Convention on Biological Diversity and Protected Areas

The conceptual framework for the Convention on Biological Diversity is largely derived from initial discussions starting in 1980 on a world conservation strategy by IUCN, the World Wide Fund for Nature (WWF), and the United Nations Environment Programme (UNEP). In 1981, IUCN's General Assembly launched the idea of a global agreement to protect the world's biodiversity and in 1984 requested the IUCN Secretariat to develop principles for a basic draft of a treaty.

This effort spurred UNEP to form an Ad Hoc Working Group of Experts on Biological Diversity in 1987. A series of meetings further developed the issues and structure for a text that was referred for review to an Ad Hoc Working Group of Legal and Technical Experts. The outcomes of these discussions were transmitted to an Intergovernmental Negotiating Committee for a Convention on Biological Diversity, which deliberated on the text of a Convention at four meetings prior to its adoption in May 1992 in Nairobi and opening for signature at UNCED in June 1992.

From the start, a few key NGOs and other intergovernmental organizations, such as IUCN, the World Resources Institute, Conservation International, the African Centre for Technology Studies, and the International Liaison Group (a global coalition of NGOs) were involved in identifying the potential elements for a framework agreement on biodiversity.[2] This involvement was ultimately trying to establish the architecture for the CBD. The initial focus of many of the larger NGOs based in developed countries (frequently referred to as Big International NGOs—BINGOs) was on strict conservation, including a listing of key protected areas identified by countries as critical for protecting global biodiversity. The proposed structure was similar to that of the 1971 Ramsar Convention on Wetlands of International Importance, which includes a mechanism to identify the conservation status of listed wetlands as well as to add new wetlands proposed by countries.

Such an approach was largely unacceptable to developing countries and the smaller southern NGOs involved in the process, which were wary of the sovereignty implications of fencing off sizeable tracts of their land in the name of conservation. The world's biodiversity hotspots coincide with some of the poorest areas on earth, and strict conservation measures could restrict the ability of local residents and governments to exploit their natural resources and develop their economies. This economic argument served as the basis for the CBD's second and third objectives (after conservation); namely, sustainable use of biodiversity and the fair and equitable sharing of benefits deriving from it. In the final agreement, reference to protected areas is limited to three provisions (establishment of protected area systems; development of guidelines for selection, establishment, and management; and regulation and management of biological resources) under Article 8 (*In Situ* Conservation). Thus, the BINGOs were largely unsuccessful in their initial bid as architects to include protected areas, whereas southern NGOs who were obvious detractors came out in the winning camp. Developing countries played the key role in this effort, yet the division within the NGO community (architects vs. detractors) on this one issue is notable.

The expansion of protected areas was thereby largely off the table during the early years of the Convention and deliberations on ecosystem-based programs of work (e.g., forests, marine and coastal areas, inland waters, dry and sub-humid lands) and cross-cutting issues (e.g., biosafety, incentives, invasive alien species). References to protected areas slowly appeared under agenda items on marine and coastal biodiversity, the ecosystem approach, and *in situ* conservation, reflecting the recognition that these sites were critical reservoirs for the conservation and sustainable use of biodiversity. It was not until COP 4 in 1998 that parties agreed to revisit the issue directly and put protected areas on the work program for COP 7 (2004), twelve years after the CBD was opened for signature at UNCED and a decade after its entry into force (ENB 1998).

At this point, a significant shift in BINGO engagement was evident. Whereas they had primarily been observers in the limited discussions around protected areas since the negotiation of the Convention, new political opportunities and resources helped to shift them back into the role of aspiring architects.

Initial preparations for discussions at COP 7 were conducted by an Ad Hoc Technical Expert Group (AHTEG), which met in June 2003 in Sweden. While the expert group was a relatively small group of approximately forty people, eight slots were filled by BINGOs, including BirdLife International, Conservation International, Greenpeace, IUCN, The Nature Conservancy (TNC), WWF, and the World Resources Institute, compared with eighteen representatives from parties. Additionally, the CBD Secretariat's designated "resource person" was a Nature Conservancy staffer (CBD 2003). There was no representation from smaller NGOs, and even the indigenous and local communities' representative was from IUCN. This group of BINGOs became a powerful force in shaping the profile and path that protected areas would take under the CBD for years to come.

The results of the AHTEG were presented to the CBD's Subsidiary Body on Scientific, Technical and Technological Advice (SBSTTA) in November 2003. Additionally, a coalition of seven BINGOs—BirdLife International, Conservation International, Greenpeace, the Nature Conservancy, the Wildlife Conservation Society, WWF, and the World Resources Institute—emerged based on initial efforts in the AHTEG. They presented a pledge including elements for a work program on protected areas (looking at protected area systems, financing, management capacity, and monitoring) as well as support for developing effective and representative protected area systems, financing, capacity building, and monitoring (BirdLife International et al. 2003). The BINGOs were thereby working to reinforce their political agenda with promises of financial and technical resources to see it implemented. The elements of this pledge were closely associated with input into the AHTEG, which then received significant support by parties as a framework for the SBSTTA 9 recommendation on protected areas. As the *Earth Negotiations Bulletin* reported, "The Joint Pledge of a number of major conservation NGOs to support the implementation of a strong programme of work was also warmly welcomed by parties, to the surprise of some NGOs themselves" (ENB 2003).

Initial efforts by these BINGOs at the AHTEG was the first major step in playing a behind-the-scenes role in crafting the framework for the program of work on protected areas. With recommendations coming from the AHTEG, the BINGO coalition was able to contribute additional reinforcement to the proposed framework in their pledge to provide additional technical resources. These roles are in keeping with the idea of NGOs serving as architects, which had a particular interest in formulating the direction of the program of work on protected areas. This international framework set the terms for national level implementation, which was where these groups' major site-level conservation efforts took place. Thus it was in their interests to have the international system align with and support their ongoing and future efforts in country.

Without a presence at the AHTEG, there were few other NGO (non-BINGO) voices around at the start of the broader discussions at SBSTTA 7. Of most interest are statements by Tebtebba, a small community-focused NGO from the Philippines, along with some of the national chapters of Friends of the Earth, which noted the need to focus on issues relevant to indigenous peoples and local communities (ENB 2003). At this point in the discussions, such groups were primarily focused on other CBD areas such as traditional knowledge and access and benefit sharing, and were thereby limiting their role in the protected areas discussion to being witnesses.

This effort faced an uphill battle given historical resistance to protected areas as fencing off biodiversity, often associated with the marginalization of local peoples, as well as the increasing realization that the growing number of COP decisions and varied work programs were more than most countries could hope to implement, let alone developing countries high in biodiversity but lacking in financial, institutional, and scientific resources. The new approach taken by these groups was to look first and foremost at the financing of protected areas work, including their own investments, and to make leveraging of additional funds conditional on a proactive and strong program of work on protected areas.

Moving into COP 7, this coalition (which had expanded to include Fauna and Flora International) had solidified a joint NGO commitment on protected areas along with a proposed number of elements and structure for a program of work on protected areas under the CBD. Collectively these groups managed approximately US$1 billion annually for conservation in over 120 countries, particularly those high in biodiversity. Additionally, they held the promise of investing additional millions of dollars in national-level efforts to implement the work program on protected areas (BirdLife International et al. 2004). Conservation International and TNC reinforced this message by pledging US$2 million each toward the implementation of the program of work on protected areas.

The promise of new funding combined with the recognition of significant existing funding was a major factor in changing government attitudes more favorably toward protected areas. With more obligations and decisions than most countries could arguably implement, the CBD has generally been regarded as soft law. Provision of funding and technical support thereby provided the added bonus of ensuring that decisions on protected areas could be implemented. So beyond simply serving as architects to the structure of the work program on paper, the BINGO coalition was going the extra step toward mobilizing countries toward implementation.

The BINGO coalition solidified its position in the negotiations in two key ways. First, there was an explicit effort to increase the presence of NGO representatives from some of these groups, such as TNC and WWF, on national

TABLE 7.1 CBD Program of Work on Protected Areas

	CBD COP Decision VII/28 (Protected Areas) (CBD 2004)	Joint NGO Statement (BirdLife et al. 2004)
Program Element 1	Direct Actions for Planning, Selecting, Establishing, Strengthening and Managing Protected Areas and Sites	Representative and Effectively Managed Protected Areas Systems
Program Element 2	Governance, Participation, Equity and Benefit-sharing	Financing for Protected Areas
Program Element 3	Enabling Activities	Capacity Development
Program Element 4	Standards, Assessment and Monitoring	Monitoring and Evaluation of Protected Area Effectiveness

delegations to the CBD and/or in work by country offices in the run up to the meeting. By integrating themselves into delegations and national positions from countries such as Costa Rica, Ecuador, Indonesia, and other Caribbean and Pacific island countries, the BINGO coalition could move their agenda forward by raising it during parties' internal discussions, and not only through explicit NGO lobbying. Second, by marketing their position as "The Joint NGO Statement" and "The Joint NGO Commitment on Protected Areas," the BINGO coalition had effectively co-opted the voice of the NGO community by representing it as theirs. While there were dissenters, their position was marginalized by what appeared to be the mainstream consensus of NGO opinion on the issue.

Through all of this work, the final decision establishing the program of work on protected areas closely mirrors the position of the BINGO coalition, as reflected in Table 7.1.

At COP 7, other NGOs and groups such as the Friends of the Earth International, the International Indigenous Forum on Biodiversity, and Kalpavriksh increased their involvement in the discussion, while mainly focusing on the rights of indigenous peoples and the role of community conserved areas (ENB 2004a, 2004b) (Figure 7.1). In some cases, these voices tried to influence the content of the discussions by including reference to areas managed by indigenous peoples and local communities. However, there was both an underlying and, at times, an explicit resistance to the broader direction that the BINGO coalition and most parties were pursuing around the identification and establishment of protected areas. This process and the significant financial and political capital behind it raised long-held fears about the disenfranchisement of locals from their homes in areas to be designated as protected. These fears have continued to shape the ebb and flow in relations between these BINGOs and smaller NGOs and indigenous groups, primarily from developing countries.

FIGURE 7.1 NGOs and groups such as the International Indigenous Forum on Biodiversity increased their involvement in CBD discussions, mainly focusing on the rights of indigenous peoples. Photo courtesy of IISD/*Earth Negotiations Bulletin*

Through 2008, groups such as WWF and TNC included representatives from indigenous groups and local communities in their delegations as a means to improve their credibility on the issue, while also taking some of the core concerns of these groups into account in their site-level conservation activities. However, groups on the other side of the fence arguably grew even more polarized, which was clearly evident at a meeting of the CBD Alliance (a group seeking to support NGO input into the CBD process) prior to SBSTTA 12 in 2007. A significant number of NGO indigenous and community-group representatives openly stated their disagreement with the present course of CBD negotiations on protected areas and, in one or two cases, were openly hostile to BINGO representatives at the meeting. Such groups were thereby embracing the role of detractor, although with an interesting twist. They were objecting to the content of the formal negotiating process, but primarily due to their fundamental disagreements with the contingent of "architect" NGOs pushing the conservation/protected areas agenda.

Since its adoption at COP 7, the program of work on protected areas has risen in stature as many of these same NGOs have further engaged as architects in the planning/implementation side as well as the financing side. Thus, many BINGOs have put significant attention and organizational resources into leveraging additional funds for protected areas work from bilateral donors and multilateral development banks.

The work under the Global Island Partnership (GLISPA), which became one of the implementing vehicles for this consortium, is a case in point. Through the development of conservation challenges and initiatives committing to protect terrestrial and marine resources, GLISPA and its partners have motivated high-level heads of state leadership and leveraged over US$20 million for the Micronesia Challenge, US$80 million for the Caribbean Challenge, and over

US$120 million for the Coral Triangle Initiative (discussions are still ongoing regarding an initiative in the Western Indian Ocean). Many of the BINGOs, such as BirdLife International, Conservation International, TNC, and WWF, are active in these areas, and such funding and close connections create positive feedback and support for the involvement of these groups in the CBD process and a much closer working relationship across involved NGOs, recipient countries, and the CBD Secretariat.

Looking back it is possible to view the various roles that NGOs played around the issue of protected areas. During the initial period of defining the issues and framework for the CBD, BINGOs aspired to the role of architect with a push for a list of priority-protected areas for conservation. Smaller NGOs from developing countries served as detractors at that time and at various points in the debate subsequently. For the next decade, BINGOs basically monitored the CBD, acting as observers and awaiting new opportunities to address protected areas (this is not to say that BINGOs were not more involved in other biodiversity issues). Then the opening arose in 2003 to put protected areas on the CBD work program, at which point BINGOs became re-engaged. Their influence in the expert groups, with the CBD Secretariat, on national delegations, and in countries at the site level formed a platform for moving their goals, and was further reinforced by the promise and delivery of technical and financial resources. Additionally, their success in aligning efforts within the protected areas program of work with their own organizational priorities provided further leverage for raising funds both internally and through other donor countries. While such an effort might seem self-serving, it was ultimately directed toward the conservation goals of those groups, which many CBD parties themselves came to champion. This campaign has arguably set a new bar for the CBD and NGO involvement, where the combination of influence on the political agenda with the provision of technical and financial resources has become a key precondition for national implementation.

Forests

There are a large number of multilateral agreements and processes that address issues related to forests (McDermott et al. 2007), all of which have had some level of NGO involvement. Here we will examine several of the most prominent ones: the International Tropical Timber Council (ITTC), UNCED, the Intergovernmental Panel on Forests/International Forum on Forests/United Nations Forum on Forests (IPF/IFF/UNFF), and UNFCCC.

International Tropical Timber Council: To Engage, or Not to Engage?

The International Tropical Timber Agreement (ITTA) was first adopted by the United Nations Conference on Trade and Development (UNCTAD) in 1983 and entered into force in 1985. It represented the first major international treaty specifically addressing forests at the international level, albeit from a trade-centric perspective. From the outset, many grass-roots environmental groups and indigenous peoples' organizations denounced the ITTA as an agreement designed to facilitate and increase trade, and expressed concern that it would result in the commodification of forests. Early ITTO sessions were attended by several large NGOs, many of which initially played an important "architect" role, facilitated by their access to significant resources and motivated by a generally optimistic outlook for the process to deliver desired outcomes. For example, WWF allocated staff resources in support of ITTC fulfilling its mandate, to the tune of 100,000 Swiss francs per year (Poore 2003, 155), and several BINGOs regularly participated as part of country delegations to the ITTC sessions: the UK, Denmark, and Malaysia all included WWF representatives, while the Netherlands included a representative from IUCN on its delegation, and the United States included a representative from the National Wildlife Federation (Humphreys 1996, 61).

However, this participation was not without incident or controversy—at the fourteenth session of the ITTC in 1993, the executive director of WWF-Malaysia was physically assaulted by the director of forests of Sarawak, with the former landing in the conference venue's swimming pool as a result, after a heated argument over deforestation in Sarawak (Humphreys 1996, 115). Although not related to the incident, in May 1994 WWF withdrew from ITTC following the conclusion of a successor agreement (ITTA, 1994), in which the council had opted not to follow WWF's recommendations that the scope of the agreement be expanded to consider other forests. In a departing address, WWF noted it would be "considering re-allocating resources to better options such as the CBD and CITES" (Poore 2003, 155).

The lack of NGO engagement with ITTO did not go unnoticed. At its thirty-second session in 2002, the Council adopted a decision "noting its concern that the views of Civil Society Organizations are still not well represented at Council sessions."[3] A Civil Society Advisory Group (CSAG) composed of mainstream groups (such as TRAFFIC, IUCN, and Forest Trends) was formed, and at ITTC 35, CSAG members decided to appoint two co-chairs, representing producer and consumer countries, as per the ITTC structure.

Nevertheless, NGO participation in Council sessions diminished significantly following WWF's departure. Other groups have gone further than non-participation to playing "detractor," openly denouncing ITTC as biased toward logging interests. At ITTC 42 in Papua New Guinea, a country known for high levels of illegal logging, Greenpeace rappelled from the roof of the hotel in which the session was being held to suspend a banner protesting forest destruction (Greenpeace 2007) (Figure 7.2). It is clear from this act and the sophistication of the accompanying press release that it was not for a lack of resources or knowledge of the issue that Greenpeace chose to detract from the outside (literally) instead of attempting to influence outcomes of the meeting taking place inside.

FIGURE 7.2 At ITTC 42 in Papua New Guinea, a country known for high levels of illegal logging, Greenpeace rappelled from the roof of the hotel in which the session was being held to suspend a banner protesting forest destruction. Photo courtesy of Peter Wood

Beginning in the early 1990s,[4] WWF and other BINGOs also allocated a substantial amount of resources toward forest certification, most importantly the Forest Stewardship Council (FSC) and the Global Forest Trade Network (GFTN). This could also be perceived as a form of "detraction"—a clear vote of non-confidence in intergovernmental responses to deforestation, throwing their support (and directing that of their constituents) behind this non-governmental alternative. Although the FSC was initially viewed with suspicion and as a potential impediment to the tropical timber trade by some ITTC countries and the industrial logging sector, it has since proven compatible with industrial logging, and has been embraced by these same actors. Certification has become a major focus of ITTC policies and projects, and some terms such as "high conservation value forests" have come to be used by the ITTC. At ITTC 46 in 2010, it was announced that the area of forest certified in producer member countries had expanded by 55 percent since the last assessment, to a total of 24.5 million hectares (ENB 2010). Thus, the FSC could be perceived as playing an "architect" role, albeit externally. At the same time, many NGOs have become increasingly uncomfortable with FSC's compatibility with industrial logging in the tropics and elsewhere. Several groups that were involved in its creation have now switched to the role of "detractor," openly critiquing the FSC[5] and other members jumping ship entirely. Nevertheless, it appears that the few NGOs that do engage with ITTC are supportive of including FSC as a way to encourage sustainable forest management, a core part of ITTC's mandate. For example, at ITTC 46 it was reported that the ITTO Civil Society/Private Partnership for SFM had initiated a collaborative project with a logging company in Indonesia to assist it in obtaining FSC certification (ENB 2010).

At the same meeting, delegates adopted a decision giving the Secretariat the mandate to pursue funding support for the organization's project work from other sources, including NGOs, since country contributions were far below that required to fund all approved projects. The response that they receive from NGOs, particularly WWF, could serve as an indicator of whether they are ready to re-engage with ITTO.

UNCED and the Forest Principles: A High Point in Engagement?

As noted above, UNCED was a critical moment for NGO engagement, and particularly within forest policy discussions. During the two years leading up to the Earth Summit, NGOs were very active in the forest negotiations, playing all three roles of witness, architect, and detractor. As architects, a coalition of Brazilian Amazon-based NGOs worked tirelessly to ensure that the rights of indigenous communities and local communities were recognized in the Forest Principles. Similarly, a group of UK NGOs put together a list of issues that they believed should be included in a treaty or agreement on the conservation and sustainable management of forests, which, among other things, included the importance of public participation in policymaking and respect for the rights of forest peoples; the need to address external causes of deforestation, including pressure to make debt payments, trade inequalities, and exploitation by foreign companies; and covers all types of forest and forest lands (Thomson 1992). As detractors, WWF expressed the frustration of many NGOs that discussions on forests in the UNCED preparatory meetings were "dilatory and confused" and that the evolving Forest Principles were "retrogressive." WWF called on UNCED to establish a process to begin formal negotiations on a Global Forest Convention immediately after UNCED, with a timetable and target date for completion and ratification (WWF 1992). Some NGOs were so frustrated with the process that they participated in the negotiation of alternative treaties, which were adopted at the parallel Global Forum, including an alternative Forest Treaty that focused heavily on the needs of local populations.[6]

In lieu of a forest treaty, in the end the Earth Summit produced a number of voluntary instruments that addressed forest management, including Chapter 11 of Agenda 21 on "Combatting Deforestation" and the "Non-legally Binding

Authoritative Statement of Principles for a Global Consensus on the Management, Conservation and Sustainable Development of All Types of Forests" (otherwise known as the "Forest Principles"). Chapter 27 of Agenda 21 also recognized the role that NGOs play within sustainable development, and established a new consultative relationship between the UN and NGOs, according them observer status within nine different "Major Groups."[7]

IPF, IFF, UNFF: From Architect to Detractor

Agenda 21 and the Forest Principles provided the basis for continued negotiations on forests at the international level beginning in 1995 when the UN Commission on Sustainable Development (CSD) was slated to review implementation of Chapter 11 of Agenda 21 and the Forest Principles. NGOs, once again, played an active role in the CSD's negotiations—this time as architects. A coalition of NGOs, the Global Forest Policy Project,[8] participated in drafting group meetings on the establishment of a new Intergovernmental Panel on Forests (IPF) and urged that the panel should: encourage the participation of Major Groups; conduct an independent assessment of existing instruments; address the underlying causes of deforestation and forest degradation; avoid discussing a global set of criteria and indicators; and prevent trade-related issues from dominating discussion (ENB 1995). The resulting IPF had a two-year mandate to analyze priority forest issues as well as to review existing international organizations and institutions and instruments to develop a clearer view on the work being carried out and to identify any gaps, areas requiring enhancement, and areas of duplication. By 1997, the end of its mandate, the IPF had identified over 150 Proposals for Action (PfA) to address global challenges to managing the world's forests sustainably.

In 1997, the CSD decided to continue the dialogue on forests by creating the Intergovernmental Forum on Forests (1997–1999), which established additional PfAs, bringing the total to nearly 200, but accomplishing very little in terms of their implementation. NGOs continued to participate both in the IFF's meetings and various intersessional meetings in an attempt to influence the process.[9] By the end of the IFF process, most NGOs held the view that there should be no further political negotiations on additional proposals for action, and that governments instead should concentrate on implementing the existing proposals. While the language in the agreed proposals was far from what the NGOs would have liked, most NGO campaigners felt that they would gain greater influence by monitoring and contesting the implementation of these proposals within individual countries and through national reporting and peer review at the UN than could be gained from further multilateral negotiations (Humphreys 2004, 68). Nevertheless, at its last session in 2000, the IFF decided to establish a new multilateral forum and called on ECOSOC to establish the United Nations Forum on Forests.

The engagement of the world's major NGOs in these processes has declined substantially during this time, most markedly during the mandate of the UNFF. Initially, NGO attendance was relatively strong during the first few sessions of UNFF, despite participation being limited to NGOs accredited by ECOSOC, and their engagement could best be described as that of witnesses, with some acting as architects (for example, an NGO representative on the Canadian delegation was known to contribute textual suggestions). However, NGO participation soon began to wane, and many stopped participating, or became detractors (such as FERN, which openly called for UNFF to be discontinued). This was due to two main factors: the low profile granted to NGOs within UNFF, and UNFF's overall lack of power.

Many NGOs came to realize that their ability to influence negotiations would be quite limited within the UNFF. Big NGOs in particular, accustomed to holding a great deal of influence in international environmental negotiations, were less than thrilled to be bracketed within one of nine "Major Groups," with considerably less standing. As one NGO complained in a release circulated at UNFF 5, "we actually do NOT appreciate to be covered under that awkward late-night-UNCED-prepcom compromise term 'Major Groups' ... it is mainly due to the persuasion of the UNFF Secretariat and their active support that you still find some observers who are prepared to attend these UNFF sessions" (GFC 2005). In contrast, this system afforded other Major Groups such as "Children and Youth" greater presence than they might otherwise have been able to attain, and were thus more inclined to participate. UNFF held multi-stakeholder dialogues (MSD) at each session to facilitate the exchange of ideas between Major Groups and with country delegations. However, while NGOs initially called for these dialogues in the IFF report, many were disenchanted with how this played out in practice, with very poor attendance and a general impression of serving as a side event to the main negotiations. For example, one NGO felt that "the 'improved' MSD was merely a means to promote a sense of 'participation' at UNFF: it provided the illusion of participation while the real negotiations went on as usual" (Caruso and Kru 2004).

NGO discontent with UNFF was also due to the fact that this contrasted with more inclusive approaches taken by other processes that NGOs had access to, namely the Convention on Biological Diversity, where NGOs are able to make interventions within plenary. The CBD was also deemed by many to be of greater consequence, due to its status as a legally binding agreement and its Programme of Work on Forests. It was also seen as a platform that could be used to influence processes that accorded less access to NGOs, such as the WTO.

Second, NGOs came to realize that the UNFF itself was limited in its mandate and its ability to enact change. This was reflected in the low level of engagement of governments (for example, the very poor response rate in National Reporting), its inability to implement the IPF/IFF Proposals for Action, and its inability to coordinate the actions of other forest-related institutions under the Collaborative Partnership on Forests (CPF).

A major turning point occurred in 2005 when the UNFF failed to agree on a successor agreement. In a document circulated just prior to UNFF 5 titled the "International Arrangement on Forests at a Crossroads," WWF stated that "Major Group participation is still felt to be a serious weakness by most NGO participants who believe the UNFF still treats them like outsiders rather than collaborators or partners" (WWF 2005). Many countries and NGOs alike believed that UNFF 5 would produce some type of decision regarding the creation of a legally binding instrument, and whether the UNFF itself would continue to exist. Even though UNFF 7 reached agreement on a "Non-legally Binding Instrument on Forests," NGO engagement in the UNFF since 2005 has been decidedly low. By UNFF 6 in 2006, the *Earth Negotiations Bulletin* reported that yet another factor detracting from the sense of urgency was the paucity of civil society engagement.

Noticeably absent from the agenda that year was the multi-stakeholder dialogue, which in previous years had provided an opportunity for civil society actors to voice their concerns and engage with governments. However, due to a decision made at UNFF 5, this event was relegated to the status of "side event," and resulted in the lowest level of NGO engagement since [UNFF] talks began. There has been little or no engagement of key indigenous and environmental groups that played a central role in pushing the forests issue into the international arena in the first place. The process and outcome of UNFF 6 hold little to entice these groups back on board, especially when they have had better luck pursuing their agenda through MEAs such as the Convention on Biological Diversity, and alternative avenues such as forest certification initiatives such as the Forest Stewardship Council (ENB 2006).

UNFCCC and REDD+: Risk or Opportunity?

Although forests had been addressed within the UNFCCC from the outset, it was only at COP 11 at Montreal in 2005 that the issue of paying developing countries to reduce deforestation and forest degradation (as opposed to increasing reforestation and afforestation) had been given serious consideration. By COP 13, this had come to be enshrined in the Bali Declaration, in what came to be known as "REDD+" (reducing emissions from deforestation and forest degradation and the role of conservation, sustainable management of forests, and enhancement of forest carbon stocks in developing countries). NGOs immediately sensed that this could be of much greater consequence to forests than the IPF/IFF/UNFF and ITTO processes, backed by much greater political will and larger sums of money. However, there was a sharp division between NGOs that welcomed this newfound attention (and were thus more likely to constructively participate as architects, most notably the BINGOs) and those that were wary of the risks of large sums of money being given to countries with poor records of governance and human rights abuses.

One result of this concern was the creation of a new coalition of environmental and social NGOs that came to be known as the Ecosystems Climate Alliance (ECA),[10] formed in 2008 at COP 14 in Poznan, Poland, which sought to take a more critical view of REDD+ than had been possible within the larger NGO coalition, the Climate Action Network. ECA's role could be described as that of witness, although its constructive engagement with country delegations occasionally brought it into the role of architect. This was particularly the case where its interests aligned with those of countries seeking to limit donor risk (e.g., Norway, Switzerland, the United States, and others); namely, the pursuit of environmental protection, social safeguards, and monitoring requirements (including of governance, something previously totally unimaginable under other forest-related agreements).

Another coalition that emerged around the same time, known as the "Accra Caucus,"[11] represented the views of twenty-six NGOs from developing countries, and urged a rights-based approach to REDD+ that put forest peoples' interests first. This coalition straddled roles, from witness at the outset, to detractor when it looked like their key demands were not reflected in the text being negotiated (for instance, recognition and respect for the rights of Indigenous Peoples and local communities to lands, territories, and resources, and their traditional uses of the forest; and prohibiting the use of carbon offsets/market-based approaches for financing REDD+). By COP 15 in Copenhagen in December 2009, the chant of "No Rights, No REDD!" was frequently heard in the halls of the conference venue, led by members of the Accra Caucus.

Complicating matters was the fact that, at the same time the REDD+ mechanism was being negotiated within the UNFCCC, there were several other related processes actively being developed, including UN-REDD (led by FAO, UNDP, and UNEP), the World Bank's Forest Carbon Partnership Facility and its Forest Investment Program, and the REDD+ Partnership (a process initiated by the governments of France and Norway in the wake of COP 15's failure to reach a decision on REDD+).[12] In addition, hundreds of voluntary "REDD+" projects were initiated around the developing world, without any formal guidance from international rules.

With so many fronts to address, many smaller NGOs' capacity to engage effectively with REDD+ processes has been stretched to the limit. This, combined with the fast pace at which these processes have moved, has resulted in less-resourced NGOs being overwhelmed and unable to respond in a meaningful, informed manner. Bigger NGOs, particularly from the North, have been better able to keep up with demands on time and resources and thus better able to engage as architects, determining what the "REDD+ rules" will look like. This has led to resentment from groups from the South, who fear that BINGOs from developed countries are driving the process, and have frequently opted instead to "detract" and oppose the whole concept of REDD+ instead of weighing in on particular details.

A decision on REDD+ was adopted at COP 16 at Cancún, Mexico, in December 2011, but much has yet to be decided, such as what types of forest management activity will be permitted, and most importantly, how it will be financed.[13] The development of these very contentious issues could further separate the NGOs involved into witnesses, detractors, and architects.

Conclusion: The Evolution of NGO Involvement

By all accounts, NGO involvement has evolved significantly over the course of multilateral environmental negotiations since 1992. As the issues on the table have multiplied and become more complex, so too has the number of NGOs participating, and their degree of engagement. Given the lack of capacity that many governments are confronted with (in both tracking issues across many negotiations and in the implementation of commitments made), it is perhaps no surprise that this has allowed NGOs to play a major role. They have become niche specialists capable of influencing processes and ensuring that commitments are fulfilled, and their role has been fine-tuned and has evolved in parallel to international environmental processes. Many NGOs are clearly interested in moving beyond discussing principles, and are increasingly involved in technical aspects of negotiations. As this occurs, some of the differences between NGOs become more apparent. For example, while few NGOs would disagree that "sustainable management" of forests is a good thing in principle, there is very little consensus in practice regarding what this should look like within REDD+, and as such details are fleshed out, it is likely that a greater divergence may be observed.

However, this evolution has not been equal across NGOs—better-resourced NGOs are more likely to act as architects and influence the ultimate outcomes of these processes. The example of the CBD clearly shows how BINGOs shifted their roles over time and were able to take advantage of an opportunity within the CBD's overall work program and bring significant resources to address protected areas. This dynamic has led to tensions between NGOs, some of which are unable to participate constructively due to lack of resources, and some of which have opted to withdraw or oppose a process due to more fundamental substantive concerns. These realities may contribute to their playing the role of observer or detractor.

Over the past two decades, NGOs have clearly embedded themselves in the process with a collective reach that spans from the negotiations themselves through to in-country and on-site implementation. This integration will likely continue as government resources to address environmental problems are increasingly limited and as the complexity and interconnections of those problems grow. Notions about the decline or porousness of the nation state have been amply discussed in the academic literature. Multilateral environmental negotiations and the participation of NGOs within these intergovernmental deliberations are but one more example of how the traditional roles of state sovereignty are being complemented by other non-state actors.

NGO involvement also lends a sense of legitimacy to environmental negotiations, particularly as groups serve the various roles of witness, architect, and detractor ostensibly in the name of the environment (vs. other political interests). Decisions by NGOs to invest significantly in an issue or, alternatively to withdraw from or boycott negotiations are taken seriously by the broader environmental community. Integration into environmental negotiations and implementation efforts arguably makes the process and governments involved more dependent on those groups, thereby increasing their influence and role as potential architects. Thus the political costs of BINGOs hypothetically withdrawing their support for CBD work on protected areas or of NGOs boycotting aspects of REDD+ to the future success of multilateral environmental processes cannot be ignored and may make states more responsive to trends within the environmental community. For many environmental issues, NGOs now have a number of international venues to "shop" among in pursuing their agenda, and given limited resources (especially smaller grass-roots organizations and those from developing countries), they are able to decide which ones are worth their time and resources, and thus vouch for their legitimacy.

Tactics, drawn from the roles of witness, architect, and detractor, will likely continue to be at the heart of future NGO strategies even as the issues and priorities of those same NGOs, both individually and collectively, evolve over time. Additionally, the roles that NGOs play will continue to change with opportunities in the political landscape as well as their ability to draw on financial, technical, and other political resources. The past twenty years saw the movement of NGOs from the fringe into the center of the debate. Now with an expected and accepted place within environmental negotiations, it remains to be seen how NGOs further integrate themselves into the policymaking and implementation processes as both a complement to and corollary of national governments.

Notes

1 It should be noted that some view the NGO category as also including business, labor, and indigenous/community organizations, as they are clearly not governmental. Given recognition of these other groups in their own right by intergovernmental processes, this chapter will narrow its conception of NGOs to environmentally, socially, and scientifically oriented non-profits focused on advocacy around and implementation of multilateral environmental agreements.

2 It should be noted that IUCN maintains a unique status in international processes as its membership includes both NGOs as well as governmental agencies. It therefore has the ability to advocate at times like an NGO, while also maintaining its status as an Intergovernmental Organization (IGO) in a number of MEAs.

3 ITTC Decision 2 (XXXII).
4 It should be noted that as far back as 1988, Friends of the Earth attempted an architect role within the ITTO. With the help of the Oxford Forestry Institute, they worked with the UK delegation to ITTO to submit a proposal to ITTO to consider certification and labeling as mechanisms for improving tropical forest management at the seventh ITTC session in November 1989. The proposal was extremely controversial and ultimately rejected by the producer countries, leading Friends of the Earth and others to pursue the certification agenda outside ITTO (Synnott 2005).
5 See, for example, www.FSC-Watch.org.
6 For the complete texts of the NGO Alternative Treaties, see http://www. earthsummit2012.org/index.php/earth-summit-history/historical-ngo/99-92-ngo.
7 Major Groups are defined by Agenda 21 as NGOs, women, youth, farmers, scientists, business and industry, indigenous peoples, local authorities, and trade unions.
8 The Global Forest Policy Project was a project of the National Wildlife Federation, Sierra Club, and Friends of the Earth—US.
9 See Humphreys 2004 for details on NGO proposals that were incorporated into the final IFF report.
10 ECA members include the Environmental Investigation Agency, Global Witness, Humane Society International, Rainforest Foundation Norway and UK, Wetlands International, the Wilderness Society, Rainforest Action Network, Nepenthes, and the Australian Orangutan Project.
11 For a complete list of Accra Caucus members, see http://www.redd-monitor. org/2008/12/08/accra-caucus-statement-on-forests-and-climate-change/.
12 See http://reddpluspartnership.org.
13 For example, there is a growing divide between NGOs that support financing REDD+ by linking it to the carbon market, and those who oppose this, and the latter appear ready to "detract" from the process if it goes in this direction (see FERN et al. 2011).

Works Cited

Betsill, Michele, and Elisabeth Corell. 2008. *NGO Diplomacy: The Influence of Nongovernmental Organizations in International Environmental Negotiations.* Cambridge, MA: MIT Press.
BirdLife International, Conservation International, Fauna and Flora International, Greenpeace, The Nature Conservancy, the Wildlife Conservation Society, WWF and the World Resources Institute. 2004. Joint NGO statement and Joint NGO commitment on protected areas: To support implementation of a strong Programme of Work on Protected Areas under the Biodiversity Convention. Seventh Conference of the Parties to the Convention on Biological Diversity. February 9–20, 2004, Kuala Lumpur, Malaysia.
BirdLife International, Conservation International, Greenpeace, The Nature Conservancy, the Wildlife Conservation Society, WWF and the World Resources Institute. 2003. Joint NGO statement and Joint NGO pledge: To Support Implementation of a Strong Programme of Work on Protected Areas under the Biodiversity Convention. Ninth Meeting of the Subsidiary Body on Scientific, Technical and Technological Advice of the Convention on Biological Diversity. November 10–14, 2003, Montreal, Canada.
Caruso, Emily and Leontien Kru. 2004. Special FERN-FPP Report: UNFF Failing its Mandate—4th Session of the United Nations Forum on Forests. *EU Forest Watch* (June). http://www.fern.org/sites/fern.org/files/pubs/fw/srjune04.pdf (accessed October 18, 2011).

CBD (Convention on Biological Diversity). 2003. Report of the Ad Hoc Technical Expert Group on Protected Areas (UNEP/CBD/SBSTTA/9/INF/3). Montreal: Secretariat of the Convention on Biological Diversity.

ENB (*Earth Negotiations Bulletin*). 1995. CSD Highlights: Monday, 24 April 1995. *Earth Negotiations Bulletin* 5(38). http://www.iisd.ca/download/pdf/enb0538e.pdf (accessed March 27, 2011).

ENB. 1998. Summary of the Fourth Meeting of the Conference of the Parties to the Convention on Biological Diversity: 4–15 May 1998. *Earth Negotiations Bulletin* 9(96). http://www.iisd.ca/download/pdf/enb0996e.pdf (accessed March 6, 2011).

ENB. 2003. Summary of the Ninth Meeting of the Subsidiary Body on Scientific, Technical and Technological Advice of the Convention on Biological Diversity: 10–14 November 2003. *Earth Negotiations Bulletin* 9(262). http://www.iisd.ca/download/pdf/enb09262e.pdf (accessed March 6, 2011).

ENB. 2004a. Summary of the Seventh Conference of the Parties to the Convention on Biological Diversity: 9–20 February 2004. *Earth Negotiations Bulletin* 9(284). http://www.iisd.ca/download/pdf/enb09284e.pdf (accessed March 6, 2011).

ENB. 2004b. CBD COP-7 Highlights: Wednesday, 11 February 2004. *Earth Negotiations Bulletin* 9(277). http://www.iisd.ca/download/pdf/enb09277e.pdf (accessed March 6, 2011).

ENB. 2006. Summary of the Sixth Session of the United Nations Forum on Forests: 13–24 February 2006. *Earth Negotiations Bulletin* 13(144). http://www.iisd.ca/download/pdf/enb13144e.pdf (accessed March 27, 2011).

ENB. 2010. Summary of the Forty-Sixth Session of the International Tropical Timber Council and Associated Sessions of the Four Committees: 13–18 December 2010. *Earth Negotiations Bulletin* 24(83). http://www.iisd.ca/download/pdf/enb2483e.pdf (accessed 2 April, 2011).

Engfeldt, Lars-Göran. 2009. *From Stockholm to Johannesburg and Beyond*. Stockholm: Government Offices of Sweden.

FERN, Greenpeace International, Rainforest Foundation UK, and Friends of the Earth. 2011. REDD+ and Carbon Markets: Ten Myths Exploded. http://www.fern.org/sites/fern.org/files/10%20myths%20exploded_0.pdf (accessed June 11, 2011).

GFC (Global Forest Coalition). 2005. UN Forest Follies: A Regular Global Forest Coalition Newsletter on UNFF5. Issue 1 (16 May). http://www.wrm.org.uy/actors/IFF/Follies.doc (accessed March 4, 2011).

Greenpeace. 2007. Greenpeace Calls on ITTO to Do More to End Tropical Forest Destruction. Press Release, May 7. http://www.greenpeace.org/international/en/press/releases/timber-trade-meeting/ (accessed June 11, 2011).

Humphreys, David. 1996. *Forest Politics: The Evolution of International Cooperation*. London: Earthscan.

Humphreys, David. 2004. Redefining the Issues: NGO Influence on International Forest Negotiations. *Global Environmental Politics* 4(2): 51–74.

Kjellén, Bo. 2008. *A New Diplomacy for Sustainable Development*. New York: Routledge.

McDermott, Constance, Aran O'Carroll, and Peter Wood. 2007. International Forest Policy—the Instruments, Agreements and Processes that Shape it. New York, NY: UN Department of Economic and Social Affairs, United Nations Forum on Forests Secretariat. http://www.un.org/esa/forests/pdf/publications/Intl_Forest_Policy_instruments_agreements.pdf (accessed October 18, 2011).

Mucke, Peter. 1997. Non-Governmental Organizations. In *The Way Forward: Beyond Agenda 21*. Edited by Felix Dodds. London: Earthscan.

Mwangi, Wagaki. 2005. Three Decades of NGO Activism in International Environmental Negotiations: Who Influences NGOs. In *Global Challenges: Furthering the Multilateral Process for Sustainable Development*. Edited by Angela Churie Kallhauge, Gunnar Sjostedt, and Elisabeth Corell. Sheffield, UK: Greenleaf Publishing.

Poore, Duncan. 2003. *Changing Landscapes: The Development of the International Tropical Timber Organization and its Influence on Tropical Forest Management*. London: Earthscan.

Synnott, Timothy. 2005. Some Notes on the Early Years of FSC. http://www.fsc.org/fileadmin/web-data/public/document_center/publications/Notes_on_the_early_years_of_FSC_by_Tim_Synnott.pdf (accessed June 11, 2011).

Thomson, Koy. 1992. *The UK NGO Agenda for the Earth Summit*. London: United Nations Environment Programme UK National Committee.

UN. 1997. UN Briefing Papers Series. *The World Conferences: Developing Priorities for the 21st Century*. United Nations Department of Public Information, 23 May (Revised January 27, 2000).

Wapner, Paul. 1996. *Environmental Activism and World Civic Politics*. Albany, NY: State University of New York Press.

Willetts, Peter. 2000. From "Consultative Arrangements" to "Partnership": The Changing Status of NGOs in Diplomacy at the UN. *Global Governance* 6(2): 191–212.

WWF. 1992. Forests. *Action for UNCED*. Gland, Switzerland: WWF International.

WWF. 2005. The IAF at the *Crossroads*: Tough Choices Ahead. http://www.panda.org/downloads/forests/iaftoughchoices30aug04.pdf (accessed January 6, 2011).

PART III
Evolution of Issues

8

WHAT'S IN A NAME?

Pamela S. Chasek, Maria Gutierrez, and Reem Hajjar

> The beginning of wisdom is the definition of terms.
>
> *(Socrates)*

Half the battle of multilateral negotiations is reaching agreement on what issues will actually be negotiated. Since acceptance of a term requires agreement by many parties, all of whom bring different interpretations to the negotiating table, the definition often starts off vague or ambiguous at best. In many cases there are few precedents for what an international response should involve, the nature of the problem itself is multifaceted, and solutions are often ill fitting and scientifically uncertain. Definitions are often even avoided initially in favor of lists of covered activities, which only later are joined under a definitional umbrella (Zartman 1994, 266). As a result, issue definition or formulation becomes an incremental process at the core of environmental negotiations, in which many definitions are proposed and combined through a process of trial and error until common ground is found and a comfortable and agreeable definition is settled upon.

This chapter looks at five cases of issue definition across different environmental negotiation processes since 1992, including: negotiations at the UN Conference on Environment and Development (UNCED) on new and additional financial resources; the implications of the definition used in the UN Convention to Combat Desertification (UNCCD) regarding definition of its objective; the change of terminology from prior informed consent to advance informed agreement in the Convention on Biological Diversity (CBD) and its Cartagena Protocol on Biosafety; the change of terminology from "avoided deforestation" to "reducing emissions from deforestation in developing countries" to "REDD+" under the United Nations Framework Convention on Climate Change (UNFCCC); and the definition of sustainable forest management. These examples demonstrate both the challenge of defining the issues and how this has been influenced by the increased linkages between economics, trade, development, and environmental issues that have characterized environmental negotiations since 1992.

New and Additional Financial Resources

While creative ambiguity is a prevailing and necessary device to reach consensus on a definition, this type of agreement often triggers years of further debate on how to actually operationalize the definition. In 1992, one of the most contentious definitional debates leading up to UNCED was over the term "new and additional financial resources." The resulting language has haunted environmental negotiations ever since.

UN General Assembly resolution 44/228, which established UNCED, contained a laundry list of objectives for the conference. It was this list of objectives that shaped the structure and negotiation of Agenda 21. One of these objectives was:

> to identify ways and means of providing new and additional financial resources, particularly to developing countries, for environmentally sound development programmes and projects in accordance with national development objectives, priorities and plans and to consider ways of effectively monitoring the provision of such new and additional financial resources particularly to developing countries, so as to enable the international community to take further appropriate action on the basis of accurate and reliable data.

The negotiations on finance ended up at the heart of the UNCED negotiations. At the beginning of the fourth meeting of the Preparatory Committee (PrepCom IV) in New York, developing countries made it clear that substantive progress on finance was a prerequisite for agreement on other issues. As the *Earth Summit Bulletin* stated in an introduction to this topic on March 4, 1992, the major controversy focused on definitions: "First, new and additional to what? Second, new and additional for what? Third, new and additional through what? And fourth, new and additional under what conditions?" (ESB 1992).

Points of discussion included whether "new and additional" meant in respect to existing multilateral and bilateral flows or whether "additional" meant that there would be no reallocation of existing funds, although there was still the question of whether additionality meant increases above the average official development assistance (ODA) of 0.35% of gross national product (GNP) or above the agreed UN target of 0.7% of GNP. The Group of 77 argued that "additionality must mean in addition to or over and above the target set by the United Nations for ODA flows" (Group of 77 1991), whereas the United States argued that "existing resources and institutions can and must be more fully and more effectively utilized" (United States 1991) and thus create new and additional resources.

On the second point, "for what," the possibilities included: simply the incremental costs of meeting obligations under new global environmental agreements or treaties; the costs of Agenda 21; or the sustainable development needs of developing countries and Agenda 21.

On the third point, "through what," there were questions about which funding mechanisms would be involved, with options including: the Global Environment Facility (GEF); a "Green Fund"; separate funds for each convention; increases in development assistance, which some called the "Earth Increment"; or innovative financial mechanisms such as pollution taxes.

Then, of course, there were the questions of conditionality and governance. How democratic and transparent would the funding mechanism be? Would the funds be assessed and mandatory or voluntary? Would the funds be compensatory and without conditions?

Discussions during five weeks of PrepCom IV and two weeks in Rio managed to reach consensus on "new and additional financial resources," but the result was ambiguous. The final text in Chapter 33 of Agenda 21 recognizes that "the implementation of the huge sustainable development programmes of Agenda 21 will require the provision to developing countries of substantial new and additional financial resources" (United Nations 1992, 250). With regard to ODA, paragraph 33.15 reads that "Developed countries reaffirm their commitments to reach the accepted United Nations target of 0.7 per cent of GNP for ODA and, to the extent that they have not yet achieved that target, agree to augment their aid programmes in order to reach that target" (United Nations 1992, 251). This language was a key component of the agreement because countries that had not committed to the UN target, such as the United States, could not reaffirm a nonexistent commitment. Other sources of funding that would maximize "the availability of new and additional resources" are listed, including the International Development Association, regional and subregional development banks, the Global Environment Facility, UN agencies, bilateral assistance programs, debt relief, and private funding. Governments committed to explore innovative sources of funding but never really outlined what this would entail. Nor did they ever define what "new and additional" actually meant.

As a result of the ambiguity of the Agenda 21 language, the issue of what "new and additional financial resources" actually means has emerged at every single environmental negotiation since 1992, as well as at meetings of the UN Commission on Sustainable Development, the 2001 UN Conference on Financing for Development, the 2002 World Summit on Sustainable Development, and the 2012 United Nations Conference on Sustainable Development. The definitional issue is compounded by including the same language in the CBD, the UNFCCC, the UNCCD, and the Stockholm Convention on

Persistent Organic Pollutants. Developing countries continue to argue that unless developed countries meet their commitment to provide "new and additional financial resources," developing countries cannot pursue environmentally sound development. But without a clear definition of "new and additional," it is difficult to prove exactly what that commitment entails.

What is Desertification?

What is desertification? This question has resulted in a vast literature and more than 100 definitions of desertification, reflecting the confusion and controversy surrounding the concept of desertification among scientists, land managers, and policymakers (Herrmann and Hutchinson 2006). The debate over this terminology and the scope of the UNCCD shows how issue definition during the negotiation of a treaty does not end with the treaty's adoption and can continue to cause confrontation after its entry into force.

The UNCCD was "born" at the Earth Summit in Rio, when delegates agreed in Chapter 12 of Agenda 21 to call for the elaboration of an international convention to combat desertification in those countries experiencing serious drought and/or desertification, particularly in Africa, with a view to finalizing such a convention by June 1994. However, its broad range of socioeconomic, political, and physical causes and effects has made desertification a complicated environmental problem to define and manage. As noted in the preamble to the UNCCD, "desertification is caused by complex interactions among physical, biological, political, social, cultural and economic factors" and "desertification and drought affect sustainable development through their interrelationships with important social problems such as poverty, poor health and nutrition, lack of food security, and those arising from migration, displacement of persons and demographic dynamics" (United Nations 1994). So, during the negotiation of the convention, the challenge was how to recognize these interrelationships, while not losing sight of the fact that this was to be a convention to combat desertification, not to eradicate poverty or mandate new international economic policies.

One area where this debate manifested itself was in the negotiation of Article 2, the objective of the convention. The stage was set for a North–South battle over socioeconomic issues from the beginning of the first session of the Intergovernmental Negotiating Committee (INCD), which was held in Nairobi, Kenya, in May–June 1993. A number of developing country delegates and NGO representatives proposed that the convention address causes of desertification emanating from poverty, external debt, trade, commodity pricing, and other external economic factors. The majority of the developed countries disagreed, stating that issues such as trade and debt should be avoided, as they are addressed in other fora (ENB 1993). Others asserted that poverty alleviation is too broad a goal for a convention on desertification on the grounds that if the convention is to be an effective and viable international instrument, it should have a narrow and specific focus, such as reversing land degradation, rather than addressing broad economic development objectives (UNSO 1994).

There was also concern that the convention would lose focus if its objectives were broadened to include all aspects of sustainable development. Some delegates argued that the emphasis should be on verifiable objectives facilitating long-term commitments, as well as on concrete actions to deal with the causes of land degradation at the local level. In other words, promotion of sustainable development should not be an end in itself but a means to combat desertification (United Nations 1993a).

After this initial sharing of views, delegates began to draft the language for the objective of the convention. At INCD 2 in September 1993, developing countries stated that the main objective of the convention should be to promote sustainable land use and sustainable development in the countries affected by desertification and drought through the eradication of poverty and the assurance of food security, energy supply, economic growth, and the stability of financial resources (United Nations 1993a). Developed countries, on the other hand, felt that the overall objective should be to marshal effective international assistance and international and national commitments to help developing countries combat desertification and mitigate the effects of drought (United Nations 1993a).

At INCD 3 in January 1994, delegates discussed the first draft of the convention (A/AC.241/15), which contained two paragraphs in Article 2 under the title "Objective." The first paragraph stated that the objective is to combat desertification in countries experiencing serious drought and/or desertification, particularly in Africa. The second paragraph, which proved to be the more contentious of the two, stated that achieving this objective would involve a long-term central strategy that focuses on both improved productivity of lands and improved living conditions at the community level, particularly through: poverty eradication; assurance of food and energy security; sustainability of economic growth and employment; and security and stability of financial resources (United Nations 1993b). Developed countries disagreed, stating that this article must be brief, deal with the subject of the convention, and not address specific socioeconomic issues. Delegates from African countries argued passionately that these issues were essential objectives of the convention (ENB 1994). In an attempt to bridge the gap, the chair of Working Group I, Ahmed Djoghlaf (Algeria), proposed a compromise. While delegates were cautious at first and not willing to accept it immediately, the compromise text was eventually adopted. The compromise text reads:

1. The objective of this Convention is to combat desertification and mitigate the effects of drought in countries experiencing serious drought and/or desertification, particularly in Africa, through effective action at all levels, supported by international cooperation and partnership arrangements, in the framework of an integrated approach which is

consistent with Agenda 21, with a view to contributing to the achievement of sustainable development in affected areas.

2. Achieving this objective will involve long-term integrated strategies
that focus simultaneously, in affected areas, on improved productivity of
land, and the rehabilitating, conservation and sustainable management
of land and water resources, leading to improved living conditions, in
particular at the community level.

(United Nations 1994)

Although the text includes reference to sustainable development as an objective,
it removed any reference to specific socioeconomic issues, ensuring that the focus
of the Convention was on combating desertification and drought, not eradicating
poverty and ensuring economic growth.

The negotiations over the scope of the Convention illustrate some of the
tensions that pervaded the work of the INCD and continue to affect the intergovernmental process and the implementation of the Convention. Ensuring that
the UNCCD was truly a sustainable development convention with a dual focus
on environment and development, on the one hand, has contributed to efforts of
the international community to bridge the distinctive worlds of environment and
development governance in the spirit of the Earth Summit. On the other hand,
the language in Article 2 and elsewhere in the Convention has led to confusion
over the Convention's focus and scope. This has affected the concrete implementation of the Convention at the national level and the overall effectiveness of
the Convention (Johnson et al. 2006, 197). This concern was noted in 2005,
more than ten years after the UNCCD's adoption, when the Joint Inspection
Unit (JIU) of the United Nations, at the request of the Conference of the Parties,
issued a report entitled "Review of the Management, Administration and
Activities of the Secretariat of the UNCCD." In the report, the inspectors
noted that:

from the outset there has been a lack of common understanding and recognition of the Convention in its true and proper perspective. It seems
unclear whether the Convention is environmental or developmental, or
both; whether it concerns problems of only a local nature or worldwide.
The very name of the Convention may perhaps be misleading since the
fundamental problem is one of land degradation, of which desertification is
a key element. The failure and/or unwillingness to recognize the
Convention in its proper perspective has inevitably led to undesirable consequences, notably:

- The marked differences in access to financial support by UNCCD and
its sister Rio Conventions;
- The lack of a clear and stable financial commitment to UNCCD by
the developed country parties;

- The failure to mainstream UNCCD programmes and activities into the respective development support initiatives among development partners; and,
- The lack of UNCCD prioritization in affected country parties, which have had little success in integrating UNCCD objectives into overall national development plans.

(Ortiz and Tang 2005)

Among other things, the JIU inspectors recommended the development of a long-term strategic framework for UNCCD implementation that may help to overcome the lack of understanding of the Convention's objectives. In 2007, the COP adopted a ten-year strategic plan for the period 2008–2018, which aimed to provide coherence and a common understanding of the Convention's objectives and implementation (Figure 8.1). The aim or "vision" of the plan is: "to forge a global partnership to reverse and prevent desertification/land degradation and to mitigate the effects of drought in affected areas in order to support poverty reduction and environmental sustainability" (UNCCD 2007). The plan also includes strategic objectives and indicators to help channel and measure implementation (see Table 8.1). The overall mission is to "provide a global framework to support the development and implementation of national and regional policies, programmes and measures to prevent, control and reverse desertification/land degradation and mitigate the effects of drought through scientific and technological excellence, raising public awareness, standard setting, advocacy and resource mobilization, thereby contributing to poverty reduction" (UNCCD 2007). Considering that work on indicators began in 1996 at INCD 8 and the Convention operated without a clear definition of its objective for well

FIGURE 8.1 In 2007, the UNCCD COP adopted a ten-year strategic plan for the period 2008–2018, which aimed to provide coherence and a common understanding of the Convention's objectives and implementation. Photo courtesy of IISD/*Earth Negotiations Bulletin*

TABLE 8.1 UNCCD Strategic Objectives and Expected Impacts: 2008–2018

Strategic Objective	Expected Impact	Indicator
1 To improve the living conditions of affected populations	1.1 People living in areas affected by desertification/land degradation and drought to have an improved and more diversified livelihood base and to benefit from income generated from sustainable land management 1.2 Affected populations' socioeconomic and environmental vulnerability to climate change, climate variability, and drought is reduced	S-1 Decrease in numbers of people negatively impacted by the processes of desertification/land degradation and drought S-2 Increase in the proportion of households living above the poverty line in affected areas S-3 Reduction in the proportion of the population below the minimum level of dietary energy consumption in affected areas
2 To improve the condition of affected ecosystems	2.1 Land productivity and other ecosystem goods and services in affected areas are enhanced in a sustainable manner contributing to improved livelihoods 2.2 The vulnerability of affected ecosystems to climate change, climate variability, and drought is reduced	S-4 Reduction in the total area affected by desertification/land degradation and drought S-5 Increase in net primary productivity in affected areas
3 To generate global benefits through effective implementation of the UNCCD	3.1 Sustainable land management and combating desertification/land degradation contribute to the conservation and sustainable use of biodiversity and the mitigation of climate change	S-6 Increase in carbon stocks (soil and plant biomass) in affected areas S-7 Areas of forest, agricultural and aquaculture ecosystems under sustainable management
4 To mobilize resources to support implementation of the Convention through building effective partnerships between national and international actors	4.1 Increased financial, technical, and technological resources are made available to affected developing country parties, and where appropriate Central and Eastern European countries, to implement the Convention 4.2 Enabling policy environments are improved for UNCCD implementation at all levels	S-8 Increase in the level and diversity of available funding for combating desertification/land degradation and mitigating the effects of drought S-9 Development policies and measures address desertification/land degradation and mitigation of the effects of drought

over a decade, many hope that the adoption of the strategic plan and the development of measurable indicators, which were adopted at COP 9 in 2009, may help resolve some of these long-standing definitional questions about what the objective of the UNCCD really is.

From Prior Informed Consent to Advance Informed Agreement

In many cases, defining a new concept can take years of negotiations and even after consensus is achieved, as demonstrated in the two cases above, some definitions are too ambiguous to be effectively operationalized. In other cases, however, delegates approach issue definition by redefining and renaming existing concepts. This was the case in the negotiations of the Cartagena Protocol on Biosafety when delegates took the concept of prior informed consent (PIC), a procedure that has been used in the hazardous chemicals sector, and renamed it "advance informed agreement" (AIA) to be applied to living modified organisms (LMOs).[1]

Issue definition began during the negotiation of the CBD in the early 1990s. One of the key issues on which delegates could not reach agreement was the inclusion of language regarding LMOs resulting from biotechnology. After months of negotiation (see McConnell 1996), Article 19.3 of the CBD simply calls on parties to consider the need for, and modalities of, a protocol setting out procedures in the field of the safe transfer, handling, and use of LMOs resulting from biotechnology that may have an adverse effect on biodiversity and its components. To this end, at the second COP to the CBD in 1995, delegates established a Biosafety Working Group to negotiate such a protocol. While much of the contentious nature of the negotiations circled around the issue of biotechnology itself, defining the procedures for LMO transfers proved just as challenging.

At the second meeting of the Biosafety Working Group in May 1997, the chair, Veit Koester (Denmark), introduced an informal aide-memoire that presented a series of questions for consideration of procedures for specific transfers of LMOs. The text asked what procedures should be included in the protocol and stated that the central question is whether protection requires explicit consent, implicit consent or both. Explicit consent, as seen in the Prior Informed Consent (PIC) procedure used with chemicals and hazardous waste, implies that the absence of a reply from the importing country within a specified time frame does not constitute consent. Implicit consent implies that consent is deemed given if no reply from the importing country has been received within the specified time (ENB 1997).

Developing countries' arguments were based on their experiences with the PIC procedure under the 1989 Basel Convention on the Control of Transboundary Movements of Hazardous Wastes and their Disposal. They pushed for PIC to serve as the linchpin of a biosafety protocol. Under the Basel Convention, the PIC procedure requires that parties not export hazardous wastes to another party unless the competent authority in the importing state has been properly informed and has consented to the trade. This information, provided by either the generator or exporter of the waste through the designated authority, or by the state itself, must enable the states of import and transit to assess the nature and risks of the intended movement. The information can include, among other things, the reason for export, the nature of the wastes, and the method of disposal. The importing state must then respond in writing to the notification and either consent to the movement, deny permission, or request more information. No transfer can begin until the exporter has received written consent[2] (Krueger 1998).

A much-publicized incident in Argentina in 1986, where a genetically altered rabies vaccine was field tested by a US institute on an Argentinean farm without the knowledge or consent of the government, provided much fodder for developing countries in their characterization of LMOs as another potential "dumping or testing of potentially toxic substances in the developing world" problem, similar to hazardous waste and toxic chemicals. In making this demand for PIC for the transfer of LMOs, developing countries implied a "moral imperative" for those with greater resources and experience in this potentially risky area to be responsible and accountable for their actions, at the very least through provision of information and solicitation of consent (Gupta 1999).

The United States objected to the use of PIC in the context of genetic engineering given the association of PIC in the international realm with hazardous and restricted substances. In keeping with their claim that LMOs posed no unique risks, the United States noted that if LMOs were not intrinsically hazardous, nor banned in the country of export, they were wholly distinct from the category of concerns for which PIC had been elaborated.

The last-minute compromise during the negotiations of the CBD in 1992 relied on creative use of language. The US proposed substituting the phrase "advance informed agreement" (AIA) for "prior informed consent" which, while ostensibly identical in meaning, was intended to be devoid of the specific institutional history, if not the set of practices, associated with PIC in other international fora (Gupta 1999). While this enabled delegates to reach agreement on Article 19 of the CBD, it did lead to protracted negotiations on the nature and parameters of such consent during the negotiation of the Cartagena Protocol, even though PIC had already been defined in the Basel Convention and was further elaborated during the negotiations of the 1998 Rotterdam Convention on the Prior Informed Consent Procedure for Certain Hazardous Chemicals and Pesticides in International Trade.

The PIC procedure in the Basel and Rotterdam Conventions is explicit and many assumed that this would be the case with AIA as well. However, debate ensued at the second meeting of the Biosafety Working Group in 1997 on whether AIA should be explicit or implicit, for which types of LMOs, under which circumstances and for which uses, and who should trigger the procedure—the exporting or importing country. Norway, New Zealand, Australia, the United States, and some developing countries, including China and Peru, argued for flexibility and a combination of implicit and explicit consent, whereas many other developing countries and NGOs stressed the need for explicit consent, stating that implicit consent at this stage is unacceptable as it could give importing countries an unfair responsibility arising from their different bureaucratic or communication conditions (ENB 1997).

The debate on AIA reflected the ongoing conflict over the need for a global biosafety regime. While the European Union (EU), developing countries, and environmental groups saw the protocol as a vehicle through which to institutionalize flexibility in decision making about trade in LMOs, derived from decisions based on the precautionary principle and/or socioeconomic considerations, the Miami Group (major grain exporting countries) and industry saw the protocol as a vehicle through which to institutionalize predictability in decision making about trade (Gupta 2001). This debate revisited the same issues time and again from 1996 until the protocol was adopted in 2000: should all LMOs be covered; should the protocol cover and should AIA apply to pharmaceuticals and other commodities, such as fabrics, detergents, food and other grains manufactured with LMOs; what were the trade implications of AIA procedures for the world's food supply and the multi-billion dollar agribusiness; and should ambiguous socioeconomic considerations be used to create trade barriers (ENB 1999) (Figure 8.2)?

FIGURE 8.2 BAM! (Bio Action Montreal), a collective of concerned parties such as Greenpeace, Friends of the Earth, students, and other interest groups organized protests in the sub-zero temperatures in Montreal and rallied through the final hours of the development of the Biosafety Protocol in January 2000. Photo courtesy of IISD/*Earth Negotiations Bulletin*

In the end, delegates succeeded in defining the AIA procedure in that it now is distinct from its origins in the PIC procedure. Under the AIA procedure, countries intending to export an LMO for direct release into the environment are required to seek consent from the potential importing countries prior to the first shipment. Importing countries are required to assess their potential risks in a scientifically sound and transparent manner. Countries can decide not to import an LMO based on the precautionary approach and may take into account socio-economic considerations that may arise from the impacts of the LMO, something distinct from PIC.

Defining and operationalizing a new concept—even one based on an existing concept and deliberately renamed—can take years of negotiations, especially when the issue is at the intersection of trade and environment. In this case, both sides of the debate stood firm in their convictions since any compromise could have potential major economic implications for major grain exporters on the one side and serious impacts on human health and the environment on the other side. However, the art of renaming existing concepts is not unique to biosafety; it is more common than many think.

From "Avoided Deforestation" to "REDD+"

It is often the case that when a party, or a group of parties, does not succeed in including an issue on the agenda of a multilateral negotiation, the next step is to bring it back under a different name or agenda item until it finds acceptance. Of course, once an issue is on the negotiating table, its definition is likely to change from the one originally intended by those who proposed it in the first place. The history of addressing deforestation in developing countries under the UNFCCC provides a good illustration of this definitional challenge.

Trees and vegetation remove carbon dioxide from the atmosphere as they grow, acting as "sinks" and contributing to climate change mitigation. Yet until 1989 international climate change negotiations addressed the sources of emissions separately from any removals.[3] It was the "comprehensive approach" to climate change, along with emissions trading, that brought them together. The "comprehensive approach" entailed collectively accounting for removals as well as emissions of different greenhouse gases and measuring them according to a single metric—that of their global warming potential (GWP).[4] Promoted initially by the US,[5] it was soon widely accepted as a pragmatic and efficient approach. Thus sinks were included alongside sources in the mitigation commitments undertaken by all parties under the 1992 Convention.[6] Yet when the time came to include them under the Kyoto Protocol and its market mechanisms, agreement on sinks proved to be much more complicated.

"Avoided deforestation" first appeared as an option under the Clean Development Mechanism (CDM), alongside other sink activities in the Land Use, Land Use Change, and Forestry (cf. p. 73, 201) (LULUCF) sector.[7] It implied calculating the emissions from deforestation to be prevented by forest conservation projects and allowing developed countries that had commitments under the Protocol to offset their emissions with the avoided ones, in the same way that the closing of a coal power plant generated credits for the emissions thus averted.

The issue was controversial at the time. The key concern was that, in contrast to the coal power plant, the removals are not permanent, since the carbon absorbed by a tree is emitted back to the atmosphere when the tree dies. There were also other problems, such as "leakage"—that is, when deforestation simply moves to an area outside the conservation project. This is the case when, for example, as a result of the establishment of a plantation that generates no employment, the displaced population clears forest land in another place, or when demand for timber, fuelwood, or other goods is simply relocated. Sinks can also have negative social and environmental effects and the greenhouse gas removals that result from them are notoriously difficult to account with precision (IPCC 2000).

The inclusion of avoided deforestation in the CDM thus proved to be a divisive issue, particularly among members of the Group of 77 and China: while most Latin American and many African and Asian countries were in favor of it, Brazil, India, and China, together with Peru and Argentina, as well as the Alliance of Small Island States (AOSIS) and others, opposed it. Although less marked, divisions appeared also among developed countries, with the United States, Japan, Canada, Australia, New Zealand, and others supporting its inclusion, while the EU as a group opposed it.[8] Many of those who opposed it did so on the grounds that it alone could offset most of the emissions from developing countries, leaving little incentive to undertake the transformational changes in the energy sector deemed necessary to respond to climate change.

In the end, avoided deforestation was traded and dealt with as part of a larger compromise political package: the 2001 Marrakesh Accords left avoided deforestation out of the CDM, allowing only afforestation and reforestation to be eligible LULUCF project activities under the CDM during the first commitment period (UNFCCC 2001). This exclusion generated great disappointment among many countries and forestry and conservation organizations, given the grand expectations of a steady source of funds for forest conservation and the belief that the carbon market might be the much sought-after golden key that would finally allow standing trees to have a price to compete with logged ones. Yet the idea was so attractive that it was only a matter of time before the issue was brought back to the negotiating table.

Indeed, four years later, at COP 11 in Montreal in 2005, Costa Rica, Papua New Guinea, and eight other parties brought the issue back as a new agenda item under the Convention, titled "Reducing emissions from deforestation in developing countries: approaches to stimulate action," shortened as "REDD" (with the second "D" initially referring to "developing countries"). Now in the larger context of the Convention, the idea was welcomed by most parties, although it was made very clear that this was very different from "avoided deforestation" (the distinction served to tell apart insiders from outsiders to the process—anyone referring to "avoided deforestation" after COP 11 was clearly an outsider). Most importantly, the fact that it was an agenda item under the Convention and not the Protocol—that is, not a project-based activity necessarily dependent on a market mechanism where one tonne of CO_2 removed in a developing country allowed for the emission of another tonne in a developed one, in a zero-sum game—facilitated its initial acceptance by key players such as Brazil and the EU. Related references were also changed to make the distinction unmistakable: "leakage," for example, became "displacement of emissions." Most importantly, while under avoided deforestation the threat to emit is what gains credits (something that is not allowed in any other sector), REDD was originally conceived as more akin to a sectoral approach for voluntary mitigation commitments; hence, the original title, "Policy approaches and positive incentives to reduce emissions from deforestation and forest degradation." And while avoided deforestation applied only to projects in delimited areas (which, once under the CDM, would be subject to the power and autonomy of the market, something that prompted sovereignty concerns in developing countries) and implied a more conservative approach to protected areas, REDD was generally conceived as support for the effective application of national forest conservation policies established by the host country. This, in principle, could allow for a more flexible approach to conservation: "reduced" emissions (as opposed to "avoided") might include sustainable forest management (Figure 8.3).

Once on the negotiating table however, parties started adding language to the REDD text so that their priorities would be reflected. The concept was first expanded to include forest degradation (with the second D in REDD now referring to degradation). Soon, the issue also explicitly included conservation (promoted notably by India), "sustainable management of forests" (not "sustainable forest management," see below), and "enhancement of forest carbon stocks" (brought up primarily by China). This expanded definition became known as "REDD+."

With such a wide-ranging definition, REDD+ soon enjoyed broad acceptance, although this too might change as the issue continues to be redefined. Two critical areas pending further clarification are the financing options for each activity and stage (i.e., fund-based, market-based, or a combination of the two), and how to incorporate subnational projects or approaches. These are precisely the questions that brought down "avoided deforestation." Thus, some of the key problems remain, even if the name is changed and the issue redefined.

The redefinition of the issue reflects the expanded coverage of mitigation commitments under the Convention—well beyond those established under the Kyoto Protocol for developed country parties—and the greater bargaining power of developing countries relative to 1997 or even 2001. It reveals the growing economic and political strength of the most advanced developing countries—particularly

FIGURE 8.3 NGOs at the United Nations Climate Change Conference in Bali in 2007 expressed concern about the status of the REDD negotiations. Photo courtesy of IISD/*Earth Negotiations Bulletin*

China, Brazil, India, and South Africa—without whom effective and concerted international climate change action will be increasingly difficult.

Meanwhile, in the Forestry Negotiations

While REDD was being defined in the climate change negotiations, delegates in fora focused on forests such as the United Nations Forum on Forests (UNFF) were concerned about how to make sure that the role of sustainable forest management (SFM) was included as an option under REDD. The forestry world saw

REDD as a potential game changer—in terms of the potential influx of money and the already apparent increased global attention being brought to the importance of forests—and wanted to make sure that REDD did not just focus on forest protection, or only on one of the multiple values and benefits of forests. They feared that without some sort of input from forestry experts, forests under the UNFCCC would be seen as nothing but "sticks of carbon," in the words of UNFF director Jan McAlpine (Figure 8.4), ignoring biodiversity, economic, social, and cultural values, and other environmental services such as watershed protection (United Nations 2009). Fears were allayed somewhat with the emergence of REDD+, which explicitly included the role of "sustainable management of forests" in reducing emissions. However, under the 2007 UNFCCC Bali Action Plan, "sustainable management of forests" (as opposed to "sustainable forest management") referred to forest management that will maintain carbon stocks at least at constant levels on average over time (Braatz 2009). In the view of foresters, this definition still narrowed the value of forests to one thing—carbon—and implied that management of carbon stocks would be the principal focus of forest management under the Bali Action Plan's definition.

This of course brought up the age-old issue of what sustainable forest management actually means. Since delegates were unable to adopt a forest convention at

FIGURE 8.4 Jan McAlpine, director of the UNFF Secretariat, stated in 2009 that without some sort of input from forestry experts, forests under the UNFCCC would be seen as nothing but "sticks of carbon." Pictured here with Sha Zukang, Under-Secretary-General for Economic and Social Affairs, at the opening of UNFF 8. Photo courtesy of IISD/*Earth Negotiations Bulletin*

the Earth Summit, but instead negotiated the "Forest Principles,"[9] what followed
in the 1990s and the early 2000s was a proliferation of ways to operationalize
and thus indirectly define SFM. These took the form of international and
regional criteria and indicators (C&I) for different forest types, the seven thematic
elements[10] that were seen as key components of SFM, and certification
schemes that further operationalized these definitions of what good forest management entailed.

When it came time to re-negotiate the international agreement on forests, in
the form of a non-legally binding instrument (NLBI), some countries, particularly Australia, the EU, New Zealand, Japan, and Mexico, felt a strong need to
finally define SFM in the NLBI, while others (African Group and Indonesia)
preferred a reference to the seven thematic elements, and yet others (Brazil,
Colombia) preferred no definition at all. The final outcome was a statement in
the agreement's scope that states: "SFM, as a dynamic and evolving concept, aims
to maintain and enhance the economic, social and environmental values of all
types of forests, for the benefit of present and future generations" (United Nations
General Assembly 2008).

This broad statement, which amounts to an overarching goal rather than a
definition, leaves to the reader's interpretation what sort of forest-related activities can be classified as SFM. NGOs have taken issue with such a definition, and
are particularly concerned with including it under REDD+, leaving the door
open for many different forestry operations saying that they are doing "SFM" and
receiving REDD money for such activities, regardless of their actual sustainability. Well-versed negotiators, however, counter by arguing that a more detailed
definition of SFM was not needed in the NLBI because of the several C&I processes that have been elaborated for such purposes. However, many criticize C&I
processes for 1) not being as widely applied as they should be; 2) being completely voluntary; 3) for the most part, not including thresholds of acceptable
behaviors, instead just pointing to aspects of forestry and forest-related impacts
that should be taken into consideration; 4) being more process-oriented than
outcome-oriented; and, perhaps most importantly for the climate debate, 5) not
giving guidance on balancing conflicting objectives of forest management.

From the start of the eighth session of UNFF (UNFF 8) in the spring of 2009,
opening plenary statements from delegations and expert panel presentations all
pointed to the importance of getting the message across that SFM should be
included under REDD, regardless of the debate on SFM definitions (see related
discussion on coalitions in Chapter 5). Some panel experts specifically said that if
anything were to come from UNFF 8, it should be a strong message to the
UNFCCC about the role of SFM in the future climate change regime. Other
countries, most notably and vocally Brazil, objected to the idea of delivering a
message on climate change issues, so as not to overstep the UNFF's mandate, or
overlap with that of the UNFCCC. After much debate, delegates finally decided
just to include a couple of paragraphs in a broader resolution on forests in a

changing environment, and addressing the message to the Secretariats of all the Rio Conventions to work together with the UNFF Secretariat. Several delegates expressed disappointment that the UNFF—considered by some as the highest international forum on forests—had little of relevance to contribute about the role of forests in a future climate change regime.

Furthermore, complaints were voiced in the corridors of UNFF 8 on the need to have more forest experts represented on delegations to the UNFCCC to avoid a potential mutual lack of understanding between forest and climate experts. As the *Earth Negotiations Bulletin* reported from the corridors of UNFF 8:

> While most UNFF delegates lamented the level of appreciation of the complexities of SFM within the climate change community, climate experts expressed dismay about the foresters' misconceptions regarding REDD. The way to find a common perspective, as some noted, would be to allow forest experts to participate in UNFCCC negotiations. "Great idea," responded others, "only that the climate people in our governments don't think that way."
>
> *(ENB 2009)*

This was exemplified in the UNFCCC negotiations held in Tianjin, China, in October 2010, at precisely the same time as the biennial meeting of the FAO's Committee on Forestry in Rome, Italy, a meeting of international forest experts. Both meetings discussed issues relevant to REDD+, but each in their own corner of the world and in their own context. Elaborating more precisely the scope of REDD+ and sustainable forest management or sustainable management of forests is ongoing, but it remains to be seen how involved the forestry world will be in this exercise.

What Does it All Mean?

The increased linkages between economic and environmental issues have had a clear impact on issue definition over the past twenty years. In fact, some of the most challenging issues, as described in this chapter, demonstrate that when issue definition has economic or trade implications, the negotiations can be protracted, the results can be ambiguous, and the impact on implementation can be harmful. Different combinations of internal and global economic and political forces influence states' positions and policies toward environmental issues. Because the actual costs and risks of environmental degradation are never distributed equally among all states, and states possess different views about what constitutes an equitable solution, achieving consensus is not easy. Since most environmental treaties are adopted by consensus instead of by voting, the result is often a "least common denominator" agreement. Because all states are sovereign entities, they can choose whether to join a global environmental agreement. However, because active participation by many if not all countries is required to address a global environmental problem, it is important for the countries to achieve consensus. Thus a regime's overall effectiveness can be undermined by the compromises made in persuading certain recalcitrant states to participate.

In the negotiations on "new and additional financial resources," developed countries, particularly the United States, did not want to write a blank check to finance Agenda 21. Yet, despite the rather inconclusive definition to "reaffirm their commitments to reach the accepted United Nations target of 0.7 per cent of GNP for ODA," this language on "new and additional financial resources" has pervaded almost every single environmental negotiation since the Earth Summit in Rio. Why? Because it was part of the overall Rio compact: developing countries would commit to more environmentally sound development and developed countries would provide new and additional financial resources, technology transfer on preferential and concessional terms, and capacity building. Thus, if the developed countries do not meet their commitments—poorly defined as they may be—the developing countries see themselves largely as off the hook.

In the desertification negotiations, the need for new and additional financial resources and the challenge of creating a truly sustainable development convention led to a rather open-ended definition of the objective of the Convention. Differing interpretations of this ambiguous objective, among other things, have prevented countries from developing and funding effective plans and programs to combat desertification, determine the relationship with land degradation, and mitigate the effects of drought. It took fourteen years before parties approved a strategic plan and set of indicators that further defined and elaborated the Convention's objective.

Sometimes when delegates cannot reach agreement on a definition or an issue is not successfully added to the agenda, the issue is often brought back under a different name. This was the case in both the biosafety negotiations, with regard to prior informed consent and advance informed agreement, and the climate change negotiations, with regard to avoided deforestation and REDD+. But even once the terms have been changed and governments are willing to work on the details of the definition, economic and trade imperatives often influence the outcome. In the biosafety negotiations, major grain exporting countries were concerned that the AIA procedure would slow down international trade. The difference in the treatment of avoided deforestation and REDD+ ten years later reflects the increased power of the most advanced developing countries in the world economy. While the Kyoto Protocol represented mainly a deal between industrialized countries, with the EU being one of the key players, in Copenhagen the center stage was taken by the BASIC group of countries—i.e., Brazil, South Africa, India and, particularly, China—and the EU appeared to be sidelined. The nationwide mitigation commitments these key emerging economies would take, perhaps on a sectoral basis, were at the center of the negotiations. Changes in the definition of the issue are thus more explicable when seen in that light; whoever has most power in a negotiation goes a long way toward explaining how the issue will be defined and redefined.

Similar power plays were seen in the forestry world when negotiating the NLBI. The Amazon Group, headed by Brazil and often supported by India, emerged as a powerful coalition that often directed negotiations toward the lowest common denominator—broad and vague definitions with no timelines or targets. Past strong players in forest negotiations such as the EU had to compromise on many issues of importance to them (see Chapter 5). However, now that the UNFCCC has attempted to define SFM in the 2010 Cancún Agreements, this definition will likely frame the activities that receive REDD+ funding. This may yet be another case of financing and political power driving definitions.

It is often said that a camel is a horse designed by a committee. In other words, the process of reaching consensus and incorporating many conflicting positions into a negotiated outcome (treaty, action program, resolution) results in an animal that may be quite different—and much more unwieldy—than what may have originally been envisioned by the different negotiators. When it comes to issue definition, the resulting language has a lasting impact on international environmental law and policy. And when the resulting camel is a case of creative ambiguity, governments can spend years trying to figure out what exactly it all means.

Notes

1 During the negotiations of the Convention on Biological Diversity, another definitional issue proved problematic. The United States and other pro-biotechnology countries refused to use the terminology "genetically modified organism" (GMO) and instead insisted on "living modified organism" (LMO) in order to exclude any non-living modified organisms from the Convention and the subsequent Biosafety Protocol. For example, an LMO will not include products derived from GMOs such as processed food derived from a genetically modified plant such as corn that may be used in a breakfast cereal.

2 The PIC procedure was also being used on a voluntary basis to help developing countries make informed decisions on the import of chemicals that have been banned or severely restricted. While the Biosafety Protocol negotiations were taking place, UNEP and FAO were also sponsoring negotiations on what was to become the 1998 Rotterdam Convention on the Prior Informed Consent Procedure for Certain Hazardous Chemicals and Pesticides in International Trade.

3 Both the Toronto and the Noordwijk Conferences focused on carbon dioxide emissions from the energy and transport sector, but only the Noordwijk Declaration had additionally called for a separate global target for forest growth of 12 million hectares per year by the beginning of 2000. This latter target was soon deemed politically unviable and abandoned. See Bodansky (1993, 520).

4 Global warming potential (GWP) serves as a common metric by equating a unit mass of a given greenhouse gas to that of carbon dioxide for a given time period (in the case of the Kyoto Protocol, a 100-year time frame). It is based on how long a greenhouse gas remains in the atmosphere and its relative effectiveness in absorbing outgoing infrared radiation.

5 In December 1989, the US government included sinks as "negative emissions" in concept papers prepared for the IPCC Response Strategy Working Group, before negotiations started for the climate change convention. See U.S. Concept Paper: Comprehensive Greenhouse Gas Approach to Addressing Climate Change. December 29, 1989 (unpublished). See also Bodansky (1993, 517).

6 The main obligation on sinks stems from UNFCCC Article 4.1(b), which calls all parties "to formulate, implement, publish and regularly update national and, where appropriate, regional programmes containing measures to mitigate climate change by addressing emissions by sources and removals by sinks of all greenhouse gases not controlled by the Montreal Protocol, and measures to facilitate adequate adaptation to climate change."

7 Although Article 12 of the Kyoto Protocol on the CDM does not include reference to removals from sinks, it is likely that the omission had to do with the fact that parties—in particular the Group of 77 and China—could not agree on the issue. But as soon as the next meeting was held, sinks were brought back to the table. See Gutierrez (2007).

8 Although the EU as a group decided to oppose it, there were different views among individual EU member states.

9 The official title is the Non-legally Binding Authoritative Statement of Principles for a Global Consensus on the Management, Conservation and Development of All Types of Forests.

10 The seven thematic elements are: extent of forest resources; biological diversity; forest health and vitality; productive functions of forest resources; protective functions of forest resources; socioeconomic functions; and legal, policy, and institutional framework.

Works Cited

Bodansky, Daniel. 1993. The U.N. Framework Convention on Climate Change: A Commentary. *Yale Journal of International Law* 18: 451–558.

Braatz, S. 2009. Sustainable management of Forests and REDD+: Negotiations need Clear terminology. FAO Information Note.

ENB (*Earth Negotiations Bulletin*). 1993. Summary of the First Session of the INCD: 24 May–3 June 1993. *Earth Negotiations Bulletin* 4(11). http://www.iisd.ca/vol04/0411000e.html (accessed December 5, 2010).

ENB. 1994. INCD Highlights: Tuesday, 18 January 1994. *Earth Negotiations Bulletin* 4(26): 1–2.

ENB. 1997. Report of the Second Meeting of the Open-Ended Ad Hoc Group on Biosafety: 12–16 May 1997. *Earth Negotiations Bulletin* 9(67). http://www.iisd.ca/download/pdf/enb0967e.pdf (accessed December 5, 2010).

ENB. 1999. Report of the Sixth Session of the Open-Ended Ad Hoc Working Group on Biosafety and the First Extraordinary Session of the CBD Conference of the Parties: 14–23 February 1999. *Earth Negotiations Bulletin* 9(117). http://www.iisd.ca/download/pdf/enb09117e.pdf (accessed December 4, 2010).

ENB 2009. UNFF Highlights: 22 April 2009. *Earth Negotiations Bulletin* 13(167). http://www.iisd.ca/download/pdf/enb13167e.pdf (accessed December 5, 2010).

ESB (*Earth Summit Bulletin*). 1992. Financial Resources. *Earth Summit Bulletin* 1(3). http://www.iisd.ca/download/asc/enb0103.txt (accessed December 5, 2010).

Group of 77. 1991. Statement by the Representative of Ghana on Behalf of the Group of 77 in the Plenary of the Third Session of UNCED on Item 2(c): Financial Resources, Geneva, 28 August 1991.

Gupta, Aarti. 1999. Framing "Biosafety" in an International Context: The Biosafety Protocol Negotiations. Belfer Center for Science and International Affairs, ENRP Discussion Paper E-99-10. http://www.hks.harvard.edu/gea/pubs/e-99-10.pdf (accessed December 5, 2010).

Gupta, Aarti. 2001. Advance Informed Agreement: A Shared Basis for Governing Trade in Genetically Modified Organisms? *Indiana Journal of Global Legal Studies* 9(1): 265–281.

Gutierrez, Maria. 2007. All that is Air Turns Solid: The Creation of a Market for Sinks under the Kyoto Protocol on Climate Change. PhD dissertation, New York: City University of New York.

Herrmann, Stephanie M. and Charles F. Hutchinson. 2006. The Scientific Basis: Links between Land Degradation, Drought and Desertification. In *Governing Global Desertification*. Edited by Pierre Mark Johnson, Karel Mayrand, and Marc Paquin. Burlington, VA: Ashgate.

IPCC (Intergovernmental Panel on Climate Change). 2000. *Land Use, Land Use Change and Forestry*. Special Report. Cambridge, UK: Cambridge University Press.

Johnson, Pierre Marc, Karel Mayrand, and Marc Paquin. 2006. Conclusion: The UNCCD at a Crossroad. In *Governing Global Desertification*. Edited by Pierre Mark Johnson, Karel Mayrand, and Marc Paquin. Burlington, VA: Ashgate.

Krueger, Jonathan. 1998. Prior Informed Consent and the Basel Convention: The Hazards of What isn't Known. *Journal of Environment and Development* 7(2): 115–138.

McConnell, Fiona. 1996. *The Biodiversity Convention: A Negotiating History*. New York: Springer.

Ortiz, Even and Guangting Tang. 2005. *Review of the Management, Administration and Activities of the Secretariat of the United Nations Convention to Combat Desertification*. Geneva: United Nations Joint Inspection Unit.

UNCCD. 2007. Report of the Conference of the Parties on its Eighth Session, held in Madrid from 3 to 14 September 2007 Addendum; Part two: Action taken by the Conference of the Parties at its Eighth Session. ICCD/COP(8)/16/Add.1 (October 23). http://www.unccd.int/cop/officialdocs/cop8/pdf/16add1eng.pdf (accessed December 5, 2010).

UNFCCC (United Nations Framework Convention on Climate Change). 2001. Land Use, Land-Use Change and Forestry. Decision 11/CP.7. http://unfccc.int/files/meetings/workshops/other_meetings/application/pdf/11cp7.pdf (accessed December 3, 2010).

United Nations. 1992. *Agenda 21*. New York: United Nations. http://www.un.org/esa/dsd/agenda21/index.shtml (accessed June 6, 2011).

United Nations. 1993a. Elaboration of an International Convention to Combat Desertification in Countries Experiencing Serious Drought and/or Desertification, Particularly in Africa. Compilation of Government Views, Statements and Drafting Proposals. A/AC.241/12 (August 23). http://www.unccd.int/cop/officialdocs/incd/pdf/24112eng.pdf (accessed December 5, 2010).

United Nations. 1993b. Negotiating Text of the Convention. A/AC.241/15 (November 19).

United Nations. 1994. Elaboration of an International Convention to Combat Desertification in Countries Experiencing Serious Drought and/or Desertification, Particularly in Africa. Final Text of the Convention. A/AC.241/27 (September 12). http://www.unccd.int/convention/text/pdf/conv-eng.pdf (accessed March 26, 2011).

United Nations. 2009. As 2009 Forum Opens, Member States to Grapple with Funding for Forest Management in Times of Changing Environment. Press Release ENV/DEV 1033 (April 17). http://www.un.org/News/Press/docs/2009/envdev1033.doc.htm (accessed March 26, 2011).

United Nations General Assembly. 2008. Non-legally Binding Instrument on All Types of Forests. A/RES/62/98. (January 31).

United States. 1991. U.S. Statement on Financial Resources, UNCED PrepCom 3, Geneva (August 28).

UNSO. 1994. *Poverty Alleviation and Land Degradation in the Drylands*. New York, NY: United Nations Development Programme.

Zartman, I. William. 1994. Lessons for Analysis and Practice. In *International Environmental Negotiation*. Edited by Gunnar Sjöstedt. Newbury Park, CA: Sage.

9

TRADE AND ENVIRONMENT

Old Wine in New Bottles?

Kati Kulovesi, Sabrina Shaw, and Stanley W. Burgiel

In the two decades since the 1992 Earth Summit in Rio de Janeiro, trade concerns have infiltrated multilateral environmental negotiations both as high-profile, contentious issues of debate and as a general subtext to ongoing discussions. In this chapter, we trace the evolution of the trade and environment debate and its increasing specialization under various multilateral environmental agreements (MEAs), including the Convention on Biological Diversity (CBD) and the United Nations Framework Convention on Climate Change (UNFCCC). We also examine the influence of linkages and substantive overlap between MEAs and international trade rules under the World Trade Organization (WTO).

This chapter takes three propositions as a starting point. First, MEAs exist in a diverse international arena, and many other considerations apart from the environment influence their negotiation. Indeed, linkages between economic, development, and environmental issues have often complicated international environmental negotiations. Second, over the course of the past two decades, the trade and environment debate has gradually shifted from a politicized general discourse on broad themes and hypothetical conflicts toward a more technical discussion focusing on specific legal questions, economics, and implementation. Yet, as illustrated in this chapter, important political differences persist, especially between developed and developing countries, such as in the agricultural sector and concerning the use of trade measures to tackle climate change. Third, while important strides have been made to enhance coordination and coherence at different levels on the various issues involved in the trade and environment debate, the legal and institutional separation of trade and environment continues to be a challenge. In other words, interaction between MEAs and the international trade regime is characterized by certain legal discrepancies and institutional barriers. At the national level, lack of coordination exists both between different ministries and different fora. Together, these factors have ensured that the trade and environment debate remains firmly on the international agenda, and controversies surrounding trade and environment continue to emerge both under MEAs and at the WTO.

The chapter begins with a brief overview of the trade and environment debate since the United Nations Conference on Environment and Development (UNCED). It then analyzes the debate in the context of biodiversity and climate change, with a special emphasis on the CBD and the UNFCCC, which feature prominent trade-related issues. This section also addresses agriculture, which continues to be a critical element for the trade and environment policy nexus. The final section presents conclusions on the trade and environment debate as it has evolved since 1992, arguing that considerable nuance has been brought to the dialogue over the past two decades. There has been progress to stabilize the trade and environment discourse resulting from a better understanding of the complexities involved. It is precisely due to these complex interlinkages and a greater focus on technical issues that has necessitated greater coordination both between international fora and within national delegations. Despite advances since UNCED in this regard, however, potential for friction between the regimes remains, while the traditional North–South dividing line has fractured as developing countries with advanced export economies have entered the debate.

Evolution of the Trade and Environment Debate

In the early 1990s, trade and environment was a popular, yet politically sensitive, topic. Debates surrounding trade and environment featured strongly in the negotiations for the North American Free Trade Agreement and during the final phase of negotiations under the Uruguay Round of global trade negotiations. At the Earth Summit, while the trade and environment debate remained largely in the back seat, principles defining the terms of interaction were inserted in the Rio Declaration and Agenda 21.[1]

Some political controversies from the context of the General Agreement on Tariffs and Trade (GATT) also surfaced at the Earth Summit. One of the drivers was the *Tuna–Dolphin* dispute in 1991, which ruled that a United States import ban on Mexican tuna aimed at supporting dolphin protection efforts violated international trade rules under the GATT (GATT 1991). In the North, the *Tuna–Dolphin* decision caused a strong environmentalist backlash against international trade cooperation. Many felt that international trade rules were undermining national environmental legislation and trade was given primacy over environment. For emerging economies in the South, however, international trade liberalization and enhanced access to industrialized countries' markets was increasingly important. Fearful of green protectionism, most developing countries strongly opposed the idea of industrialized countries using trade bans to impose their higher environmental standards on developing country producers.

In the end, the Rio Declaration was accepted subject to formal reservation by the United States concerning Principle 12, on cooperation to promote a supportive and open international economic system. The United States' interpretive statement indicates that, in certain situations, trade measures may provide effective and appropriate means of addressing environmental concerns.

Overall, at the time of the Earth Summit, the trade and environment communities were unfamiliar and uncomfortable with each other's territories and they came from two "clashing" cultures and paradigms (Esty 1994, 36). However, awareness of linkages between trade and environment were growing and some attempts were made to reflect this at the institutional level. In 1991, the European Free Trade Association requested the establishment of a working group on trade and environment under the GATT. At the same time, the GATT Contracting Parties debated how best to respond to the request from UNCED Secretary-General Maurice Strong to make a contribution to the Earth Summit. Trade negotiators were, however, generally reluctant to dwell on environmental questions at a crucial moment in the negotiations to conclude the Uruguay Round, after over a decade of deliberations. Developing countries, while not alone in expressing reservations about the competence of the GATT to take environmental issues on board, voiced serious concerns about the risk of green protectionism. Many developed countries, in turn, worried about the possibility of a "race to the bottom" concerning environmental standards. The scene was set for the introduction of environment and sustainable development into the legal construct of the international trade regime.

The Uruguay Round was completed in April 1994 and a new organization was created to administer international trade liberalization. The establishment of the WTO in 1995 had an important impact on the legal and institutional framework in which the trade–environment debate takes place. The GATT, which focuses on trade in goods, retained its central place, while new areas, such as services and intellectual property, were also brought under the WTO and rules were strengthened in areas such as agriculture, food safety, and technical barriers to trade. Also remarkable was the establishment of a new system for settling trade disputes. All WTO members undertook to recognize the jurisdiction of the dispute settlement system and granted it powers to authorize trade sanctions against states that were not complying with its rulings. They also established a permanent Appellate Body, which has come to play a key role in developing the WTO regime. Given the absence of equally powerful dispute settlement bodies under MEAs, the WTO dispute settlement system continues to play a prominent role in resolving legal aspects at the intersection of trade and environment.

While focusing on trade, the Uruguay Round outcome includes elements reflecting the growing environmental awareness and commitment to sustainable development expressed at UNCED. In Rio, developing countries attached considerable importance to the references in Agenda 21 to the need to conclude the Uruguay Round of trade negotiations as a contribution to achieving sustainable development. In this context, the mandate of the WTO was crafted to reflect the role that the trading system could play toward accelerating sustainable development. The preamble of the Marrakesh Agreement Establishing the World Trade Organization refers to the importance of working toward sustainable development—a notion absent from the GATT. Ministers also adopted a Decision on Trade and Environment, indicating that: "There should not be, nor need be, any policy contradiction between upholding and safeguarding an open, non-discriminatory and equitable multilateral trading system on the one hand, and acting for the protection of the environment, and the promotion of sustainable development on the other" (WTO 1995).

The decision called for the establishment of a WTO Committee on Trade and Environment, which has a broad mandate to look at the relationship between trade and environment in order to promote sustainable development. To date, it has examined issues including the effects of environmental measures on market access, labeling requirements for environmental purposes, and relations with multilateral environmental agreements. With these reforms, the international trade regime made its borders more permeable to environmental interests and began to alleviate some of the political tensions between the trade and environment communities (Najam et al. 2007). Yet, environmentalists' unhappiness that the Uruguay Round had not addressed trade and environmental issues adequately was no secret and calls were made to further "green" the GATT in light of the broad commitment to sustainable development voiced at the Earth Summit.

The outcome of the Uruguay Round also influenced the relationship between the WTO and MEAs. It expanded the substantive scope of international trade rules and made the trade regime institutionally more powerful than any MEA. From the mid-1990s to the early 2000s, the discourse around trade issues within MEAs was thus replete with arguments over the "chilling effect" of the WTO, which appeared in several different forms (Marceau 1999). Questions emerged both concerning the general relationship between WTO rules and MEAs, as well as the extent to which WTO rules constrain the application of trade measures under MEAs (WTO 1996). During preparations for the eighth session of the UN Commission on Sustainable Development (CSD 8) in 2000, the European Union (EU) emphasized the ability of WTO members to pursue levels of environmental protection they deem appropriate and called for greater legal clarity regarding the relationship between trade measures pursuant to MEAs and WTO agreements, and for WTO accommodation of such agreements, citing the Biosafety Protocol (ENB 2000b).

In the specific case of intellectual property rights, a number of developing countries and civil society groups specifically argued that the WTO Agreement on Trade-related Aspects of Intellectual Property Rights (TRIPS) was being implemented in a manner contrary to biodiversity protection (ENB 1998). At CSD 8, the Group of 77 and China, supported by Norway, proposed text referring to the equal status of the CBD and TRIPS, while the United States preferred language stating that there is no preordained hierarchy between the two (ENB 2000d). Delegates agreed to language introduced by Canada, noting that "both trade agreements and MEAs are developed and negotiated in pursuit of legitimate multilateral objectives in support of sustainable development" (ENB 2000d). Debates concerning the impact of the TRIPS Agreement also continued to affect the negotiations on access and benefit sharing under the CBD (see ENB 2000b, 2000c, 2001, 2006, 2010a).

The trade and environment communities also put forward different understandings concerning the role and meaning of the precautionary principle (WTO Appellate Body 1998). These debates were particularly prominent during the later stages of negotiations of the Cartagena Protocol on Biosafety where questions emerged concerning pre-eminence in the event of a dispute and the legal weight of a national measure based on precaution came to the fore (ENB 1999b).

The WTO, in turn, continued to be criticized by environmentalists and the anti-globalization movement. Environmental issues took on a growing and dramatic public profile at the contentious WTO Ministerial Conferences in Seattle (1999) and Cancún (2003). The 1999 Battle for Seattle around the WTO ministerial became a symbol for anti-trade sentiments as environmental and labor lobbies brought their concerns both to the delegates and to the streets through rallies, protests, and civil disobedience. The failure to conclude a new round of negotiations at both these ministerial conferences highlighted the simple fact that the WTO process has its own internal problems and faults, and therefore may not be the monolith that environmentalists had initially feared.

In the face of such protests, the turn of the millennium marked a more conciliatory tone regarding trade and environment by WTO institutions. The 2001 *Shrimp–Turtle* decision confirmed that the United States could lawfully ban imports of shrimp and shrimp products from countries that were not implementing adequate policies to protect endangered migratory species of sea turtles (WTO Appellate Body 2001). The Doha Round of trade negotiations contained, for the first time, a narrow but explicit environmental mandate geared at enhancing "the mutual supportiveness of trade and environment," and discussion of environmental issues in other areas, such as services, agriculture, and intellectual property. Trade negotiators were also mandated to consider the relationship between WTO rules and MEAs, particularly those containing specific trade obligations (WTO 2001). With the adoption of the Cartagena Protocol on Biosafety and evolution of WTO jurisprudence, discussions on the precautionary principle also became more legalistic and arguably less politicized.

Overall, recent years have seen a decrease in the fervor around discussions of trade-related issues. This normalization or more subdued tone may reflect a greater degree of comfort with the boundaries between environmental and trade rules, as well as increased experience with the implementation of relevant provisions that have not actualized fears of unjustifiable trade barriers. This should not, however, be regarded as lack of concern over the issue. As the following section illustrates, issues surrounding trade and environment continue to surface under MEA negotiations and in the WTO.

Biodiversity, Climate Change, and Agriculture: Trade and Environment Debate in Context

Biodiversity

Since the beginning of the negotiation of the CBD, trade-related issues have percolated beneath the surface. This should be no surprise as the major drivers of biodiversity loss—whether deforestation, overfishing, habitat conversion for agriculture, and other methods of resource exploitation—were and still are trade-related activities. To reverse these trends, the CBD would eventually have to address issues of global consumption of resources, habitat destruction, and the underlying trading system. While the CBD arguably has not made sufficient inroads on the consumption issue (witness the failure to achieve the CBD's 2010 goal to significantly reduce the rate of biodiversity loss), in some newer areas of international law and policy it has carved out a space for environmental concerns.

Early discussions on a range of ecosystem-based themes and cross-cutting issues under the CBD highlighted the need for work on issues related to trade and overconsumption, including deforestation and illegal logging, overfishing and fishing subsidies, as well as the role of perverse incentives promoting the unsustainable use of biological resources. However, the ability of the CBD to address these issues in depth was compromised by a tendency to label these behaviors as the result of particular national economic actions and not necessarily a broader legal issue with the international trade regime. For example, during discussions at the second meeting of the Conference of the Parties (COP 2) in 1995, some countries, such as the Republic of Korea, thought the draft program of work on marine and coastal biodiversity overemphasized resource exploitation and that references to fisheries subsidies extended too far into trade-related issues (ENB 1995a). Similarly, discussions at COP 4 in 1998 on the forest biodiversity program of work replaced proposals addressing the underlying causes of forest biodiversity loss with a blander reference to "positive and negative" human influences (ENB 1998).

Successive generations of NGOs have publically pressed for the CBD to take a stronger stand to push for the reform of elements of the trading system that are clearly unsustainable. Such debates were quite explicit at COP 4, where numerous NGOs and NGO coalitions called on CDB parties to address WTO rules that threaten biodiversity (ENB 1998). At other CBD meetings, NGOs focused on specific examples of unsustainable resource use (e.g., fishing on sea mounts, dam developments in the Mekong Region, clear-cutting of the boreal forest), but did not succeed in getting these issues adequately addressed. Without the political will to address these trade-related impacts on biodiversity, the only areas in which the CBD could have an impact on trade were new issues, such as genetically modified organisms (GMOs) and biosafety, the precautionary principle, and access and benefit sharing.

Under the CBD, the friction between trade and the environment came to a climax around the conclusion of the Cartagena Protocol on Biosafety in 2000. The Biosafety Protocol established a new set of rules around the international movement of GMOs with definite trade implications both for countries interested in developing and marketing genetically modified (GM) crops and for countries pursuing or maintaining GM-free markets. The fear of countries with major GM business interests was that such decisions would be political and not science-based, and that those averse to GMOs could use the provisions of the Protocol to skirt their obligations under the WTO, particularly under the Agreement on the Application of Sanitary and Phytosanitary Measures (SPS Agreement).

For the most part, these allegations and fears were hypothetical given the lack of significant trade in GM goods at the time. Yet for the purposes of developing a new international legal agreement, they were increasingly given voice in the closing deliberations. The collapse of the "final" negotiating session in Cartagena, Colombia in 1999 can, in part, be traced to language over trade and the issue of whether WTO rules or the Biosafety Protocol would take precedence in cases of national implementation or international disputes. More specifically, text on the Protocol's relationship to other international agreements (e.g., the WTO), non-discrimination of trade in GM products, relations with non-parties (e.g., the United States), and treatment of products derived from GMOs (e.g., corn flour from GM maize) all raised a series of "what if" questions regarding the extent of the Protocol's legal application (ENB 1999b). These issues constituted the elements of the core package of outstanding provisions considered at the closed informal consultations held in Vienna later in 1999, which led into the final negotiating session in Montreal in January 2000 (ENB 1999a, 2000a). The final compromise language arguably did little to clarify the picture with its three preambular components:

1. Trade and environment agreements should be mutually supportive to achieve sustainable development;
2. The Protocol should not be interpreted as implying a change in the rights and obligations of a party under existing international agreements; and
3. The phrase above is not intended to subordinate the Protocol to other international agreements.

For several years, the inability to resolve the relationship between the Biosafety Protocol and the WTO had a "chilling effect" on other MEA discussions where any language that was suspected of impacting trade became a sticking point. This was most visible in the negotiations on the CBD's Guiding Principles on Invasive Alien Species from the late 1990s into the early 2000s. Within language relating to the use of risk assessment and the precautionary approach, major trading countries again feared that these guidelines could provide cover for national regulations that would unjustifiably restrict international trade. By their nature, invasive alien species are generally moved with commodities as well as with the ships and planes that transport them. Preventing the movement of invasive alien species can thereby require measures that affect the import, transport, and processing of goods. These concerns came to a head during the final plenary of COP 6 in 2002, where the Australian delegation objected to the final text after overnight consultations with its trade ministry in Canberra (Figure 9.1). Despite hours of additional discussions, the issue was not resolved and Decision VI/23 was adopted over these Australian objections (ENB 2002a).

As decisions under the CBD can only be taken by consensus (as the rules of procedure for voting have not been approved), this objection contributed a new set of procedural issues on top of the existing substantive concerns over trade-related language. Legal discussions over the validity of Decision VI/23 escalated

FIGURE 9.1 The inability to resolve the relationship between the Biosafety Protocol and the WTO had a "chilling effect" on other MEA discussions where any language that was suspected of impacting trade became a sticking point. During the negotiations on the CBD's Guiding Principles on Invasive Alien Species, these concerns came to a head during COP 6 in 2002, where the Australian delegation objected to the final text because of the impact on trade. Photo courtesy of IISD/*Earth Negotiations Bulletin*

up to the UN General Assembly. In the end, the UN's legal advisors maintained that the decision was valid, which furthered the concerns and aggravations of Australia and other countries holding similar concerns. The issue also had ripple effects beyond the CBD. The Ramsar Convention removed discussion of the principles from the agenda of its subsequent COP meeting and did not raise the issue of reconsidering guidance on invasive alien species for wetlands for over eight years. These actions were taking place at the same time that environmental issues were growing in profile at the contentious WTO Ministerial Conferences in Seattle (1999) and Cancún (2003).

While time has not healed all wounds, the nature of both legal realities and the commercial world has moved along. Within the CBD, Australia still insists on inserting a footnote to any reference to Decision VI/23 on invasive alien species that highlights its procedural concern over the decision's adoption. However, discussions on invasive alien species have moved forward and include positive involvement by Australia and other countries that held similar concerns. While one WTO dispute over US concerns with the EC's process for the review and approval of GM varieties arose prior to the Biosafety Protocol's entry into force (WTO Dispute Settlement Panel 2006), much of the public concern and political furor over the issue has died down.

The United States, not a party to the CBD or to the Biosafety Protocol, continues to export GMOs, while also working with countries implementing the Protocol. Other countries, such as Brazil, that were not pro-GMO during the Protocol negotiations, are now major producers, a change that has shifted the power balance among developing countries. Markets for GM commodities never collapsed, although new markets for GM-free goods expanded. By example, the EU, which had significant concerns over the approval of GM goods during the negotiations, has subsequently approved the import and sale of many of these GM varieties. The Fifth Meeting of the Parties to the Cartagena Protocol on Biosafety in 2010 highlighted this shift from opposed positions around the application of biotechnology toward a more cooperative approach for managing risks associated with living modified organisms (ENB 2010c). On the other side of the fence, environmental and social concerns did leave their mark on the WTO, yet the WTO's inability to agree on larger trade issues generally overshadowed such matters and provided evidence of the trade regime's own deficiencies. Ultimately, events sorted themselves out, trade in GM and non-GM goods were normalized in accord with the Protocol's provisions and, some could argue, negotiators got a better sense of the real areas of intersection between trade and the environment.

This is not to say that trade–environment issues have disappeared in the CBD. The adoption at CBD COP 10 in 2010 of the Nagoya Protocol on Access to Genetic Resources and the Fair and Equitable Sharing of Benefits Arising from their Utilization raised a suite of issues (Figure 9.2). The Nagoya Protocol has been described as a "masterpiece in creative ambiguity." Vague language on key issues, which was necessary to obtain general acceptance by the negotiators, will

FIGURE 9.2 Negotiations on the Nagoya Protocol on Access to Genetic Resources and the Fair and Equitable Sharing of Benefits Arising from their Utilization raised a suite of trade-related issues that continue after its adoption at COP 10 in October 2010. Photo courtesy of IISD/*Earth Negotiations Bulletin*

likely raise future questions around implementation. Likely concerns to look out for are discrimination between compliant and non-compliant users, disclosure of origin and certificates of compliance for patent applications, and possibly procedures for access and monitoring that could become technical barriers to trade. While legal discussions around these issues will continue, particularly with regard to their trade implications, it is doubtful that the first recourse will be to dispute settlement under the WTO. The history of negotiations around biosafety and invasive alien species has shown how the CBD can engage in a more technical and productive manner on the margins of trade-related issues.

Climate Change

Influenced by growing global awareness that preventing catastrophic climate change necessitates a fundamental economic and energy transition in the coming decades, climate change and trade is emerging as one of the most prominent sub-themes in the trade and environment debate. Trade issues have recently resurfaced in the high-profile international negotiations under the UNFCCC on long-term issues. At the same time, climate change has also lifted its profile under the WTO.

When negotiating the UNFCCC in the early 1990s, states were aware of the potential linkages between climate change and trade. Reflecting language of Principle 12 of the Rio Declaration, Article 3.5 of the UNFCCC came to include a general provision on promoting a supportive and open international economic system leading to sustainable economic growth and development in all parties. Mirroring both Principle 12 of the Rio Declaration and Article XX of the GATT, the UNFCCC also indicates that measures to combat climate change, including unilateral ones, should not constitute arbitrary or unjustifiable discrimination, or a disguised restriction on international trade. The trade linkage became more prominent during the negotiation of the Kyoto Protocol in 1997 (ENB 1995b, 1996), with some parties expressing concern that the Protocol should not be subordinate to the WTO while others sought to establish that the Protocol would not prejudice rights and obligations of WTO members (ENB 1997). The Protocol requires developed countries to cut their greenhouse gas emissions by an average of 5.2% from 1990 levels in 2008–2012 without specifying how these cuts are to be achieved. Countries thus have at their disposal a wide range of climate mitigation policies and measures in various economic sectors. Many of the possible options—trade restrictions, subsidies, labeling requirements, and standards—have trade implications and are governed by WTO rules. In addition, the Kyoto Protocol contains provisions on carbon trading through three market-based flexibility mechanisms designed to ensure cost-effective emission reductions. Despite its potential trade implications, the Protocol does not contain specific provisions addressing trade, apart from requiring developed countries "to strive to implement" their emission reductions "in such a way as to minimize adverse effects, including … on international trade" (Article 2.3). Given that both contain only vaguely formulated provisions on trade-related issues, the UNFCCC and the Kyoto Protocol left room for future differences over permissibility of trade-related climate measures.

Such differences did not, however, surface as quickly as some had feared. After the adoption of the Kyoto Protocol, linkages between trade and climate change took a secondary role in UN climate negotiations for nearly a decade. Attention focused on detailed rules for the Protocol's implementation[2] and uncertainties surrounding the Protocol's entry into force. But with the launch in 2007 of a new, comprehensive negotiation process on long-term climate cooperation, the debate on trade and climate change was reinvigorated. The Bali Action Plan (UNFCCC 2007) identified adaptation, finance, mitigation, and technology, as well as a shared vision for long-term cooperative action, as the key areas for the negotiations. Trade linkages surfaced in various specific contexts, including in climate technology negotiations. Some developing countries, strongly opposed by major developed countries, have advocated taking advantage of provisions on compulsory licensing and other flexibilities in the TRIPS Agreement to make low-carbon technologies more accessible to developing countries. Such views emerged during the first round of negotiations on the Bali Action Plan in early 2008. Cuba, Tanzania, and India stressed the need to address intellectual property rights (IPRs) as barriers to technology transfer; Saudi Arabia identified compulsory licensing under the WTO TRIPS Agreement as an option to access climate-friendly technologies, suggesting such technologies should not necessarily be patented (ENB 2008b). The United States, in turn, emphasized IPRs were not a barrier but a catalyst for technology transfer, and said IPR critics were those very countries who have taken advantage of the IPR regime (ENB 2008b). The debate on the TRIPS Agreement, IPRs, and technology transfer under the UNFCCC then continued largely without resolution (ENB 2009d). To pave the way for agreement, references to the controversial issue of IPRs were dropped from the Cancún Agreements (UNFCCC 2010) at COP 16 in 2010. Bolivia, however, opposed the Cancún Agreements on various grounds, mentioning the lack of reference to intellectual property rights as one of the problems. The Agreements were adopted, despite Bolivia's objection (ENB 2010d).

Links between climate change mitigation and trade have also surfaced in other contexts during the ongoing long-term negotiations under the UNFCCC. Some developing countries have voiced serious concerns over trade measures contemplated by the United States and European Union against carbon-intensive imports from major developing countries to address concerns over economic competitiveness and environmental integrity. These debates intensified in the spring of 2009 after the United States outlined plans to launch a federal cap-and-trade scheme (ENB 2009a) and awareness grew that in the US domestic debate, measures targeting carbon-intensive imports from developing countries played an important role. Saudi Arabia highlighted the significant negative impacts of carbon taxes and tariffs, while India and others proposed prohibiting unilateral measures against exports from developing countries (ENB 2009c). Subsequently, China, supported by Saudi Arabia and Argentina, introduced text stating, inter alia, that "Annex I parties shall not resort to unilateral measures against imports from developing countries" and Saudi Arabia stressed that developed countries must not be allowed to use environmental protection as a pretext to impose tariffs or trade barriers (ENB 2009e.) On the other side of the controversy, the United States, Singapore, and Japan, enjoying support from many developed countries, maintained that UNFCCC Article 3.5 adequately addresses trade concerns (ENB 2009d). While the issue remains controversial, language on trade in the recent Cancún Agreements reflects the existing wording in UNFCCC Article 3.5 (ENB 2010d).

The negotiations have also witnessed some more fundamental debates over links between trade, markets, capitalism, and climate change mitigation. Countries belonging to the ALBA coalition (Bolivarian Alliance for the Americas[3]) have voiced ideological opposition to the use of carbon trading and market mechanisms as tools to mitigate climate change. While more moderate, many other developing countries have also expressed serious concerns over the emphasis by developed countries on market-based solutions and finance flowing from the

FIGURE 9.3 Bolivian President Evo Morales at COP 16 in Cancún in December 2010: We came to Cancún to save nature, forests and planet earth, not to convert nature into a commodity, not to revitalize capitalism with carbon markets.
Photo courtesy of IISD/*Earth Negotiations Bulletin*

private sector. In negotiations leading to the historic 2009 United Nations Climate Change Conference in Copenhagen, Venezuela highlighted a lack of consensus on the use of market mechanisms to mitigate climate change and Bolivia identified a structural link between climate change and markets (Figure 9.3). Venezuela also argued that trading obligations under the Convention are not consistent with the Convention's principles and called for principled discussions on the use of market mechanisms to mitigate climate change (ENB 2009e).

The question of market-based approaches was one of several issues that contributed to the failure of the Copenhagen Conference. The negotiating text on the table contained a number of proposals from both developed and developing countries concerning existing and new market mechanisms. However, during the final days of the Conference, Venezuela, with Angola for the African Group, highlighted the option in the negotiating text of not taking any decision on market approaches, while the United States stressed the centrality of market approaches. Ultimately, Venezuela (with Bolivia, Cuba, Nicaragua, and Tuvalu) opposed the adoption of the Copenhagen Accord, stressing that the accord had been negotiated by a non-transparent and unrepresentative group and that the parties did not give a mandate to the COP presidency to negotiate the accord (ENB 2009f).

Apart from ideological debates on the use of market mechanisms from a limited number of countries, discussions on climate change and trade under the UNFCCC have tended to move from a relatively abstract North–South debate in the 1990s toward the consideration of more specific proposals on facilitating access to climate technologies, prohibiting trade measures on developing county imports and the role of carbon trading in climate change mitigation. Despite its more detailed content, the debate remains politically sensitive and is, to a large extent, polarized along North–South lines.

Climate change has also raised its profile at the WTO. In 2009, UNEP and the WTO completed a widely publicized joint report on trade and climate change (WTO-UNEP 2009). There have also been attempts to find synergies between international climate change cooperation and trade liberalization. One example is trade liberalization for environmental goods and services under the Doha Round of trade negotiations, which could facilitate access to climate-friendly technologies for both adaptation and mitigation. This link between trade and climate change is increasingly relevant and the trade and climate communities have begun to look for synergies to make the two objectives—climate cooperation and trade liberalization—mutually supportive. At the same time, the broad range of possible policies and measures means that climate policies will need to be reconciled with the trade rules at some point. In other words, political debates over climate and trade are not likely to disappear.

Agriculture

Agriculture is critical to development prospects and poverty alleviation, but also is a key driver of many environmental problems. The agricultural sector, thus, illustrates an inherent tension between the different pillars of sustainable development. As a focus of the WTO and a cross-cutting issue in several MEAs, agriculture has been a central component of the trade and environment debate since UNCED. It links the sustainable development agenda from trade (subsidies and market access), environment (sustainable agricultural practices), and development (poverty alleviation, food security, energy poverty) perspectives. Agricultural policy has direct and indirect impacts on a range of issues, including biodiversity, deforestation, and climate change. The many developing countries that rely on agricultural exports to underpin economic growth and prosperity are at the forefront of adapting more integrated farming practices as a matter of necessity. This section outlines key issues linking the agricultural sector to the trade and environment discussions, arguing that the way in which agriculture is addressed under the multilateral environmental and trade regimes will influence effective outcomes in both arenas.

The Uruguay Round succeeded in bringing agriculture under the rules of the multilateral trading system to address trade-distorting subsidies in developed countries. Including environmental considerations in the negotiations in the WTO Agreement on Agriculture, however, complicated the issues even further, partly because developed countries use green measures as loopholes to continue subsidizing production.

The recent food crises and developments concerning biofuels and climate change mitigation have injected new dimensions into the discussions, while providing policy space to consider potentially mutually beneficial outcomes for development, trade, and the environment. Since its inception, there has been recognition in the WTO of the "triple win" opportunities from removing trade-distorting and environmentally harmful agricultural subsidies—with little movement to implement these outcomes. Capturing these potential benefits necessitates more holistic thinking, requiring a shift in the prevailing system that pits "agriculture for development" against "agriculture for environment" in a way that moves from focusing on the trade-offs to capturing the opportunities. The trade nexus has a role to play in reconciling these two divides and making agriculture part of the solution to the multiple challenges of sustainable development, rather than a part of the multiple problems.

Agriculture contributes to environmental concerns primarily due to *market failures*, whereby environmental costs of agricultural production are not taken into account or factored into prices. These are further compounded by *policy failures* related to both trade (subsidies) and environment (water, land, and biodiversity). Calling for a major adjustment to agricultural, environmental, and macroeconomic policy in developed and developing countries to create the conditions for sustainable agriculture and rural development, Agenda 21 identified the nature of these market and policy failures and suggested ways to get the prices right in the agricultural sector (United Nations 1992: see Chapter 2 on trade and Chapter 14 on agriculture). As reiterated during sessions of the UN Commission on Sustainable Development (CSD), UNCED supported reform of the international trading system in a twofold process: to reduce support and export subsidies in the agricultural sector, and to increase market access for developing countries. Discussions in the CSD have been consistently supportive of agricultural trade liberalization in the WTO. Delegates have systematically called for countries to fulfill their commitments to improve market access, specifically to phase out trade-distorting agricultural subsidies in the WTO (ENB 2009b).

In various multilateral processes, on the one hand, there is support for the WTO and recognition of the importance of enhanced market access and reduction in subsidies, especially for developing countries to achieve sustainable development. On the other hand, trade-offs cannot be avoided in achieving triple win outcomes. A transition to more resilient and sustainable agriculture involves less intensive agricultural production and new uses of agricultural land. Agriculture is one of the main drivers of deforestation, pitting agricultural development against forest and biodiversity conservation. In this context, forestry constitutes an important means of rural development either by afforestation of abandoned agricultural land or by employing existing forests for more than just timber production as well as consideration of environmental services (e.g., the role of forests in climate change mitigation). There is no area more controversial in this respect than multilateral negotiations related to forests. In this sense, tensions between trade and environment in the forestry or biodiversity sectors are strongly linked with agricultural trade. To this point, a delegate at the CSD session dedicated to agriculture questioned "how preservation of forests and agricultural development could be reconciled" (ENB 2009b).

Reconciliation between trade and environment is based first and foremost on coordination and common understanding. Coordination continues to improve both between different UN agencies and within countries. However, coordination does not mean that conflict disappears and consensus is achieved. Yet, it does help remove institutional barriers to reaching a common understanding on the optimal way to transition to more sustainable and resilient agricultural systems. It is interesting to note that the role of biofuels and agricultural trade was as controversial at the CSD and the World Food Security Conference as in the WTO (IISD RS 2008).

The prospects for achieving greater agricultural sustainability through the development agenda are linked, in turn, to a combination of both trade and environmental policies primarily for two reasons. First, in most developing countries, agriculture continues to account for 20 percent to 60 percent of gross domestic product and employs a significant portion of the labor force, particularly of the rural poor (De Schutter 2008). For low-income, resource-rich developing countries, agricultural exports are an important source of livelihoods. In this sense, poverty continues to exacerbate environmental degradation of land, forests, biodiversity, and water in developing countries. That is why ensuring market access in their main markets in the developed world is a prerequisite to address both poverty alleviation and environmental sustainability—a core message of the trade and environment debate since UNCED encapsulated in the concept of sustainable development or, more recently, the transition to a green economy (Cosbey 2011; ENB 2010b).

Second, market access is being driven by a growing array of environment-related conditions. As illustrated by the discussion above on GMOs and climate change, these standards are linked to the product itself (e.g., food safety and quality standards), as well as the production and processing methods used (e.g., energy efficiency). This is an aspect of the debate that is shifting the terms of engagement toward greater convergence over time, despite the continuing objections of many developing countries that trade-related environmental measures are unjustifiable barriers to trade. The market reality, however, is that even voluntary environmental labeling and certification effectively acts to restrict market access, as demonstrated by the work of the Forest Stewardship Council.

In the climate change debate, agriculture is at the same time a source of greenhouse gases and a sink enhancing their removals from the atmosphere. The emerging consensus in diverse multilateral fora ranging from the UNFCCC, the UN Forum on Forests, the World Food Security Conference, and the CSD, as well as the WTO, is that agriculture is as much a part of the problem as it is a component of the solution to climate change, especially in developing countries

FIGURE 9.4 Gerald Nelson, International Food Policy Research Institute, at a press briefing launching a report on food security and climate change during the Cancún Climate Change Conference in 2010. Photo courtesy of IISD/*Earth Negotiations Bulletin*

(ENB 2009b) (Figure 9.4). On the one hand, agriculture and other land-use change are responsible for nearly one-third of global greenhouse gas emissions, more than twice that of the transport sector (IPCC 2007). On the other hand, agriculture can contribute to sequestering carbon through sustainable farming practices, such as low tillage and restoration of degraded and saline land. Agriculture is one of the main drivers of deforestation in many countries, as forests are converted to produce food and other agricultural products. For example, rapid expansion of agriculture in Brazil, which has become a global bread basket and a major commodities trader over the past few decades, has been a key driver of deforestation. Deforestation, in turn, is the main source of Brazil's greenhouse gas emissions. Brazil's policy objective has been to enforce environmental legislation to curb illegal logging and reduce perverse incentives to clear cut forests to expand agricultural production. This policy response illustrates the way in which targeted policies are being used to address concerns in the context of global agricultural trade, deforestation, and climate change in an integrated manner—as called for at the Earth Summit two decades ago.

As more attention is given to developing agricultural systems on existing crop lands to help reduce poverty and food insecurity, and the pressure on forests, opportunities are emerging for triple win outcomes flowing from more resilient *climate-smart* agriculture—for adaptation, mitigation, and food security, starting with more efficient use of inputs and diffusion of technologies to farmers (Delgado 2011). In this context, for example, trade in genetically modified crops (as noted in the section on biodiversity above) may be seen in a more favorable light as more drought-tolerant crop varieties contribute to increasing the resilience of agriculture to climatic changes.

Despite the challenges to reaching consensus witnessed in multilateral fora, a new vision for agriculture is emerging from the interlinked global food, fuel, and financial crisis (ENB 2009b; IISD RS 2008). Empirical evidence confirms the importance of agriculture as an engine of growth, a tool for poverty reduction, and a critical entry point for environmental stewardship (UNF 2008). Recalling the report of the International Assessment of Agricultural Knowledge, Science and Technology for Development (IAASTD 2009), the CSD session devoted to agriculture in 2009 highlighted that the objective of agriculture goes beyond simply maximizing production, to optimize the sector's contribution to a more complex landscape of production, rural development, environment, and social justice outcomes (ENB 2009b).

In the energy debate, agriculture has thus acquired yet another dimension that further complicates the drivers facing global agricultural trade (FAO 2009). For those countries that rely on increasingly costly oil imports to underpin economic opportunities, lack of access to energy to meet basic needs—referred to as *energy poverty*—has significant impacts on livelihoods and the environment. As noted at the World Food Security Conference, this aspect emerged in the food crisis of 2008 and generated political and scientific controversy over the role of biofuels (Abdel Motaal 2008; Steenblik 2008) and, essentially, the use of agricultural crops as fuel in a world of growing food insecurity (FAO 2008; IISD RS 2008).

Negotiations related to agriculture also illustrate the challenges of coordination between negotiating fora and within national delegations—both by neglect (e.g., difficulty in bringing the relevant ministries to the negotiations) and by design (e.g., so-called forum shopping, whereby countries defend different positions in different bodies based on national interest) (see Chapter 2).

Agriculture is an area of the WTO where there was an immediate convergence between trade and environmental objectives through the removal of trade-distorting and environmentally harmful subsidies (Jones and Steenblik 2010). Despite the potential for complementarity, it has been difficult to implement the triple win opportunities for trade, environment, and development that were already identified at UNCED. Moreover, failure to get at the root of developing country concerns continues to push a solution to more specific issues beyond our collective grasp, whether at the WTO or pursuant to MEAs. As a direct result, trade is likely to exacerbate the prospects for short-run crop failures and long-run production declines, increasing concerns of food security, particularly in the most vulnerable countries. In this sense, agriculture has the potential to shift from being part of the problem to an essential element of the solution *if and only if* the essentially misplaced divide between trade and environment is addressed.

There is increasing recognition of a false divide in the agricultural sector precisely due to growing resource scarcity and declining environmental quality of inputs (i.e., water, forests, biodiversity, and land). The divide is false precisely because agriculture—as with environment as a whole—cannot be viewed in isolation from a holistic discussion of the three pillars of sustainable development.

Integration of trade and environment—in agriculture or other linked areas—is finding greater policy space and political will in the multilateral discourse, slowly but surely. As evidenced in the agricultural sector, trade and environmental policies need to go hand in hand in a mutually supportive manner to move toward sustainable development.

Trade and Environment: 1992–2012 …

Over the past twenty years, controversies relating to trade and environment have surfaced in multilateral negotiations, both under MEAs and under the WTO. In the 1990s, the trade and environment debate was more political and focused on general themes, such as the legality and economic desirability of environmentally motivated trade measures, or on the relationship between the WTO and MEAs in general. Toward the end of the 1990s and early 2000s, the focus gradually shifted toward finding ways to make the trade and environment regimes mutually compatible through a better understanding of the issues involved, and lowering some of the institutional barriers; for example, through the WTO Committee on Trade and Environment, and greater interaction between the WTO and MEA Secretariats (Najam et al. 2007). While some experts argue that the WTO has had a chilling effect on the use of trade measures in MEAs, effectively taking the bite out of environmental enforcement efforts, there is counter evidence that the trade rules have been interpreted to recognize a gradual accommodation of the multilateral environmental consensus.

Coordination of trade and environment in multilateral fora continues to be an issue in at least two aspects: (1) top-down coordination between different UN bodies working on related aspects of the topic area; and (2) bottom-up coordination at the national level to bring in the negotiating voice of trade ministries, environment ministries and—in the case of agriculture—agriculture ministries. As a direct reflection of the complexity and breadth of the discussion, "delegations of countries with a greater stake have grown to include trade, agriculture, environment and foreign affairs ministries" (ENB 2008a). That is to say, increasing technical emphasis has necessitated greater coordination.

Beyond the evident gap in coordination, there is a third and arguably more fundamental issue inhibiting greater consistency—competing objectives in the international arena. MEAs exist in an international arena that is not only focused on sustainable development. Whereas global environmental negotiations are generally propelled by cooperation toward a common environmental goal, the multilateral trading system operates mainly from a confrontational, mercantilist perspective.

That is to say, for example, that competition—not cooperation—in global agricultural markets underpins obligations in the WTO. As noted at the outset, discussion of trade-related issues in MEAs continues to be a sensitive area both in MEAs and in the WTO. This relates to the broader point made in this chapter with reference to coordination between MEAs and the WTO and the fact that the WTO has a legally binding enforcement mechanism with the authority to impose economic sanctions. This has led to the perception that resort to dispute settlement in the WTO acts as a trump card with respect to MEAs.

Over the past twenty years, greater transparency—notably through *Earth Negotiations Bulletin* coverage of these multilateral negotiations—has illuminated converging and, often, diverging discourses on trade and environment issues both between various fora and within national delegations. This has illuminated a continuing lack of coordination between international fora and within national delegations. This illustrates a lack of political will to devise strategies to increase policy coherence amongst competing issues on the international agenda—to effectively tackle the trade-offs and create opportunities to integrate trade and environment. Clearly, there are no quick fixes to integrating trade and environmental policies or greening the trading system. While progress on the substantive technical agenda is possible, as noted in the seminal report of the WTO Committee on Trade and Environment (WTO 1996), it remains difficult for countries to appreciate that improved trade opportunities—a vital component of their prospects for development or economic recovery—may be held to ransom in the process.

In sum, negotiations since 1992 have revealed difficulties in achieving greater coordination on trade and environment and are rooted in three basic factors: (1) the nature and design of the negotiating forum (i.e., based on cooperation or competition); (2) the interplay of national interests (i.e., linkages with other issues); and (3) the shifting negotiating dynamics and relative voice of developing countries; for example, on agriculture, forests, biodiversity, and climate change. In this respect, since the 1990s, developing countries have taken on a stronger voice commensurate with the increasing weight of emerging economies such as Brazil, China, and India. The coalition of these emerging economic powerhouses has shifted the priority toward sustaining growth and development through trade, with environment often a secondary consideration.

In more recent years, the debate has become less heated and more obvious. In other words, the parameters of the discourse, to a large extent, are now well established and widely accepted. With the evolution of environmental regimes, the focus has also shifted toward more technical questions, such as the compatibility of a particular MEA provision with a certain WTO agreement (e.g., the intersection between the Cartagena Protocol and the WTO SPS Agreement; or the compatibility of certain climate policies designed to implement the legally binding emission reduction targets under the Kyoto Protocol with WTO rules). There have also been more serious attempts to find synergies and win–win solutions, for instance, concerning trade and climate change (e.g., a WTO and UNEP joint report in 2009 put ideas forward under both the WTO and UNFCCC on lowering trade barriers for climate-friendly technologies). Biodiversity and agriculture illustrate the broadening of the trade and environment debate, precisely because environmental policy has increasingly become inseparable from economic and trade policy. Moreover, the economic stakes and trade implications of climate change linked with resource scarcity and loss of biodiversity and agricultural productivity are significant and growing. Our understanding of these costs is a driver for action to reconcile the trade and environment discourse.

This normalization of the discourse does not mean that either regime has emerged as superior or that concerns are not likely to arise anew. Many institutional discrepancies and barriers remain. As both environmental and trade law move into new areas, substantive controversies surrounding their governance and implementation will likely continue to emerge in an effort to balance the inevitable trade-offs in achieving sustainable development. The hope is that their consideration will be more nuanced and constructive, thereby reinforcing the notion that at least the dialogues on trade and environment can be mutually supportive.

... and Beyond

This chapter has highlighted three trends that are important for understanding the interplay of multilateral trade and environment negotiations. First, recognizing the multisectoral nature of environmental issues and the diverse international arena in which MEAs exist, one can expect that developing the broader linkages with economic and development issues will complicate multilateral environmental negotiations.

Second, this chapter illustrates that important political differences persist—particularly between, and, increasingly, amongst developed and developing countries, such as in environmental negotiations linked with the agricultural sector and concerning the use of trade measures to tackle climate change. Nevertheless, as a general point, since 1992 the trade and environment debate has gradually shifted from a politicized general discourse on broad themes and hypothetical conflicts toward a more technical discussion focusing on specific legal questions, economics, and implementation.

Third, there continues to be a legal and institutional separation of trade and environment regimes, despite significant improvement in coordination and coherence at different levels on various aspects of the trade and environment debate. This is why interaction between the environmental and trade regimes continues to be controversial. At the national level, lack of coordination exists both between different ministries and different fora. At the international level, communication between the secretariats of trade and environmental agreements is limited to informal exchanges or the lengthy negotiation of formal decision language.

These illustrative trends suggest that the trade and environment debate is likely to remain firmly on the international agenda, with controversies continuing to emerge in the negotiations both under MEAs and at the WTO. The discourse surrounding the transition to a green economy and an ever-increasing focus on private sector involvement also suggest that there is money to be made in being green, which may help move the trade–environment debate from its zero-sum roots to a more complex interplay of interests that can realize gains on both sides of the policy debate. These gains are not likely to come without scrutiny or criticism, as illustrated by the early forays of biotechnology company investment in developing countries. Further integration of trade and environment requires finding policy space and political will in the multilateral discourse, both out of design and necessity. Over the past twenty years, the horizon for the trade and environment discourse has broadened to include larger issues relating to globalization. To this end, strengthening global environmental governance in a way that reinforces the synergies between trade and environmental policymaking should be high on the agenda of Rio+20 and for years to come.

Notes

1 Principle 12 of the Rio Declaration provides, inter alia, that: Trade policy measures for environmental purposes should not constitute a means of arbitrary or unjustifiable discrimination or a disguised restriction on international trade. Unilateral actions to deal with environmental challenges outside the jurisdiction of the importing country should be avoided. Environmental measures addressing transboundary or global environmental problems should, as far as possible, be based on an international consensus.
2 Detailed rules on the implementation of the Protocol were agreed in 2001 in a package known as the Marrakesh Accords. They were formally adopted by CMP in 2005. Decisions 1- 36/CMP.1, in FCCC/KP/CMP/2005/8/Adds.1–4, 30 March 2006.
3 ALBA members include Antigua and Barbuda, Bolivia, Cuba, Dominica, Ecuador, Nicaragua, St. Vincent and the Grenadines, and Venezuela.

Works Cited

Abdel Motaal, Doaa. 2008. The Biofuels Landscape: Is There a Role for the WTO? *Journal of World Trade* 42(1): 61–86.
Cosbey, Aaron. 2011. Trade, Sustainable Development and a Green Economy: Benefits, Challenges and Risks. In *Report by a Panel of Experts to the Second Preparatory Committee Meeting for the UN Conference on Sustainable Development*. Geneva: United Nations Conference on Trade and Development and United Nations Environment Programme. http://www.uncsd2012.org/rio20/index.php?page=view&type=400&nr=12&menu=45 (accessed June 17, 2011).
Delgado, Christopher. 2011. Food Security: The Need for Multilateral Action. In *Post-Crisis Growth and Development: A Development Agenda for the G20*. Edited by Shahrokh Fardoust, Yongbeom Kim, and Claudia Sepúlveda. Washington, DC: World Bank.

De Schutter, Olivier. 2008. *Statement of the Special Rapporteur on the Right to Food*. Rome: Food and Agriculture Organization of the United Nations (18 November).

ENB (*Earth Negotiations Bulletin*). 1995a. Report of the Second Meeting of the Conference of the Parties to the Convention on Biological Diversity: 6–17 November 1995. *Earth Negotiations Bulletin* 9(39). http://www.iisd.ca/download/pdf/enb0939e.pdf (accessed February 27, 2011).

ENB. 1995b. Report of the Second Session of the Ad Hoc Group on the Berlin Mandate: 30 October–3 November 1995. *Earth Negotiations Bulletin* 12(24). http://www.iisd.ca/download/pdf/enb1224e.pdf (accessed March 1, 2011).

ENB. 1996. Report of the Third Session of the Ad Hoc Group on the Berlin Mandate: 5–8 March 1996. *Earth Negotiations Bulletin* 12(27). http://www.iisd.ca/download/pdf/enb1227e.pdf (accessed March 1, 2011).

ENB. 1997. Report of the Meeting of the FCCC Subsidiary Bodies: 20–31 October 1997. *Earth Negotiations Bulletin* 12(66). http://www.iisd.ca/download/pdf/enb1266e.pdf (accessed March 1, 2011).

ENB. 1998. Summary of the Fourth Meeting of the Conference of the Parties to the Convention on Biological Diversity: 4–15 May 1998. *Earth Negotiations Bulletin* 9(96). http://www.iisd.ca/download/pdf/enb0996e.pdf (accessed February 27, 2011).

ENB. 1999a. Briefing Note on the Informal Consultations Regarding the Resumed Session of the Extraordinary Meeting of the Conference of the Parties for the Adoption of the Protocol on Biosafety to the Convention on Biological Diversity: 15–19 September 1999. http://www.iisd.ca/biodiv/bswg6/excop_informals.html (accessed February 27, 2011).

ENB. 1999b. Report of the Sixth Extraordinary Sessions of the Open-Ended Ad Hoc Working Group on Biosafety and the First Extraordinary Session of the CBD Conference of the Parties: 14–23 February 1999. *Earth Negotiations Bulletin* 9(117). http://www.iisd.ca/download/pdf/enb09117e.pdf (accessed February 27, 2011).

ENB. 2000a. Report of the Resumed Session of the Extraordinary Meeting of the Conference of the Parties for the Adoption of the Protocol on Biosafety to the Convention on Biological Diversity: 24–28 January 2000. *Earth Negotiations Bulletin* 9(137). http://www.iisd.ca/download/pdf/enb09137e.pdf (accessed February 27, 2011).

ENB. 2000b. CSD Intersessional Working Group: Wednesday, 23 February 2000. *Earth Negotiations Bulletin* 5(135). http://www.iisd.ca/download/pdf/enb05135e.pdf (accessed June 17, 2011).

ENB. 2000c. Fifth Meeting of the Conference of the Parties to the Convention on Biological Diversity: 15–26 May 2000. *Earth Negotiations Bulletin* 9(160). http://www.iisd.ca/download/pdf/enb09160e.pdf (accessed June 17, 2011).

ENB. 2000d. Summary of the Eighth Session of the UN Commission Sustainable Development: 24 April–5 May 2000. *Earth Negotiations Bulletin* 5(157). http://www.iisd.ca/download/pdf/enb05157e.pdf (accessed March 1, 2011).

ENB. 2001. Summary of the Second Experts Panel Meeting on Access and Benefit-sharing: 19–22 March 2001. *Earth Negotiations Bulletin* 9(190). http://www.iisd.ca/download/pdf/enb09190e.pdf (accessed March 1, 2011).

ENB. 2002a. Sixth Meeting of the Conference of the Parties to the Convention on Biological Diversity: 7–19 April 2002. *Earth Negotiations Bulletin* 9(239). http://www.iisd.ca/download/pdf/enb09239e.pdf (accessed February 27, 2011).

ENB. 2002b. Summary of the World Summit on Sustainable Development: 26 August–4 September 2002. *Earth Negotiations Bulletin* 22(51). http://www.iisd.ca/download/pdf/enb2251e.pdf (accessed March 1, 2011).

ENB. 2006. Summary of the Fourth Meeting of the Working Group on Access and Benefit-Sharing of the Convention on Biological Diversity: 30 January–3 February 2006.

Earth Negotiations Bulletin 9(344). http://www.iisd.ca/download/pdf/enb09344e.pdf (accessed June 6, 2011).

ENB. 2008a. Summary of the Fifth Meeting of the Open-ended Ad Hoc Working Group of Legal and Technical Experts on Liability and Redress in the Context of the Cartagena Protocol on Biosafety: 12–19 March 2008. *Earth Negotiations Bulletin* 9(435). http://www.iisd.ca/download/pdf/enb09435e.pdf (accessed March 1, 2011).

ENB. 2008b. Summary of the First Session of the Ad Hoc Working Group on Long-term Cooperative Action under the UNFCCC and the Fifth Session of the Ad Hoc Working Group on Further Commitments by Annex I Parties under the Kyoto Protocol: 31 March–4 April 2008. *Earth Negotiations Bulletin* 12(362). http://www.iisd.ca/download/pdf/enb12362e.pdf (accessed March 1, 2011).

ENB. 2009a. Summary of the Fifth Session of the Ad Hoc Working Group on Long-term Cooperative Action and the Seventh Session of the Ad Hoc Working Group on Further Commitments for Annex I Parties under the Kyoto Protocol: 29 March–8 April 2009. *Earth Negotiations Bulletin* 12(407). http://www.iisd.ca/vol12/enb12407e.html (accessed March 1, 2011).

ENB. 2009b. Summary of the Seventeenth Session of the Commission on Sustainable Development: 4–15 May 2009. *Earth Negotiations Bulletin* 5(281). http://www.iisd.ca/download/pdf/enb05281e.pdf (accessed March 1, 2011).

ENB. 2009c. Summary of the Bonn Climate Change Talks: 1–12 June 2009. *Earth Negotiations Bulletin* 12(421). http://www.iisd.ca/download/pdf/enb12421e.pdf (accessed March 1, 2011).

ENB. 2009d. Summary of the Bonn Climate Change Talks: 10–14 August 2009. *Earth Negotiations Bulletin* 12(427). http://www.iisd.ca/download/pdf/enb12427e.pdf (accessed March 1, 2011).

ENB. 2009e. Summary of the Bangkok Climate Change Talks: 28 September–9 October 2009. *Earth Negotiations Bulletin* 12(439). http://www.iisd.ca/download/pdf/enb12439e.pdf (accessed March 1, 2011).

ENB. 2009f. Summary of the Copenhagen Climate Change Conference: 7–19 December 2009. *Earth Negotiations Bulletin* 12(459). http://www.iisd.ca/download/pdf/enb12459e.pdf (accessed March 1, 2011).

ENB. 2010a. Summary of the Ninth Meeting of the Working Group on Access and Benefit-Sharing of the Convention on Biological Diversity: 22–28 March 2010. *Earth Negotiations Bulletin* 9(503). http://www.iisd.ca/download/pdf/enb09503e.pdf (accessed June 6, 2011).

ENB. 2010b. Summary of the Eighteenth Session of the Commission on Sustainable Development: 3–14 May 2010. *Earth Negotiations Bulletin* 5(292). http://www.iisd.ca/download/pdf/enb05292e.pdf (accessed March 1, 2011).

ENB. 2010c. Summary of the Fifth Meeting of the Parties to the Cartagena Protocol on Biosafety: 11–15 October 2010. *Earth Negotiations Bulletin* 9(533). http://www.iisd.ca/download/pdf/enb09533e.pdf (accessed February 28, 2011).

ENB. 2010d. Summary of the UN Climate Change Conference in Cancún: 29 November–11 December 2010. *Earth Negotiations Bulletin* 12(488). http://www.iisd.ca/download/pdf/enb12498e.pdf (accessed March 1, 2011).

Esty, Daniel. 1994. *Greening the GATT: Trade, Environment and the Future.* Washington, DC: Institute for International Economics.

FAO. 2008. *State of Food and Agriculture—Biofuels: Prospects, Risks and Opportunities.* Rome: Food and Agriculture Organization of the United Nations.

FAO. 2009. *The State of Food Insecurity and the World.* Rome: Food and Agriculture Organization of the United Nations.

GATT. 1991. US—Restrictions on Imports of Tuna. Panel report BISD 39S/155 (September 3). Unadopted.

IAASTD. 2009. *Agriculture at a Crossroads.* Washington, DC: Island Press.

IISD RS (International Institute for Sustainable Development Reporting Services). 2008. Report of the High-Level Conference on World Food Security: The Challenges of Climate Change and Bioenergy: 5 June 2008. *High-Level Conference on World Food Security Bulletin* 150(1). http://www.iisd.ca/download/pdf/sd/ymbvol150num1e.pdf (accessed February 18, 2011).

IPCC. 2007. *Climate Change 2007 Synthesis Report: Summary for Policymakers.* http://www.ipcc.ch/pdf/assessment-report/ar4/syr/ar4_syr_spm.pdf (accessed June 17, 2011).

Jones, Darryl and Ronald Steenblik (eds.). 2010. *Subsidies Manual.* Geneva: Global Subsidies Initiative, International Institute for Sustainable Development.

Marceau, Gabrielle. 1999. A Call for Coherence in International Law—Praises for the Prohibition against "Clinical Isolation" in WTO Dispute Settlement. *Journal of World Trade* 33(5): 87–152.

Najam, Adil, Mark Halle, and Ricardo Melendez Ortiz. 2007. *Trade and Environment: A Resource Book.* Winnipeg and Geneva: International Institute for Sustainable Development and the International Centre for Trade and Sustainable Development. http://www.iisd.org/pdf/2007/trade_and_env.pdf (accessed June 17, 2011).

Steenblik, Ronald. 2008. *Biofuels: Is the Cure Worse than the Disease?* Paris: Organization for Economic Cooperation and Development.

UNF (United Nations Foundation). 2008. *Sustainable Bioenergy Development in the West African Economic and Monetary Union Member Countries.* Washington, DC: UNF. http://www.unfoundation.org/press-center/publications/sustainable-bioenergy-report.html (accessed March 28, 2011).

UNFCCC. 2007. Report of the Conference of the Parties on its Thirteenth Session, Held in Bali from 3 to 15 December 2007: Addendum (FCCC/CP/2007/6/Add.1). http://unfccc.int/resource/docs/2007/cop13/eng/06a01.pdf (accessed June 17, 2011).

UNFCCC. 2010. Report of the Conference of the Parties on its Sixteenth Session, Held in Cancún from 29 November to 10 December 2010: Addendum (FCCC/CP/2010/7/Add.1). http://unfccc.int/resource/docs/2010/cop16/eng/07a01.pdf (accessed March 28, 2011).

United Nations. 1992. *Agenda 21.* New York: United Nations.

WTO. 1995. Marrakesh Agreement Establishing the World Trade Organization. Geneva: WTO. http://www.wto.org/english/docs_e/legal_e/04-wto.pdf (accessed June 17, 2011).

WTO. 1996. Report of the WTO Committee on Trade and Environment to the Singapore Ministerial Conference. Geneva: WTO.

WTO. 2001. Doha Ministerial Declaration of 14 November (WT/MIN(01)/DEC,/1) 20 November. http://www.wto.org/english/thewto_e/minist_e/min01_e/mindecl_e.htm (accessed June 17, 2011).

WTO Appellate Body. 1998. European Community—Measures Concerning Meat and Meat Products (WT/DS26/AB/R and WT/DS/48/AB/R) 16 January.

WTO Appellate Body. 2001. United States—Import Prohibition of Certain Shrimp and Shrimp Products, Recourse to Article 21.5 of the DSU by Malaysia (WT/DS58/AB/RW) 22 October.

WTO Dispute Settlement Panel. 2006. *European—Measures Affecting the Approval and Marketing of Biotech Products* (WT/DS291/R, WT/DS292/R, WT/DS293/R) 29 September.

WTO-UNEP. 2009. *Trade and Climate Change.* Geneva: WTO. http://www.wto.org/english/res_e/booksp_e/trade_climate_change_e.pdf (accessed March 28, 2011).

10

CLIMATE CHANGE BANDWAGONING

Climate Change Impacts on Global Environmental Governance[1]

Sikina Jinnah and Alexandra Conliffe

The political landscape that surrounds global environmental issues has become increasingly crowded since 1992 when the Earth Summit focused the international spotlight on a variety of widely shared environmental challenges. Hundreds of existing bilateral, regional, and global environmental agreements now challenge countries' capacities to allocate adequate resources to effectively participate in this increasingly chaotic international political space (Chasek 2001; Najam 2005). Further stressing already-overburdened countries, many of these environmental agreements deal independently with related and/or linked issues. These activities, carried out in parallel rather than in tandem, have led to duplication of effort, further stretching already-scarce problem-solving resources. Resulting in part from these two factors, many environmental agreements now suffer incomplete or weak implementation, with financial resources falling short of problem-solving needs and objectives (see Chapter 2).

From the midst of this crowded political landscape, climate change issues have gained significant political importance and have attracted an unprecedented amount of media attention and resources for mitigation and adaptation-related initiatives. As a result, actors working on many other international environmental issues have tried to strategically link their activities to climate change. Reflecting this trend, it is now difficult to find an international organization, corporation, non-governmental organization (NGO), university, foundation, religious organization, or government agency that does not have a climate-relevant program or focus. Indeed, with over 1,300 observers now accredited to attend the United Nations Framework Convention on Climate Change (UNFCCC) negotiations (UNFCCC 2010), representing over twenty-two issue areas (Muñoz 2011), it seems that everyone from OPEC to Oxfam is jumping on the proverbial climate change bandwagon.

This chapter argues that climate bandwagoning has altered global environmental governance by influencing pathways charted by a wide variety of environmental treaties and regimes. According to Jinnah (2011a), climate bandwagoning occurs when linking agents purposefully expand an international treaty or regime's mission to include new climate-oriented goals, typically by foregrounding potential climate mitigation or adaptation benefits of these linkages. Linking agents usually bandwagon because they believe that doing so will further their own agendas, regardless of whether the linkages detract from the common good (Jinnah 2011a). Thus, while bandwagoning can make good sense when climate change and the linking regime's environmental issue are interconnected, we demonstrate here that linking agents often bandwagon for a variety of other reasons too.

In the sections that follow, we first introduce four case studies—desertification, biodiversity, deforestation, and ozone—to reflect on *how* and *why* bandwagoning occurs. We chose our case studies to include both major environmental issues in the UN system as well as examples that demonstrate different styles of bandwagoning and different impacts. The analysis draws together the lessons learned from the cases and helps to illuminate when bandwagoning makes sense, when it can have negative effects, and what to strive for in the future as we necessarily continue to build linkages between multilateral environmental agreements (MEAs).

Case Studies: Bandwagoning on the Ground

Desertification[2]

Historical Context

The UN Convention to Combat Desertification (UNCCD) is the only UN convention to explicitly address land. While its sister Rio Conventions on biodiversity and climate change were created to address what, at that time, were largely developed country *environmental* concerns, it was developing countries that pushed for the negotiation of the UNCCD. Apprehensive that newly established MEAs were neglecting the very real *development* challenges caused by disastrous droughts such as those in the Sahel in the 1970s, and that attempts by the UN to address desertification and drought since the 1970s had been inadequate, African countries, in particular, pressed for establishing the UNCCD (Chasek 1997).

Bandwagoning Evolution

The UNCCD has always engaged in bandwagoning. Its dual development–environment focus necessitates linkages across regimes that address a wide variety of cross-cutting issues, including climate change, biodiversity loss, poverty, poor health and nutrition, food insecurity, and environmental migration and displacement

(UNCCD 1994, Article 2). Moreover, frequently called the "poor sister" of the Rio Conventions, the UNCCD has seen bandwagoning as critical for mobilizing finances to combat desertification. Unsurprisingly then, negotiators have called for linkages to anything from the World Trade Organization (ENB 2000) to the Millennium Development Goals (ENB 2003) and the Ramsar Convention on Wetlands (ENB 2007a).

At COP 1, some delegates breathed a sigh of relief that "the process of combating desertification has reached its most important phase: implementation" (ENB 1997). But in 2007, more than ten years after the UNCCD's adoption, UNCCD parties were still talking about moving "from assessment to action" (ENB 2007a). Warned by an external review by the UN Joint Inspection Unit that without significant reforms the UNCCD might slip into "sclerosis" (Ortiz and Tang 2005, 9), parties adopted a ten-year strategy to enhance the convention's implementation (the strategy). As part of a broad package of reforms, the strategy seeks to "actively influence relevant international ... processes and actors in adequately addressing [desertification]" (UNCCD 2007, 8). In short, the strategy re-emphasizes the importance of bandwagoning.

Also in 2007, Al Gore and the Intergovernmental Panel on Climate Change (IPCC) jointly won the Nobel Peace Prize, and UNFCCC parties established the Ad Hoc Working Group on Long-term Cooperative Action under the UNFCCC to negotiate a potential post-2012 climate regime. Hoping to cash in on some of the political and financial attention that climate change was garnering, and believing that a new round of climate change negotiations constituted good timing to do so, the UNCCD Secretariat took its mandate of actively influencing relevant international processes and engaged in what we consider a "classical" bandwagoning strategy. Specifically, the UNCCD Secretariat sought to demonstrate to UNFCCC parties how activities that combat desertification also have climate change benefits.

The UNCCD Secretariat has pursued a wide range of desertification–climate change linkages, searching for one that "sticks" (Conliffe 2011). Between 2007 and 2009, the UNCCD Secretariat recognized that funding for climate change mitigation exceeded that for adaptation. Accordingly, it sought to convince UNFCCC parties that activities to combat desertification can also help mitigate climate change. Stressing that these linkages were scientifically based (ENB 2007b), it promoted key findings from the 2005 Millennium Ecosystem Assessment (MA), including estimates that 4 percent of global carbon emissions result from desertification in drylands and that restoring degraded lands can enhance soil carbon sequestration and thus help mitigate climate change (MA 2005).

Having presented the science, the Secretariat sought to unleash financing from the carbon markets into the drylands by lobbying to include new Land Use, Land-Use Change, and Forestry (LULUCF) activities under a post-2012 market mechanism (afforestation and reforestation are the only LULUCF activities eligible under the Kyoto Protocol's Clean Development Mechanism (CDM)).

In addition to broader inclusion of agricultural activities, at a side event at UNFCCC COP 13 in Bali in 2007, the UNCCD Secretariat pitched the inclusion of biochar, a soil carbon enhancing technology, for inclusion under the CDM. A UNCCD representative passionately argued that the additionality and permanence of sequestration from biochar were assured and the baseline simple (ENB 2007b). Policymakers within the UNFCCC have largely deplored efforts by biochar advocates to scale up a technology that requires more research (Conliffe 2011).

Following the 2009 Copenhagen climate change talks, the UNCCD Secretariat realized that issues related to permanence and leakage from soil carbon—among other issues (Conliffe 2011)—make LULUCF's inclusion in post-2012 market mechanisms highly uncertain.[3] Simultaneously, it noticed that funding for, and attention to, adaptation—previously second fiddle to mitigation (Schipper 2006)—were on the rise. Starting in 2010, when parties took note of the Copenhagen Accord, the UNCCD Secretariat shifted its attention to desertification–adaptation linkages (Conliffe 2011). While the UNFCCC text highlights that dryland populations are among the most vulnerable to climate change impacts (UNFCCC 1992), the UNCCD Secretariat in particular seized on language in the 2009 Copenhagen Accord which states that developing countries most vulnerable to the impacts of climate change need urgent assistance to adapt to climate change (2/CP.15). The UNCCD Secretariat wants to ensure that adaptation funding indeed flows to these regions.

Bandwagoning Evaluation

Desertification–climate change linkages make sense when they help to combat desertification and mitigate and/or adapt to climate change. Unfortunately, in its desire to tap financial resources, the UNCCD Secretariat has sometimes advocated linkages that may not yield the desired results. While scientific evidence suggests that restoring degraded drylands (i.e., combating desertification) may sequester large amounts of carbon (i.e., contribute to climate change mitigation), important uncertainties and controversies remain. The long-term sequestration potential of soils remains contested (see Gutierrez 2007 for an overview of this literature). Whether linkages to carbon markets would unleash financial flows to poor dryland farmers, how it would affect their behaviors, and whether this would indeed incentivize activities that result in enhanced soil carbon sequestration remains uncertain, a point the UNCCD Secretariat now seems more willing to concede (UNDP, UNCCD, and UNEP 2009). The potential environment and development impacts of large-scale biochar promotion are particularly uncertain; even advocates agree that there exists insufficient science to justify scaling up at this time (Conliffe 2011).

That the UNCCD Secretariat has tried to advance desertification–climate change linkages for which sound science remains underdeveloped (as yet), and that could potentially exacerbate climate change and desertification, brings into question whether the secretariat is seeking linkages that will help it to better address interlinked environmental challenges or whether it is seeking financial resources for institutional survival, irrespective of problem-solving impacts. In this regard, its more recent attempts to establish desertification–adaptation linkages are more promising. That adaptation is core to addressing climate change and combating desertification is virtually uncontested (UNCCD 1994; UNFCCC 1992). Many countries identified as requiring urgent adaptation support under the Copenhagen Accord (and subsequently the Cancún Agreements) encompass drylands; the foundation for desertification–adaptation linkages is thus solid. Furthermore, many socioeconomic factors that undermine populations' adaptive capacities are beyond the UNFCCC's scope (Schipper 2006). Therefore, the UNFCCC will need support to implement adaptation effectively. The UNCCD should be well positioned to offer this support; it is founded on the very bottom-up principles, including its livelihoods approach and the value it attributes to traditional knowledge and participatory processes (UNCCD 1994), that the IPCC highlights as critical to successful adaptation implementation (Adger et al. 2007).

The UNCCD case suggests that climate bandwagoning founded on uncertain science for the sake of mobilizing resources can have negative consequences. At best, it is a waste of resources (to date, the UNCCD Secretariat's attempts have yielded no tangible results). At worst, such linkages can exacerbate the very environmental challenges they were intended to address, potentially tarring the reputations of the institutions established to address them.

Biodiversity

Historical Context

Global biodiversity governance is extremely diffuse. It is scattered across over 200 multilateral agreements (Mitchell 2002–2010), dealing with a wide range of specific issues surrounding species and habitat loss. The Convention on Biological Diversity (CBD), which emerged in 1992, is essentially (albeit unofficially) a framework convention, as its norms and goals encompass and expand upon other international biodiversity agreements (Figure 10.1). Specifically, the CBD aims to ensure: conservation of biodiversity; sustainable use of its resources; and equitable sharing of benefits arising from the use of biodiversity. As the de facto hub of the biodiversity "regime complex" (Raustiala and Victor 2004), we focus our attention on the CBD.

Bandwagoning Evolution

Much like those observed in the UNCCD, the CBD Secretariat's bandwagoning efforts constitute a "classical" case wherein a weaker regime goes to great lengths

FIGURE 10.1 Ahmed Djoghlaf, Executive-Secretary, Convention on Biological Diversity, and Luc Gnacadja, Executive-Secretary, UN Convention to Combat Desertification, at the Cancún Climate Change Conference in 2010. Photo courtesy of IISD/*Earth Negotiations Bulletin*

to strategically forge linkages to a stronger one with the intention of accruing institutional and problem-solving benefits. Largely "marketed" by the CBD Secretariat and, in some instances, scientists, these linkages fall into four general categories: (1) climate change negatively impacts biodiversity; (2) conservation helps people adapt to climate change; (3) conservation-based adaptation enhances human security; and (4) inadequately conceived climate change mitigation activities can negatively impact biodiversity (Jinnah 2011b).[4]

Scientific linkages demonstrating that climate change negatively impacts biodiversity are clear and well established. After habitat loss, climate change will likely become the leading cause of biodiversity loss in coming years (MA 2005). By increasing the frequency of extreme weather events, heating ocean waters, inundating coastal areas, and altering the availability of freshwater supplies, climate change is expected to test the resilience capacity of many species. Given these documented scientific linkages, the CBD has addressed the effects of climate change on biodiversity loss in regular COP decisions, beginning in 1998 at COP 4 with a decision on the impacts of climate change on coral reefs.

By 2007 at the twelfth CBD Subsidiary Body on Scientific, Technical and Technological Advice (SBSTTA) meeting in Paris, France, scientific information about the biodiversity–climate linkage was prolific. Politically, however, parties were divided over how to frame the linkage, in particular over the appropriate way to discuss mitigation and adaptation within the CBD, and if and/or how to cooperate with the UNFCCC on these issues. Although they could not agree on how, this meeting nevertheless highlighted that parties to the CBD wanted to ramp up climate bandwagoning. Yet despite the prominence of climate issues on the agenda, no UNFCCC representatives attended this meeting. Some delegates noted that this was because the UNFCCC lacked a mandate to cooperate with the CBD, and was less enthusiastic to do so because of the CBD's scarce resources (ENB 2007b). Particularly notable was one delegate who said the UNFCCC COP saw the CBD as having "climate envy," seeking operational linkages to tap into the climate change spotlight (ENB 2007b).

As discussed in Chapter 6, the then new CBD Executive-Secretary, Ahmed Djoghlaf, played an important role in this process, attempting to shift the discourse from the dominant "climate impacts on biodiversity" to one that foregrounds climate impacts on culture and food security, and later the role of biodiversity in climate adaptation.

Rather than passively focusing on the impacts of climate change on biodiversity loss and lobbying exclusively for mitigation under the UNFCCC, in recent years the CBD Secretariat has shifted its discourse to highlight the capacity of conservation itself to aid in mitigation and adaptation. Indeed, Jinnah's analysis of CBD Executive-Secretary Djoghlaf's public speeches reveals a trend in linkage framings away from exclusive focus on climate impacts on biodiversity toward one that includes the role of, for example, wetland conservation in human adaptation and forest conservation in carbon mitigation (2011b).

In addition to highlighting conservation's potential contribution to mitigation and adaptation, the CBD Secretariat has also begun to strategically use the discourse of human security to explain the implications of the biodiversity-climate linkage. After clearly establishing the link between climate change and biodiversity loss, the CBD Secretariat's discourse has increasingly related this linkage to human security concerns such as freshwater access and resiliency of agricultural systems. In its aim of decreasing human vulnerability to climate impacts, adaptation is implicitly bound up with ideas of human security (Detraz 2011). The CBD Secretariat's strategic use of a human security discourse is notable, however, because it moves beyond discussions of this topic in the UNFCCC, which tends to avoid a security discourse and, critically, because it aims to explicitly *humanize* biodiversity loss. In so doing, the Secretariat reconstructs this issue as one that impacts people rather than solely non-human systems, which have understandably been lower on the priority list for many developing countries. This reframing of biodiversity is critical to overcoming the "priorities barrier" that has stymied many countries' interest in substantively addressing biodiversity loss under the CBD or elsewhere (Jinnah 2011b).

The more recent discussions surrounding the linkages between biodiversity and climate change within the CBD have refocused attention on the potentially negative impacts of climate mitigation activities under the UNFCCC on biodiversity. Specifically, CBD climate linkage discussions in recent years have revolved around issues such as biofuel production, geo-engineering, and reducing emissions from deforestation and forest degradation in developing countries (REDD) (ENB 2008, 2010a). Whereas both of these activities have attracted much attention for their potential climate mitigation benefits,[5] they each also present potential dangers to biological (and social) systems depending on how they are implemented (Fargione et al. 2008; Righelato and Spracklen 2007). For example, increased demand for biofuels has resulted in the clearing of tropical forests for palm plantations (Danielsen et al. 2009), and conservation of high carbon forests does not always correlate with high priority conservation areas (Wright and Jinnah 2010). Ongoing discussions within the CBD are focused on ameliorating these impacts, as well as on the role of biodiversity in contributing to climate change mitigation and adaptation. For example, at CBD COP 10 in Nagoya, Japan, the COP requested that the Secretariat convene an expert working group to explore the latter, and passed a de facto moratorium on geo-engineering (ENB 2010a) (Figure 10.2).

Bandwagoning Evaluation

Because biodiversity and climate change are closely linked, fostering political linkages is logical and imperative. However, the *way* in which these linkages are created has important implications for both regimes. Whereas "climate change

FIGURE 10.2 At the fourteenth meeting of the CBD's Subsidiary Body on Scientific, Technical and Technological Advice in 2010, a side-event looked at geo-engineering and the challenges faced by the CBD. Photo courtesy of IISD/*Earth Negotiations Bulletin*

causes biodiversity loss" and "mitigation measures can cause biodiversity loss" are robust and well-established linkages that biodiversity actors should continue to reiterate, other linkage frames stand on less solid ground.[6]

Specifically, as in the desertification case above, it remains unclear if framing biodiversity conservation as a promising adaptive safeguard is fully accurate (Thomas et al. 2004; Worm et al. 2006). Similarly, with respect to human security, it has not yet been established that increased species diversity will necessarily lead to livelihood benefits (Lewis and Antony 2010). As in the desertification case, over-emphasizing open scientific debates may be dangerous because it could arguably fuel the flames of climate skepticism in the aftermath of "Climategate" and other attacks on the climate science community.

Deforestation

Historical Context

Global forest management ostensibly began in 1945 with the establishment of the UN Food and Agriculture Organization (FAO) and its Committee on Forestry, which held its first meeting in 1972. Since then, much effort has been focused on forest issues, with a plethora of public and private initiatives and bodies emerging to guide forest management, including: the International Tropical Timber Agreement (1983); the Tropical Forest Action Plan (1985); Agenda 21's Chapter 11 on "Combating Deforestation" (1992); private certification systems such as the Forest Stewardship Council (FSC); and the United Nations Forum on Forests (UNFF) (2000).

Despite this crowded governance space, UN forest governance, comprising the UNFF and its predecessors—the Intergovernmental Panel on Forests (1995–1997) and the Intergovernmental Forum on Forests (1997–2000)—has failed to deliver a legally binding convention.[7] Rather, to a much greater extent than observed in the other cases examined here, non-state, market-driven governance systems have proliferated to fill this governance gap. Chief among these are voluntary forest certification schemes, such as the FSC, which employs mostly performance-based standards to assess ecological and social impacts of forest management systems (Gulbrandsen 2004). However, these schemes have also fallen short in adequately addressing global forest loss, in part because they do not fully integrate the drivers of deforestation into governance approaches and objectives (McDermott et al. 2011).

Bandwagoning Evolution

This failure in international cooperation has created a ripe policy space for forest–climate bandwagoning. As opposed to the CBD and UNCCD cases, however, advocates for forest conservation have not had to bang quite as loudly at the

UNFCCC's door, jockeying for negotiator time and attention. Rather, forest issues have in many ways been subsumed into the UNFCCC's ongoing work. Forest–climate linkages have manifested within the UNFCCC in three ways: (1) LULUCF activities in developed countries; (2) afforestation and reforestation projects under the CDM; and (3) the evolving mechanism for REDD+ in developing countries. Since REDD+ discussions have garnered the most interest within the UNFCCC and CBD, we focus on this forest–climate linkage.

By incentivizing developing countries not to cut down their trees, REDD+ aims to create a framework to reduce emissions from deforestation and forest degradation. REDD-related discussions began in 2005 with a proposal to UNFCCC COP 11 by Papua New Guinea, Costa Rica, and others. The mechanism became fully integrated into the UNFCCC negotiations, with a decision at COP 13 in 2007. In negotiations on long-term cooperative action, UNFCCC member states continued to hammer out how best to operationalize REDD-related activities on the ground.

This strong forest–climate platform provided fertile ground for a third-party bandwagoner: biodiversity. Forest conservation, as it relates to REDD, had been an ongoing subject of discussion within the UNFCCC since at least COP 13 in Bali (1/CP.13). However, many biodiversity organizations were quick to point out that reducing emissions from deforestation and forest degradation does not necessarily correlate with conservation of biodiversity. Specifically, conservation biologists have expressed concern that if REDD+ implementation focuses exclusively on maximizing climate mitigation, key biodiversity benefits may not accrue. This is in part because forests that have potentially large carbon flow benefits (e.g., single tree plantations) are not necessarily those with the most urgent conservation needs (e.g., biodiversity hot spots) (Association for Tropical Biology and Conservation and the Society for Tropical Ecology 2009; Grainger et al. 2009).

As such, conservation organizations became very concerned that REDD+ would result in countries prioritizing forest conservation in ways that managed for carbon flows without adequately accounting for the biodiversity implications of these decisions. This coupled with the fact that REDD+ has attracted significant funding (including potentially long-term finance for forests) and political resources—an enduring struggle for biodiversity organizations—made REDD+ a very attractive "wagon" to jump on. And jump they did.

Biodiversity conservation organizations have become very involved with REDD+ discussions surrounding safeguards and co-benefits. Muñoz (2011) finds that between 1995 and 2009 conservation organizations represented the largest NGO constituency at UNFCCC COPs. They have participated through lobbying governments, hosting side events, and when possible participating directly in discussions on REDD+ safeguards and co-benefits (Figure 10.3). Further, REDD+ discussions have also made their way into CBD negotiations, with REDD+ featuring prominently at the 2010 CBD COP in Nayoga, Japan (ENB 2010a).

FIGURE 10.3 NGOs at UNFCCC COP 15 calling for an end to deforestation—another form of bandwagoning. Photo courtesy of IISD/*Earth Negotiations Bulletin*

This bandwagoning effort has already yielded some success. Many biodiversity organizations mark the Copenhagen Conference (2009) a victory of their efforts, with COP 15's decision on the matter formally acknowledging *biodiversity* conservation as a REDD+ co-benefit (4/CP/15). COP 16 (2010) further reified their efforts, requiring that REDD+ activities be consistent with the conservation of biological diversity (1/CP.16 para 70 and Appendix para 2(e)). In short, in their efforts to both avoid potential negative biodiversity impacts of REDD+ *and* benefit from growing REDD-related resources, a third-party (i.e., biodiversity) jumped on the forest–climate bandwagon.

Bandwagoning Evaluation

In contrast to the other cases examined in this chapter, linkages between forest and climate governance are relatively mature, and housed primarily in the UNFCCC. This difference reflects the fact that, unlike our observations on the CBD and UNCCD, bandwagoning efforts are not necessarily aimed at sustaining existing institutions. Rather, forest–climate bandwagoning is about creating governance structures (including financial ones) where these have been politically intractable elsewhere. In this sense, forest–climate bandwagoning is not of the "classical" variety discussed above, but more akin to "forum shopping," wherein actors strategically place issues in venues that have the potential to yield favorable results, in this case new institutions.[8] Indeed, this forum shopping endeavor has been successful for the forest–climate linkage, as evidenced through the formal institutionalization of forest–climate linkages within the UNFCCC through REDD+. Importantly, this does not imply that new institutions are necessarily "good" for forest conservation. Indeed, there is ongoing debate within the forest community about whether governing forests primarily on the basis of their carbon value will have detrimental impacts on forests.

This case of successful (institutional) bandwagoning is explained by a variety of factors. Most importantly, the forest–climate linkage created through REDD+ is based on strong scientific understandings of the relationship between deforestation, forest management, and carbon emissions. Trees remove carbon dioxide (CO_2) from the atmosphere through photosynthesis, storing it as carbon in biomass. Alongside oceans, forests serve as one of the largest sinks for CO_2, storing more carbon than the total stored in the atmosphere (FAO 2005, 14). Moreover, deforestation, primarily through burning for agricultural purposes, accounts for more than 17% of global emissions, following the burning of fossil fuels as the largest source of global CO_2 emissions (IPCC 2007a, 36). In short, addressing climate mitigation through forest management makes scientific sense.

Linking forest issues to climate change politics also makes economic sense. The forest sector holds great promise for cost-effective climate mitigation. The Stern Review stated that "curbing deforestation is a highly cost-effective way of reducing greenhouse gas emissions" (Stern 2006, 25), a point also made by the IPCC (2007b) and Kindermann et al. (2008). This combination of a good scientific and economic fit between climate and forest issues has allowed global forest protection advocates to successfully bandwagon the *en vogue* governance framework: the UNFCCC.

It is less clear if the recent expansion of forest–climate linkages to include biodiversity conservation through REDD+ will be successful. Although this tripartite bandwagoning effort holds great potential for benefits to accrue to the three issues, balancing biodiversity benefits with climate–forest benefits means that climate and forest benefits will suffer to some extent. This is because, as noted above, areas with high-density carbon and high deforestation rates do not closely correlate with areas urgently in need of conservation. As such, successful bandwagoning requires careful consideration of balancing priorities. Although biodiversity conservation is a worthy goal in itself, institutionally linking it to climate change requires careful consideration of whether bandwagoning these two issues is the best way to yield maximum benefits for either regime.

Ozone

Historical Context

The Montreal Protocol, adopted in 1987, responded to concerns first raised in the 1970s that chlorofluorocarbons (CFCs) and other anthropogenic substances were damaging the stratospheric ozone layer.[9] The Protocol seeks to phase down and out the production and consumption of many of these ozone depleting substances (ODS) by establishing schedules for developing and developed countries.[10] We focus on those substances that most closely linked the Montreal Protocol to the climate change regime at the time of writing: CFCs and hydrochlorofluorocarbons (HCFCs).

The Montreal Protocol established that developed countries should phase out production and consumption of CFCs by 1996, and developing countries by 2010. In the medium term, HCFCs were seen as the best substitute for many applications. Yet because these are also ozone depleting, in 1992 parties agreed to add them to the list of chemicals controlled under the Montreal Protocol. In 2007, they agreed to an accelerated schedule to phase HCFCs down and out.

Bandwagoning Evolution

The Montreal Protocol is often touted as one of the most successful MEAs. It enjoys universal ratification and has been relatively successful in phasing down ODS use. Additionally, 2008 estimates suggested that the Montreal Protocol had achieved approximately five times the greenhouse gas (GHG) reductions that countries pledged to meet under the Kyoto Protocol (Norman et al. 2008). This is because many ODS also have a high global warming potential. The initial relationship between the Montreal Protocol and the UNFCCC and Kyoto Protocol might, therefore, be categorized as "Montreal Protocol envy"; the Montreal Protocol did not need to bandwagon (Nicholson and Chong 2011).

As the world's attention has shifted from plugging the hole in the ozone layer to tackling climate change, however, so the Montreal Protocol has had to take climate change concerns on board. This became particularly evident in the 2000s, when a key contradiction emerged between the goals of the Montreal and Kyoto Protocols. Under the Montreal Protocol, parties phasing out CFCs and HCFCs have often replaced these with non–ozone depleting hydrofluorocarbons (HFCs), which are considered the best substitute in many applications. But scientific evidence shows that some HFCs have a global warming potential thousands of times greater than CO_2. As such, the phase-out schedules under the Montreal Protocol have actually incentivized increased use of a substance that exacerbates climate change.

Because HFCs do not deplete the ozone layer, they are not currently controlled under the Montreal Protocol. Instead, they are one of the six GHGs whose emissions are considered under the Kyoto Protocol. At the Montreal Protocol's 21st Meeting of the Parties (MOP) in 2009, parties considered two proposals, advanced by the Federated States of Micronesia and Mauritius, and by the United States, Canada, and Mexico, to amend the Protocol to include a phase-down of HFCs.[11] Parties who supported this idea noted that the 1985 Vienna Convention (from which the Montreal Protocol emerged) obligates such activity under the Montreal Protocol because the Convention contains language on preventing the negative environmental consequences of phase-out decisions. Amendment advocates also argued that because the Montreal Protocol has reduced ODS production and consumption more successfully than the Kyoto Protocol has reduced GHG emissions, the Montreal Protocol is more likely to achieve its governance targets and should therefore be used to address the HFC-climate issue that it exacerbated. Finally, some advocates recognize that for their institution to remain relevant, they can no longer consider only the ozone impact of the chemicals they seek to control (ENB 2010b).

Objections to the proposed amendments, however, have been significant. Led by India, China, and Brazil, many countries have argued that because HFCs are not ozone depleting, their control is beyond the scope of the Montreal Protocol and should instead be addressed under the climate regime. At MOP 22 in 2010, India suggested that addressing HFCs under the Montreal Protocol would amount to "an amalgamation of the Vienna Convention and the UNFCCC" (ENB 2010b). Led by Kuwait and Saudi Arabia, at MOP 21 many developing countries argued that financial resources for phasing down and out ODS, and in particular HCFCs under the accelerated schedule agreed to in 2007, are already limited, and would be further stretched if they had to be used to control HFCs as well (ENB 2009, 2010b). These parties argued that by diverting finances to non-ozone depleting substances, the Montreal Protocol's ability to achieve its own governance target, namely minimizing ozone depletion, would be diluted.

A much more cynical reason for blocking action on HFCs under the Montreal Protocol may be at play. Under the accelerated schedule, developed countries must phase out HCFC production and consumption by 2020, but developing countries can *increase* production through 2013. One such HCFC is the refrigerant HCFC-22, which creates GHG HFC-23 as a byproduct. Under the Kyoto Protocol's CDM, developing country parties can gain credits for destroying HFC-23 due to its high global warming potential (the heat trapped in one tonne is equivalent to that trapped in 11,700 tonnes of carbon dioxide) (IPCC 2001). Poor coordination between the mechanisms developed by the two Protocols creates a perverse incentive for developing countries to overproduce HCFC-22 (which is bad for the ozone layer and also for the climate because HCFC-22 has a global warming potential of 1,810) to profit from destroying the resultant HFC-23 (which is bad for climate change because developed countries are buying "hot air" on the carbon markets).

Although there are only nineteen registered HFC-23 destruction projects under the CDM, by 2010 they accounted for 52.6% of total CDM credits because of HFC-23's high climate impact. While the cost of HFC-23 destruction will total €80 million, Certified Emissions Reductions (CERs) from HFC-23 are expected to be worth €6 billion in 2012 (Environmental Investigation Agency and CDM-Watch 2010). Eleven of these projects are in China and five in India; the economic benefits these countries stand to gain from misalignment between the Kyoto and Montreal Protocol mechanisms likely explains their interest in ensuring that HFCs fall between the Protocols' gaps. Indeed, at the Barcelona climate talks leading up to the 2009 Copenhagen climate negotiations, India blocked discussions on HFCs saying that these would be addressed at the upcoming Montreal Protocol MOP 21, which also took place prior to Copenhagen (ENB 2009). As noted, however, India blocked discussion within the Montreal Protocol negotiations, stating that HFCs were to be addressed in the climate talks.

Bandwagoning Evaluation

The links between climate change and ozone depletion are unambiguous and, consequently, so too is the need for two-way linkages. In the ozone case, however, this is not only because of scientific linkages, but also because the mechanisms established by two institutions to meet their respective governance targets have, over time, become inextricably linked. This changes the nature of the bandwagoning.

In contrast to the biodiversity and desertification cases, in which these regimes bandwagoned onto the climate regime, and more in line with the forestry case, the ozone case is more akin to "reverse" bandwagoning (Nicholson and Chong 2011). Specifically, the latter are examples whereby effectively tackling climate change requires action on issues that were originally largely beyond the climate regime's mandate. Yet whereas forestry is being consumed within the UNFCCC, the Montreal Protocol has demonstrated that it can be more effective at tackling climate change than the Kyoto Protocol. Because many ODS and some of their substitutes have high global warming potential, the climate regime *needs* the ozone regime to effectively tackle—or at least account for the effects of its activities on—climate change.

The Montreal Protocol also presents an example of what some consider "forced" bandwagoning. Due to the political attention to climate change, the Montreal Protocol can no longer operate in a vacuum where it can carry out activities that address ozone depletion without considering climate impacts. Parties are at a crossroads: they can focus on existing commitments only, and then phase out their institution, or they can increase the Montreal Protocol's scope by taking on new obligations that necessarily require them to work at the messy climate–ozone interface. Some parties lament that their Protocol is being *forced* into the world of climate politics. Others, such as the United States, see that the Montreal Protocol could be an additional tool for addressing climate change and see this as an opportunity rather than a hindrance (ENB 2010b).

At the heart of this impasse are issues of prioritization and financing. Because substances that most effectively prevent ozone depletion (e.g., HFCs) have a high global warming potential, it is not possible to optimize ozone and climate goals simultaneously; unless replacements to ODS that do not negatively affect the climate are found, achieving the goals under one of the Protocols will slow progress in the other. A "win–win" solution—the favorite kind in the UN system—does not seem possible at this time; someone will have to dilute their governance target in the name of bigger-picture environmental sustainability.

Finally, the Montreal/Kyoto Protocol debacle over HCFC-22 demonstrates the urgent need for regimes to coordinate the mechanisms they establish to attain their governance targets. The huge profits that a few actors are making at the expense of both the ozone layer and the climate due to misalignments in the Montreal Protocol's phase-out schedule and the Kyoto Protocol's CDM could lead to a "Climategate" not of science but of mechanisms. While the CDM Executive Board's decision in 2010 to delay CER issuance to several HFC projects and to disqualify five chemical plants in China from obtaining CERs until further review was a promising start to addressing this issue, parties' failure to make progress at MOP 22 on the HFC issue due to continued blocking on the part of China, India, Brazil, and others was disheartening. How continued efforts, both within and outside of the Montreal Protocol, will play out remains to be seen. While many parties understandably do not want to wade into this messy political territory, if the ozone and climate regimes seize the opportunity to work together to close these loopholes, they could set a positive example for other MEAs. Hitting closer to home, the fate of the Montreal Protocol likely rests on its ability to navigate the turbulent airways ahead.

Why Bandwagon?

There are many motivations to jump on the climate change bandwagon. First and foremost, bandwagoning happens because scientific evidence increasingly supports the claim that climate change is inextricably intertwined with a wide variety of other environment- and development-related problems. In other words, the scope of climate change impacts on human and natural systems is expected to be broad and deep (IPCC 2007b). As shown in the case studies above, projected climate changes will likely exacerbate biodiversity loss, desertification, deforestation, and ozone depletion.[12] These impacts are of course not unidirectional. For example, deforestation is a primary driver of climate change, while desertification makes climate change adaptation more difficult.

Second, bandwagoning occurs because international regimes that address discrete environmental issues using discrete mechanisms have had spillover effects. For example, the Montreal Protocol's phase-out schedule for CFCs and HCFCs initially led to significant climate change mitigation benefits. More recently, the replacement of HCFCs with HFCs has exacerbated climate change, a negative impact that necessitates coordination between the ozone and climate regimes. Increased demand for biofuels in order to mitigate climate change has resulted in the clearing of tropical forests for palm plantations, which has also contributed to biodiversity loss. As scientists discover a growing number of climate linkages, and as regimes designed to address single issues increasingly develop regulatory and management mechanisms that affect other environmental issues, bandwagoning is becoming a necessity for effective global environmental problem solving.

Third, bandwagoning is used to capture additional problem-solving resources. Limited state and, accordingly, institutional (e.g., underfunded secretariats) capacity coupled with high environmental regime density and uneven distribution of financial and political resources across regimes has facilitated proactive linking agents to engage in what we refer to as "classical" bandwagoning. Our case studies corroborate recent studies of secretariat politics (e.g., Jinnah 2010), which suggest that genuine problem-solving interests drive secretariats to forge climate linkages. For example, the UNCCD Secretariat seeks to tap climate adaptation funding because such funds could be used to support climate adaptation initiatives in drylands and hence improve dryland livelihoods (which is core to its governance target). Similarly, in marketing adaptation benefits of conservation, the CBD Secretariat and others have likely recognized the financial opportunities available to its member states that could successfully link these two issues in CBD and/or UNFCCC implementation. Stakeholders within the UNCCD and CBD regimes are likely eyeing the significant financing that is expected to flow through the new Green Climate Fund, and that could address cross-cutting issues. The strong climate–forest–biodiversity linkage within the UNFCCC's REDD+ discussions further highlights a "classical" case in its utilization of clear power differentials between regimes to attract resources in support of a weaker regime's problem-solving objectives.

Nevertheless, the case studies clearly demonstrate that bandwagoning is not always so altruistic. In some instances, "classical" bandwagoning is about institutional survival itself; this form of bandwagoning often proves more problematic in practice. Agreeing with some parties to the UNCCD who felt that the UNFCCC and CBD could get money at the "snap of their fingers" (ENB 2003), the UNCCD Secretariat has at times pushed for linkages between desertification and mitigation that are poorly supported by science. A similar dynamic may have driven the CBD Secretariat to pursue biodiversity–adaptation linkages, and, as suggested in related studies, secretariats of regional fisheries management organizations only bandwagon when doing so has the potential to increase their budgets and institutional relevancy (Axelrod 2011). Irrespective of the rationale of the linking agents, taken together these cases further highlight that actors with the most to lose from institutional collapse or weakening, namely treaty secretariats, often play a central role in this type of bandwagoning.

A fourth bandwagoning rationale is forum shopping. As demonstrated by the deforestation case above, failures in international cooperation to create an overarching framework convention for forests spurred forest conservation actors to seek governance under the UNFCCC. These efforts have contributed to the emergence of an emerging REDD+ framework, which, if carefully conceived, holds potential to do more for forest conservation than the loose network of voluntary forest agreements that date back to the mid-1940s.

Conclusions: Implications of Bandwagoning

Climate bandwagoning has had mixed results. On the one hand, bandwagoning allows for other environmental issues to benefit from the contemporary political/ financial attention on climate politics. Deforestation presents the most promising case of institutional bandwagoning, whereby the tight scientific and economic rationale for linking deforestation and climate change has resulted in a new forum for forest conservation under the UNFCCC. The tangible benefits of this new institutional home remain to be seen.

Although as yet most bandwagoning efforts have had little problem-solving success, in some cases bandwagoning has resulted in success as measured by political metrics, such as expanding interest and participation in relatively weak environmental regimes. For instance, the CBD's reframing of the biodiversity–climate linkage attempts to expand interest and participation in CBD activities in developing countries by recasting conservation-based adaption as a development and human security strategy.

Of course, bandwagoning also has potentially negative effects. "Forced" bandwagoning under the Montreal Protocol, for example, means that this institution may have to dilute attainment of its own governance target in the interests of tackling environmental sustainability writ large. Yet more worrying are the perverse incentives that can develop when mechanisms designed to tackle one environmental issue inadvertently have negative impacts on another. For example, the incentives for developing countries to overproduce harmful chemicals under the Montreal Protocol to create "hot air" to sell on the carbon markets have negative environmental impacts for both the climate and the ozone regimes. Finally, bandwagoning that overemphasizes the strength of scientific consensus surrounding a specific climate linkage (e.g., desertification–mitigation linkages) could produce backlashes that further exacerbate climate skepticism in the wake of "Climategate" and other scientifically related scandals. This type of bandwagoning is particularly dangerous in that it wastes precious problem-solving resources and undermines the legitimacy of linking regimes, while potentially worsening the very environmental issues the regimes in question were designed to address.

On balance, then, is climate bandwagoning a good thing? On the one hand, it can involve political maneuvering that dilutes climate or linking regimes' policy and wastes already-scarce resources available for environmental problem solving. On the other hand, the term "bandwagoning" may denote an overly negative connotation, when in fact this process may lead to positive environmental outcomes. After all, climate change bandwagoning could be seen as a phenomenon in which environmental and other communities rally behind, arguably, the most pressing problem of our lifetimes. Examined from the perspective of how this phenomenon (whatever its label) affects climate politics, linkages to other issues further expand climate change's global salience. By connecting to issues such as biodiversity, forests, desertification, ozone, fisheries, and even security, we remove climate change exclusively from the technocratic UNFCCC discussions of additionality and carbon accounting in order to explore the expansive, textured, and diverse nature of a problem that will affect us for generations.

Climate change is solidly positioned on center stage within contemporary international environmental politics (and beyond). Given the scarcity of resources available to address many linked environmental issues, bandwagoning is likely to remain a prominent feature of multilateral environmental negotiations. In short, climate change and the bandwagoning it has precipitated have permanently altered the landscape of international environmental politics. The trick will be to ensure that bandwagoning is done strategically to ensure that already scarce resources are not wasted on tangentially linked issues.

Ultimately, carefully designed bandwagoning that is based on solid scientific evidence and provides clear benefits to both regimes is best. Certainly there will be trade-offs, due both to the interlinked nature of the environmental challenges of our time and to the mechanisms we are increasingly creating to tackle them. A delegate at Montreal Protocol MOP 22 perhaps said it best when discussing the imperative of addressing the HFC debacle that the ozone and climate regimes face: "we will stand or fall together" (ENB 2010b). In other words, we will have to learn to bandwagon where environmental issues are interlinked, even if the political decision making is difficult. If we fail to do so, our (grand)children may find themselves in a world where (for example) crops have the climatic conditions to grow but lack the pollinators necessary to bear fruit.

Notes

1 This chapter expands on a special issue of *Global Environmental Politics* (Jinnah 2011a).
2 This case study is based on Conliffe 2011.
3 Given the uncertainty surrounding the future of market mechanisms under the UNFCCC more broadly, the UNCCD Secretariat has also shifted attention to the possibility of addressing soil carbon sequestration in Nationally Appropriate Mitigation Actions.
4 The analysis that follows draws from Jinnah 2011b.
5 The mitigation benefits of biofuels are debatable. See, for example, Farrell et al. 2006 and Searchinger et al. 2008.
6 See Jinnah 2011b for an in-depth discussion of the universe of frames used in this case.
7 See Chapters 3, 5 and 7 for examinations of the effort to negotiate such a convention.
8 See Shany 2005 for more on forum shopping.
9 See Morrisette 1991 for a historical overview.
10 The Montreal Protocol sets schedules for Article 5 (developing) countries and non-Article 5 (predominantly developed) countries.
11 See ENB 2009 for a detailed analysis of these negotiations.
12 On the latter, see UNEP 2010 at 1.

Works Cited

Adger, W.N., S. Agrawala, M.M.Q. Mirza, C. Conde, K. O'Brien, J. Pulhin, R. Pulwarty, B. Smit, and K. Takahashi. 2007. Assessment of Adaptation Practices, Options, Constraints and Capacity. *Climate Change 2007: Impacts, Adaptation and Vulnerability: Contribution of Working Group II to the Fourth Assessment Report of the Intergovernmental Panel on Climate Change.* Edited by M.L. Parry, O.F. Canziani, J.P. Palutikof, P.J. van der Linden, and C.E. Hanson. Cambridge, UK: Cambridge University Press.

Association for Tropical Biology and Conservation, Society for Tropical Ecology. 2009. The Marburg Declaration. Marburg, Germany.

Axelrod, Mark. 2011. Climate Change and Global Fisheries Management: Linking Issues to Protect Ecosystems or Save Political Interests? *Global Environmental Politics* 11(3).

Chasek, Pamela S. 1997. The Convention to Combat Desertification: Lessons Learned for Sustainable Development. *Journal of Environment and Development* 6(2): 147–169.

Chasek, Pamela S. 2001. NGOs and State Capacity in International Environmental Negotiations: The Experience of the Earth Negotiations Bulletin. *Review of European Community and International Environmental Law* 10(2):168–176.

Conliffe, Alexandra. 2011. Combating Ineffectiveness: Climate Change Bandwagoning and the UN Convention to Combat Desertification. *Global Environmental Politics* 11(3).

Danielsen, F., H. Beukema, N.D. Burgess, F. Parish, C.A. Brühl, P.F. Donald, D. Murdiyarso, B. Phalan, L. Reijnders, M. Struebig, and E.B. Fitzherbert. 2009. Biofuel Plantations on Forested Lands: Double Jeopardy for Biodiversity and Climate. *Conservation Biology* 23(2): 348–358.

Detraz, Nicole. 2011. Threats or Vulnerabilities? Assessing the Link Between Climate Change and Security. *Global Environmental Politics* 11(3): 104–120.

ENB (*Earth Negotiations Bulletin*). 1997. Summary of the First Conference of the Parties to the Convention to Combat Desertification: 29 September–10 October 1997. *Earth Negotiations Bulletin* 4(116). http://www.iisd.ca/download/pdf/enb04116e.pdf (accessed February 15, 2011).

ENB. 2000. Summary of the Fourth Conference of the Parties to the Convention to Combat Desertification: 11–22 December 2000. *Earth Negotiations Bulletin* 4(149). http://www.iisd.ca/download/pdf/enb04149e.pdf (accessed February 15, 2011).

ENB. 2003. Summary of the Sixth Conference of the Parties to the Convention to Combat Desertification: 25 August–6 September 2003. *Earth Negotiations Bulletin* 4(173). http://www.iisd.ca/download/pdf/enb04173e.pdf (accessed June 20, 2011).

ENB. 2007a. Summary of the Fifth Session of the Committee for the Review of Implementation of the UNCCD: 12–21 March 2007. *Earth Negotiations Bulletin* 4(195). http://www.iisd.ca/download/pdf/enb04195e.pdf (accessed June 20, 2011).

ENB. 2007b. Summary of the 12th Meeting of the Subsidiary Body on Scientific, Technical and Technological Advice and 2nd Meeting of the Ad Hoc Open-ended Working Group on Review of Implementation of the Convention on Biological Diversity: 2–13 July 2007. *Earth Negotiations Bulletin* 9(382). http://www.iisd.ca/download/pdf/enb09382e.pdf (accessed June 20, 2011).

ENB 2008. Summary and Analysis of the Ninth Conference of the Parties to the Convention on Biological Diversity: 19–30 May 2008. *Earth Negotiations Bulletin* 9(452) http://www.iisd.ca/download/pdf/enb09452e.pdf (accessed February 7, 2011).

ENB. 2009. Summary and Analysis of the Twenty-First Meeting of the Parties to the Montreal Protocol: 4–8 November 2009. *Earth Negotiations Bulletin* 19(73). http://www.iisd.ca/download/pdf/enb1973e.pdf (accessed February 20, 2011).

ENB. 2010a. Summary of the 10th Conference of the Parties to the Convention on Biological Diversity: 18–29 October 2010. *Earth Negotiations Bulletin* 9(554) http://www.iisd.ca/download/pdf/enb09544e.pdf (accessed February 7, 2011).

ENB. 2010b. Summary and Analysis of the 22nd Meeting of the Parties to the Montreal Protocol: 8–12 November 2010. *Earth Negotiations Bulletin* 19(79). http://www.iisd.ca/download/pdf/enb1979e.pdf (accessed June 20, 2011).

Environmental Investigation Agency and CDM-Watch. 2010. HFC-23 Offsets in the Context of the EU Emissions Trading Scheme. Policy Brief. http://www.cdm-watch.org/wordpress/wp-content/uploads/2010/07/HFC-23_Policy-Briefing1.pdf (accessed October 25, 2010).

FAO (Food and Agriculture Organization of the United Nations). 2005. *Global Forest Resources Assessment 2005.* http://www.fao.org/forestry/fra/fra2005/en/ (accessed May 27, 2011).

Fargione, Joseph, Jason Hill, David Tilman, Stephen Polasky, and Peter Hawthorne. 2008. Land Clearing and the Biofuel Carbon Debt. *Science* 319(5867): 1235–1238.

Farrell, Alexander E., Richard J. Plevin, Brian T. Turner, Andrew D. Jones, Michael O'Hare, and Daniel M. Kammen. 2006. Ethanol Can Contribute to Energy and Environmental Goals. *Science* 311(5760): 506–508.

Grainger, Alan, Douglas H. Boucher, Peter C. Frumhoff, William F. Laurance, Thomas Lovejoy, Jeffrey McNeely, Manfred Niekisch, Peter Raven, Navjot S. Sodhi, Oscar Venter, and Stuart L. Pimm. 2009. Biodiversity and REDD at Copenhagen. *Current Biology* 19(21): R974–R976.

Gulbrandsen, Lars H. 2004. Overlapping Public and Private Governance: Can Forest Certification Fill the Gaps in the Global Forest Regime? *Global Environmental Politics* 4(4): 75–99.

Gutierrez, Maria. 2007. All that is Air Turns Solid: The Creation of a Market for Sinks Under the Kyoto Protocol on Climate Change. Unpublished PhD dissertation, New York: The City University of New York.

IPCC. 2001. *Third Assessment Report (TAR), Working Group III.* Geneva: Intergovernmental Panel on Climate Change.

IPCC. 2007a. *Climate Change 2007: Synthesis Report.* Geneva: Intergovernmental Panel on Climate Change.

IPCC. 2007b. *Fourth Assessment Report (AR4), Working Group III, Summary for Policy Makers.* Geneva: Intergovernmental Panel on Climate Change.

Jinnah, Sikina. 2010. Overlap Management in the World Trade Organization: Secretariat Influence on Trade-Environment Politics. *Global Environmental Politics* 10(2): 64–79.

Jinnah, Sikina. 2011a. Introduction to Climate Change Bandwagoning: The Impacts of Strategic Linkages for Regime Design, Maintenance, and Death. *Global Environmental Politics* 11(3): 1–9.

Jinnah, Sikina. 2011b. Marketing Linkages: Secretariat Governance of the Climate-Biodiversity Interface. *Global Environmental Politics* 11(3): 23–43.

Kindermann, Georg, Michael Obersteiner, Brent Sohngen, Jayant Sathaye, Kenneth Andrasko, Ewald Rametsteiner, Bernhard Schlamadinger, Sven Wunder, and Robert Beach. 2008. Global Cost Estimates of Reducing Carbon Emissions Through Avoided Deforestation. *PNAS* 105(30): 10302–10307.

Lewis, Sian and Naomi Antony. 2010. Poor Want More Biomass, not Biodiversity. *Science and Development Network* (April 30).

MA. 2005. *Ecosystems and Human Wellbeing: Desertification Synthesis.* Washington, DC: World Resources Institute.

McDermott, Constance, Kelly Levin, and Benjamin Cashore. 2011. Building the Forest-Climate Bandwagon: REDD+ and the Logic of Problem Amelioration. *Global Environmental Politics* 11(3): 85–103.

Mitchell, Ronald B. 2002–2010. International Environmental Agreements Database Project (Version 2010.2). http://iea.uoregon.edu/page.php?file=home.htm&query=static (accessed October 17, 2010).

Morrisette, Peter M. 1991. The Montreal Protocol: Lessons for Formulating Policies for Global Warming. *Policy Studies Journal* 19: 152–161.

Muñoz, Miquel. 2011. Strategic Linkages to Climate Change Measured through NGO Participation in the UNFCCC. *Global Environmental Politics* 11(3): 10–22.

Najam, Adil. 2005. Developing Countries and Global Environmental Governance: From Contestation to Participation to Engagement. *International Environmental Agreements* 5: 303–321.

Nicholson, Simon and Daniel Chong. 2011. Jumping on the Human Rights Bandwagon: How Rights-based Linkages are Reshaping Climate Politics. *Global Environmental Politics* 11(3): 121–136.

Norman, Catherine S., Stephen J. DeCanto, and Lin Fan. 2008. The Montreal Protocol at 20: Ongoing Opportunities for Integration with Climate Protection. *Global Environmental Change* 18: 330–340.

Ortiz, Even, and Guangting Tang. 2005. *Review of the Management, Administration and Activities of the Secretariat of the United Nations Convention to Combat Desertification.* Geneva: United Nations Joint Inspection Unit.

Raustiala, Kal and David G. Victor. 2004. The Regime Complex for Plant Genetic Resources. *International Organization* 58: 277–309.

Righelato, Renton and Dominick Spracklen. 2007. Carbon Mitigation by Biofuels or by Saving and Restoring Forests? *Science* 317(5840): 902.

Schipper, E.L.F. 2006. Conceptual History of Adaptation in the UNFCCC Process. *Review of European Community and International Environmental Law* 15(1): 82–92.

Searchinger, Timothy, Ralph Heimlich, R.A. Houghton, Fengxia Dong, Amani Elobeid, Jacinto Fabiosa, Simla Tokgoz, Dermot Hayes, and Tun-Hsiang Yu. 2008. Use of U.S. Croplands for Biofuels Increases Greenhouse Gases Through Emissions from Land-Use Change. *Science* 319(5867): 1238–1240.

Shany, Yuval. 2005. *The Competing Jurisdiction of International Courts and Tribunals.* New York, NY: Oxford University Press.

Stern, Nicholas. 2006. *Stern Review: The Economics of Climate Change Executive Summary.* London: UK Treasury.

Thomas, Chris D., Alison Cameron, Rhys E. Green, Michel Bakkenes, Linda J. Beaumont, Yvonne C. Collingham, Barend F.N. Erasmus, Marinez Ferreira de Siqueira, Alan Grainger, Lee Hannah, Lesley Hughes, Brian Huntley, Albert S. van Jaarsveld, Guy F. Midgley, Lera Miles, Miguel A. Ortega-Huerta, A. Townsend Peterson, Oliver L. Phillips, and Stephen E. Williams. 2004. Extinction Risk from Climate Change. *Nature* 427(6970): 145–148.

UNCCD. 1994. *United Nations Convention to Combat Desertification in Countries Experiencing Serious Drought and/or Desertification, Particularly in Africa.* Nairobi: UNEP.

UNCCD. 2007. The 10-year Strategic Plan and Framework to Enhance the Implementation of the Convention (2008–2018). (ICCD/COP(8)/16/Add.1/Dec.3). http://www.unccd.int/cop/officialdocs/cop8/pdf/16add1eng.pdf#page=8 (accessed June 18, 2011).

UNDP, UNCCD, and UNEP. 2009. *Climate Change in the African Drylands: Options and Opportunities for Adaptation and Mitigation.* New York, Bonn and Nairobi: UNDP, UNCCD, and UNEP.

UNEP. 2010. *Environmental Effects of Ozone Depletion and its Interactions with Climate Change: 2010 Assessment.* http://ozone.unep.org/Assessment_Panels/EEAP/eeap-report2010.pdf (accessed May 23, 2011).

UNFCCC. 1992. *United Nations Framework Convention on Climate Change.* New York, NY: UN.

UNFCCC. 2010. Cumulative Admission of Observer Organizations. http://unfccc.int/files/parties_and_observers/ngo/application/pdf/cumulative_admissions_of_observer_organizations_cop_1–16.pdf (accessed June 20, 2011).

Worm, Boris, Edward B. Barbier, Nicola Beaumont, J. Emmett Duffy, Carl Folke, Benjamin S. Halpern, Jeremy B.C. Jackson, Heike K. Lotze, Fiorenza Micheli, Stephen R. Palumbi, Enric Sala, Kimberley A. Selkoe, John J. Stachowicz, and Reg Watson. 2006. Impacts of Biodiversity Loss on Ocean Ecosystem Services. *Science* 314(5800): 787–790.

Wright, Heather and Sikina Jinnah. 2010. Effectiveness, Efficiency, and Equity in REDD Implementation: What Can We Learned from Past Experience? In *Advances in Environmental Research*. Edited by J.A. Daniels. New York, NY: Nova Science Publishers.

11

IMPLEMENTATION CHALLENGES AND COMPLIANCE IN MEA NEGOTIATIONS

Elisa Morgera, Elsa Tsioumani, Soledad Aguilar, and Hugh S. Wilkins

Since the Earth Summit, international environmental obligations have expanded both through the development of protocols to multilateral environmental agreements (MEAs), and through expanding interpretations of their objectives. Challenges in implementing these growing obligations have created increasing tensions in negotiating dynamics related to these MEAs. This chapter seeks to identify trends across multilateral environmental negotiations, over the last twenty years, in relation to capacity issues and approaches to facilitating compliance in the face of increasing implementation challenges. It does so by analyzing related issues within selected MEAs; namely, the Convention on International Trade in Endangered Species (CITES), the Convention on Biological Diversity (CBD) and its Protocols on biosafety (Biosafety Protocol) and on access and benefit-sharing (ABS) (the ABS Protocol), the International Treaty on Plant Genetic Resources for Food and Agriculture (ITPGR), and the United Nations Framework Convention on Climate Change (UNFCCC) and its Kyoto Protocol.

The chapter first examines the evolution of implementation challenges under each of these MEAs, discussing how questions of implementation have been addressed through action at the international and national levels (Bodansky 2010). Then, it looks at the evolution of compliance procedures under these agreements. While much literature has focused on the creation and functioning of compliance mechanisms (Beyerlin et al. 2006; Treves et al. 2009), this chapter examines the little-studied question of how compliance challenges have affected multilateral environmental negotiations. It analyzes the tensions in negotiating dynamics and seeks to outline trends in negotiations resulting from the growing complexity and scope of implementation of the selected MEAs.

Evolution of Implementation Challenges

While negotiations on MEAs leading into the Earth Summit and earlier had generally resulted in succinct provisions related to the objectives of MEAs, successive interpretations of those objectives in the context of the periodic meetings of MEA Conferences of the Parties (COPs) have resulted in an expansion of their areas of activities beyond what was originally envisaged. This section discusses how the growing mandate of MEAs has brought about ever-increasing demands for implementation and how this has affected COP negotiations.

CITES

In the 1970s, when CITES was adopted, its main focus was the control of international trade in rapidly vanishing flagship species. At the time, wild species and their products were not part of wholesale trade, but instead were mostly shipped individually. CITES was thus construed as an international standardized system for national authorities to issue permits to accompany international wildlife and plant shipments.

More than three decades later, however, CITES has grown to regulate trade in more than 30,000 species of animals and plants, and confronts new challenges; namely, international trade in commodities such as live flowers, fish, and timber. Several examples of "growing implementation pains" may be found in CITES' recent history. For example, the CITES Secretariat proposed in 2002 to eliminate the term "endangered species" from the Convention's title, to take into account its widened scope in addressing species that may not be in danger of extinction but nevertheless require regulation. In presenting this proposal, the then CITES Secretary-General, Willem Wijnstekers, appealed to parties to bear in mind that Appendix II species, which are species that are not in danger of extinction but could be if trade were unregulated, constitute the vast majority of CITES-listed species (Figure 11.1). He cautioned that the Convention's reputation as regulating trade in endangered species does not facilitate the listing of species that are the basis of economically important consumer goods, and said this has "stood in the way of CITES becoming involved in the regulation of trade in economically important species, such as commercial fish and timber species, even in cases where such species are subject to unsustainable levels of exploitation" (CITES 2002). Even though countries did not present their views openly, two large groups opposed the measure. First, EU member states, which held positions close to non-governmental organizations (NGOs) on this issue, reflected concerns over possible effects that the proposal might have on the market, as the "endangered species" label limits consumer demand on such wildlife products. Second, Latin American and Caribbean countries traditionally expressed concern over the expansion of CITES' scope toward economically important timber and fish

FIGURE 11.1 The CITES Secretariat proposed at CoP 12 in 2002 to eliminate from the convention's title the term "endangered species" to take account of its widened scope in addressing species that may not be in danger of extinction but nevertheless require regulation. Photo courtesy of IISD/*Earth Negotiations Bulletin*

species in the region (including Bigleaf Mahogany and Patagonian Toothfish). As a result, the Secretariat withdrew its proposal (ENB 2002c).

As the parties to CITES confront new threats to wildlife, they push the convention to go beyond the impacts of trade. Today, the interconnection between wildlife and livelihoods, as well as habitat loss, are among the main concerns for biodiversity conservation, stretching CITES' mandate even farther beyond its originally intended scope. In response, new concepts have entered the CITES legal system: the precautionary principle was incorporated into CITES Appendix amendment criteria (CITES CoP 2010c); the ecosystem approach and the Addis Ababa Principles and Guidelines on Sustainable Use of Biodiversity (developed under the CBD) were included in non-detriment findings (CITES CoP 2007b); and livelihoods issues were incorporated into the CITES agenda (CITES 2004).

As a result of these evolving objectives, CITES parties have increased the demands on human resources and capacities of both exporter and importer governments to enforce these provisions on the ground, and existing resources are often considered insufficient. National authorities in wildlife exporting developing countries in particular lament limitations in their ability to regulate wildlife trade, as most costs fall on them, while the benefits from CITES implementation flow to all parties. In 2010, for example, the chairperson of the Bigleaf Mahogany Working Group affirmed that a lack of financial and human resources in range countries had limited the implementation of the Bigleaf Mahogany Plan of Action

(ENB 2010a). In particular, a lack of funding affects developing countries' capacity to: perform scientific studies needed to determine the adequate level of harvest to be allowed for listed species ("non-detriment findings"); train customs authorities to identify products of different biological origin at border points; and train judicial authorities to understand international obligations and prosecute offenders.

Alongside these changes, the approach to implementation within the CITES treaty regime has evolved. Initially, the treaty relied solely on national-level implementation—that is, control of individual shipments by national authorities of member countries. More recently, the system has increasingly relied on international monitoring and support. This evolution, however, has not occurred without encountering some state resistance.

One example concerns the attempt to develop international guidelines on non-detriment findings (NDFs)—the process to ensure trade in listed species does not jeopardize the species' existence based on an assessment by national authorities in interpreting impacts of trade on vulnerable species. NDFs are considered the heart of CITES implementation, but insufficient guidance is provided by the CITES text or COP resolutions regarding how they should be carried out, and as a result national practice is uneven or insufficient. While parties acknowledged the need for international guidance, they have cautioned against developing binding or overly prescriptive guidelines that could be used as a tool to "name and shame" governments, or that would not allow for national experimentation and understanding of different capabilities (ENB 2011b). Another concern, expressed by the representative from Malaysia, was that guidelines on NDFs could be used to expand international surveillance over national decision-making processes (ENB 2010a).

Another example of increasing reliance on international monitoring is CITES National Legislation Project, which since 1992 has enabled the Secretariat, in the absence of strict prescriptions in the Convention in this regard, to analyze parties' national legislation and determine whether it adequately implements CITES, and then to categorize each country's legislation as meeting all, some, or none of the requirements for implementing CITES. Countries in the latter category have to develop a "CITES Legislation Plan," which identifies agreed steps and a time frame for the adoption of national legislation. Failing to submit the plan or to adopt adequate legislation by set deadlines may result in the recommended suspension of commercial trade with the party, although the Secretariat may withhold action if good legislative progress has been made by a party (CITES CoP 2010b).

In addition, the CITES Secretariat has assisted countries in developing or revising their implementing legislation. Upon request, it reviews and comments on draft legislation. It has also developed a legislative guidance package (containing a model law, legislative checklist, and format for legislative analysis), convenes regional and national workshops on drafting CITES-implementing legislation, fields experts to assist countries in developing legislation, and has set up various bilateral and multilateral legislative projects.[1]

CITES' increased reliance on international surveillance and monitoring of national implementation has thus been coupled with the possibility for parties to obtain advisory services from the Secretariat. Tensions, however, still persist. For example, in 2002, while Saint Lucia highlighted the benefits of technical assistance on national legislation, Chile, China, and the Dominican Republic called for more flexible deadlines in the context of the National Legislation Project, and Namibia noted that enhancing national legislation to comply with CITES is costly (ENB 2002a).

CBD

As opposed to earlier conservation conventions, the CBD has a wider subject-matter scope, based on its comprehensive concept of "biodiversity" as "the variability among living organisms," including "diversity within species, between species and of ecosystems" (Article 2). The treaty text also establishes broader objectives: in addition to the conservation of biodiversity, the CBD aims to ensure the sustainable use of biodiversity components, as well as the equitable sharing of the benefits arising out of the utilization of genetic resources (Article 1).

The fact that the CBD provisions are largely expressed as overall goals allows a variety of flexible approaches for implementation at the national and local levels, so long as these goals are achieved. The innovative features of the CBD, nevertheless, require major developments in national laws regarding conservation and sustainable use of biodiversity, which in many respects still remain unattained. This is particularly the case of the holistic and people-centered approach to nature conservation that emerges from the third CBD objective on benefit-sharing, CBD provisions on the participation of indigenous and local communities, traditional knowledge and customary use (Articles 8(j) and 10(c)), and numerous guidelines developed to facilitate implementation in several areas of environmental protection and human activities (CBD 2004a, 2004b, 2004c).

At the international level, the Convention has developed a multitude of sub-processes for the further refinement of its provisions, through the development of thematic and cross-cutting programs of work. In addition, the notion of ecosystem services, following the release in 2005 of the Millennium Ecosystem Assessment (a UN study providing the first global scientific evidence of the urgent need to address environmental sustainability and its link to poverty reduction), has tightened the link between biodiversity and human wellbeing, thereby contributing to the further growth of the CBD agenda. These linkages, however, still encounter resistance from some parties; for instance, in 2010, New Zealand, India, and Turkey opposed references to the role of biodiversity in water security, arguing that the CBD should focus on ecosystems rather than on poverty reduction and human wellbeing (ENB 2010b, 2010c).

Following the expansion of work under the CBD, the capacities required for its full implementation have increased and become more comprehensive over time, with higher expectations placed on parties for the resources and actions to be taken on the ground. As is the case with most of the 1992 and post-1992 conventions, the CBD specifically includes an obligation for developed country parties to provide new and additional financial resources to enable developing country parties to meet the agreed full incremental implementation costs of complying with commitments under the CBD (Article 20). This obligation has consistently been considered unmet by developing countries (see Chapter 8), and in 2010, during COP 10, developing countries dramatically backed up their long-standing demands for sufficient financing for CBD implementation by conditioning their support for the post-2010 Strategic Plan for the Convention (containing new targets for improved implementation of the CBD) on the further refinement of the CBD Resource Mobilization Strategy and the adoption of the ABS Protocol (Figure 11.2). Considering that one of the main aims of the ABS Protocol is to generate benefits for biodiversity conservation and sustainable use at the local level, the success of the entire meeting could be viewed to have been dependent on finance-related issues (ENB 2010d). Also during COP 10,

FIGURE 11.2 During CBD COP 10, developing countries dramatically backed up their long-standing demands for sufficient financing for CBD implementation by conditioning their support for the post-2010 Strategic Plan for the Convention to the further refinement of the CBD Resource Mobilization Strategy and the adoption of the ABS Protocol. Photo courtesy of IISD/*Earth Negotiations Bulletin*

developing countries called for developing targets and indicators to assess financing flows, and thus monitoring developed countries' compliance with their financial solidarity obligations. Developed countries proposed instead to prioritize innovative financing mechanisms, possibly attempting to shift at least part of the burden toward the private sector or ensuring that their climate financing also serves, and is accounted for, biodiversity conservation (ENB 2010d).

Another international avenue to support CBD implementation was the creation of a dedicated program on technology transfer and scientific and technological cooperation (Articles 16, 18, and 19) in 2004 (CBD COP 2004a). Negotiations, however, have been complicated by the concern that technology transfer also may imply transferring traditional knowledge without ensuring its adequate protection (which is called for in Article 8(j)), and the implications of intellectual property rights (IPRs) for technology transfer (ENB 2003, 2004a). Already in 2003, delegates had agreed to delete all references to traditional knowledge from the scope of the work program on technology transfer (ENB 2003) and to address exchanges of traditional knowledge in the framework of the work program on Article 8(j). IPR implications, however, continue to attract attention (ENB 2008a). Another difficulty in these negotiations concerns the potential of the CBD Secretariat to guide and facilitate technology transfer. COP 10 discussions regarding the proposed establishment of a biodiversity technology initiative reflected this divide, with the African Group preferring the CBD Secretariat as future host, and the EU favoring the UN Environment Program the (UNEP) because it was already working on technology transfer (ENB 2010d).

With regard to implementation at the national level, CBD provisions are quite open-ended in relation to the type of action needed, rarely pointing unequivocally to the enactment of national legislation. The CBD "in-depth reviews" of areas of activities to implement the Convention have only occasionally, and to varying extents, assessed implementation through national legislation (CBD 2010a, 2010b), resulting in "light-touch" identification of good practice, rather than a systematic "naming, shaming or praising" approach that has been used by other MEAs.

The main tool for CBD implementation at the national level (Article 6) is the National Biodiversity Strategy and Action Plan (NBSAP). To date, 171 countries have adopted their NBSAPs. However, a 2010 comprehensive assessment of NBSAPs indicates that, while they are indeed an indispensable step toward implementation and have generated concrete results in many countries, they have not attenuated the main drivers of biodiversity loss or contributed to mainstreaming biodiversity in a broader development policy context (Prip et al. 2010). Until recently, international guidance on NBSAPs has been limited and almost exclusively based on COP decisions. However, a series of regional and subregional workshops on NBSAPs, held during 2008–2010, proved to be of significant assistance in guiding the drafting and reviewing of national legislation and implementation in general, highlighting participants' views that the

CBD should focus more on implementation, moving away from policy development in the form of the negotiation, adoption, and revision of decisions (Prip et al. 2010). The Revised NBSAP Training Modules, prepared by the CBD Secretariat and currently under consultation, could assist in that regard and even evolve into something akin to the support provided under the CITES Legislation Project.

Biosafety Protocol

Implementation of the Cartagena Protocol on Biosafety, the first protocol developed under the CBD, primarily requires the development of technical capacity. It requires, for instance, parties to make decisions on imports of living modified organisms (LMOs) for intentional introduction into the environment in accordance with scientifically sound risk assessment (Article 15), and to adopt measures and strategies for preventing adverse effects and for managing the risks identified by risk assessments (Article 16). Initially, parties' concerns, particularly in the case of developing countries, centered on receiving technical assistance and building their research and LMO detection capacity, while ensuring autonomous decision making at the time of import (ENB 2002b). In this context, the Global Environment Facility (GEF) has been instrumental in funding the development and implementation of national biosafety frameworks.[2]

The Biosafety Protocol provides detailed procedures to ensure implementation at the national level through the operation of the advance informed agreement (AIA) procedure (Articles 4–7), which lies at the heart of the Protocol, requiring designation of a national competent authority responsible for all administrative functions required by the Protocol (Article 19) and reaching and communicating a decision on the import, within set deadlines, on the basis of a risk assessment. However, although the Protocol sets out a specific AIA procedure, it allows parties significant flexibility in the way it is applied. A party of import may: apply its own domestic regulatory framework, as long as this is consistent with the Protocol (Articles 9(3) and 14(4)); adopt simplified procedures for certain LMOs (Article 13); enter into bilateral, regional, or multilateral agreements regarding the intentional transboundary movement of LMOs (Article 14); or take action for the conservation and sustainable use of biodiversity that is more protective than that provided in the Protocol. These are options with complex legal implications that make the drafting and operationalization of national legislation particularly challenging. On the other hand, implementation at the national level has been facilitated by the Biosafety Clearing House (BCH), an electronic resource that facilitates the exchange of scientific, technical, environmental, and legal information on, and experience with, LMOs. In 2010, developed and developing countries alike praised the improvements made to the digital and communications structure of the BCH, underscoring nevertheless the continued need for capacity building in using it (ENB 2010f).

FIGURE 11.3 Co-Chairs Jimena Nieto and René Lefeber celebrated the adoption of the Nagoya-Kuala Lumpur Supplementary Protocol on Liability and Redress to the Cartagena Protocol on Biosafety in Nagoya in October 2010. Photo courtesy of IISD/*Earth Negotiations Bulletin*

Concerns have, however, evolved in recent years, potentially reflecting increased country experience with the use of modern biotechnology and the need for increased agricultural production. In 2010, more countries expressed interest in the safe *use* of modern biotechnology as such, while the adoption of the Supplementary Protocol on Liability and Redress has created new demands for national-level measures (ENB 2010f) (Figure 11.3). Thus, new legal challenges have emerged with regard to implementation, as future parties to the Supplementary Protocol will be expected to develop national legislation on liability from damage resulting from LMOs—a complex and uncharted legal field. The issue of financial security (Article 10) was among the last ones to be resolved during the negotiations because of the complex legal, technical, and economic issues it raised (ENB 2010g).

ABS Protocol

Implementation challenges dominated the negotiations of the Nagoya Protocol on Access to Genetic Resources and the Fair and Equitable Sharing of Benefits Arising from their Utilization, adopted under the CBD in October 2010. While it may take several years before the ABS Protocol enters into force, CBD parties already anticipate difficulties with regard to: the drafting of national legislation and measures to implement requirements regarding the organizational and decision-making structures needed to grant prior informed consent (PIC); building the capacity of national institutes and indigenous and local communities to negotiate mutually agreed terms; and enforcing national legislation, particularly through building the ability of selected authorities to monitor genetic resources in the established checkpoints (Article 17).

Critical implementation issues are also expected to arise with regard to the extra-territorial application of provider countries' ABS legislation: the Protocol requires parties to take measures to ensure that genetic resources and traditional knowledge utilized within their jurisdiction have been accessed in accordance with the legislation and requirements of the party that provided them (Article 15 and 16). Implementation of such provisions would require the establishment of some kind of mechanism in countries with users in their jurisdiction (potentially all) to ensure that they receive relevant information and recognize the legislation of the countries that have provided the genetic resources or traditional knowledge. Because of the in-built flexibility in the Protocol, capacity-building activities will vary greatly from one country to another. In 2011, parties discussed the need to develop a strategy for capacity building under the Protocol that will balance a bottom-up approach to allow countries and communities to determine their own needs with overarching global coordination of the various multilateral and bilateral initiatives on ABS (ENB 2011c).

The fact that only a few countries have drafted domestic legislation on ABS despite the adoption of the non-binding Bonn Guidelines on ABS in 2002 (CBD COP 2002) indicates that these earlier efforts were not successful in lessening the complexities of implementing ABS at the national level, and innovative solutions are still to be found for the Protocol to be operationalized. To address these challenges, the Protocol specifically calls for cooperation in capacity building, capacity development and strengthening of human resources and institutional capacities, based on needs and priorities identified through national capacity self-assessments (Article 22), technology transfer (Article 23), and support from the financial mechanism based on the CBD Article 20 (Article 25). It is therefore no surprise that the last-minute adoption of the Protocol was made possible, among other things, by the pledge of US$2 billion of Japanese aid over three years on ABS (ENB 2010d).

ITPGR

While the CBD deals with biodiversity as a whole, the ITPGR addresses specific issues raised by the conservation and sustainable use of plant genetic resources for food and agriculture. Because its objectives are therefore more related to food and agriculture than to the environment, the ITPGR was adopted as an independent international agreement under the UN Food and Agriculture

Organization (FAO), rather than as a protocol to the CBD, as was suggested during its negotiations (ENB 2001a).

Structures at the international level have been put into place to ensure implementation of the Treaty's Multilateral System (MLS) of facilitated access and fair and equitable benefit sharing. The MLS has become operational through the use of a standard material transfer agreement (SMTA) specifying the terms for access and benefit-sharing provisions. The access component of the system is to a large degree automated, using the SMTA in combination with previously operating networks of national gene banks and the international agricultural research centers of the Consultative Group on International Agricultural Research (CGIAR). The benefit-sharing component is, in turn, to be implemented through payments upon commercialization of products developed on the basis of material accessed through the system. However, mandatory payments are not expected to take place soon, taking into consideration the time required for research, development, and commercialization. Their control and enforcement, when that time comes, will also be done at the international level under the authority of the Treaty's Governing Body and will certainly represent a challenge requiring innovative solutions. Until then, the benefit-sharing through information exchange, technology transfer, and capacity building, accompanied by an appropriate use of the Treaty's funding strategy, will need to support implementation.

As a response to developing countries' concerns about implementation costs, a Benefit-Sharing Fund was established in the framework of the treaty's funding strategy (Article 18). The fund is currently based largely on voluntary contributions, providing certain means to build capacities for conservation and sustainable use of plant genetic resources at the national and local levels. Norway provided an annual contribution equivalent to 0.1% of the total sales of seeds in the country (ITPGR 2008). Challenges, however, remain with regard to the selection of projects to be supported by the fund, including the determination of which communities or groups will be able to have access to an international mechanism detached from their realities, and under which conditions (ENB 2009a).

The Benefit-Sharing Fund could also serve as a means to promote implementation of farmers' rights (Article 9)—an innovative concept enshrined in the treaty but left to be implemented at the national level. Additional international support for farmers' rights derives from the treaty provision about sharing benefits under the MLS primarily with farmers (Article 13(3)) and ensuring that farmers also benefit from plans and programs implemented in the framework of the treaty's funding strategy (Article 18(8)). Controversy over the balance between national action and international guidance (mainly provided by the Treaty's Governing Body) on farmers' rights was reflected in heated discussions between developed countries such as Canada and Australia insisting that this was an issue strictly within the national purview, and many other countries calling for enabling measures at the international level, including the financial assistance and technical advice required for national implementation of these rights (ENB 2009a, 2011a).

UNFCCC and the Kyoto Protocol

The UNFCCC embodies general agreement regarding the need to address climate change, and a commitment by developed countries to take the lead in this, including by stabilizing emissions at 1990 levels. It does not, however, set out clear-cut binding commitments that are strictly enforceable. Its main mechanisms for fostering implementation are policy tools such as technology transfer, funding, capacity building, and support for national reporting (Articles 4.3, 4.5, 4.8, 4.9, 8, and 11; Wang and Wiser 2002). The Kyoto Protocol, in turn, established unprecedented legally binding and time-bound targets for developed countries to reduce greenhouse gas emissions, while key political and technical details were later smoothed out through subsequent COP decisions, such as the 2001 Marrakesh Accords.[3]

Implementation tools under the Convention include the Least Developed Countries (LDC) Fund and Special Climate Change Fund for climate adaptation activities, the creation of an Expert Group on Technology Transfer to facilitate and provide advice and funding for technology transfer, and the creation of guidance for capacity-building efforts. More recently, the establishment of the Technology Mechanism, Adaptation Committee, and the Green Climate Fund has further expanded these innovative tools (ENB 2010i). Furthermore, the UNFCCC's Subsidiary Body on Implementation (SBI) was designed to assist the regime's Conference of the Parties "in the assessment and review of the effective implementation of the Convention" (Article 10.1), but its effectiveness is hampered somewhat by the restriction laid on it to "assess the overall aggregated effect of the steps taken by the parties" (Article 10.1). Thus, it does not generally address implementation issues that are being confronted by specific parties. A more practical international mechanism for the resolution of questions regarding implementation was envisioned in the UNFCCC (Article 13), but was never established.

The Protocol was "revolutionary" for its comprehensiveness and the nature of its legally binding targets, as well as for its ground-breaking use of innovative market mechanisms to facilitate implementation and compliance: the Joint Implementation (JI), Clean Development Mechanism (CDM), and international emissions trading market mechanisms and the use of land use, land-use change and forestry (LULUCF) activities. With the UNFCCC, the Protocol (and the decisions made under it) provides significant support for national implementation through the provision of technical support from the Secretariat, and additional capacity building, technology transfer, and financing tools (Article 11), including the Adaptation Fund, for developing country parties.[4] The Protocol further enhances the implementation and compliance tools used under the UNFCCC with compliance-related commitments for developed countries, compliance-related commitments on supplementary reporting of greenhouse gas (GHG) emissions to ensure compliance with the emission reduction target (Article 7.1), independent review of developed country implementation reporting by expert review teams (Article 8), strict rules for the Protocol's market-based mechanisms (Articles 6, 12, and 17 and the Marrakesh Accords), and commitments to establish national systems for estimating GHG emissions and removals (Article 5). The Protocol's Facilitative Branch of its Compliance Committee is also designed to provide advice, financial and technical assistance, and recommendations to parties implementing the Protocol (Yamin and Depledge 2004). The Committee's Enforcement Branch, as discussed below, provides strong incentives for implementation as well as through its powers to adjudicate over compliance matters and to issue binding decisions.

Given the urgency of the threat of climate change, the necessary engagement of the private sector in reducing emissions, and the highly technical nature of the detailed rules and methodologies set out in the Marrakesh Accords, the enactment of binding domestic law at the national level should have an important role in the implementation of the Kyoto Protocol. And in most cases it does. Most countries with emission reduction commitments under the Protocol have passed binding legislation and are making headway in fulfilling their commitments. But this is not technically a requirement of the Protocol. The Protocol requires developed country parties to ensure that their emissions do not exceed their emission targets (Article 3), and in doing so, "to implement and/or elaborate policies and measures" (Article 2.1) and requires the setting up of domestic programs, systems and/or institutions, in areas including estimating emissions, advancing implementation, emissions reporting, and flexible mechanism operation. But there are no binding requirements for the passage or implementation of binding domestic laws and there is no real specificity regarding what policies and measures must contain. Unsurprisingly, the differences in the legislative approaches of parties are reflected in their success in reducing domestic GHG emissions. Those developed country parties that have enacted binding measures, such as the EU's Emissions Trading Scheme, are generally on the road to compliance, while those that have not, such as Canada, are not (NRTEE 2007) (Figure 11.4).

Without emission reduction targets, developing countries do not have the same pressing need for national implementation legislation. However, to participate in the CDM and also to attract funding, technology transfer, and other resources to address climate issues at home, developing countries need to adopt policies that facilitate CDM projects and other international initiatives. Thus, implementation of the protocol through binding national law is practically necessary, although rarely done.[5]

FIGURE 11.4 NGOs protesting Canada's position opposing a reference to the need to reduce GHG emissions by 25–40% at UNFCCC COP 13 in Bali, Indonesia. Photo courtesy of IISD/*Earth Negotiations Bulletin*

Finally, differentiated implementation requirements have significantly impacted the negotiation of further GHG emission reduction commitments. One of the key attributes of the climate treaties is their entrenchment of the principle of common but differentiated responsibilities. This principle not only led to text in the UNFCCC and the Protocol on the provision of funding and technical assistance to developing countries, but also on differentiated legal obligations with regard to mitigation. The resulting differences in the level of commitments and types of implementation that are required between developed countries and large emerging developing countries such as India, China, and Brazil has led to serious consequences for the effectiveness of the Protocol and in the negotiations for a second commitment period or successor agreement. The United States highlighted the lack of developing country commitments as one of the reasons why it withdrew its support of the Protocol in 2001 and the Canadian, Japanese, EU, and other governments consider this a problem that must be addressed in any agreement on a post–2012 regime.

Despite its innovative tools, the depth and scale of the climate change problem has made implementation of the Protocol through domestic emissions reductions challenging for many states, particularly for those that adopted aggressive targets. The extent of the challenges in implementing their existing climate change commitments is reflected in the positions and difficulties the international community is presently having in agreeing on a follow-up or successor agreement to the Protocol (ENB 2009c).

Negotiating Compliance Mechanisms

While significant variations characterize the balance between international and national action for the implementation of MEAs, the processes under all the selected treaties have engaged in discussions on international compliance systems. And while the establishment of non-compliance mechanisms under MEAs seems to be a common trend, these mechanisms have been set up in different ways in the MEAs addressed in this chapter. Discussions on compliance mechanisms have emerged as key deal-makers and breakers in MEA negotiations, often with significant spill-over effects to various items under discussion. In addition, the difficulty in negotiating compliance mechanisms has reflected the increasing volume in implementation challenges: parties are less willing to undertake mandatory obligations and allow for international oversight over national-level implementation if such obligations are not met by sustainable financing, capacity building, and technology transfer.

CITES

The compliance system under CITES was not part of its original design, but gradually resulted from decisions and resolutions of its Conference of the Parties, eventually developing into a complex machinery with the possibility to impose trade sanctions on parties. The COP and the Secretariat, as well as the Scientific Committees and Standing Committee created by the COP, not only supervise but also monitor national action and propose actions, including trade suspensions as a last resort, to guarantee efficient implementation of the Convention. These powers were derived from a provision in CITES enabling the COP to make recommendations to improve the effectiveness of the Convention (Article XI), coupled with majority-voting decision making. This means that—unlike most MEAs working by consensus—decisions in CITES COPs are regularly taken notwithstanding the opposition of a specific party or group of parties.

The compliance system in place relies on data provided by parties through annual submissions on legal trade statistics and information (Article VIII(7)) and biennial reports on legislative, regulatory, and administrative measures taken to enforce the Convention, in order to protect species at risk from international trade. The CITES scientific committees regularly review the Convention's functioning through two main procedures: the Review of Significant Trade (RST) and the Periodic Review of the CITES Appendices.

The Periodic Review of the Appendices can be described as a regular "updating" exercise, identifying listed species or families that may no longer be traded internationally, and thus may be removed from the appendices to ensure that only species that actually need CITES' protection receive appropriate attention and a share of CITES' limited resources. The review entails verifying whether the criteria for listing species on the appendices are still met by listed species, and deciding whether such species should be de-listed or down-listed (but also possibly up-listed). Both the Plants and Animals Committee chairs, however, have highlighted the difficulty in finding parties to volunteer to carry out the review of species, noting that "periodic reviews keep the appendices alive and support the Convention's implementation" (ENB 2008b). But parties prefer to devote their limited resources to the identification of new species threatened by trade that should be listed or to listed species that should be better managed (such as those under the RST), rather than to find out whether listed species should be expunged from the Appendices (ENB 2011b). Many of these reviews are thus financed by researchers in universities or NGOs, which provides a point of entry for independent scientific advice and relevant stakeholders into CITES international compliance process.

The RST looks at trade trends in species listed in Appendix II and identifies those cases that provide a cause for concern over potential unsustainable harvest levels. Trade statistics, generated at points of exit and entry, allow the identification of loopholes in implementation, as well as trends that may give cause for concern. The UNEP World Conservation Monitoring Centre (WCMC) keeps track of international trade in wildlife trends generated by national reports through a public registry that allows all stakeholders including NGOs to bring issues of concern to the attention of the Secretariat or the CITES committees (UNEP-WCMC 2011). These allow CITES' scientific organs to monitor and follow up on countries that have enforcement problems, suggesting, together with the secretariat and Standing Committee, alternatives to bring wildlife trade back to sustainable levels.

Parties concerned are required to present additional information to back their extraction levels and CITES scientific committees evaluate whether a sound "non-detriment finding procedure," based on a scientific assessment of the impact of trade on such species, has been performed prior to allowing exports in that country. In 2010, for example, the Standing Committee evaluated the results of RST processes for Saker falcons from Mongolia, and pursuant to Mongolia's explanations on conservation actions undertaken decided to lift the recommendation to suspend trade in falcon specimens from Mongolia on the condition that an export quota of 300 specimens is maintained for 2009 and 2010 (ENB 2009b).

Some NGOs, most notably TRAFFIC, collaborate actively with CITES in bringing to the attention of Convention parties those cases where illegal trade, or unrestricted legal trade places species at the brink of extinction. In these cases, to support parties in improving their internal procedures to ensure that use is sustainable, CITES (through the Secretariat, the COP or the Standing or Scientific Committees) may suggest the establishment of zero quotas, the adoption of specific regulations and/or management plans, etc. It is important to note that only in cases where all possible efforts do not achieve the desired result are trade suspensions recommended, and that suspensions may derive not only from failure to implement CITES regulations on the ground, but also from failure to adopt national legislation.

Based on recommendations by the Scientific and Standing Committees, the COP may also adopt decisions on measures to bring extraction levels or trade levels in line with the convention, on the adoption of adequate regulation at the national level, or on requesting parties, for example, to review species which would benefit from a CITES-listing (CITES CoP 2010a) or establishing international trade standards, such as the treatment of live specimens (CITES CoP 2007a) on transport of live specimens. Sustained non-compliance by a party may also lead to the Standing Committee recommending, and the COP adopting, a recommendation for CITES parties to refrain from engaging in trade with a specific country, such as those which are in place for Somalia, Rwanda, Djibouti, and Mauritania (October 2010).[6] Countries must then internalize the decisions taken at the international level through their own national legislative processes.

Parties, however, are not completely comfortable with these procedures. In 2007, a proposal to instruct the Standing Committee to consider sanctions against parties not complying with requirements to improve CITES legislation at the national level was opposed by several Latin American countries, which preferred measures "to facilitate" compliance: the proposal supported by the United States and the David Shepherd Wildlife Foundation eventually garnered the needed majority of votes (CITES 2007).

Tensions also emerged when a proposal was made in 2007 to codify CITES compliance procedures. The initiative failed to achieve sufficient support by parties, who decided to "take note of" the guidelines rather than adopt them.[7] This may well indicate that countries seeking stronger compliance most likely preferred keeping the reasonably effective compliance mechanism emerged through practice uncodified (ENB 2006, 2007a), rather than risking a watering down of the compliance mechanism in striking a deal with countries such as Japan (a country with strong whaling interests) that opposed such an initiative (ENB 2007b).

CBD

As opposed to CITES and notwithstanding the preponderance of national implementation for the effectiveness of the CBD, the Convention itself and subsequent COP decisions have not created a mechanism to systematically and effectively monitor compliance at the national level. The SBSTTA was created to provide timely advice relating to the CBD implementation (Article 25), and has engaged in the analysis of national reports (Article 26) and the undertaking of so-called "in-depth reviews" of areas of activities of the Convention. It is questionable, however, that these exercises are effectively keeping tabs on implementation in various countries. The creation by the CBD COP of a Working Group on

Review of Implementation (WGRI) (CBD COP 2004b) did not necessarily provide any added value in terms of compliance monitoring by parties, as the WGRI has mostly focused on streamlining the processes within the CBD and ensuring cooperation between the CBD and other international or national non-state actors (ENB 2005, 2007d, 2010e).

An inversion to this trend, however, may have started in 2010, when the COP was explicitly tasked not only to review progress in the implementation of the Strategic Plan but also to provide guidance on means to address obstacles encountered in its implementation, and to consider in 2012 the possible development of additional mechanisms to facilitate compliance with the convention and the plan, or strengthening of SBSTTA or WGRI to that end (CBD COP 2010).

Biosafety Protocol

The negotiations of the Biosafety Protocol showed clearly that setting up non-compliance mechanisms may result in a deal-maker or -breaker. Reflecting a lack of consensus on whether a provision on compliance should be included in the Protocol at all, agreement could only be achieved on an enabling clause providing that the first meeting of the parties shall "consider and approve cooperative procedures and institutional mechanisms to promote compliance" with the provisions of the Protocol and address cases of non-compliance (Article 34). Indeed, such consensus was made possible only when the compliance procedures were qualified as "cooperative" (ENB 1999) making the Biosafety Protocol part of a trend toward non-adversarial compliance procedures in MEAs. Accordingly, the first meeting of the parties adopted a decision establishing a compliance committee (BS 2004; ENB 2004b).

The Compliance Committee has focused mainly on an analysis of national reports and information contained in the BCH, without having addressed a case of non-compliance to date. At its sixth meeting it concluded that it had no mandate to consider a submission made by an NGO alleging non-compliance of a party, as its mandate only allowed a party to trigger the procedure with respect to itself or with respect to another party (BS 2009). As opposed to the practice under CITES, this seems to confirm that more formalized rules on compliance tend to disfavor participatory mechanisms at the international level.

ABS Protocol

Compliance was one of the three key elements on which the success of the negotiations of the ABS Protocol depended: the Co-Chairs of the negotiations on the Protocol, Fernando Casas (Colombia) and Timothy Hodges (Canada), referred to the "ABC" of ABS so as to highlight the importance of compliance (C) on equal footing with access to genetic resources (A) and benefit-sharing (B) (ENB 2010h).

As a result, the ABS Protocol includes several compliance-related provisions operating at different levels.

A framework provision on monitoring compliance at the international level foresees the possible future establishment of a compliance mechanism similar to those adopted by other MEAs—that is, of a cooperative and non-adversarial nature (Article 30). In earlier negotiations, certain parties had argued for the establishment of a subsidiary body under the Protocol to assist in the assessment of implementation, considering information communicated by parties (IISD RS 2010). Another idea that had emerged in earlier negotiations of the Protocol but did not make it into its agreed text was the proposed establishment of an international ombudsperson to support developing countries and indigenous and local communities to identify breaches of rights and provide technical and legal support in ensuring effective redress of such breaches (Draft Article 14 bis, in CBD 2010c; ENB 2010h). If established, such an innovative feature in the MEA landscape (which is more familiar in the human rights context) would essentially constitute an international institution able to work on the ground directly with communities, while enabling communities to have immediate access to an international avenue to address alleged disrespect of their rights protected under the Protocol (Morgera and Tsioumani 2011). In 2011, CBD parties realized that they may need to take inspiration not only from MEAs, but also from other international treaties, thus possibly opening the door for some features of human rights compliance mechanisms to be taken into account in devising the compliance mechanism for the Protocol (ENB 2011c).

One of the key provisions that made it into the agreed text of the ABS protocol, as the result of a series of compromises by all players involved, was the monitoring of the utilization of genetic resources at the national level, including through the designation of checkpoints, to support compliance (Article 17). With developed and developing countries having directly opposing views on the necessity of mandatory checkpoints, the kind of information such checkpoints would manage, disclosure requirements, and consequences of non-compliance, the final text appears to combine an international law obligation to establish checkpoints, as appropriate, with flexibility to select those checkpoints most suited to national circumstances (ENB 2010d).

In addition, the link between national and international levels of implementation is guaranteed by an internationally recognized certificate of compliance (Article 13(3)), aiming to serve as evidence at the international level that the genetic resource it covers has been accessed in accordance with prior informed consent and that mutually agreed terms have been established at the national level. The certificate basically consists in a national permit on ABS that is made available on the ABS clearinghouse—an international centralized information system that is expected to give certainty to both users and providers, and provide some sort of independent verification of access and benefit-sharing decisions on the ground. Parties will thus be able to use the clearinghouse to monitor compliance or perhaps even use that information as defense against non-compliance allegations (ENB 2011c).

ITPGR

Although the decision to establish a compliance committee was adopted at the first session of the Treaty's Governing Body (ITPGR 2006), the procedures and operational mechanisms to promote compliance and address issues of non-compliance were eventually agreed upon five years later (ENB 2011a). Debated over three Governing Body sessions, and tied by developing countries to simultaneous progress on implementation of the Treaty's Funding Strategy (ENB 2007c, 2009a), the discussions provide another example of the links between compliance and the need for assistance to address implementation challenges.

The treaty text mandates the Governing Body to consider and approve cooperative and effective procedures and operational mechanisms to promote compliance and address issues of non-compliance, including monitoring, and offering advice or assistance, including legal advice or legal assistance (Article 21). The reference to "monitoring" created the opportunity for the governing body to adopt far-reaching international compliance procedures, at least in comparison with the CBD and the Biosafety Protocol. The final outcome was thus described by delegates as "second-generation compliance procedures": the Compliance Committee will not only consider information submitted to it on issues of compliance and non-compliance, but will have additional duties on monitoring implementation, considering parties' reports, and presenting a synthesis and analysis of such reports, as well as recommendations, to the Governing Body. The functions of the committee also include the ability to answer questions and statements addressed to it: the only exceptions seem to be questions related to the SMTA raised by parties to a specific SMTA, although arguably the committee could address general questions by the Governing Body regarding the SMTA (ENB 2011a).

Illustrating the links between implementation challenges and compliance-related debates, one of the main issues hampering negotiations under the treaty was related to recognition of the special needs of developing countries and countries with economies in transition. Participants from North America took a principled stance that compliance obligations apply equally to all parties, whereas a distinction could potentially be drawn when it comes to remedies. On the other hand, developing countries insisted that the principle of common but differentiated responsibilities applies to compliance, too. Consensus was only made possible on the last day of the fourth Governing Body meeting in 2011 after an all-night session, using compromise text based on the Basel Convention Compliance Mechanism, noting that the operation of the compliance procedures shall pay particular attention to the special needs of developing country parties and parties with economies in transition (ENB 2011a).

UNFCCC and Kyoto Protocol

Compliance is one of the key and innovative elements of the international climate change regime, which is among the few MEAs (together with CITES) where negative consequences for non-compliance are envisaged. Under the Kyoto Protocol, a Compliance Committee was created to promote compliance, determine cases of non-compliance, and apply appropriate consequences. Another key feature of this compliance system is that compliance proceedings to be brought before the committee may be triggered by reports of expert review teams on parties' national communications.

The committee has two branches with different functions: the Facilitative Branch assists parties in implementing their Kyoto commitments by requiring the provision of advice and assistance, facilitating financial and technical assistance, and making non-binding recommendations; while the Enforcement Branch determines whether an Annex I party has met its emissions target, complied with its monitoring and reporting requirements, and met the eligibility tests for participating in the Protocol's market mechanisms. Although proposals were made at negotiations in Bonn in 2001 to permit a broader range of consequences available to the Enforcement Branch (including for instance the ordering of payments to repair damage to the environment) (ENB 2001b), in the end the branch may apply consequences only when a developed country party has failed to: comply with its monitoring and reporting requirements (KP Articles 5.1, 5.2, and 7.1); meet the eligibility tests for participating in the Kyoto flexible mechanisms; or meet its emissions target (Article 3.1). Where there is non-compliance with monitoring and reporting requirements, the Enforcement Branch may require the party to submit an action plan analyzing the causes of non-compliance and setting out corrective measures to remedy the non-compliance and a timetable to assess progress. When a developed country is found to be out of compliance with the eligibility requirements for the Kyoto market mechanisms, the Enforcement Branch will order suspension of the party's eligibility to participate in the market mechanisms pending the return to compliance with those requirements.

Developed country parties that fail to meet their emissions target may face the most serious consequences: a deduction of 1.3 tonnes from their emissions allocation (assigned amount) for the subsequent compliance period, for every tonne of emissions by which a party exceeds its target; the obligation to prepare a detailed plan explaining how it will meet its reduced target for the subsequent compliance period—the Enforcement Branch may review the plan and assess whether or not it is likely to work, but it cannot approve the plan or order a party to undertake specific measures; and a prohibition on using international emissions trading to sell parts of its emissions allocation until it has demonstrated that it will be able to comply with its current target.

Enforcement of commitments is by no means easy. First, although the compliance rules in the Marrakesh Accords were unanimously adopted, the consequences are not technically "legally binding" (UNFCCC 2006). The question of whether the compliance text would be made binding was a divisive issue in several stages of the negotiations (ENB 2001b). Based on the wording of Article 18 of the Protocol, compliance procedures and mechanisms "entailing binding consequences shall be adopted by means of an amendment to this Protocol." Although, it was called for by developing countries (ENB 2001b), no such amendment has yet been adopted.

Second, even if the Protocol were amended, some commitments may be difficult to enforce. For instance, Article 3.2 states that "each Party included in Annex I shall, by 2005, have made demonstrable progress in achieving its commitments under this Protocol." Unfortunately, although there are several requirements under the UNFCCC necessitating that parties report on it (UNFCCC Articles 4.2(b) and 7.2(e)), there are no indicators in the Protocol on how to assess "demonstrable progress."[8]

Third, political issues may complicate proceedings. As the Protocol's first commitment period spans from 2008 to 2012, compliance with the Protocol's key emission reduction commitments under its Article 3.1 will only be formally assessed after 2012. In fact, the Canadian government has stated that "measuring compliance involves extensive expert review and submissions by the Parties, and cannot be completed until 2015" (Department of Justice 2009). Thus, there is little a country can do to enforce non-compliance until several years after the violation has been committed—and possibly several years after the responsible government has been out of power. Moreover, until a follow-up or successor climate change agreement is concluded, parties may be unwilling to enter into enforcement proceedings and Compliance Committee members may be unwilling to vote for ordering strict measures that may jeopardize the goodwill needed to negotiate a new climate deal.

Fourth, without a continuation of the Kyoto regime, the compliance tools set out for meeting the first commitment period targets are undermined as some of the key consequences for non-compliance relate to a second commitment period of the Kyoto Protocol. Thus compliance has become a critical question in the ongoing negotiations on the post-2012 international climate change regime. With the emergence of the Copenhagen Accord, the likelihood of a second commitment period under the Kyoto Protocol is questionable (ENB 2009c). Moreover, even if there is a second commitment period, recalcitrant states will likely factor their penalties from the first commitment period into the setting of their subsequent commitments, thus diluting the effectiveness of the regime.

Conclusions

The expansion of country obligations under, and increased scope of, MEAs through the development of protocols and the broad interpretation of treaty objectives has been evident over the last twenty years. CITES' scope has gone beyond the regulation of trade in endangered species, by addressing trade in commodities and threats that are not related to trade. The CBD now includes three protocols and several extensive programs of work targeting not only biodiversity, but also ecosystem services and human wellbeing. The climate change regime, with the Kyoto Protocol's strict implementation requirements, extends well beyond the UNFCCC's general obligations.

This expansion has brought with it considerable implementation challenges, leading in turn to tensions in negotiating dynamics and distinct trends in the negotiation of means to address them. A significant trend in this regard is the increasing openness among negotiators to use innovative solutions to address implementation challenges. The CITES Secretariat has increasingly offered its advisory services to parties. Under the CBD, regional and subregional workshops have been used in an effort to enhance effectiveness of NBSAPs. Under the Biosafety Protocol, implementation at the national level has been greatly facilitated by the Biosafety Clearing House. In the context of the ITPGR, the multilateral benefit-sharing fund is put in use to assist implementation at the national and community levels. And under the climate change regime, flexible implementation measures have been established in direct response to the challenges in implementing the Kyoto Protocol's emission reduction targets.

A second general trend in negotiations relates to a general reluctance of negotiators to agree to effective binding measures to ensure compliance with treaty commitments. Certainly, this trend is not new, but the expanding scope and comprehensiveness of many MEAs adds to this by broadening the risk of non-compliance. While CITES has a non-codified compliance mechanism that has evolved over time and remains dynamic, negotiation of a compliance mechanism under the other biodiversity-related conventions has been difficult and remains strictly facilitative and non-adversarial. Under the climate change regime, the Kyoto Protocol's compliance tools are comprehensive, but non-binding. Attempts at setting-up non-compliance mechanisms have shown their potential to "break" broader deals in the negotiations of the Biosafety and ABS Protocols, as well as under the ITPGR, notwithstanding the fact that parties have in those frameworks clearly chosen a non-confrontational and purely supportive model. As a result, while implementation becomes more complex, parties are less willing to agree on far-reaching compliance mechanisms, particularly if their compliance is not supported by sufficient and sustainable financing, technology transfer, and capacity building.

More prominence and systematic discussions of financing, technology transfer, and capacity-building issues under different MEAs can thus be identified as a third trend. This is in part due to the recognition by parties of the gravity of many environmental problems and the challenges in addressing them. Despite optimism and progress in the early 1990s in the development of international environmental law, the reality of the implementation challenges raised by

MEAs resulted in slow progress in the negotiation and entry into force of more comprehensive subsidiary agreements. This has led to an increasingly technical focus and specialization in many of these negotiations, which has led to reduced accessibility of the negotiations to non-experts in specific MEAs (or even sub-processes under the same MEA) and had made comparison across MEAs more difficult.

Despite these trends, there are also significant divergences. A pertinent example is the extent to which implementation relies on international action as opposed to national efforts. The attention devoted to the enactment and enforcement of national legislation in ensuring the implementation of MEAs therefore varies significantly. For example, CITES has gradually institutionalized a complex system of international oversight and support for the development and application of national legislation, while the ITPGR only provides for a more limited approach to international assistance in that respect, and the CBD opts for a light-touch system of aggregate information gathering with a view to identifying best practices.

For the past twenty years, MEA parties have entertained discussions on the complex and increasing implementation challenges related to multilateral environmental objectives. Yet with the expansion of the scope of these agreements and the general deepening severity of environmental degradation, implementation challenges have only increased over time. These developments have changed the dynamics of negotiations resulting in the development of a variety of new practices. Negotiators have become more innovative; financial, technological, and capacity-building assistance issues have been afforded greater significance; and negotiations have become more complex and technical. These factors do not necessarily mean that environmental negotiations have become less effective due to the increased scope of these treaties, but rather they have become more sophisticated, as the seriousness and extent of the environmental and development challenges faced have become more apparent and the need to address them has become more pressing.

Notes

1 See http://www.unep.org/dec/onlinemanual/Enforcement/NationalLawsRegulations/Resource/tabid/780/Default.aspx.
2 Following the adoption of the Biosafety Protocol in 2000, the GEF Council approved in November 2000 an initial strategy for assisting countries to prepare for the Protocol's entry into force, together with a global UNEP-GEF project to assist all eligible countries to develop national biosafety frameworks. The project was launched in June 2001, and has assisted 123 countries. Under the initial strategy, the GEF also provided support to twelve demonstration projects for capacity building in implementation of national biosafety frameworks. In November 2003, the GEF approved an add-on project to the UNEP-GEF project on the development of national biosafety frameworks entitled Building Capacity for Effective Participation in the Biosafety Clearing House (BCH) of the Cartagena Protocol. See http://bch.cbd.int/protocol/gefprojects.shtml.

3 The Marrakesh Accords set out detailed rules, guidelines, and methodologies for implementing the protocol.

4 See also Marrakesh Accords, Decision 3/CP.7, Capacity Building in Countries with Economies in Transition, at 15; UNFCCC, Articles 4.3, 4.5, 4.8, 4.9, 8 and 11.

5 Presently, over 115 developing country parties have designated national authorities for CDM projects and over sixty-five have registered projects. See http://cdm.unfccc.int/Statistics/dna/DNAByRegionBarChart.html.

6 See http://www.unep.org/dec/onlinemanual/Enforcement/NationalLawsRegulations/Resource/tabid/780/Default.aspx.

7 This process derived from CoP 12 (2002) instructing the secretariat to draft a set of guidelines on compliance with implementation of the convention for consideration by the Standing Committee. Further to the establishment of an open-ended compliance working group, in 2007 the CoP considered the guidelines on CITES compliance procedures, and in a clear effort by parties not to adopt a legally binding procedure, the guidelines were renamed "Guide for Compliance," which the COP took note of—rather than adopted (CITES 2007c).

8 There is also the question as to whether the Article 3.2 requirements are simply procedural obligations or substantive ones. If they are procedural, then the production of a report may be sufficient (Anderson 2003). If they are substantive, then the content of the report may be subject to scrutiny when determining compliance (Verheyen 2006).

Works Cited

Anderson, M. 2003. "Demonstrable Progress" on Climate Change: Prospects and Possibilities. In VERTIC (ed.), *Verification Yearbook*, London: VERTIC Baird House 171.

Beyerlin, U., P.T. Stoll, and R. Wolfrum (eds.). 2006. *Ensuring Compliance with Multilateral Environmental Agreements.* Leiden, The Netherlands: Martinus Nijhoff Publishers.

Bodansky, Daniel. 2010. *The Art and Craft of International Environmental Law.* Cambridge, MA: Harvard University Press.

BS (Biosafety Protocol). 2004. Establishment of Procedures and Mechanisms on Compliance under the Cartagena Protocol on Biosafety. Decision I/7. http://bch.cbd.int/protocol/decisions/decision.shtml?decisionID=8289 (accessed June 21, 2011).

BS. 2009. Report of the Compliance Committee under the Cartagena Protocol on Biosafety on the Work of its Sixth Meeting (UNEP/CBD/BS/CC/6/4). http://www.cbd.int/doc/meetings/bs/bscc-06/official/bscc-06-04-en.pdf (accessed June 21, 2011).

CBD (Convention on Biological Diversity). 2004a. *Addis Ababa Principles and Guidelines for the Sustainable use of Biodiversity.* Montreal: Secretariat of the Convention on Biological Diversity. http://www.cbd.int/doc/publications/addis-gdl-en.pdf (accessed June 21, 2011).

CBD. 2004b. *Guidelines on Biodiversity and Tourism Development.* Montreal: Secretariat of the Convention on Biological Diversity. http://www.cbd.int/doc/publications/tou-gdl-en.pdf (accessed June 21, 2011).

CBD. 2004c. *Akwé: Kon Guidelines.* Montreal: Secretariat of the Convention on Biological Diversity. http://www.cbd.int/doc/publications/akwe-brochure-en.pdf (accessed June 21, 2011).

CBD. 2010a. In-depth Review of the Implementation of the Programme of Work on Mountain Biodiversity. UNEP/CBD/SBSTTA/14/2. http://www.cbd.int/doc/meetings/sbstta/sbstta-14/official/sbstta-14-02-en.pdf (accessed June 21, 2011).

CBD. 2010b. In-depth Review of the Implementation of the Programme of Work on Protected Areas. UNEP/CBD/SBSTTA/14/5. http://www.cbd.int/doc/meetings/sbstta/sbstta-14/official/sbstta-14-05-en.pdf (accessed June 21, 2011).

CBD. 2010c. Report of the Third Part of the Ninth Meeting of the Ad Hoc Open Ended Working Group on Access and Benefit-Sharing. UNEP/CBD/COP/10/5/Add.5. http://www.cbd.int/doc/meetings/cop/cop-10/official/cop-10-05-add5-en.pdf (accessed June 21, 2011).

CBD COP (Convention on Biological Diversity Conference of the Parties). 2002. Bonn Guidelines on Access to Genetic Resources and Fair and Equitable Sharing of the Benefits Arising out of their Utilization. Decision VI/24. http://www.cbd.int/decision/cop/?id=7198 (accessed June 21, 2011).

CBD COP. 2004a. Transfer of Technology and Technology Cooperation (Articles 16 to 19). Decision VII/29. http://www.cbd.int/decision/cop/?id=7766 (accessed June 21, 2011).

CBD COP. 2004b. Strategic Plan: Future Evaluation of proGress. Decision VII/30. http://www.cbd.int/decision/cop/?id=7767 (accessed June 21, 2011).

CBD COP. 2010. The Strategic Plan for Biodiversity 2011–2020 and the Aichi Biodiversity Targets. Decision X/2. http://www.cbd.int/decision/cop/?id=12268 (accessed June 21, 2011).

CITES. 2002. Title of the Convention. Document CoP12 Doc.14 Rev.1. http://www.cites.org/eng/cop/12/doc/E12–14.pdf (accessed June 21, 2011).

CITES. 2004. Recognition of the Benefits of Trade in Wildlife. Resolution Conf. 8.3 (Rev. COP13). http://www.cites.org/eng/res/08/08–03R13.shtml (accessed June 21, 2011).

CITES. 2007. Summary Record of the Seventh Session of Committee II: 8 June 2007: 9h05–12h15. Document COP14 Com. II Rep. 7 (Rev. 1). http://www.cites.org/eng/cop/14/rep/E14-Com-II-Rep-07.pdf (accessed June 21, 2011).

CITES COP. 2007a. Transport of Live Specimens. Resolution Conf. 10.21 (Rev. COP14). http://www.cites.org/eng/res/10/10–21R14.shtml (accessed June 21, 2011).

CITES COP. 2007b. Sustainable Use of Biodiversity: Addis Ababa Principles and Guidelines. Resolution Conf. 13.2 (Rev. COP14). http://www.cites.org/eng/res/13/13–02R14.shtml (accessed June 21, 2011).

CITES COP. 2007c. CITES compliance procedures. Res. Conf. 14.3. http://www.cites.org/eng/res/14/14–03C15.shtml (accessed June 21, 2011).

CITES COP. 2010a. Madagascar. http://www.cites.org/eng/dec/valid15/15_97–98.shtml (accessed June 21, 2011).

CITES COP. 2010b. National Laws for Implementation of the Convention. Resolution Conf. 8.4 (Rev. COP15). http://www.cites.org/eng/res/08/08–04R15.shtml (accessed June 21, 2011).

CITES COP. 2010c. Criteria for Amendment of Appendices I and II. Resolution Conf. 9.24 (Rev. COP15). http://www.cites.org/eng/res/09/09–24R15.shtml (accessed June 21, 2011).

Department of Justice. 2009. *Factum* in *Friends of the Earth v. Governor in Council* (Federal Court of Appeal of Canada).

ENB (*Earth Negotiations Bulletin*). 1999. Report of the Sixth Session of the Open-ended Ad Hoc Working Group on Biosafety and the First Extraordinary Session of the CBD Conference of the Parties: 14–23 February 1999. *Earth Negotiations Bulletin* 9(117). http://www.iisd.ca/download/pdf/enb09117e.pdf (accessed June 21, 2011).

ENB. 2001a. Summary of the Sixth Extraordinary Session of the Commission on Genetic Resources for Food and Agriculture: 24 June–1 July 2001. *Earth Negotiations Bulletin* 9(197). http://www.iisd.ca/download/pdf/enb09197e.pdf (accessed June 21, 2011).

ENB. 2001b. Summary of the Resumed Sixth Session of the Conference of the Parties to the UN Framework Convention on Climate Change: 16–27 July 2001. *Earth Negotiations Bulletin* 12(176). http://www.iisd.ca/download/pdf/enb12176e.pdf (accessed June 21, 2011).

ENB. 2002a. The Twelfth Conference of the Parties to the Convention on International Trade in Endangered Species of Wild Fauna and Flora: 3–15 November 2002.

Earth Negotiations Bulletin 21(30). http://www.iisd.ca/download/pdf/enb2120e.pdf (accessed June 21, 2011).

ENB. 2002b. Third Meeting of the Intergovernmental Committee on the Cartagena Protocol on Biosafety: 22–26 April 2002. *Earth Negotiations Bulletin* 9(244). http://www.iisd.ca/download/pdf/enb09244e.pdf (accessed June 21, 2011).

ENB. 2002c. CITES COP-12 Highlights: Tuesday, 5 November 2002. *Earth Negotiations Bulletin* 21(22). http://www.iisd.ca/download/pdf/enb2122e.pdf (accessed June 21, 2011).

ENB. 2003. Summary of the Ninth Meeting of the Subsidiary Body on Scientific, Technical and Technological Advice of the Convention on Biological Diversity: 10–14 November 2003 *Earth Negotiations Bulletin* 9(262). http://www.iisd.ca/download/pdf/enb09262e.pdf (accessed June 21, 2011).

ENB. 2004a. Summary of the Seventh Conference of the Parties to the Convention on Biological Diversity: 9–20 February 2004. *Earth Negotiations Bulletin* 9(284). http://www.iisd.ca/download/pdf/enb09284e.pdf (accessed June 21, 2011).

ENB. 2004b. Summary of the First Meeting of the Conference of the Parties to the Convention on Biological Diversity serving as the Meeting of the Parties to the Cartagena Protocol on Biosafety: 23–27 February 2004. *Earth Negotiations Bulletin* 9(289). http://www.iisd.ca/download/pdf/enb09289e.pdf (accessed June 21, 2011).

ENB. 2005. Summary Report of the First Meeting of the Ad Hoc Open-ended Working Group on Review of Implementation: 5–9 September 2005. *Earth Negotiations Bulletin* 9(327). http://www.iisd.ca/download/pdf/enb09327e.pdf (accessed June 21, 2011).

ENB. 2006. Summary of the 54th Meeting of the CITES Standing Committee: 2–6 October 2006. *Earth Negotiations Bulletin* 21(50). http://www.iisd.ca/download/pdf/enb2150e.pdf (accessed June 21, 2011).

ENB. 2007a. CITES COP-14 Highlights: Thursday, 14 June 2007. *Earth Negotiations Bulletin* 21(60). http://www.iisd.ca/download/pdf/enb2160e.pdf (accessed June 21, 2011).

ENB. 2007b. CITES COP-14 Highlights: Wednesday, 6 June 2007. *Earth Negotiations Bulletin* 21(54). http://www.iisd.ca/download/pdf/enb2154e.pdf (accessed June 21, 2011).

ENB. 2007c. Summary of the Second Session of the Governing Body of the International Treaty on Plant Genetic Resources for Food and Agriculture: 29 October–2 November 2007. *Earth Negotiations Bulletin* 9(410). http://www.iisd.ca/download/pdf/enb09410e.pdf (accessed June 21, 2011).

ENB. 2007d. Summary of the 12th meeting of the Subsidiary Body on Scientific, Technical and Technological Advice and 2nd Meeting of the Ad Hoc Open-ended Working Group on Review of Implementation of the Convention on Biological Diversity: 2–13 July 2007. *Earth Negotiations Bulletin* 9(382). http://www.iisd.ca/download/pdf/enb09382e.pdf (accessed June 21, 2011).

ENB. 2008a. Summary of the Ninth Conference of the Parties to the Convention on Biological Diversity: 19–30 May 2008. *Earth Negotiations Bulletin* 9(452). http://www.iisd.ca/download/pdf/enb09452e.pdf (accessed June 21, 2011).

ENB. 2008b. Summary of the 57th Meeting of the CITES Standing Committee: 14–18 July 2008. *Earth Negotiations Bulletin* 21(63). http://www.iisd.ca/download/pdf/enb2163e.pdf (accessed June 21, 2011).

ENB. 2009a. Summary of the Third Session of the Governing Body of the International Treaty on Plant Genetic Resources for Food and Agriculture: 1–5 June 2009. *Earth Negotiations Bulletin* 9(471). http://www.iisd.ca/download/pdf/enb09471e.pdf (accessed June 21, 2011).

ENB. 2009b. Summary of the 58th Meeting of the CITES Standing Committee: 6–10 July 2009. *Earth Negotiations Bulletin* 21(66). http://www.iisd.ca/download/pdf/enb2166e.pdf (accessed June 21, 2011).

ENB. 2009c. Summary of the Copenhagen Climate Change Conference: 7–19 December 2009. *Earth Negotiations Bulletin* 12(459). http://www.iisd.ca/download/pdf/enb12459e. pdf (accessed June 21, 2011).

ENB. 2010a. Summary of the Fifteenth Conference of the Parties to the Convention on International Trade in Endangered Species of Wild Fauna and Flora: 13–25 March 2010. *Earth Negotiations Bulletin* 21(67). http://www.iisd.ca/download/pdf/enb2167e. pdf (accessed June 21, 2011).

ENB. 2010b. CBD COP 10 Highlights Friday, 22 October 2010. *Earth Negotiations Bulletin* 9(539). http://www.iisd.ca/download/pdf/enb09539e.pdf (accessed June 21, 2011).

ENB. 2010c. Summary of the Fourteenth Meeting of the Subsidiary Body on Scientific, Technical and Technological Advice to the Convention on Biological Diversity: 10–21 May 2010. *Earth Negotiations Bulletin* 9(514). http://www.iisd.ca/download/ pdf/enb09514e.pdf (accessed June 21, 2011).

ENB. 2010d. Summary of the Tenth Conference of the Parties to the Convention on Biological Diversity: 18–29 October 2011. *Earth Negotiations Bulletin* 9(544). http:// www.iisd.ca/download/pdf/enb09544e.pdf (accessed June 21, 2011).

ENB. 2010e. Summary of the Third Meeting of the CBD Ad Hoc Open-ended Working Group on Review of Implementation: 24–28 May 2010. *Earth Negotiations Bulletin* 9(519). http://www.iisd.ca/download/pdf/enb09519e.pdf (accessed June 21, 2011).

ENB. 2010f. Summary of the Fifth Meeting of the Parties to the Cartagena Protocol on Biosafety: 11–15 October 2010. *Earth Negotiations Bulletin* 9(533). http://www.iisd.ca/ download/pdf/enb09533e.pdf (accessed June 21, 2011).

ENB. 2010g. Fifth Meeting of the Cartagena Protocol on Biosafety: 11–15 October 2010. *Earth Negotiations Bulletin* 9(528). http://www.iisd.ca/download/pdf/enb09528e.pdf (accessed June 21, 2011).

ENB. 2010h. Summary of the Resumed Ninth Meeting of the Ad Hoc Open-ended Working Group on Access and Benefit-sharing (ABS) of the Convention on Biological Diversity: 10–16 July 2010. *Earth Negotiations Bulletin* 9(527). http://www.iisd.ca/ download/pdf/enb09527e.pdf (accessed June 21, 2011).

ENB 2010i. Summary of the Cancún Climate Change Conference: 29 November–11 December 2010. *Earth Negotiations Bulletin* 12(498). http://www.iisd.ca/download/ pdf/enb12498e.pdf (accessed June 21, 2011).

ENB. 2011a. Summary of the Fourth Session of the Governing Body of the International Treaty on Plant Genetic Resources for Food and Agriculture: 14–18 March 2011. *Earth Negotiations Bulletin* 9(550). http://www.iisd.ca/download/pdf/enb09550e.pdf (accessed June 21, 2011).

ENB. 2011b. Summary of the 19th Meeting of the Plants Committee of the Convention on International Trade in Endangered Species of Wild Fauna and Flora: 18–21 April 2011. *Earth Negotiations Bulletin* 21(68). http://www.iisd.ca/download/pdf/enb2168e. pdf (accessed June 21, 2011).

ENB. 2011c. Summary of the First Meeting of the Intergovernmental Committee for the Nagoya Protocol: 5–10 June 2011. *Earth Negotiations Bulletin* 9(551). http://www.iisd. ca/download/pdf/enb09551e.pdf (accessed June 21, 2011).

IISD RS (International Institute for Sustainable Development Reporting Services). 2010. Summary of the Interregional Negotiating Group on Access and Benefit-Sharing: 18–21 September 2010. Briefing Note. http://www.iisd.ca/biodiv/absing/brief/ absing_briefe.pdf (accessed June 21, 2011).

ITPGR. 2006. Compliance. Resolution 3/2006. *First Meeting of the Governing Body of the International Treaty on Plant Genetic Resources for Food and Agriculture.* ftp://ftp.fao.org/ ag/agp/planttreaty/gb1/gb1repe.pdf (accessed June 21, 2011).

ITPGR. 2008. Norway Announces Annual Contribution to the Benefit-Sharing Fund of the International Treaty. Secretariat Press Release (3 March).

Morgera, Elisa and Elsa Tsioumani. 2011 (forthcoming). Yesterday, Today and Tomorrow: Looking Afresh at the Convention on Biological Diversity. *Yearbook of International Environmental Law* 21. Oxford: Oxford University Press.

NRTEE (National Round Table on the Environment and the Economy). 2007. *Response of the National Round Table on the Environment and the Economy to its Obligations Under the Kyoto Protocol Implementation Act.* http://www.nrtee-trnee.com/eng/publications/KPIA-2007/NRTEE-C288-Response-2007-eng.pdf (accessed June 21, 2011).

Prip, C., T. Gross, S. Johnston, and M. Vierros. 2010. *Biodiversity Planning: An Assessment of National Biodiversity Strategies and Action Plans.* Tokyo: United Nations University Institute of Advanced Studies.

Treves, Tullio, Laura Pineschi, Atilla Tanzi, Cesare Pitea, Chiara Ragni, and Francesa Romanin Jacur (eds.). 2009. *Non-compliance Procedures and Mechanisms and the Effectiveness of International Environmental Agreements.* The Hague: TMC Asser Press.

UNEP-WCMC. 2011. United Nations Environment Programme World Conservation Monitoring Centre Website. http://www.unep-wcmc.org/ (accessed June 10, 2011).

UNFCCC. 2006. Procedures and Mechanisms Relating to Compliance under the Kyoto Protocol. Kyoto Protocol Decision 27/CMP.1, as contained in UNFCCC/KP/2005/8/Add.3. http://unfccc.int/resource/docs/2005/cmp1/eng/08a03.pdf#page=92 (accessed June 21, 2011).

Verheyen, Roda. 2006. Legal Opinion on Whether Canada is Currently in Violation of, or is Likely to Violate, its Obligations under the UNFCCC and/or the Kyoto Protocol. http://www.climateactionnetwork.ca/e/cop-12/canada-legal-obligations-unfccc.pdf (accessed June 21, 2011).

Wang, Xueman and Glenn Wiser. 2002. The Implementation and Compliance Regimes under the Climate Change Convention and its Kyoto Protocol. *RECIEL* 11(2): 181–198. http://www.ciel.org/Publications/Wang_Wiser.pdf (accessed June 21, 2011).

Yamin, Farhana and Joanna Depledge. 2004. *The International Climate Change Regime: A Guide to Rules, Institutions and Procedures.* Cambridge, UK: Cambridge University Press.

Conclusions

12

LESSONS LEARNED ON THE ROADS FROM RIO

Pamela S. Chasek, Lynn M. Wagner, and Peter Doran

At the United Nations Conference on Environment and Development in Rio de Janeiro in June 1992, world leaders attempted to turn their backs on the old world order and a "Cold War" security paradigm. Instead, they sought to operationalize a new "sustainable development" paradigm that promised to enhance environmentally sound economic and social development throughout the world. In a concrete manifestation of this new paradigm, the Earth Summit launched an era of rapid development of international environmental law through multilateral negotiations. New conventions, protocols, and amendments to existing treaties emerged on climate change, biodiversity, desertification, high seas fisheries, migratory species, trade in chemicals, persistent organic pollutants, biosafety, plant genetic resources for food and agriculture, hazardous wastes, oil pollution at sea, ozone depletion, and air pollution. Since 1992, these multilateral environmental agreements (MEAs), as they are collectively known, which were once at the periphery of international law, have started to move to the center of international affairs—an achievement that was best illustrated by the active engagement of 119 world leaders in drafting the final agreement during the Copenhagen Climate Change Conference in December 2009 (UNFCCC 2009).

Yet at the same time, it is not possible to understand the evolution of multilateral environmental negotiations since 1992 without a closer look at the global context within which these negotiations have taken place. The costs of environmental degradation and measures to reverse it are growing, in part because it is core economic activities that have caused the identified problems. Governments have realized that greater changes in economic and social development strategies and production techniques must be taken if their collective efforts to implement MEAs are to be effective. However, because of the acceleration of the globalization of investment and the liberalization of trade, global economic forces and the policies that support them can threaten the role of MEAs in shifting the international community onto a sustainable development path (Chasek et al. 2010). This concluding chapter looks at the global context of multilateral environmental negotiations, specifically the impact of globalization. Then, within this context, we examine the challenges and lessons learned from the past twenty years of multilateral environmental negotiations.

Globalization and Governance

Globalization is the accelerating and complex process by which governments, companies, individuals, information, and knowledge are integrated and interconnected on a global scale (Dierks 2001, 2). On the one hand, globalization could be considered beneficial for the environment because it is an "engine of wealth creation" that can fund environmental improvements and facilitate the implementation of MEAs. As societies become wealthier, there is a greater concern for pollution reduction and environmental protection. And because of the wealth creation, society has the ability to implement the necessary measures to achieve these goals. Globalization, by delivering the development side of the sustainable development equation, can solve the social problems that contribute to environmental degradation. The contrary argument, however, sees most aspects of globalization as bad for the environment; globalization is responsible for rapidly accelerating the overconsumption of natural resources and overproduction of waste on a global scale. It has advanced the movement of capital, technology, goods, and labor to areas with high returns on investment without regard for the impact on the communities and people who live there (Chasek et al. 2010, 367).

The exact relationship between globalization and the environment is far more complex than either of these two archetypal arguments and probably contains elements of both. The environment itself is inherently global, with life-sustaining ecosystems and watersheds crossing national boundaries, air pollution moving across entire continents and oceans, and a single shared atmosphere providing a hospitable global climate and ozone layer shielding us from harsh ultraviolet rays. Moreover, the environment is intrinsically linked to economic development, providing natural resources that fuel growth and ecosystem services that underpin lives and livelihoods. Thus while it is important to highlight how globalization impacts the environment, we must also remember that the environment impacts the pace, direction, and quality of globalization. At the very least, this happens because environmental resources provide the fuel for economic globalization, but it also happens because our social and policy responses to global environmental problems constrain and influence the context in which globalization happens (Najam et al. 2007, 6–7).

So how do we come to terms with this complex problem? It is generally recognized that better global governance is the key to managing both globalization and the global environment. More importantly, it is also the key to managing the relationship between the two (Najam et al. 2007, 29). However, it is also quite clear that both globalization and environmental protection challenge the architecture of the international system as it now exists. The term "governance" has a number of meanings, referring, for example, to regimes and common property resources management. Within the UNCED process, the term "governance" was linked to three developments: the participation of states in international law-making; the evolution of the decision-making mechanisms of international institutions; and the participation of non-governmental entities in national and international decision making. Indeed, the very concept of sustainable development came to be associated with notions of governance, and "good governance" (referring to state reform, especially anti-corruption safeguards, in developing countries, often promoted by international financial institutions) in particular.

Three years after the Earth Summit, the Commission on Global Governance published its report, *Our Global Neighborhood* (1995), in an attempt to bring some clarity to the new distributions and flows of power in the wake of economic and financial globalization. In keeping with the UNCED discourse, the Commission on Global Governance was constrained by a consensual discourse, describing governance as the "sum of the many ways individuals and institutions, public and private, manage their common affairs" (1995, 2), while doing little to acknowledge shifts in power toward transnational institutions and the instrumentalizing of national and local actors. Ironically, in the wake of UNCED, the environmentalists' adage that we should "think globally and act locally" suffered a profound loss of innocence as financial and strategic power migrated upwards and away from national and local actors, prompting a decade of global activism targeting the so-called "Washington Consensus"[1] and its institutional agents of globalization. In contrast with the optimistic calls by Kofi Annan, former UN Secretary-General, to make globalization work for sustainable development, critics argued that the post-Earth Summit process had been superseded by neo-liberal globalization and blocked by the resulting rivalries and conflicting interests (Brand et al. 2010).

In addition, the decades since 1992 have witnessed an important transformation of the modern state itself, with major consequences for its capacity to respond to environmental crises. After the Cold War and the intensification and spread of industrial development on a newly globalized scale, the rise of transnational corporations saw many private entities become more powerful than states and begin to instrumentalize states for their own financial–development purposes. Nation-states were transformed from their role as "developmental" actors to "regulatory" states (Majone 1996) with the chief aim of basically controlling operations within their territories. National governments increasingly saw their role as subcontracting out the lucrative, wealth creation parts of its operation to the private sector while the non-lucrative activities were handed over to the non-profit sector. The state began to limit itself to regulating the operations performed by others, seeking to maintain control via regulation. As such, the state became increasingly dependent on and vulnerable to the very actors and organizations it was supposed to regulate, including the transnational corporations and newly empowered financial institutions.

This geopolitical backdrop to the 1990s played a decisive role in delimiting and shaping multilateral environmental negotiations and the way in which problems would be posed in the course of those negotiations. The collapse of the Soviet Union and the disintegration of communism signaled the disappearance of the "last envelope" that had, until then, separated the First from the Second and Third Worlds. With the collapse of communism, developing countries were, more or less, compelled to become "emerging markets" open to various forms of Western investment, while the former Soviet satellites were designated "countries with economies in transition." Corporate mergers went global, civilian high tech was promoted as a new panacea, and market indices and equity valuations went stratospheric as the winds of neoliberalism, deregulation, and openness became the watchwords of a new world order (Nitzan and Bichler 2004).

In the process, the United Nations' role in the international system has diminished, as its historic development role has migrated to the Bretton Woods institutions, with global trade responsibilities falling to the World Trade Organization, created just two years after the Earth Summit. The UN itself has sought to maintain a role, chiefly through the prism of security and humanitarian intervention. Finger (2002) concludes that globalization has not only led the world away from sustainability, but that it has also transformed our global institutions and approaches to the environment. Far from a holistic, precautionary, and non-incremental approach, which was once deemed a requirement, the environment has instead been fragmented and instrumentalized into a series of security, investment, and regulatory dimensions and problematiques.

Thus, a good number of the weaknesses and challenges identified in the chapters of this volume cannot be explained entirely by looking within the negotiating chambers. Rather, they are linked to globalization, the shift in the organization of capitalism, and a neoliberal orientation of society. Brand et al. (2010) have observed, at the international level, the emergence of a cooperation–competition paradox as a central condition of international environmental policy. On one side, they argue, there has been growing pressure for cooperative treatment of transnational environmental problems. However, these international environmental agreements do not eliminate the competition between states and between different economic sectors and regions. In fact, it is evident that within international environmental agreements and processes, completely different and partly contradictory interests are often articulated, which carry the competition between various national and international interest groups into the wording of agreements and further into processes of negotiation (Brand et al. 2010). The oft-cited contradictions to be found within the discourse of sustainable development are supremely functional in facilitating the paradox of cooperation *and* competition. The dispute over meaning, however, is neatly bound within certain parameters so that questions are seldom raised about existing power relations and the economic sphere. Competitive and conflictive relationships are, meanwhile, either ignored or treated as surmountable.

Escobar (1996, 328) identified this dynamic soon after the Earth Summit, observing that the sustainable development discourse purports to reconcile two old enemies—economic growth and the preservation of the environment—without any significant adjustments in the market system. In the sustainable development discourse, nature is reinvented as environment so that capital, not nature and culture, may be sustained. A good deal of the history of multilateral environmentalism, under the rubric of sustainable development, has been a story of denial in an attempt to create the impression that only minor corrections to the market system are needed to launch an era of environmentally sound development, hiding the fact that the economic framework itself cannot hope to accommodate environmental concerns without substantial reforms. Themes such as consumption and equity remain the Cinderella left outside the door at most negotiations, while the logic of the market and trade demand both deference and institutional innovation. Instead, a large proportion of existing global environmental policy instruments are, in fact, based on the creation, regulation, and management of markets (Najam et al. 2007). The most obvious examples are the direct trade-related instruments such as CITES and the Rotterdam and Basel Conventions. The climate change regime, too, notably the emissions trading provisions, and the Convention on Biological Diversity, operates largely within created or existing market logic.

As Kulovesi, Shaw, and Burgiel point out in Chapter 9, this dynamic has played out in multilateral negotiations, both under MEAs and under the WTO. In the 1990s, the trade and environment debate was more political and focused on general themes, such as the legality and economic desirability of environmentally motivated trade measures, or on the relationship between the WTO and MEAs in general. Toward the end of the 1990s and early 2000s, the focus gradually shifted toward finding ways to make the trade and environment regimes mutually compatible through a better understanding of the issues involved, and promoting greater interaction between the WTO and MEA Secretariats. Yet, without the political will to reform the system and devise the necessary strategies to increase policy coherence among competing environment and economic issues on the international agenda, there will be no quick fixes.

Along these lines, the International Forum on Globalization doubts that global environmental challenges can be addressed unless much is done to curb corporate power and reshape the present process of economic globalization. They believe that globalization exacerbates harmful environmental trends and not much can be done without far-reaching changes in the economic and political distribution of power in modern society (Chasek et al. 2010, 374). Others believe that a much more fundamental change is needed—a change in basic values, actions, and habits of thought. The transition they seek, the acceptance of a broad new paradigm, is captured well in the "Earth Charter," which urges us "to bring forth a sustainable global society founded on respect for nature, universal human rights, economic justice and a culture of peace" (Speth 2007, 16). Not until we have abandoned the values and practices that produced today's global problems, this line of reasoning maintains, will we truly be able to solve them.

Whither Multilateral Environmental Negotiations?

Given this backdrop, where do multilateral negotiations fit in? The development of the MEA system—with treaties, secretariats, conferences of the parties, subsidiary body meetings, reports, scientific advisory panels, technology transfer, financial obligations, and capacity building—has led to an unprecedented level of international cooperation in the field of the environment (Engfeldt 2009). Yet, as noted above, without addressing the global economic system, some fear that little progress on environmental and human wellbeing will be possible. In fact, in some respects the environment is no better off today than it was in 1992. As reported in UNEP's Global Environmental Outlook (2007), concentrations of the greenhouse gas CO_2 are roughly a third higher now than twenty years ago. Twenty years ago, approximately 15 percent of global fish stocks were classified as collapsed; this has roughly doubled to 30 percent. Twenty years ago, around one-fifth of fish stocks were deemed over-exploited; this has now risen to about 40 percent. Globally, more than two million people may be dying prematurely as a result of outdoor and indoor air pollution.

Land use intensity, with links to land degradation, soil erosion, water scarcity, nutrient depletion, and pollution, has increased. In Latin America and the Caribbean, desertification—caused by deforestation, overgrazing, and inadequate irrigation—affects one-quarter of the region. Ecuador's Antisan glacier retreated eight times faster in the 1990s than in earlier decades, and Bolivia's Chacaltava glacier has lost over one-half its entire area since 1990. Energy consumption per head in Canada and the United States has grown by 18 percent since 1987. Available freshwater resources are declining; by 2025, close to two billion people are likely to live with absolute water scarcity. Populations of freshwater vertebrates have declined on average by nearly 50 percent since 1987, as compared with an around 30 percent decline for terrestrial and marine species (UNEP 2007).

According to the Millennium Ecosystem Assessment (2005), since 1980, 35 percent of the world's mangroves have been lost, and 20 percent of the world's coral reefs have been destroyed. Since the adoption of the CBD, the species extinction rate is still 1,000 times higher than what would be occurring naturally, without human impact. Despite dozens of regional and global fisheries agreements, an estimated 90 percent of tuna, sharks, swordfish, and other large predators have disappeared.

These facts do not lie. Much of the optimism generated by the political and media spectacle of the Earth Summit dissipated as the international community encountered the complex realities that arise from competing objectives, agenda items, and interests. While the proliferation of MEAs, summits, and global assessments that report on the state of the environment that followed 1992 points to an achievement in international diplomacy and an engagement of more countries and non-state actors than any other global issue area, and it is possible that the condition of the environment could have been even worse off if these agreements had not been negotiated, its legacy requires careful examination for both its accomplishments and shortcomings. The chapters in this volume have examined the evolution of multilateral environmental negotiations that accompanied the increasing attention to environmental issues on the global stage and demonstrate that, while the results have been impressive, many obstacles still stand in the way of efforts to develop international environmental law and policies. So what have we actually learned from our observations of these negotiations? Close scrutiny of the processes and methods used by the international community to reach agreements, the roles and alliances formed among actors, and the texture of the debates and linkages among issues do offer lessons for future efforts.

Evolution of the Process of Multilateral Environmental Negotiations: How are the Negotiations Conducted?

Since 1992, the number of negotiating days and the number of MEAs has increased dramatically. As Depledge and Chasek describe in Chapter 2, barely a fortnight goes by without an environmental meeting somewhere on the planet. At stake is not just the number of negotiating sessions, but also the pace and complexity of these sessions, characterized by a proliferation of agenda items, documents, informal groups, late nights, and, of course, political controversies. These factors have contributed to high levels of stress on negotiators, particularly those from developing countries or with smaller delegations to rely on. At the same time, there has been an escalation in the level at which many negotiations are conducted, with ministers and even heads of state becoming involved in day-to-day talks that used to be the preserve of diplomats and other officials. These trends in the evolution of global environmental negotiations have also coincided with extraordinary advances in information technology, which have dramatically accelerated the speed and extent of communications. As a result, participants have adapted their strategies, the composition of their delegations, their use of scientific advice, and their sleep patterns.

Lesson 1: The interconnections between global environmental problems are increasingly apparent at the same time that the negotiations and MEAs are becoming increasingly fragmented. In Chapter 2, Depledge and Chasek examined the intensification of negotiations and the impact it has had on both negotiators and outcomes. The implications of this intensification for both global environmental policymaking and for the future of multilateral solutions to transboundary environmental problems are not always positive. Intensification and increasing fragmentation have resulted in conflicting agendas and inconsistencies. In the ozone regime, for example, connections with the response to climate change have come to the fore, notably in dealing with hydrofluorocarbons. The CBD and forest regimes are also major stakeholders in the evolving commitments under the climate change regime on land-use change and forests. As debates over global environmental governance reflect the need for more urgent synergistic implementation, responsibility for negotiating and implementing solutions to global environmental problems is becoming more dispersed.

In response to this fragmentation, many have called for greater cooperation and coordination among secretariats and even holding joint meetings of the Conferences of the Parties, as has been done with the three chemicals conventions (Basel, Rotterdam, and Stockholm Conventions). Others have called for the creation of a new United Nations Environment Organization or World Environment Organization or a strengthening of UNEP to better manage the body of MEAs,[2] with the hope that interlinkages would be better captured and incorporated into implementation processes through a reorganized institutional structure. While the pros and cons of these institutional adjustments are under debate, this volume's review of the current system suggests that continuing fragmentation could lead to a situation where none of the interlinked issues are being adequately addressed.

Lesson 2: At the same time, however, there are some positive outcomes to this intensification, as chairpersons and negotiators alike have had the opportunity of experimenting with innovative trust-building techniques that have facilitated consensus building. Global environmental negotiators have been pioneers in the development of innovative negotiating practices aimed at reconciling the dual imperatives of efficiency and transparency—with varying degrees of success. While these techniques, as described by Davenport, Wagner, and Spence in Chapter 3, may not guarantee a successful outcome, in some cases a well-formulated approach may help generate the trust and "space" needed for negotiators to find common ground. Innovative approaches can help to build a sense of inclusion, participation, and, ultimately, ownership, whether through a change of venue to a more relaxing location or seating arrangement, or the intentional ordering of participation in small working groups, such as the Vienna Setting.

However, we cannot underestimate the important role of the chairperson of the negotiations. Without the presence of a skilled chair who understands the importance of timing, when to propose compromises, and when to pull out the innovations, it is unlikely that trust can be built or consensus can be found. Chairs such as Colombia's Juan Mayr, during the final stage of the negotiations on the Cartagena Protocol on Biosafety, are able to incorporate a creative approach to organize negotiating coalitions and set up procedural controls that can reinvigorate talks and build trust in the process. However, other chairs have not been as inclusive; and if negotiators believe that these chairs' "innovations" decrease transparency or leave out key states or coalitions, as was the case with Danish presidency of the Copenhagen Climate Change Conference, trust is lost and the negotiations can collapse or result in a contested outcome.

Lesson 3: The increasing role of science in coaching environmental policy has greatly reinforced the status of science; however, its credibility depends on the perception of neutrality. As environmental issues under negotiation become more complex, negotiations have increasingly involved scientific advisors and scientists, although their participation can take many forms and be couched in competing political interests and institutions. As noted by Kohler, Conliffe, Jungcurt, Gutierrez, and Yamineva in Chapter 4, MEAs have established a variety of scientific panels and bodies, with the goal of providing scientific advice to policymakers. The experiences of these panels and bodies provide lessons for the way in which science advice has and has not succeeded in serving as an arbiter and shaped (or not) the policymaking process.

The public is sensitive about being influenced by special interests and developing countries are often suspect of scientific bodies that are dominated by industrialized countries. Conversely, given the influence of science, governments are sensitive to the opinion of scientists and may attempt to control them. Within this context, the rise in prominence of and the awarding of the Nobel Peace Prize to the IPCC—despite the controversies that developed in late 2009—has led to a case of "IPCC envy," where other multilateral environmental forums (including the CBD and the UNCCD) see the IPCC model as a panacea to the science deficit in environmental decision making. It remains to be seen to what extent it is feasible for several parallel institutions to provide the necessary politically neutral expertise, and the extent to which experts can, on a largely pro bono basis, continually prepare state-of-the-art assessments of knowledge relating to every overarching environmental challenge. And perhaps even more important is the receptiveness to and acceptance of this scientific advice by political negotiators. The successful integration of science and policymaking, while more developed since 1992, is still not guaranteed.

Evolution of Actors: Who is at the Table?

While the conduct of international negotiations within the UN system is still mainly the prerogative of national governments, since 1992 environmental negotiations have featured an ever-growing panoply of actors. When the Montreal Protocol and the Basel Convention were concluded in the late 1980s, there were 159 members of the United Nations. Today there are 192 members. In addition, there has been an increasing number of international organizations, secretariats, NGOs, other Major Groups, the media, and even high-profile individuals who all have their own stakes and interests in the negotiations, further complicating and enriching the decision-making process.

Lesson 4: Among governments, issue-based coalitions have multiplied and are increasingly becoming more influential than traditional geo-political coalitions in environmental negotiations, adding complexity to the process. To some extent these new formations are a function of the newly articulated interests—and convergences of interests—that resulted from the collapse of the old Cold War designations, and have resulted in a blurring of the traditional North–South division. As discussed by Wagner, Hajjar, and Appleton in Chapter 5, from a division of countries into four main negotiating groups in the 1990s—the Group of 77 developing countries and China, the European Union, the JUSSCANNZ coalition of non-EU industrialized countries, and former Soviet-bloc countries—to more issue-specific arrangements, it is now necessary to understand the organization and composition of these groups in order to better understand the nature of the negotiations as well as the outcomes.

The presence of a larger number of smaller coalitions adds complexity to negotiations. More government delegates must speak in order to get all views on the table. More delegates must be present in contact groups that do the actual negotiating. And the more people there are in a room, the more difficult it is to reach a meaningful agreement. Thus, the result is often a proliferation of least common denominator agreements with ambiguous language, often reached after all-night sessions.

As the issues addressed in the post-1992 treaty regimes have moved from the initial framework agreements for cooperation to stronger obligations through protocols and COP decisions, the traditional coalitions have not served so well. While environmental negotiations remain a North–South battleground, as the negotiations on biosafety, climate change, and forests show, coalitions can and do cross traditional boundaries. In addition, issue-based coalitions that are active in one MEA, such as the Like-minded Megadiverse Countries in the CBD negotiations, may not be in another, such as in the Montreal Protocol. However, in recent years we have seen some new coalitions, such as the Bolivarian Alliance for the Americas (ALBA), becoming increasingly active across multiple MEAs. The bottom line is that an appreciation of the use of issue-based coalitions, through which countries have attempted to influence the outcome based on their power vis-à-vis the specific issue under discussion, is required to truly understand the negotiation dynamics.

Lesson 5: The proliferation of MEAs has also led to the emergence of secretariats as key actors in managing the mismatch between the large number of obligations that states have taken on and their limited capacity to effectively implement those obligations. Fragmenting global environmental governance into discrete, highly specialized agreements may facilitate consensus building, but it has also increased the number of obligations that parties must undertake. State capacity has not always kept pace with this evolution and increasing complexities dissipate already low political will to live up to commitments. Furthermore, overlap, duplication, and uncoordinated approaches to solving interlinked problems abound between MEAs. The result is that secretariats have moved beyond the mere administrative role that historically characterized their activities.

As pointed out by Jinnah in Chapter 6, secretariat functions have evolved in response to their surrounding governance architecture, including the increased use of the Convention–Protocol framework, the inclusion of financial mechanisms into many treaties, and the emerging focus on regional initiatives. States increasingly rely on secretariats to carry out core regime tasks, including verification missions, drafting decisions, and capacity-building workshops, as well as governance objectives such as overlap management. This has occurred in part because many states, particularly developing ones, lack the capacity to effectively juggle the continually growing and often overlapping set of obligations laid out in these agreements. Secretariats are in a unique position to drive this governance process due to their expertise, social networks, and "veils of legitimacy" (Depledge 2005). As a result, secretariats have increasingly become actors in their own right in negotiations as they often play a role in setting the agenda, drafting decisions, and advising delegates. However, all this is not without complications. It is not easy for secretariats to tread that fine line between promoting the objectives of the MEA they serve, while maintaining impartiality and the trust of all parties. Some secretariats have been criticized for alleged overstepping of mandates, and are facing resulting backlashes, notably the squeezing of budgets, even in the face of increasing workloads.

Lesson 6: When NGOs participate more extensively in multilateral environmental negotiations, they have the potential to exert influence and bring legitimacy to the negotiations, depending on the role they play and the resources they can bring to bear. Since the 1992 Earth Summit, the nature of NGO influence and action in MEA negotiations has increased greatly, although it does vary with the NGOs' roles and resources and across negotiating fora. The objective of an NGO is not ultimately to play a specific role of witness, architect, or detractor, as described by Burgiel and Wood in Chapter 7, but instead to use those strategies to influence the negotiations. But it is not so simple. Not all processes or NGOs are created equal.

The extent to which an NGO is permitted to play a role depends on factors such as the openness of a process to NGO participation. On the one hand, while more and more NGOs have been attending environmental negotiations, there has been a concomitant increase in contact group and other "closed" meetings when the negotiations become more legal and technical or deal with financial matters (i.e., the biosafety and access and benefit-sharing negotiations). However, when a process is open to NGO participation, NGOs have often been used to play a legitimizing role. When NGOs attend a negotiating session in great numbers, such as the Convention on Biological Diversity and the UNFCCC COPs, it can give greater attention and perceived legitimacy to the process. But when NGO participation significantly diminishes, as has been the case with the International Tropical Timber Organization and the United Nations Forum on Forests, their actions or lack thereof may call the legitimacy of the process into question.

At the same time, it is not only environmental NGOs that have been involved in negotiations. From the earliest days of the UNCED preparations (Doran 1993), business and industry NGOs, led by the Business Council for Sustainable Development and the International Chamber of Commerce, have been remarkably successful in advocating market-friendly solutions with the endorsement of key players, dating back to UNCED Secretary-General Maurice Strong who encouraged their participation. Thus, as environmental NGOs and civil society organizations have increased their participation and influence in MEA negotiations, so too has the business and industry community, who often place greater emphasis on the economic development over the environmental protection and social development legs of the sustainable development platform.

Evolution of Issues: What is Under Discussion?

As environmental issues have become an important component of both international law and negotiations, the issues have become more complex and increasingly necessitate continuous and inevitable trade-offs between the three pillars of sustainable development—economic, social, and environmental. Moreover, the negotiations have not taken place in a vacuum. They have often been framed by a powerful set of economic issues unleashed during the late 1980s and early 1990s that have affected the roles and priorities of states and international institutions.

Lesson 7: Environmental problems and our understanding of them are constantly evolving and, thus, definitions must be permitted to evolve. However, to understand the outcomes in often protracted debates over issue definition, it is important to examine global economic and trade imperatives, and those countries with the most economic power in the negotiations, rather than just the environmental issue at hand. Defining environmental issues in a vacuum is challenging in itself, but when they are examined in the context of the related economic, development, or trade implications, the issue definition process can become protracted, trade-offs are inevitable, and the resulting language may be an exercise in creative ambiguity. In some cases, as Chapter 8 illustrates, a definition agreed upon in one forum pervades other fora and complicates implementation far beyond its original intention. For example, when delegates agreed on the need for "new and additional financial resources" in Agenda 21 in 1992, delegates could not foresee that this important, yet ambiguous, definition would pervade environmental negotiations for the following twenty years. Developing countries ever since 1992 have claimed that they are not responsible for Agenda 21 or MEA implementation if developed countries do not keep their part of the bargain to provide the "new and additional" resources, while developed countries have tried to focus on the better use of existing resources. Yet because "new and additional" to what and how these resources would be mobilized was not clearly defined, this definition has led to endless, and often fruitless, debates that proliferate virtually all MEAs.

But even once there is an emerging agreement on a definition and governments are willing to work on the details, economic and trade imperatives (as described by Chasek, Gutierrez, and Hajjar in Chapter 8) often have a greater priority on the outcome, which can be years in the making. For example, in the biosafety negotiations, major grain exporting countries were concerned that the definition and implementation of "advance informed agreement" in the Cartagena Protocol could slow down international trade. The challenges in defining and operationalizing "avoided deforestation" and REDD+ in the climate change negotiations reflects in many ways the increasing power of the emerging economies in the developing world, as they have changed the economic terms of the debate. Thus, issue definition is often more explicable when it is recognized that if you know who has most economic power in a negotiation, you can better explain how the issue will be defined and redefined. However, it is worth noting that these definitional debates contribute to the incrementalism that has characterized negotiations and treaty implementation, which in turn has come to be viewed as anachronistic in view of the urgency and scale of the environmental and associated development and security challenges.

Lesson 8: Negotiations since 1992 have revealed difficulties in achieving greater coordination on trade and environment and are rooted in three basic factors: (1) the nature and design of the negotiating forum (i.e., based on cooperation or competition); (2) the interplay of national interests (i.e., linkages with other issues); and (3) the shifting negotiating dynamics and relative voice of developing countries. As discussed by Kulovesi, Shaw, and Burgiel, in Chapter 9, over the past twenty years, controversies relating to trade and environment have surfaced in multilateral negotiations, both under MEAs and under the WTO. Greater coordination has been inhibited, in part, due to competing objectives in the trade and in the environmental arenas. Whereas global environmental negotiations are generally propelled by cooperation toward a common environmental goal, the multilateral trading system operates mainly from a confrontational, mercantilist perspective. That is to say, for example, that competition—not cooperation—in global agricultural markets underpins obligations in the WTO. Discussion of trade-related issues in MEAs continues to be a sensitive area for both the MEAs and the WTO. This sensitivity relates to the broader point made in Chapter 9 with reference to coordination between MEAs and the WTO and the fact that the WTO has a legally binding enforcement mechanism with the authority to impose economic sanctions. This situation has led to the perception that resorting to the WTO's dispute settlement mechanism acts as a trump card with respect to MEAs.

There is also a lack of political will to devise strategies to increase policy coherence amongst competing issues on the international agenda—to effectively tackle the trade-offs and create opportunities to integrate trade and environment. Clearly, there are no quick fixes to integrating trade and environmental policies or greening the trading system. While progress on the substantive technical agenda is possible, it remains difficult for countries to appreciate that improved trade opportunities—a vital component of their prospects for development or economic recovery—may be held as ransom in the process. In this respect, since the 1990s, developing countries have taken on a stronger voice commensurate with the increasing weight of emerging economies such as Brazil, China, and India. The coalition of these emerging economic powerhouses has shifted the priority toward sustaining growth and development through trade, with environmental protection often viewed as a secondary consideration.

Lesson 9: When one issue captures the international stage and gains significant political importance and media attention, actors working on other international environmental issues will try to strategically link their activities to it. This lesson has definitely been the case with climate change, as has been demonstrated by Jinnah and Conliffe in Chapter 10. Negotiations on desertification, forests, biodiversity, and ozone depleting chemicals have all bandwagoned with climate change, not only because of the issue linkage, but also to gain attention as well as much needed financial support. Jinnah and Conliffe argue that given the scarcity of resources available to address many linked environmental issues, bandwagoning is likely to remain a prominent feature of multilateral environmental negotiations. In short, climate change and the bandwagoning it has precipitated have permanently altered the landscape of international environmental negotiations. The powerful pull of climate change as an issue that permeates many other negotiations is, undoubtedly, a harbinger of the paradigmatic shifts that will be demanded across economics, governance, and security institutions when effective responses are finally embraced. Climate change is conclusive evidence of the provocative nature of global environmental problems, provoking transformations beyond the field of environmental governance.

Lesson 10: The expansion of country obligations under, and increased scope of, MEAs has translated into considerable implementation challenges and tensions in negotiating dynamics, but has also led to increasing openness among negotiators to use innovative solutions to address these challenges. In Chapter 11, Morgera, Tsioumani, Aguilar, and Wilkins note several of these innovative solutions that have been used to facilitate implementation, including CBD regional and subregional workshops to enhance effectiveness of National Biodiversity Strategies and Action Plans. Under the

Biosafety Protocol, implementation at the national level has been greatly facilitated by the Biosafety Clearing House and the protocol's roster of experts on biosafety with regard to risk assessment. In the context of the ITPGR, the multilateral benefit-sharing fund is used to assist implementation at the national and community levels. Under the climate change regime, flexible implementation measures and innovative compliance tools have been established in direct response to the challenges in implementing the Kyoto Protocol's emission reduction targets.

Along these lines, parties have also had more prominent and systematic discussions of financing, technology transfer, and capacity-building issues under different MEAs. These discussions have resulted, in part, due to the recognition by parties of the gravity of many environmental problems and the challenges in addressing them. Despite optimism and progress in the early 1990s in the development of international environmental law, the reality of the implementation challenges in achieving success on the ground has resulted in slow progress in the negotiation and entry into force of more comprehensive subsidiary agreements. This has led to an increasingly technical focus and specialization in many of these negotiations, which has reduced accessibility of the negotiations to non-experts in specific MEAs (or even sub-processes under the same MEA). These factors do not necessarily mean that environmental negotiations have become less effective due to the increased scope of these treaties, but rather they have become more advanced as the seriousness and extent of the environmental and development challenges that we face have become more apparent and the need to address them has become more pressing.

Concluding Thoughts

This collection of observations on the evolution of multilateral environmental negotiations since 1992 is meant to be just that—a collection of insights that writers and editors of the International Institute for Sustainable Development's *Earth Negotiations Bulletin* have developed over twenty years of reporting on and analyzing the development of international environmental law and policy-making. While global environmental governance is clearly an underlying theme of this volume, we have deliberately shied away from making any policy prescriptions about how or whether to address the increasing fragmentation of governance architecture through the development and evolution of MEAs. While we acknowledge the importance of the different concerns over priorities and trade-offs in the negotiations, we are not here to propose a new organization of the international system. Nor is this an effectiveness study that is trying to measure how effective negotiated outcomes are on solving the environmental problems they are meant to address.

Instead, we have captured ways in which the process of negotiating multilateral environmental agreements has evolved since 1992, why this is important, and how this may affect current and future global environmental policymaking.

Multilateral environmental negotiations have grown significantly more complex. Many more issues, treaties, negotiating bodies, institutions, and policy initiatives exist in this system that integrates environment into a broad array of international economic, trade, and development issues. Beyond the MEAs, there is also recognition that legally binding instruments are not the only way to address environmental and sustainable development issues. Soft law, including declarations, principles, and codes of conduct, exist for a number of global environmental problems, including land-based sources of marine pollution, fisheries, and sustainable forest management, with varying degrees of success.[3] In addition, the WSSD in 2002 recognized the importance of public–private partnerships and multi-stakeholder approaches to attain sustainable development, a point that was reiterated by the UN Commission on Sustainable Development (United Nations 2003, 9). In some ways, this growth and variety of approaches demonstrate progress over the past twenty years as environmental issues are now a prominent part of the international system.

However, caution is necessary. Despite the ascendency of environmental issues on the international stage, and both the consequent and inciting evolution of the MEA processes to address these issues, progress is still limited by the dominant economic paradigm of the twentieth century that featured two assumptions of neoclassical economics: the free market will always maximize social welfare and there exists an infinite supply of both natural resources and "sinks" for disposing of the wastes that accrue from exploiting those resources—providing that the free market is operating (Chasek et al. 2010, 31). Corporations, government ministries dealing with trade and finance, the leaders of some political parties, and some of the top officials of the World Bank and other multilateral institutions have been slow to change. Increasingly grass roots and NGO efforts to challenge this dominant economic paradigm that has framed so much of multilateral environmental discourse has led to a great deal of skepticism about the ability of governments and international institutions to honestly acknowledge, let alone address, the most compelling questions around the future of "growth" and consumption/debt-driven capitalism. Over the next twenty years, the multilateral process will be judged by the extent to which it shows willing to meet these profound economic (even existential) questions head on.

But, the trends and lessons learned from observing multilateral environmental negotiations show some signs that a new paradigm based on sustainable development may still be on the rise. Industrialized countries have joined their developing country counterparts in reaching tentative agreement on changing unsustainable consumption and production patterns within the context of the UN Commission on Sustainable Development in 2011.[4] Developing countries have also shown a greater willingness to negotiate on a number of key issues, including climate change. In some respects, developing countries have adapted to the new paradigm by necessity. Experts agree that developing countries will be disproportionately affected by the environmental impacts of climate change.

So the South has been almost forced out of necessity to show a greater willingness to negotiate. As an example, during the 2009 Copenhagen Climate Conference, Brazil shifted its position after a political realization and a greater domestic appetite to accept the inevitable trade-offs implicit in choosing environment over growth (Lula da Silva 2009). Chinese leaders have acknowledged that many benefits of their country's unparalled economic growth are threatened by a failure to control environmental degradation (Jacobs 2011).

However, it is not just political will that will lead to a paradigm shift. It is also a greater understanding of the economic costs of destroying the environment as well as the national security implications. With regard to the former, there are some signs of hope, with the important work of the Sarkozy-commissioned Stiglitz Commission on alternative measures of economic activity (see Stiglitz et al. 2009) and the Tim Jackson report on prosperity without growth (see Jackson 2009). New think tanks are also emerging to raise far-reaching questions about the future of economics, and even Harvard economist Stephen A. Marglin is doing battle with the titans of neoclassical economics (see Marglin 2010).

There is also a greater understanding that environmental degradation, resource depletion, and climate change can impact national security. For example, changing climate conditions contributed to the devastating ethnic conflict in Darfur, Sudan. Severe changes in rainfall patterns and deteriorating soils caused many farmers to block off the remaining fertile land from herders, which led to violent clashes. While environmental factors alone did not cause the violence, they pushed other factors, including poverty, increasing ethnic and political divisions, and the territorial ambitions of certain groups, past the tipping point. Climate change could also produce large numbers of refugees from flooded coastal areas, increase water and food scarcity, spread disease and weaken economies in parts of the world that are already vulnerable, unstable, or prone to extremism, or that suffer significant cultural, ethnic, or economic divisions (Chasek et al. 2010, 42–43).

The future is far from clear. As economies, populations, cities, energy production, and resource demands continue to grow, the paradigms that influence current and future policy debates—and multilateral environmental negotiations—could go a long way toward determining what the world will look like in the future. What we do know is that today's environmental challenges are global in nature and unprecedented in scope, and they will require innovative and creative global solutions. The lessons learned reveal a few fundamental trends that are likely to permeate the path forward:

- Integration of environmental issues with development and trade imperatives is slowly but surely finding greater policy space and political will in the MEA discourse.
- The emerging narrative is likely to involve devising strategies to increase policy coherence between competing interests to effectively tackle the trade-offs that underpin integration of the three pillars of sustainable development.

- With the economic stakes and trade implications of climate change linked with resource scarcity and loss of biodiversity and agricultural productivity significant and growing, there will be a greater understanding of these costs as a driver for action to reconcile the discourse/integrate environmental concerns in green growth strategies. This is likely to impact multilateral environmental negotiations for the better.

Perhaps with these issues in mind, in 2009, the UN General Assembly adopted resolution 64/236 establishing the United Nations Conference on Sustainable Development to mark the twentieth anniversary of the 1992 Earth Summit. The objective of the conference is to secure renewed political commitment for sustainable development, assess the progress to date and the remaining gaps in the implementation of the outcomes of the major summits on sustainable development, and address new and emerging challenges. The conference is focusing on two themes: (a) a green economy in the context of sustainable development and poverty eradication; and (b) the institutional framework for sustainable development. Together these two themes address the major challenges that we have addressed here, notably the need to change the economic paradigm and the need to rationalize global governance in this area. Perhaps the lessons learned over the past twenty years can guide us toward a better understanding of how to move forward and address these challenges on the new roads from Rio.

Notes

1 The "Washington Consensus" is a term used to describe ten policy prescriptions coined by economist John Williamson in 1989. The Washington Consensus is meant as a baseline of directions for nations in need of assistance from international economic entities such as the World Bank and the International Monetary Fund. The ten points of the Washington Consensus include: fiscal discipline, reordering public expenditure priorities, tax reform, liberalizing interest rates, a competitive exchange rate, trade liberalization, liberalization of inward foreign direct investment, privatization, deregulation, and property rights. See http://www.iie.com/publications/papers/williamson0904-2.pdf.
2 See for example, Daniel Esty 2004, 287–307; Frank Biermann 2005, 117–144.
3 See, for example, the Global Programme of Action for the Protection of the Marine Environment from Land-Based Activities (http://www.gpa.unep.org), the FAO Code of Conduct for Responsible Fisheries (http://www.fao.org/docrep/005/v9878e/v9878e00.HTM), the Akwé: Kon Voluntary guidelines for the conduct of cultural, environmental, and social impact assessments regarding developments proposed to take place on, or which are likely to impact on, sacred sites and on lands and waters traditionally occupied or used by indigenous and local communities (http://www.cbd.int/doc/publications/akwe-brochure-en.pdf) and the FAO Voluntary Guidelines for Responsible Management of Planted Forests (http://www.fao.org/docrep/009/j9256e/j9256e00.htm).
4 While the Ten Year Framework of Programmes on Sustainable Consumption and Production Patterns was not adopted by CSD 19, this was due to a failure to reach agreement on other issues on the CSD's agenda. See ENB 2011.

Works Cited

Biermann, Frank. 2005. The Rationale for a World Environment Organization. In *A World Environmental Organization: Solution or Threat for Effective Environmental Governance*. Edited by Frank Biermann and Steffen Bauer. Aldershot, UK: Ashgate.

Brand, Ulrich, Christoph Görg, Joachim Hirsch, and Markus Wissen. 2010. *Conflicts in Environmental Regulation and the Internationalization of the State: Contested Terrains*. New York, NY: Routledge.

Chasek, Pamela S., David L. Downie, and Janet Welsh Brown. 2010. *Global Environmental Politics*, 5th edition. Boulder, CO: Westview.

Commission on Global Governance. 1995. *Our Global Neighborhood*. New York, NY: Oxford University Press.

Depledge, Joanna. 2005. *The Organization of Global Negotiations: Constructing the Climate Change Regime*. London: Earthscan.

Dierks, Rosa Gomez. 2001. *Introduction to Globalization*. Chicago: Burnham Publishers.

Doran, Peter. 1993. The Earth Summit: Ecology as Spectacle. *Paradigms: The Kent Journal of International Relations* 7(1): 55–65

ENB (*Earth Negotiations Bulletin*). 2011. Summary of the Nineteenth Session of the Commission on Sustainable Development: 2–14 May 2011. *Earth Negotiations Bulletin* 5(304). http://www.iisd.ca/download/pdf/enb05304e.pdf (accessed June 23, 2011).

Engfeldt, Lars-Göran. 2009. *From Stockholm to Johannesburg and Beyond*. Stockholm: Government Offices of Sweden.

Escobar, Arturo, 1996. Construction Nature: Elements for a Post-structuralist Political Ecology. *Futures* 28(4): 325–343.

Esty, Daniel. 2004. The Case for a Global Environmental Organization. In *Managing the World Economy: Fifty Years after Bretton Woods*. Edited by Peter B. Kenen. Washington, DC: Institute for International Economics.

Finger, Matthias, 2002. Rio Plus Ten Years of Globalization. *Politics and the Life Sciences* 21(2): 51–52.

Jackson, Tim. 2009. *Prosperity Without Growth: Economics for a Finite Planet*. London: Earthscan.

Jacobs, Andrew. 2011. China Issues Warning on Climate and Growth. *The New York Times* (March 1). http://www.nytimes.com/2011/03/01/world/asia/01beijing.html (accessed June 23, 2011).

Lula da Silva, Luiz Inácio. 2009. Statement at the Joint High-Level Segment of COP/CMP. Copenhagen, Denmark (17 December). http://www.cop15brasil.gov.br/en-US/?page=noticias/pres-lula-speech (accessed June 23, 2011).

Majone, Giandomenico. 1996. *Regulating Europe*. London: Routledge.

Marglin, Stephen A. 2010. *The Dismal Science: How Thinking Like an Economist Undermines Community*. Cambridge, MA: Harvard University Press.

Millennium Ecosystem Assessment. 2005. *Ecosystems and Human Wellbeing: Synthesis Report*. Washington, DC: Island Press.

Najam, Adil, David Runnalls, and Mark Halle. 2007. *Environment and Globalization: The Five Propositions*. Winnipeg: IISD. http://www.iisd.org/pdf/2007/trade_environment_globalization.pdf (accessed May 23, 2011).

Nitzan, Jonathan and Shimson Bichler. 2004. New Imperialism or New Capitalism? http://bnarchives.yorku.ca/124/01/041214NB_NewImperialismNewCapitalism (Ver2).pdf (accessed June 23, 2011).

Speth, James Gustave. 2007. Beyond Reform. *Our Planet* (February). http://www.unep.org/pdf/OurPlanet/OP_Feb07_GC24_en.pdf (accessed June 11, 2011).

Stiglitz, Joseph E., Amartya Sen, and Jean-Paul Fitoussi. 2009. Report by the Commission on the Measurement of Economic Performance and Social Progress. http://www.stiglitz-sen-fitoussi.fr/documents/rapport_anglais.pdf (accessed June 23, 2011).

UNEP. 2007. *Global Environmental Outlook 4*. Nairobi: UNEP.

UNFCCC (United Nations Framework Convention on Climate Change). 2009. Copenhagen United Nations Climate Change Conference Ends with Political Agreement to Cap Temperature Rise, Reduce Emissions and Raise Finance. Press Release (19 December). http://unfccc.int/files/press/news_room/press_releases_and_advisories/application/pdf/pr_cop15_20091219.pdf (accessed April 2, 2011).

United Nations. 2003. Commission on Sustainable Development Report on the Eleventh Session (27 January 2003 and 28 April–9 May 2003). E/CN.17/2003/6. http://www.un.org/esa/dsd/resources/res_docucsd_11.shtml (accessed October 19, 2011).

APPENDIX

Summaries of Selected Multilateral Environmental Agreements

This appendix contains summaries of the multilateral environmental agreements discussed in this book. The treaties are listed in chronological order. The information is accurate as of the time of publication.

Ramsar Convention on Wetlands of International Importance especially as Waterfowl Habitat

Adopted: 2 February, 1971
Entered into force: 21 December, 1975
Number of parties: 160

Objective: The conservation and wise use of all wetlands through local and national actions and international cooperation, as a contribution toward achieving sustainable development throughout the world.

Summary of the Convention: The Ramsar Convention provides a framework for national action and international cooperation for the conservation and wise use of wetlands and their resources. Parties accept four main commitments. First, parties agree to designate at least one wetland at the time of accession for inclusion in the List of Wetlands of International Importance (the Ramsar List) and to promote its conservation, in addition to continue to designate suitable wetlands within its territory for the List (Article 2). Second, parties include wetland conservation considerations in their national land-use planning and to promote the "wise use" of wetlands in their territory (Article 3). Third, parties undertake to establish nature reserves in wetlands and promote training in the fields of wetland research, management, and wardening (Article 4). Fourth, parties agree to consult with other parties about the implementation of the Convention, especially in regard to transboundary wetlands, shared water systems, and shared species (Article 5).

To date there are 1933 sites designated on the List of Wetlands of International Importance that cover 189,362,942 hectares of surface area.

Structure and meetings: The Ramsar Convention Secretariat is based at the headquarters facilities of IUCN (the International Union for the Conservation of Nature) in Gland, Switzerland. Secretariat staff members are legally considered to be employees of IUCN. The United Nations Educational, Scientific and Cultural Organization (UNESCO) serves as Depositary for the Convention, but the Ramsar Convention is not part of the United Nations and UNESCO system of environment conventions and agreement.

The Conference of the Contracting Parties (COP) is the policymaking organ of the Convention. Government representatives from each of the contracting parties meet every three years to receive national reports on the preceding triennium, approve the work program and budgetary arrangements for the next three years, and consider guidance for the parties on a range of ongoing and emerging environmental issues. The Standing Committee is the intersessional executive body that represents the COP between its triennial meetings, within the framework of the decisions made by the COP. The Scientific and Technical Review Panel was established in 1993 as a subsidiary body of the Convention to provide scientific and technical guidance to the Conference of the Parties, the Standing Committee, and the Ramsar Secretariat.

Information sources: http://www.ramsar.org; http://www.iisd.ca/vol17.

Convention on International Trade in Endangered Species of Wild Fauna and Flora (CITES)

Adopted: 3 March, 1973
Entered into force: 1 July, 1975
Number of parties: 175

Objective: To protect certain endangered species from over-exploitation by means of a system of import/export permits.

Summary of the Convention: CITES has three conservation objectives: to end commercial trade in endangered species; to maintain species' ecological roles in the face of commercial exploitation; and to assist countries in implementing their own species conservation programs if assistance is requested in the form of an Appendix II listing.

CITES is charged with regulating wildlife trade through controls on species listed in three Appendices, which form the scientific core of the Convention. The criteria for inclusion in the Appendices are set out in the treaty text as follows:

- *Appendix I* includes all species "threatened with extinction which are or may be affected by trade." Particularly strict regulation is to be employed to prevent further endangerment, with trade authorized "only in exceptional circumstances." Commercial trade in wild specimens of these species is generally prohibited (CITES, Article III).
- *Appendix II* includes all species for which strict regulation of trade flows is required to prevent unsustainable utilization, as well as look-alike species. Controls are intended "to maintain that species throughout its range at a level consistent with its role in the ecosystems in which it occurs and well above the level at which that species might become eligible for inclusion in Appendix I" (CITES, Article IV).
- *Appendix III* includes "all species which any Party identifies as being subject to regulation within its jurisdiction for the purpose of preventing or restricting exploitation, and as needing the cooperation of other parties in the control of trade" (CITES, Article V).

The appendices to the Convention have been amended multiple times and two specific amendments to other sections of the treaty have been adopted. The first, which relates to financial provisions and amends Article XI, was adopted in Bonn in 1979 and entered into force on April 13, 1987. The second, which is related to accession to the Convention by regional economic integration organizations, and amends Article XXI, was adopted in Gaborone in 1983, but is not yet in force. It will enter into force when it has been formally accepted by fifty-four of the eighty states that were Parties to the Convention on April 30, 1983. Roughly 5,000 species of animals and 28,000 species of plants are protected by CITES against over-exploitation through international trade.

Structure and meetings: The CITES Secretariat is based in Geneva and is administered by UNEP. CITES has three committees. The Standing Committee provides policy guidance to the Secretariat concerning the implementation of the Convention and oversees the management of the Secretariat's budget. It carries out tasks given to it by the Conference of the Parties and drafts resolutions for consideration by the Conference of the Parties. The Plants and Animals Committees are composed of experts to fill gaps in biological and other specialized knowledge regarding species of animals and plants that are (or might become) subject to CITES trade controls. The Conference of the Parties meets every two to three years to review progress in the conservation of species included on the appendices, consider proposals to amend the lists of species, consider documents and reports from parties, the committees, the Secretariat and others, recommend measures to improve the effectiveness of the Convention, and adopt a budget and other decisions to improve functioning of the Secretariat.

Information sources: http://www.cites.org; http://www.iisd.ca/vol21.

Convention on Migratory Species of Wild Animals (CMS)

Adopted: 23 June, 1979
Entered into force: 1 November, 1983
Number of parties: 116

Objective: To conserve terrestrial, marine, and avian migratory species throughout their range.

Summary of the Convention: The CMS recognizes that states must be the protectors of migratory species that live within or pass through their national jurisdictional boundaries and aims to conserve terrestrial, marine, and avian migratory species throughout their range. The Convention constitutes a framework through which parties may act to conserve migratory species and their habitat by: adopting strict protection measures for migratory species that have been characterized as being in danger of extinction throughout all or a significant portion of their range (species listed in Appendix I of the Convention); concluding agreements for the conservation and management of migratory species that have an unfavorable conservation status or would benefit significantly from international cooperation (species listed in Appendix II); and joint research and monitoring activities. At present, over 100 endangered migratory species are listed in Appendix I of the Convention. The CMS prohibits the taking of species listed in Appendix I with exemptions for: scientific purposes; improvement of propagation or survival of the species; traditional subsistence use; and extraordinary circumstances.

CMS also provides for the development of specialized regional agreements for Appendix II species. To date, seven agreements and nineteen memoranda of understanding (MOUs) have been concluded. The seven agreements aim to conserve: populations of European bats; cetaceans of the Mediterranean Sea, Black Sea and contiguous Atlantic area; small cetaceans of the Baltic and North Seas; seals in the Wadden Sea; African-Eurasian migratory waterbirds; albatrosses and petrels; and gorillas and their habitats. The MOUs aim to conserve: the Siberian crane; the slender-billed curlew; marine turtles of the Atlantic coast of Africa; marine turtles of the Indian Ocean and Southeast Asia; the Middle-European population of the great bustard; the bukhara deer; the aquatic warbler; West African populations of the African elephant; the Saiga antelope; cetaceans of Pacific island states; dugongs; the Mediterranean monk seal; the ruddy-headed goose; grassland birds in South America; birds of prey in Africa and Eurasia, small cetaceans and manatees of West Africa, high Andean flamingos; sharks and Andean deer. These agreements and MOUs are open to all range states of the species, regardless of whether they are parties to the Convention.

Structure and meetings: The CMS Convention Secretariat is based in Bonn, Germany and is administered by UNEP. In addition to the Conference of the Parties, which meets every three years, the Standing Committee provides policy and administrative guidance between regular meetings of the COP and the

Scientific Council advises the COP on scientific matters and priorities for research and conservation.

The Conference of the Parties meets to review progress in the implementation of the Convention, adopt the budget, resolutions, and recommendations, amend Appendix I and II, and determine priorities for future CMS activities. Most of the CMS agreements have their own meetings of the parties and some of them have their own advisory committees, steering committees, and standing committees.

Information sources: http://www.cms.int; http://www.iisd.ca/vol18.

International Tropical Timber Agreement (ITTA)

Adopted: 18 November, 1983 (revised in 1994 and 2006)
Entered into force: 1 April, 1985 (ITTA 1994 entered into force in 1997; ITTA 2006 entered into force in 2011)
Number of parties: 62

Objective: To promote the conservation and sustainable management, use, and trade of tropical forest resources.

Summary of the convention: The original 1983 Agreement was established to (a) provide an effective framework for cooperation and consultation between countries producing and consuming tropical timber; (b) promote the expansion and diversification of international trade in tropical timber and the improvement of structural conditions in the tropical timber market; (c) promote and support research and development with a view to improving forest management and wood utilization; and (d) encourage the development of national policies aimed at sustainable utilization and conservation of tropical forests and their genetic resources, and at maintaining the ecological balance in the regions concerned.

The 1994 successor agreement to the ITTA continues the agreement's focus on the world tropical timber economy. In addition, it contains broader provisions for information sharing, including non-tropical timber trade data and allows for consideration of non-tropical timber issues as they related to tropical timber.

In 2003, negotiations began on a successor agreement to the ITTA, 1994. The ITTA, 2006 was adopted in Geneva on January 27, 2006. The ITTA, 2006 builds on the foundations of the previous agreements and focuses on promoting the expansion and diversification of international trade in tropical timber from sustainable managed and legally harvested forests and promoting the sustainable management of tropical timber producing forests. The 2006 agreement also: provides an effective framework for consultation, international cooperation, and the development of timber economy policies; contributes to the process of sustainable development; promotes the expansion and diversification of international trade in tropical timber from sustainable sources; improves forest management and the efficiency of wood utilization; provides members with new financial resources; and encourages information-sharing on the international timber market, through the ITTO.

The agreement established the International Tropical Timber Organization (ITTO):

- to provide an effective framework for consultation, international cooperation and policy development among all members with regard to all relevant aspects of the world timber economy;
- to provide a forum for consultation to promote non-discriminatory timber trade practices;
- to contribute to the process of sustainable development;
- to enhance the capacity of members to implement a strategy for achieving exports of tropical timber and timber products from sustainably managed sources;
- to promote the expansion and diversification of international trade in tropical timber from sustainable sources by improving the structural conditions in international markets, by taking into account, on the one hand, a long-term increase in consumption and continuity of supplies, and, on the other, prices which reflect the costs of sustainable forest management and which are remunerative and equitable for members, and the improvement of market access;
- to promote and support research and development with a view to improving forest management and efficiency of wood utilization as well as increasing the capacity to conserve and enhance other forest values in timber-producing tropical forests;
- to develop and contribute toward mechanisms for the provision of new and additional financial resources and expertise needed to enhance the capacity of producing members to attain the objectives of this agreement;
- to improve market intelligence with a view to ensuring greater transparency in the international timber market, including the gathering, compilation, and dissemination of trade related data, including data related to species being traded;
- to promote increased and further processing of tropical timber from sustainable sources in producing member countries with a view to promoting their industrialization and thereby increasing their employment opportunities and export earnings; and
- to encourage members to support and develop industrial tropical timber reforestation and forest management activities as well as rehabilitation of degraded forest land, with due regard for the interests of local communities dependent on forest resources.

Structure and meetings: The ITTO is located in Yokohama, Japan and administers the provisions and supervises the operation of the agreement. Member states are divided into two caucuses: producing countries and consuming countries.

The ITTO's membership represents 90% of the world trade in tropical timber and 80% of the world's tropical forests. The governing body of the ITTO is the International Tropical Timber Council (ITTC), which includes all members. Annual contributions and votes are distributed equally between producers and consumers. The Council is supported by four committees, which are open to all members and provide advice and assistance to the Council on issues for consideration and decision on: Economic Information and Market Intelligence (CEM); Reforestation and Forest Management (CRF); Forest Industry (CFI); and Finance and Administration (CFA). The Council historically met twice a year, once in Yokohama and once in a producing country. However, beginning in 2008 the Council and its committees have only met once a year in Yokohama, unless funding is provided to hold a second meeting in a producing country.

Information sources: http://www.itto.int; http://www.iisd.ca/vol24.

Montreal Protocol to the Vienna Convention for the Protection of the Ozone Layer on Substances that Deplete the Ozone Layer

Adopted: 16 September, 1987
Entered into force: 1 January, 1989
Number of parties: 196

Objective: To protect the ozone layer by taking precautionary measures to control global emissions of ozone depleting substances.

Summary of the Protocol: The Protocol, as adopted in September 1987 under the 1985 Vienna Convention on the Protection of the Ozone Layer, controls eight substances: five CFCs (numbers 11, 12, 113, 114, and 115) and three bromine compounds (halons 1211, 1301, and 2402). Within ten years, production and consumption of the CFCs was to be cut back, in three stages, to 50 percent of their 1986 levels. Production and consumption of the halons would be frozen within three years, except for essential uses such as fire retardants, because no satisfactory substitute was yet available. Qualifications to the agreement were built into the Protocol to meet the special circumstances of several nations. Additional controls limiting trade with non-parties were adopted to give these nations an incentive to become parties. Developing countries were given a ten-year grace period before they had to comply with the control measures, provided that their annual consumption of the eight substances during that period did not exceed 0.3 kilograms per capita.

- *London Amendment and Adjustments:* Delegates to the second Meeting of the Parties (MOP 2), which took place in London, UK, in 1990, tightened control schedules and agreed to add ten more CFCs to the list of ODS, as well as carbon tetrachloride (CTC) and methyl chloroform. To date, 195 parties have ratified the London Amendment. MOP 2 also established the Multilateral Fund (MLF), which meets the incremental costs incurred by Article 5 parties in implementing the Protocol's control measures and finances clearinghouse functions.

- *Copenhagen Amendment and Adjustments:* At MOP 4, held in Copenhagen, Denmark, in 1992, delegates tightened existing control schedules and added controls on methyl bromide, hydrobromofluorocarbons, and hydrochlorofluorocarbons (HCFCs). To date, 192 parties have ratified the Copenhagen Amendment.

- *Montreal Amendment and Adjustments:* At MOP 9, held in Montreal, Canada, in 1997, delegates agreed to a new licensing system for the import and export of ODS, in addition to tightening existing control schedules. They also agreed to ban trade in methyl bromide with non-parties to the Copenhagen Amendment. To date, 182 parties have ratified the Montreal Amendment.

- *Beijing Amendment and Adjustments:* At MOP 11, held in Beijing, China, in 1999, delegates agreed to controls on bromochloromethane and additional controls on HCFCs, and to reporting on methyl bromide for quarantine and pre-shipment (QPS) applications. At present, 167 parties have ratified the Beijing Amendment.

Under the amendments to the Montreal Protocol, non–Article 5 parties were required to phase out production and consumption of: halons by 1994; CFCs, CTC, hydrobromochlorofluorocarbons, and methyl chloroform by 1996; bromochloromethane by 2002; and methyl bromide by 2005. Article 5 parties were required to phase out production and consumption of hydrobromochlorofluorocarbons by 1996 and bromochloromethane by 2002. Article 5 parties must still phase out: production and consumption of CFCs, halons, and CTC by 2010; and methyl chloroform and methyl bromide by 2015. Under the accelerated phaseout of HCFC adopted at MOP-19, HCFC production and consumption by Article 2 countries was to be frozen in 2004 and phased out by 2020, while in Article 5 parties, HCFC production and consumption is to be frozen by 2013 and phased out by 2030 (with interim targets prior to those dates, starting in 2015 for Article 5 parties). There are exemptions to these phase-outs to allow for certain uses lacking feasible alternatives.

Structure and meetings: The Ozone Secretariat is based in Nairobi and is administered by UNEP. There are currently three scientific panels that carry out periodic assessments on the scientific issues of ozone depletion; environmental effects of ozone depletion; status of alternative substances and technologies as well as their economic implications: the Technology and Economic Assessment Panel, the Scientific Assessment Panel, and the Environmental Effects Assessment Panel. Other temporary subsidiary bodies are established and dissolved according to the needs for specialized assessments as required by the parties. The Meeting of the

Parties convenes every year to review the implementation of the Protocol, assess control measures, decide on any adjustments or reductions, or changes to control measures or substances, consider proposals for amendments, and, among other things, adopt a budget and other decisions to improve functioning of the Secretariat.

Information sources: http://ozone.unep.org/; http://www.iisd.ca/vol19.

Basel Convention on the Control of Transboundary Movements of Hazardous Wastes and their Disposal

Adopted: 22 March, 1989
Entered into force: 5 May, 1992
Number of parties: 178

Objective: To prevent developing countries from becoming repositories for improperly identified and improperly managed hazardous wastes: to pinpoint what constitutes illegal traffic; to ensure mechanisms for redress in case of illegal or inappropriate exports of hazardous wastes to developing countries; and, in general, to ensure environmentally sound management of hazardous wastes subject to transboundary movement.

Summary of the Convention: The Basel Convention strictly regulates the transboundary movements of hazardous wastes and provides obligations to its parties to ensure that such wastes are managed and disposed of in an environmentally sound manner. The main principles of the Basel Convention are:

- Transboundary movements of hazardous wastes should be reduced to a minimum consistent with their environmentally sound management.
- Hazardous wastes should be treated and disposed of as close as possible to their source of generation.
- Hazardous waste generation should be reduced and minimized at source.

In order to achieve these principles, the Convention aims to control the transboundary movement of hazardous wastes, monitor and prevent illegal traffic, provide assistance for the environmentally sound management of hazardous wastes, promote cooperation between parties in this field, and develop technical guidelines for the management of hazardous wastes.

In 1995 the parties adopted an amendment to ban hazardous wastes exports for final disposal and recycling from what are known as Annex VII countries (Basel Convention parties that are members of the European Union, OECD, Liechtenstein) to non-Annex VII countries (all other parties to the Convention). In 1999, the parties adopted the Protocol on Liability and Compensation for Damage Resulting from the Transboundary Movement of Hazardous Wastes and their Disposal. To date, neither has entered into force.

Structure and meetings: The Basel Convention Secretariat is based in Geneva and is administered by UNEP. The Conference of the Parties meets every two years to review and evaluate the effective implementation of the Convention, and adopt amendments and protocols, provide guidance to the Secretariat and adopt a budget, among other things. It has an Open-Ended Working Group to assist the Conference of the Parties in developing and keeping under continuous review the implementation of the Convention's work plan, specific operational policies and decisions taken by the Conference of the Parties for the implementation of the Convention. The Compliance Committee assists parties to comply with their obligations under the Convention and to facilitate, promote, monitor, and aim to secure the implementation of and compliance with the obligations under the Convention.

Information sources: http://www.basel.int; http://www.iisd.ca/vol20.

Convention on Biological Diversity (CBD)

Adopted: 22 May, 1992
Entered into force: 29 December, 1993
Number of parties: 193

Objective: The 1992 Convention on Biological Diversity addresses the conservation of biological diversity, the sustainable use of its components and the fair and equitable sharing of the benefits arising out of the utilization of genetic resources, including by appropriate access to genetic resources and by appropriate transfer of relevant technologies, taking into account all rights over those resources and technologies, and by appropriate funding.

Summary of the Convention: The CBD restates the principle of national sovereignty over domestic natural resources, subject to respect for the rights of other states. The Convention, however, places a duty on parties to conserve biological diversity within their jurisdiction, as well as outside their jurisdiction in certain cases. Parties are required to cooperate in the preservation of biological diversity in areas out of national jurisdiction. Parties are also given the responsibility to:

- formulate and implement strategies, plans or programs for the conservation and sustainable use of biological diversity;
- monitor the elements of biological diversity, determining the nature of the urgency required in the protection of each category, and in sampling them, in terms of the risks to which they are exposed;
- conserve both *in-situ* and *ex-situ* biological diversity;
- provide for research, training, general education, and the fostering of awareness, in relation to measures for the identification, conservation, and sustainable use of biological diversity;

- provide for environmental impact assessment of projects that are likely to have significant adverse effects on biological diversity;
- exchange information and undertake consultation with other states in all cases where proposed national projects are likely to have adverse effects on biological diversity in other states.

There are also provisions concerning access to genetic resources as well as access to transfer of technology, for application in the conservation and sustainable use of biological diversity. The convention also places a duty on parties to provide, in accordance with their individual capabilities, financial support for the fulfillment of the objectives of conservation and sustainable use of biological diversity.

On January 29, 2000, the Conference of the Parties adopted the Cartagena Protocol on Biosafety, which aims to ensure the safe handling, transport, and use of living modified organisms (LMOs) resulting from modern biotechnology that may have adverse effects on biological diversity, taking also into account risks to human health. It establishes an advance informed agreement (AIA) procedure for ensuring that countries are provided with the information necessary to make informed decisions before agreeing to the import of such organisms into their territory. The Protocol also establishes a Biosafety Clearing House to facilitate the exchange of information on living modified organisms and to assist countries in the implementation of the Protocol. It entered into force on September 11, 2003. To date, 159 countries plus the European Union have ratified the Cartagena Protocol.

On October 15, 2010, at the fifth meeting of the Meeting of the Parties to the Cartagena Protocol, the Nagoya-Kuala Lumpur Supplementary Protocol on Liability and Redress to the Cartagena Protocol on Biosafety was adopted. The supplementary Protocol provides international rules and procedure on liability and redress for damage to biodiversity resulting from LMOs. The supplementary Protocol will enter into force ninety days after being ratified by at least forty parties to the Cartagena Protocol on Biosafety.

On October 29, 2010, the Conference of the Parties adopted the Nagoya Protocol on Access to Genetic Resources and the Fair and Equitable Sharing of Benefits Arising from their Utilization. The Protocol aims at sharing the benefits arising from the utilization of genetic resources in a fair and equitable way, including by appropriate access to genetic resources and by appropriate transfer of relevant technologies, taking into account all rights over those resources and technologies, and by appropriate funding, thereby contributing to the conservation of biological diversity and the sustainable use of its components. The Nagoya Protocol will enter into force ninety days after receipt of the fiftieth instrument of ratification.

Structure and meetings: The CBD Secretariat is based in Montreal and is administered by UNEP. The Conference of the Parties meets every two years, or as needed, to review progress in the implementation of the Convention, to adopt programs of work, to achieve its objectives, and provide policy guidance. The COP is assisted by the Subsidiary Body on Scientific, Technical and Technological Advice, which provides recommendations to the COP on the technical aspects of the implementation of the Convention. Three ad hoc working groups are currently established to deal with specific issues, including the Working Group on Review of Implementation of the Convention, the Working Group on Article 8(j) (traditional knowledge), and the Working Group on Protected Areas. Other ad hoc bodies can be established by the COP, as needed.

Information sources: http://www.cbd.int; http://www.iisd.ca/vol09.

United Nations Framework Convention on Climate Change (UNFCCC)

Adopted: 9 May, 1992
Entered into force: 21 March, 1994
Number of parties: 195

Objective: To achieve stabilization of carbon dioxide and other greenhouse gas concentrations in the atmosphere at a level that would prevent dangerous anthropogenic interference with the climate system.

Summary of the Convention: The UNFCCC sets forth a number of commitments for its parties, including the preparation of national inventories on greenhouse gas emissions and on actions taken to remove them. Parties are also required to: formulate and implement programs for the control of climate change; undertake cooperation in technology for the control of change in the climate system; incorporate suitable policies for the control of climate change in national plans; and undertake education and training policies that will enhance public awareness in relation to climate change.

Developed country parties (and other parties listed in Annex I) commit themselves to take special measures to limit their anthropogenic emissions of greenhouse gases, and to enhance the capacity of their sinks and reservoirs for the stabilization of such gases. The developed country parties (and other parties listed in Annex II) undertake to accord financial support to developing country parties, to enable the latter to comply with the terms of the Convention. Parties are required to cooperate in the establishment and promotion of networks and programs of research into and systematic observation of climate change.

On December 11, 1997, the Conference of the Parties adopted the Kyoto Protocol. The Protocol sets binding targets for thirty-seven industrialized countries and the European community for reducing greenhouse gas emissions. These targets amount to an average of 5 percent against 1990 levels over the five-year period 2008–2012. The Kyoto Protocol entered into force on February 16, 2005.

To date there are 193 parties to the Protocol. The detailed rules for the implementation of the Protocol were adopted at COP 7 in Marrakesh in 2001, and are called the "Marrakesh Accords."

Structure and Meetings: The UNFCCC Secretariat is based in Bonn, Germany, and is administered by the United Nations. The Conference of the Parties is responsible for keeping international efforts to address climate change on track. It reviews the implementation of the Convention and examines the commitments of parties in light of the Convention's objective, new scientific findings and experience gained in implementing climate change policies. A key task for the COP is to review the national communications and emission inventories submitted by parties. Based on this information, the COP assesses the effects of the measures taken by parties and the progress made in achieving the ultimate objective of the Convention. The COP meets once a year, unless the parties decide otherwise. The Convention established two permanent subsidiary bodies: the Subsidiary Body for Scientific and Technological Advice (SBSTA) and the Subsidiary Body for Implementation (SBI). These bodies give advice to the COP and each has a specific mandate. They are both open to participation by any party and governments often send representatives who are experts in the fields of the respective bodies. Two other ad hoc working groups have been established to address the need for commitments after the Kyoto Protocol's first commitment period ends in 2012. The Ad Hoc Working Group on Further Commitments for Annex I Parties under the Kyoto Protocol was set up in 2005 and the Ad Hoc Working Group on Long-term Cooperative Action was established in 2007 to address climate change by enhancing implementation of the Convention.

Information sources: http://unfccc.int; http://www.iisd.ca/vol12.

United Nations Convention to Combat Desertification (UNCCD)

Adopted: 17 June, 1994
Entered into Force: 26 December, 1996
Number of parties: 194

Objective: To combat desertification and mitigate the effects of drought in countries experiencing serious drought and/or desertification, particularly in Africa, through effective action at all levels, supported by international cooperation and partnership arrangements, in the framework of an integrated approach which is consistent with Agenda 21, with a view to contributing to the achievement of sustainable development in affected areas.

Summary of the Convention: The Convention recognizes the physical, biological, and socioeconomic aspects of desertification, the importance of redirecting technology transfer so that it is demand-driven, and the importance of local populations in efforts to combat desertification. The core of the convention is the development of national and subregional/regional action programs by national governments in cooperation with donors, local populations, and NGOs, as well as its implementation through action programs. At the national level, they address the underlying causes of desertification and drought and identify measures of preventing and reversing it. National programs are complemented by subregional and regional programs, particularly when transboundary resources such as lakes and rivers are involved. Action programs are detailed in the five regional implementation annexes to the convention—Africa, Asia, Latin America and the Caribbean, the Northern Mediterranean, and Central and Eastern Europe.

Structure and meetings: The UNCCD Secretariat is based in Bonn, Germany, and is administered by the United Nations. The Conference of the Parties is the supreme decision-making body. The COP has been meeting biannually since 2001. The COP is responsible for reviewing reports submitted by the parties detailing how they are carrying out their commitments. The COP then makes recommendations on the basis of these reports. It also has the power to make amendments to the Convention or to adopt new annexes.

The COP is assisted by two subsidiary bodies: the Committee on Science and Technology and the Committee for the Review of the Implementation of the Convention. The Global Mechanism, which is based in Rome at the International Fund for Agricultural Development, was created by the UNCCD and helps the COP promote funding for Convention-related activities and programs.

Information sources: http://www.uncccd.int; http://www.iisd.ca/vol04.

Rotterdam Convention on the Prior Informed Consent (PIC) Procedure for Certain Hazardous Chemicals and Pesticides in International Trade

Adopted: 10 September, 1998
Entered into Force: 24 February, 2004
Number of parties: 143

Objective: To promote shared responsibility and cooperative efforts among parties in the international trade of certain hazardous chemicals in order to protect human health and the environment from potential harm; and to contribute to the environmentally sound use of those hazardous chemicals, by facilitating information exchange about their characteristics, by providing for a national decision-making process on their import and export, and by disseminating these decisions to parties.

Summary of the Convention: The Convention covers pesticides and industrial chemicals that have been banned or severely restricted for health or environmental reasons by parties and which have been notified by parties for inclusion in the PIC procedure. One notification from each of two specified regions triggers consideration of addition of a chemical to Annex III of the Convention. Severely hazardous pesticide formulations that present a hazard under conditions of use in developing countries or countries with economies in transition may also be nominated for inclusion in Annex III.

There are forty chemicals listed in Annex III of the Convention and subject to the PIC procedure, including twenty-five pesticides, four severely hazardous pesticide formulations and eleven industrial chemicals. More chemicals are expected to be added in the future. The Conference of the Parties decides on the inclusion of new chemicals.

Once a chemical is included in Annex III, a "decision guidance document" containing information concerning the chemical and the regulatory decisions to ban or severely restrict the chemical for health or environmental reasons is circulated to all parties. Parties have nine months to prepare a response concerning the future import of the chemical. The response can consist of either a final decision (to allow import of the chemical, not to allow import, or to allow import subject to specified conditions) or an interim response. Decisions by an importing country must be trade neutral (i.e., apply equally to domestic production for domestic use as well as to imports from any source). The Convention also promotes the exchange of information on a very broad range of chemicals.

Structure and meetings: The Rotterdam Convention Secretariat is based in Rome and Geneva, co-administered by the UN Food and Agriculture Organization and the United Nations Environment Programme. The Conference of the Parties is the supreme decision-making body. The COP meets every two to three years. The COP is responsible for reviewing reports submitted by the parties detailing how they are carrying out their commitments. The COP then makes recommendations on the basis of these reports. It also has the power to make amendments to the Convention and add new chemicals to the PIC procedure.

The COP is assisted by the Chemical Review Committee, which evaluates information provided by parties and recommends to the COP whether the chemical in question should be made subject to the Prior Informed Consent procedure and, accordingly, be listed in Annex III.

In 2010, at simultaneous extraordinary Conferences of the Parties to the Basel, Rotterdam, and Stockholm Conventions in Bali, Indonesia, delegates adopted an omnibus synergies decision on joint services, joint activities, synchronization of the budget cycles, joint audits, joint managerial functions, and review arrangements between the three chemicals conventions. As a result of the section of the decision on Joint Managerial functions, Jim Willis was appointed as the Joint Head of the Basel and Stockholm Convention Secretariats and UNEP–part of the Rotterdam Convention Secretariat in April 2011.

Information sources: http://www.pic.int; http://www.iisd.ca/vol15.

Stockholm Convention on Persistent Organic Pollutants (POPs)

Adopted: 22 May, 2001
Entered into force: 17 May, 2004
Number of parties: 173

Objective: To protect human health and the environment from chemicals that remain intact in the environment for long periods, become widely distributed geographically, accumulate in the fatty tissue of humans and wildlife, and have adverse effects to human health or to the environment.

Summary of the Convention: The Stockholm Convention initially called for international action on twelve POPs grouped into three categories: 1) pesticides: aldrin, chlordane, DDT, dieldrin, endrin, heptachlor, mirex, and toxaphene; 2) industrial chemicals: hexachlorobenzene (HCB) and polychlorinated biphenyls (PCBs); and 3) unintentionally produced POPs: dioxins and furans. Governments are to promote best available techniques and best environmental practices for replacing existing POPs while preventing the development of new POPs. Provision was also made for a procedure to identify additional POPs and the criteria to be considered in doing so.

Key elements of the treaty include: the requirement that developed countries provide new and additional financial resources; measures to eliminate production and use of intentionally produced POPs, eliminate unintentionally produced POPs, where feasible, and manage and dispose of POPs wastes in an environmentally sound manner; and substitution involving the use of safer chemicals and processes to prevent unintentionally produced POPs. Precaution is exercised throughout the Stockholm Convention, with specific references in the preamble, the objective, and the provision on identifying new POPs.

The Convention can list chemicals in three annexes: Annex A contains chemicals to be eliminated; Annex B contains chemicals to be restricted; and Annex C calls for the minimization of unintentional releases of listed chemicals.

In May 2009, the Conference of the Parties decided to list nine new chemicals: two pesticides (chloredecone and lindane); four industrial chemicals: hexabromobiphenyl, commercial pentabromodiphenyl ether, commercial octabromodiphenyl ether, and perfluorooctane sulfonic acid (PFOS), its salts and perfluorooctane sulfonyl fluoride (PFOS-F); and two by-products of lindane (alpha hexachlorocyclohexane and beta hexachlorocyclohexane). In April 2011, the fifth meeting of the Conference of the Parties added endosulfan to the list of chemicals, bringing the total number of controlled chemicals to twenty-two.

Structure and meetings: The Stockholm Convention Secretariat is based in Geneva and is administered by UNEP. The Conference of the Parties meets every two to three years to review progress in the implementation of the Convention and take decisions including whether or not to add new chemicals. The POPS Review Committee, which consists of government-designated experts, meets once a year to review chemicals proposed for addition to the Convention.

In 2010, at simultaneous extraordinary Conferences of the Parties to the Basel, Rotterdam, and Stockholm Conventions in Bali, Indonesia, delegates adopted an omnibus synergies decision on joint services, joint activities, synchronization of the budget cycles, joint audits, joint managerial functions, and review arrangements between the three chemicals conventions. As a result of the section of the decision on joint managerial functions, Jim Willis was appointed as the joint head of the Basel and Stockholm Convention Secretariats and UNEP–part of the Rotterdam Convention Secretariat in April 2011.

Information sources: http://www.pops.int; http://www.iisd.ca/vol15.

International Treaty of Plant Genetic Resources for Food and Agriculture (ITPGR)

Adopted: 3 November, 2001
Entered into force: 29 June, 2004
Number of parties: 127

Objective: The purpose of treaty is to: recognize the enormous contribution of farmers to the diversity of crops that feed the world; establish a global system to provide farmers, plant breeders, and scientists with access to plant genetic materials; and ensure that recipients share benefits they derive from the use of these genetic materials with the countries where they have been originated.

Summary of the Convention: The main components of the treaty are the provisions relating to conservation and sustainable use of plant genetic resources for food and agriculture (PGRFA) (Part II), the provisions on Farmers' Rights (Part III), the Multilateral System of Access and Benefit Sharing (Part IV), supporting components (Part V) and financial provisions (Part VI). Article 5 sets out the main tasks that the parties are to carry out with respect to the conservation, exploration, collection, characterization, evaluation, and documentation of PGRFA. Article 6 requires parties to develop and maintain appropriate policy and legal measures that promote the sustainable use of PGRFA. Article 9 recognizes the contribution of local and indigenous communities and farmers to the conservation and development of plant genetic resources as a basis for food and agriculture production and places the responsibility for realizing those rights on national governments.

A key part of the treaty is the Multilateral System of Access and Benefit-sharing, which was established to facilitate access to genetic resources of major food crops and forage species and to share, in a fair and equitable way, the benefits arising from the utilization of these benefits. Annex I lists crops to be included; however, only those crops for which some PGRFA are under the management and control of the parties and are in the public domain are part of the Multilateral System, as described in Article 11. Article 12 states that parties should take the necessary legal or other appropriate measures to provide facilitated access through the Multilateral System to other parties and to "legal and natural persons under their jurisdiction," pursuant to a Standard Material Transfer Agreement. Article 13 sets out the terms for benefit sharing.

Structure and meetings: The Secretariat is based in Rome and is administered by the FAO. In addition to the Governing Body, which meets at least once every two years, there are several ad hoc and advisory committees that have been established to examine the funding strategy, the standard material transfer agreement and the Multilateral System, and third party beneficiaries.

Information sources: http://www.planttreaty.org; http://www.iisd.ca/vol09.

CONTRIBUTORS

Soledad Aguilar is IISD Reporting Services' thematic expert on finance and trade for sustainable development, and founder and editor of the Latin American Forum on Climate Change and Trade. Since 2000, she has participated in more than fifty meetings of multilateral environmental agreements, as a writer and team leader for the *Earth Negotiations Bulletin*, and as a negotiator for the Argentine government, focusing on climate change, biodiversity, chemicals and biosafety. She is a regular contributor to the *Environmental Law and Policy Journal* and the *Yearbook of International Environmental Law*.

Asheline Appleton is a lawyer and previously worked in private practice and the public sector. She holds an LL.M. degree from University College London and a law degree from the University of Nairobi. She focuses on international environmental law and policy, particularly climate change and biodiversity, and has consulted for various organizations and development consultancies, including UNEP, UNDP, and the UNFCCC. She has also been a team leader, writer, and editor for the *Earth Negotiations Bulletin* since December 2005.

Stanley W. Burgiel, PhD, has more than two decades of experience with international environmental negotiations and has worked and consulted for a variety of non-governmental, intergovernmental, and governmental organizations. He wrote for the *Earth Negotiations Bulletin* from 1997 to 2002, covering issues related to biodiversity, biosafety, genetic resources, intellectual property rights, and traditional knowledge. He has published on a range of issues including biodiversity conservation and sustainable use, invasive species, trade and the interface between science and policymaking, and currently serves as assistant director for the U.S. National Invasive Species Council.

Pamela S. Chasek, PhD, is a professor of political science and director of the international studies program at Manhattan College in New York. She is the co-founder and executive editor of the *Earth Negotiations Bulletin*. She has consulted for the UN Environment Programme, the UN Development Programme, the UN Forum on Forests and the UN Department on Economic and Social Affairs. She is the author or editor of numerous articles and books on international environmental policy and negotiations, including *Global Environmental Politics*, 5th edition and *Earth Negotiations*.

Alexandra Conliffe, PhD, is a visiting research associate at the University of Oxford, and was a writer/editor for the *Earth Negotiations Bulletin* from 2005 to 2010. Her recent research has focused on regime linkages in global environmental governance. A former Rhodes scholar, Alexandra has published in *Global Environmental Politics*.

Deborah Davenport, PhD, is author of *Global Environmental Negotiations and US Interests* and numerous other publications, including, as convening lead author, Chapter 5 of the recent second assessment report of the UN Collaborative Partnership on Forests' Global Forest Expert Panel. After directing the environmental work of the Carter Presidential Center in Atlanta, followed by seven years in academia, she is now an independent consultant to various national governments and intergovernmental bodies including FAO and the World Bank. She is also a visiting senior research associate at the Environmental Change Institute of the University of Oxford. She has been a writer/editor for the *Earth Negotiations Bulletin* since 1996.

Joanna Depledge, PhD, is an affiliated lecturer at the Department of Politics and International Studies, Cambridge University (UK). She has published widely on climate change and other environmental issues, including as author of *The Organization of Global Negotiations: Constructing the Climate Change Regime* and co-author of *The International Climate Change Regime: A Guide to Rules, Institutions and Procedures*. Joanna also worked for several years with the UN Climate Change Secretariat, and was a writer/editor for the *Earth Negotiations Bulletin* from 1999 to 2003.

Peter Doran, PhD, is a lecturer in sustainable development and environmental law at the School of Law, Queens University Belfast. His current research and publications address consumerism and sustainable development, critical approaches to green growth and the "Green New Deal," and the introduction of Buddhist philosophical ideas and practices to critical theoretical reflections on politics of transition. He has worked for a number of non-governmental organizations, the Green Party parliamentary team in Dail Eireann in Dublin, and as a researcher in the Northern Ireland Assembly. He has been a writer/editor for the *Earth Negotiations Bulletin* since 1995.

Maria Gutierrez, PhD, works mainly as a consultant to the UNFCCC secretariat on matters related to land use, land-use change, and forestry. She is also in the roster of experts conducting reviews of national communications for the UNFCCC, specializing on adaptation, finance and technology transfer, and education. Her more recent work has centered on building capacity in developing countries, particularly in regards to climate change and forests. She has been a writer for the *Earth Negotiations Bulletin* since 2003.

Reem Hajjar, PhD, is a post-doctoral research fellow at the Faculty of Forestry of the University of British Columbia. Her recent research has focused on community forestry in the Neotropics. Her scholarly articles have recently been published in *Journal of Environmental Management, International Forestry Review, Forests*, and *Agriculture, Ecosystems and Environment*. She has been a writer for the *Earth Negotiations Bulletin* since 2005, as well as the thematic expert on Forests for IISD Reporting Services.

Sikina Jinnah, PhD, is an assistant professor of international relations at the School of International Service at American University, and has written for the *Earth Negotiations Bulletin* since 2007. Her research focuses on the politics of overlapping regimes, and in particular on the role the international secretariats in managing this emerging area of international politics. Her recent work has been published in the *Journal of Environment and Development, Berkeley Journal of International Law Publicist, Environmental Research Letters, Global Environmental Politics, Georgetown International Environmental Law Review*, and *Science*.

Stefan Jungcurt, PhD, is a research fellow at the Institute for Advanced Sustainability Studies (IASS) in Potsdam, Germany. His doctoral studies were in agricultural sciences and he has performed research on the institutional interplay in global environmental governance in the area of genetic resource management. He currently works on knowledge management of global environmental governance issues. Stefan has written for the *Earth Negotiations Bulletin* on biodiversity and related issues since 2003 and has worked as the thematic expert on biosafety for the Biodiversity Policy and Practice knowledge base since 2008.

Pia M. Kohler, PhD, is assistant professor of environmental studies at Williams College. She has been a writer and editor for the *Earth Negotiations Bulletin* since 2002. Her research examines how science is incorporated into global environmental negotiations, in particular within chemicals management treaties.

Her work is published in *International Negotiation* and the *Review of European Community and International Environmental Law.*

Kati Kulovesi, PhD, is post-doctoral researcher at the Law Department of the University of Eastern Finland, and affiliated research fellow at the Erik Castrén Institute of International Law and Human Rights, University of Helsinki. She has been team leader/writer for the *Earth Negotiations Bulletin* since 2004, focusing on climate change negotiations. Her current research focuses on climate change law and her recent publications include the book *WTO Dispute Settlement System: Challenges of Environment and Legitimacy*. She also advises the Finnish government on legal issues related to carbon funds and the Kyoto Protocol's flexibility mechanisms, and participates in an IUCN research project on climate change adaptation law.

Elisa Morgera, PhD, is a lecturer in European environmental law and director of the masters programme in global environment and climate change law at the University of Edinburgh School of Law, UK. She previously worked for the Food and Agriculture Organization and the United Nations Development Programme. Her publications include journal articles on "Corporate Accountability in International Environmental Law" and "The Evolution of Benefit-sharing: Linking Biodiversity and Community Livelihoods," and *Environmental Integration in the EU External Relations: Beyond Multilateral Dimensions*. She has been a writer and team leader for the *Earth Negotiations Bulletin* since 2004.

Sabrina Shaw, PhD, is an IISD associate and has been a writer for the *Earth Negotiations Bulletin* since 2004. Her research focuses on the political economy of sustainable development in the Mekong and Mercosul regions. She taught environmental policy and politics at Chulalongkorn University, Bangkok. Sabrina was a member of the secretariat of the World Trade Organization from 1992 to 2004, serving as secretary to the Committee on Trade and Environment and secretary to several dispute settlement panels (Brazil Aircraft and US Shrimp–Turtle).

Chris Spence is deputy director of IISD Reporting Services. He has also managed the *Earth Negotiations Bulletin*, reporting on climate change from major UN negotiations (1999–2002 and 2005–2009). Chris has written widely on climate change, including *Global Warming: Personal Solutions for a Healthy Planet*. A book chapter on "Climate Change and Energy Insecurity" focused on the role of various UN bodies, including the UN Security Council. He has consulted for various United Nations agencies and other organizations, and was a special advisor to IUCN (2006–2011).

Elsa Tsioumani is a lawyer and consultant in international and European environmental law and policy, with a focus on biodiversity, biosafety, and genetic resources. She has been a team leader, writer, and editor for the *Earth Negotiations Bulletin* since December 1999, and has consulted for several organizations including FAO, IUCN, and the Foundation for International Environmental Law and Development (FIELD). She is also a regular contributor to the *Yearbook on International Environmental Law*, *Environmental Policy and Law*, and UNU Institute of Advance Studies' *Traditional Knowledge Bulletin*.

Lynn M. Wagner, PhD, is the manager/editor of knowledge management projects for IISD Reporting Services. She has also written for the *Earth Negotiations Bulletin* since 1994. She has authored *Problem Solving and Bargaining in International Negotiations*, co-edited a special issue of *International Negotiation Journal* focused on international development negotiations, and authored several other journal articles and book chapters on topics related to international negotiations.

Hugh S. Wilkins is a lawyer with Ecojustice Canada, and specializes in the areas of climate change and natural resources law. Over the past decade, he has worked for the Foundation for International Law and Development (FIELD) and the World Wide Fund for Nature (WWF) (International). Hugh has been a writer and editor for the Earth Negotiations Bulletin since 2002. He is also the managing editor of the *Review of European Community* and *International Environmental Law (RECIEL)* and an adjunct professor at Osgoode Hall Law School in Toronto.

Peter Wood, PhD, is a forest policy consultant and has been a writer and team leader for the *Earth Negotiations Bulletin*, since 2004. He recently contributed as a lead author to the IUFRO Global Forest Expert Panel book *Embracing Complexity: Meeting the Challenges of International Forest Governance*. He has served as an advisor to a number of different policy actors, including the government of British Columbia, West Coast Environmental Law Association, the UNFF, and Global Witness. His areas of interest include forest governance and trade, certification, and reducing emissions from deforestation and forest degradation.

Yulia Yamineva, PhD, was a writer for the *Earth Negotiations Bulletin* from 2007 to 2010, where she primarily covered meetings of the UNFCCC and IPCC. Her PhD research examined the extent to which the IPCC takes a post-normal science approach in its scientific assessments and analyzes five areas of the panel's work: participation, basis for the assessment and policy relevance, treatment of uncertainties, interdisciplinarity, and learning. She is currently working on publications based on the findings of her doctoral thesis. She has also recently consulted for the UNFCCC Secretariat on climate finance issues.

INDEX

References to figures are shown in *italics*. References to tables are shown in **bold**.

ABS Protocol *see* Nagoya Protocol on Access to Genetic Resources and the Fair and Equitable Sharing of Benefits (CBD)

Accra Caucus 143

ACIA (Arctic Climate Impact Assessment) 62

actors, evolution of 12–13, 261–64; *see also* coalitions; non-governmental organizations (NGOs); secretariats

Adaptation Fund/funding 52, 202, 215, 233

Addis Ababa Principles and Guidelines on Sustainable Use of Biodiversity 116, 224

Ad Hoc Joint Working Group on Enhancing Cooperation and Coordination (AHJWG) 121–22, 260; *see also* Basel Convention on the Control of Transboundary Movements of Hazardous Wastes and their Disposal; Rotterdam Convention on the Prior Informed Consent Procedure For Certain Hazardous Chemicals and Pesticides in International Trade; Stockholm Convention on Persistent Organic Pollutants (POPs)

advance informed agreement (AIA) 159–62, 169, 229; *see also* prior informed consent (PIC)

Advisory Group on Greenhouse Gases 64

Africa: CDM projects 25; desertification 154, 155, 200

African Centre for Technology Studies 131

African Group 46, 90, 94–95, 98, 186, 228

African Union 22

Agenda 21 (United Nations): agriculture 188; desertification 154–55, 156; environment-trade debate 175, 176; financial resources 152–53, 169, 264–65; forests 92, 139–40, 207; international law 3; major groups 2; NGOs 140

Agrawala, Shardul 74

agriculture 13, 73–74, 174, 175, 187–92; *see also* International Treaty on Plant Genetic Resources for Food and Agriculture (ITPGR)

Aguilar, Soledad 13, 266

AHJWG *see* Ad Hoc Joint Working Group on Enhancing Cooperation and Coordination (AHJWG)

AIA *see* advance informed agreement (AIA)

Akmuradov, Makhtumkuli *118*

Akwé: Kon Guidelines on Cultural, Environmental and Social Impact Assessments 72

ALBA (Bolivarian Alliance for the
    Peoples of Our America) 99–100,
    185–86, 262
Alliance of Small Island States (AOSIS)
    90, 98, 163; *see also* small island
    developing states (SIDS)
Amazon Group 94–95, 102, 170
Annan, Kofi 255
Appleton, Asheline 12, 262
Arctic Climate Impact Assessment
    (ACIA) 62
Arctic Monitoring and Assessment
    Programme (AMAP) 62, 67
Asia-Pacific Economic Cooperation
    (APEC) 22
Australia: invasive alien species 181–82,
    181; *see also* CANZ; JUSSCANNZ
awareness raising 66–67, 128–29

Bali Action Plan (UNFCCC 2007) 23,
    98, 166, 184
Bali Climate Change Conference
    (UNFCCC COP 13, 2007):
    negotiation process 26, 27, 30; NGOs
    165, *235*; REDD+ 142, *165*, 208;
    trust building 47, 52, 54; *see also*
    Cancún Climate Change Conference
    (UNFCCC COP 16, 2010); climate
    change; Copenhagen Climate Change
    Conference (UNFCCC COP 15,
    2009); United Nations Framework
    Convention on Climate Change
    (UNFCCC)
Bali Declaration 142
Bali Road Map 52, 53
BAM! (Bio Action Montreal) *161*
bandwagoning 13, 119–200, 214–17;
    biodiversity 203–7, 215, 216;
    deforestation 207–10; desertification
    200–203, 216; lessons learned 266;
    ozone 210–14, 216; *see also* issue
    definition; linkages
Basel Convention on the Control
    of Transboundary Movements of
    Hazardous Wastes and their Disposal:
    compliance mechanisms 241; market
    system 257; negotiation process 20, 21,
    24; secretariats 108; *see also* Ad Hoc
    Joint Working Group on Enhancing
    Cooperation and Coordination
    (AHJWG);
BASIC 54, 85, 99, *100*, 164–65, 169
BCH (Biosafety Clearing House) 229,
    239, 244, 266, 283

Big International NGOs (BINGOs)
    131–36, 137–38, 141, 142, 143,
    144–45
biochar 202
biodiversity: bandwagoning 203–7;
    climate change linkages 114–16;
    coalitions 90–91; concept 67, 68–69;
    expert advice 77; NGOs and protected
    areas 130–36, **134**; and trade 179–83;
    treaties and overlap management
    111–16, **112**, 123; trust building 43–46,
    54–55; *see also* Addis Ababa Principles
    and Guidelines on Sustainable Use of
    Biodiversity; Cartagena Protocol on
    Biosafety; climate change; Convention
    on Biological Diversity (CBD);
    Convention on International Trade in
    Endangered Species of Wild Fauna and
    Flora (CITES)
Biodiversity Liaison Group (BLG)
    116, 122
biofuels 24, 188, 189, 191, 206, 214–15
Biosafety Clearing House (BCH) 229,
    239, 244, 266, 283
Biosafety Protocol *see* Cartagena Protocol
    on Biosafety
BirdLife International 132, 136
bloggers, impact on international
    negotiations 31
Bolin, Bert 71
Bolivarian Alliance for the Peoples of
    Our America (ALBA) 99–100,
    185–86, 262
Bonn Agreements on climate change
    (2001) 29
Bonn Convention on Migratory
    Species *see* Convention on Migratory
    Species (CMS)
Boutros-Ghali, Boutros 1
Brand, Ulrich 256
Brazil: climate change 268; deforestation
    190; GMOs 182; *see also* BASIC
Bretton Woods institutions 256
Brundtland, Gro Harlem 2–3
Burgiel, Stanley W. 12, 13, 257, 263, 265
business, and the environment 2, 6,
    77, 264
Business Council for Sustainable
    Development 264

Canada: forests 94, 102; greenhouse
    gases 234, *235*; *see also* CANZ;
    JUSSCANNZ
Cancún Agreements 100, 170, 185, 203

Cancún Climate Change Conference
(UNFCCC COP 16, 2010): agriculture
190; ALBA 99–100; CBD and
UNCCD executive secretaries *204*;
negotiation process 23, 25, 30, 34–35,
200; REDD+ 144, 170, 209; trade
185, *186*; trust building *51*, 53,
54–55; *see also* Bali Climate Change
Conference (UNFCCC COP 13,
2007); climate change; Copenhagen
Climate Change Conference
(UNFCCC COP 15, 2009); United
Nations Framework Convention on
Climate Change (UNFCCC)
CANZ 89
capitalism: and climate change 185–86;
see also market system
carbon capture and storage (CCS) 24
CarbonTradeWatch 77
carbon trading 184, 185–86, 187, 234,
257; *see also* desertification; greenhouse
gases; REDD+; sinks
Caribbean Challenge 135
Caribbean Community 90
Cartagena Dialogue/Group of Progressive
Countries 100–101
Cartagena Protocol on Biosafety:
coalitions 90–91; implementation
and compliance mechanisms 229–30,
239, 244; informal groups 26; issue
definition (LMOs and PIC/AIA)
159–62; negotiation process 20, 21, 28;
trade-environment debate 177, 178,
180, 182; trust building 43–46, 54–55;
see also biodiversity; Convention on
Biological Diversity (CBD)
Casas, Fernando 239
Cash, D. 61
CBD *see* Convention on Biological
Diversity (CBD)
CBD Alliance 135
CCS (carbon capture and storage) 24
CDM *see* Clean Development Mechanism
(CDM)
CDMWatch 77
CEB (Chief Executives Board) 120
cellular phones, impact on negotiations
29, 30–31
Central American Integration System
(SICA) 94–95
CFCs (chlorofluorocarbons) 66, 210–11
Chasek, Pamela S. 10, 13, 259, 265
chemicals governance 120–22, **121**,
123; *see also* Basel Convention on the

Control of Transboundary Movements
of Hazardous Wastes and their Disposal;
Rotterdam Convention on the Prior
Informed Consent Procedure For
Certain Hazardous Chemicals and
Pesticides in International Trade;
Stockholm Convention on Persistent
Organic Pollutants (POPs)
Chief Executives Board (CEB) 120
China: environment versus growth 268;
HFCs 212–13, 214; *see also* BASIC;
G-77 group
chlorofluorocarbons (CFCs) 66, 210–11
Christ, Renata *63*
CITES *see* Convention on International
Trade in Endangered Species of Wild
Fauna and Flora (CITES)
Clean Development Mechanism (CDM):
CDMWatch 77; desertification 201–2;
forests 162–64, 208; HFCs 212, 214;
implementation challenges 233–34;
specialization 24–25
climate change: Adaptation Fund/
funding 52, 202, 215, 233; Bonn
Agreements (2001) 29; coalitions
96–101; and developing countries 50,
54–55, 85, 98–99, 102, 268; linkages
with CBD 114–16; reframing of issue
68–69; and trade 183–87; trust building
50–54; *see also* Bali Climate Change
Conference (UNFCCC COP 13,
2007); biodiversity; Cancún Climate
Change Conference (UNFCCC
COP 16, 2010); Copenhagen Climate
Change Conference (UNFCCC COP
15, 2009); ozone; United Nations
Framework Convention on Climate
Change (UNFCCC)
"Climategate" 207, 214, 216
CMS *see* Convention on Migratory
Species (CMS)
coalitions 12, 39, 54, 85–86, 101–4, **103**;
biodiversity 90–91; climate change
96–101; CSD (sustainable development)
87–90; forests 92–96; lessons learned
262; *see also* trust building
COFO *see* FAO Committee on Forestry
(COFO)
Coimbra, Fernando *96*
Collaborative Partnership on Forests 48
"Comfy Armchair Theory" 51–52, *51*
Commission on Global Governance 255
compliance mechanisms 222, 236,
244; ABS Protocol 239–41, 244;

Cartagena Biosafety Protocol 239, 244;
CBD 238–39; CITES 236–38, 244;
ITPGR 241, 244; UNFCCC and the
Kyoto Protocol 242–43, 244; *see also*
implementation challenges
Compromise Group 43–44, 91, 102
conflict resolution *see* "Track II-type"
techniques; trust building
Conliffe, Alexandra 12, 13, 261, 266
consensus-based model 9, 29, 168–69,
181, 236; *see also* trust building
conservation *see* biodiversity; protected
areas; Saiga antelope conservation;
Saker falcon conservation
Conservation International 131, 132,
133, 136
constructivism, social 41
Convention on Biological Diversity
(CBD): bandwagoning 203–7, 215,
216; COP 2 (1995) 159, 179;
COP 4 (1998) 114, 131, 179;
COP 6 (2002) 181, *181*; COP 7
(2004) 131–32, 133, 134, 135; COP 9
(2008) 25, 75; creation of 2, 130–31;
ExCOP 1 (1999/2000) 28, 43, 45;
forestry 47, 208; genetic resources
75; implementation and compliance
mechanisms 226–29, 238–39, 244,
245; indigenous and local communities
72, 75, 76; living modified organisms
(LMOs) 43, 159–62; and market
system 257; negotiation process 20, 21,
22, 23, 25, 36; and NGOs (protected
areas) 130–36, **134**, *135*, 141;
Open-ended Ad Hoc Working Group
on Biosafety 43; overlap management
with CMS 117; Resource Mobilization
Strategic Plan 227–28; secretariat 108,
113–16; technology transfer 228; and
TEEB Study 69; and trade 174, 175,
179–83; *see also* Biodiversity Liaison
Group (BLG); Cartagena Protocol on
Biosafety; International Indigenous
Forum on Biodiversity; Nagoya CBD
Meeting (COP 10, 2010); Nagoya
Protocol on Access to Genetic
Resources and the Fair and Equitable
Sharing of Benefits (CBD); Subsidiary
Body on Scientific, Technical and
Technological Advice (SBSTTA,
CBD); United Nations Environment
Programme (UNEP)
Convention on International Trade in
Endangered Species of Wild Fauna
and Flora (CITES) 20; expert advice
60; implementation and compliance
mechanisms 223–26, *224*, 236–38,
243–44, 245; and market system 257;
overlap management with CMS 116,
117–18, 120; secretariat 119; *see also*
Biodiversity Liaison Group (BLG)
Convention on Long-Range
Transboundary Air Pollution 67
Convention on Migratory Species (CMS)
3, 116, 117–20, *118*, 123; *see also*
Biodiversity Liaison Group (BLG)
Convention-Protocol framework 110, 263
cooperation-competition paradox
256–57, 265
Copenhagen Accord: coalitions 99;
compliance mechanisms 243;
desertification 202, 203; market
approach 186; negotiation process 29,
31, 52
Copenhagen Climate Change Conference
(UNFCCC COP 15, 2009): ALBA 99,
186; BASIC 85, *100*, 169; European
Union 169; heads of state involvement
35, *35*, 253; HFCs 213; market
system issue 186; negotiation process
21, 23, 25, 29, 31, 33–34; NGOs
(deforestation) *209*; REDD+ 143,
209; trust building 52–53, 54–55,
261; *see also* Bali Climate Change
Conference (UNFCCC COP 13,
2007); Cancún Climate Change
Conference (UNFCCC COP 16,
2010); climate change; United Nations
Framework Convention on Climate
Change (UNFCCC)
Coral Triangle Initiative 136
Countries with Economies in Transition
87, 89, 256
cross-breeding 73–74
CSD *see* United Nations Commission on
Sustainable Development (CSD)

Davenport, Deborah 12, 260
David Shepherd Wildlife Foundation 238
deforestation 162–68, 169, 188–89, 190,
207–10, 216; *see also* desertification;
forests; REDD+; United Nations
Forum on Forests (UNFF)
Depledge, Joanna 10, 259
desertification 154–59, 169, 200–203,
216, 258; *see also* United Nations
Convention to Combat Desertification
(UNCCD)

developing countries: ABS Protocol
(CBD) 240; Adaptation Fund/funding
52, 202, 215, 233; agriculture 174, 189;
Biosafety Protocol (Cartagena) 90–91;
carbon trading 185; CBD Resource
Mobilization Strategy 227–28, 227;
CDM 234; climate change negotiations
50, 54–55, 85, 98–99, 102, 268;
deforestation 162–63; desertification
155, 200; expert identity issues 70–72,
76; finance negotiations (UNCED)
152–54, 169, 264–65; forests and
REDD+ 98, 142, 163–65; GMOs 182;
greenhouse gases 235; LMOs and PIC/
AIA 159–61; MBTOC process 68;
negotiation process 22, 24–25, 26, 33,
36; overlap management 123; protected
areas 131, 133; trade-environment
debate 174, 175, 176, 193, 265; TRIPS
177–78, 184–85; value of human life
issue 73; wildlife trade 224–25; see also
Accra Caucus; G-77 group; Group of
Landlocked Developing Countries;
Group of Mountain Landlocked
Developing Countries; Least Developed
Countries; North-South divide; Pacific
Small Island Developing States; small
island developing states (SIDS)
Djoghlaf, Ahmed 114–15, 115, 155,
204, 205
documentation, proliferation of 25–26

Earth Charter 258
Earth Negotiations Bulletin (ENB): creation
and role xviii–xx, 10, 193, 267; on
financial resources debate 152; on
forests 168; on negotiation process 23,
24, 29, 31, 32, 36; on NGOS 132, 142;
on trust building 45, 51
Earth Summit see Rio Earth Summit
(UNCED 1992)
Earth Summit Bulletin xviii, xix, 10, 29
"Econet," impact on negotiations
29–30
ECOSOC (United Nations Economic and
Social Council) 47, 127, 140–41
Ecosystems Climate Alliance (ECA) 143
EIG (Environmental Integrity Group) 97
Elista International Workshop on the
Saiga antelope 117–18
email, impact on negotiations 29–30
ENB see Earth Negotiations Bulletin (ENB)
endangered species see Convention on
International Trade in Endangered

Species of Wild Fauna and Flora
(CITES)
energy see biofuels
English language, dominance of 25–26, 36
Environmental Integrity Group (EIG) 97
Escobar, Arturo 257
European Commission 88–89
European Community 85, 87, 89
European Free Trade Association 176
European Union (EU): Adaptation Fund
52; Biosafety Protocol negotiations
43–44, 90–91; carbon trading 185, 234;
conferring delegates 88; Copenhagen
Climate Change Conference 169; CSD
negotiations 85–86, 87–89; forests
94–95, 163, 170; GMOs 182; Kyoto
Protocol 169; LMOs 161; technology
transfer 228; trade-environment debate
177; UNFCCC negotiations 97
expert advice see scientific advice
ExxonSecrets 77

Facebook, impact on negotiations 30
FAO (United Nations Food and
Agriculture Organization) 231–32
FAO Committee on Forestry (COFO)
47, 143, 168, 207
farmers' rights 232–33
Fauna and Flora International 133
FERN 141
Figueres, Christiana 53
financial resources (new and additional)
debate 152–54, 169, 264–65
Finger, Matthias 256
food crisis (2008) 191; see also agriculture
Forest Principles 2, 92, 93, 139–40, 167
forests: bandwagoning 207–10; coalitions
92–96; deforestation 162–68, 169,
188–89, 190, 207–10, 216; NGOs
and ITTO 129, 136–39, 138; NGOS
and UNCED (Forest Principles)
139–40; NGOs and UNFF 140–42;
trust building 47–50, 54–55; see also
desertification; Land Use, Land-Use
Change and Forestry (LULUCF);
Non-Legally Binding Instrument on
Forests (NLBI); REDD+; United
Nations Forum on Forests (UNFF)
Forest Stewardship Council (FSC)
138–39, 142, 189, 207
Forest Trends 137
forum shopping 191, 209–10, 215–16;
see also negotiations, intensification of
fragmentation 36, 259–60

"Friends of the Chair" group 27, 34
Friends of the Earth 133, *161*
Friends of the Earth International 134
FSC (Forest Stewardship Council)
    138–39, 142, 189, 207

G-77 85, 102; Biosafety Protocol
    negotiations (Cartagena) 44, 90–91;
    CSD negotiations 87, 89–90; Kyoto
    Protocol negotiations 27–28, 40;
    UNCED finance negotiations 152;
    UNFCCC climate change negotiations
    97–99; UNFF forest negotiations 92,
    93–94, 95
GEF (Global Environment Facility)
    153, 229
General Agreement on Tariffs and Trade
    (GATT) 175, 176–77, 184; *see also*
    World Trade Organization (WTO)
genetically modified organisms (GMOs)
    180, 182–83, 191
genetic resources *see* International
    Treaty on Plant Genetic Resources
    for Food and Agriculture (ITPGR);
    Nagoya Protocol on Access to Genetic
    Resources and the Fair and Equitable
    Sharing of Benefits (CBD)
genetic use-restriction technologies
    (GURTs) 73–74
geo-engineering 24, 114, *206*
Global Environmental Outlook (UNEP
    2007) 258
Global Environment Facility (GEF)
    153, 229
Global Forest Policy Project 140
Global Forest Trade Network (GFTN)
    138
Global Island Partnership (GLISPA)
    135–36
globalization, and governance
    253–58, 270
GMOs (genetically modified organisms)
    180, 182–83, 191
Gnacadja, Luc *204*
Gonzalez, Marco 74
González García, Ginés *51*
Gore, Al 201
Gören-Engfeldt, Lars 40
governance, and globalization
    253–58, 270
green economy 189, 195, 270
greenhouse gases 64, 73, 189–90, 211–14,
    234–35, 258; *see also* carbon trading;
    sinks

Greenpeace 132, 137, *138, 161*
green protectionism 175, 176
Group of 10 (biosafety negotiations)
    43–45, 91
Group of 77 (developing countries)
    see G-77
Group of Landlocked Developing
    Countries 90, 98
Group of Mountain Landlocked
    Developing Countries 100
growth-environment debate 268–69;
    see also trade-environment debate
GURTs (genetic use-restriction
    technologies) 73–74
Gutierrez, Maria 12, 13, 261, 265

Hajjar, Reem 12, 13, 262, 265
heads of state, greater involvement of
    34–36, *35*
Hepworth, Robert *118*
Hodges, Timothy 239
hydrochlorofluorocarbons (HCFCs)
    211–12, 214
hydrofluorocarbons (HFCs) 24, 36, 74,
    211–14, 217

IAF (international arrangement on
    forests) 47, 48–49, 93
identity formation 41–42
IFF (Intergovernmental Forum on
    Forests) 92, 93, 140, 141, 207
IISD (International Institute for
    Sustainable Development) 10
implementation challenges 13, 222–23,
    243–45; ABS Protocol 230–31;
    Biosafety Protocol (Cartagena) 229–30,
    239, 244; CBD 226–29, 244, 245;
    CITES 223–26, *224*, 243–44, 245;
    ITPGR 231–33, 244, 245; lessons
    learned 266–67; UNFCCC and
    the Kyoto Protocol 233–35; *see also*
    compliance mechanisms
India: and HFCs 212–13; *see also*
    BASIC
indigenous and local communities
    (ILCs): expert advice 72, 75, *76*;
    forests negotiations 137, 139, 142,
    143; implementation issues 226, 240;
    protected areas 133–35
industry *see* business
informal groups 26–27
information and communication
    technology (ICT) *see* technological
    revolution

intellectual property rights 177–78,
184–85, 228
Intergovernmental Forum on Forests
(IFF) 92, 93, 140, 141, 207
Intergovernmental Panel Oon Climate
Change (IPCC): adaptation
implementation 203; deforestation 210;
expert advice 63–64, 73, 77; expert
identity issues 70–72; issue framing 67;
Nobel Peace Prize *63*, 71, 201, 261
Intergovernmental Panel on Forests (IPF)
92, 93, 140, 207
Intergovernmental Science-Policy
Platform on Biodiversity and Ecosystem
Services (IPBES) 77
interlinkages *see* linkages
international arrangement on forests
(IAF) 47, 48–49, 93
International Chamber of Commerce 264
International Food Policy Research
Institute *190*
International Forum on Globalization 257
International Indigenous Forum on
Biodiversity 134, *135*
International Institute for Sustainable
Development (IISD) 10
international law 3
International Liaison Group 131
International Panel on Chemical Pollution
(IPCP) 63
International Treaty on Plant Genetic
Resources for Food and Agriculture
(ITPGR) 20, 231–33, 241, 244, 245;
see also genetically modified organisms
(GMOs); genetic use-restriction
technologies (GURTs); International
Tropical Timber Agreement (ITTA)
20, 136–37, 207
International Tropical Timber
Organization (ITTO) 47, 129, 136–37,
138–39, *138*
internet, impact on negotiations 29–30, 31
invasive alien species 181–82
IPBES (Intergovernmental Science-Policy
Platform on Biodiversity and Ecosystem
Services) 77
IPCC *see* Intergovernmental Panel on
Climate Change (IPCC)
IPCP (International Panel on Chemical
Pollution) 63
IPF (Intergovernmental Panel on Forests)
92, 93, 140, 207
issue-based coalitions *see* coalitions

issue definition 13, 72, 129, 151–52,
168–70; deforestation (REDD+)
162–68, 169; desertification (UNCCD)
154–59, *157*, **158**, 169; financial
resources (UNCED) 152–54, 169;
lessons learned 264–65; living modified
organisms (PIC/AIA) 159–62, 169;
see also linkages
issues: evolution of 13, 264–67;
proliferation of 23–25
ITPGR *see* International Treaty on Plant
Genetic Resources for Food and
Agriculture (ITPGR)
ITTA (International Tropical Timber
Agreement) 20, 136–37, 207
ITTO (International Tropical Timber
Organization) 47, 129, 136–37,
138–39, *138*
IUCN (International Union for
Conservation of Nature) 117, 130–31,
132, 137

Jackson, Tim 269
Jasanoff, Sheila 61
Jiabao, Wen *35*
Jinnah, Sikina 12, 13, 200, 205, 263, 266
Johannesburg Plan of Implementation 34
Johannesburg Summit *see* World
Summit on Sustainable Development
(WSSD)
Jungcurt, Stefan 12, 261
JUSCANZ 89
JUSSCANNZ 86, 87, 89, 90–91,
97, 102

Kalpavriksh 134
Kazakhstan: Saiga antelope conservation
117–18, 120
Kindermann, Georg 210
Koester, Veit *46,* 159
Koh, Tommy 3, 40, 44
Kohler, Pia M. 12, 261
Kulovesi, Kati 13, 257, 265
Kyoto Protocol: Adaptation Fund 52,
233; carbon and land use 73; and the
EU 169; greenhouse gases 211–14;
implementation and compliance
mechanisms 233–36, 242–43, 244;
limitations of 50; negotiation process
20, 27–28, 30; trade-climate change
linkage 184; *see also* Bali Action Plan
(UNFCCC 2007); Clean Development
Mechanism (CDM); Marrakesh

Accords; United Nations Framework
Convention on Climate Change
(UNFCCC)

landlocked countries *see* Group of
Landlocked Developing Countries;
Group of Mountain Landlocked
Developing Countries
Land Use, Land-Use Change and
Forestry (LULUCF) 73, 162, 163,
201–2, 208, 233; *see also* forests;
REDD+; United Nations Forum
on Forests (UNFF)
language problems 25–26, 36
laptops, impact on negotiations 31, 32
LBI (legally binding instrument) 93–95
League of Nations 109, 110
"least common denominator agreement"
9, 168, 170
Least Developed Countries (LDCs) 71,
90, 97, 98, 233
Lefeber, René *230*
legally binding instrument (LBI) 93–95
lessons learned 14, 267–70; bandwagoning
266; fragmentation 259–60;
implementation challenges 266–67;
issue-based coalitions 262; issue
definition 264–65; NGOs' increasing
role 263–64; scientific advice 76–78,
261; secretariats' increasing role
262–63; trade-environment
coordination 265–66, 269; trust
building 54–55, 260–61
liberal economics 41
Like-minded Group 43–44, 46, 91
limited membership subsidiary bodies
65–66; *see also* operational advice
linkages: and scientific advice 66–67,
68–69; *see also* bandwagoning;
fragmentation; issue definition;
secretariats, and overlap management;
trade-environment debate
Lisbon Treaty (2009) 88
living modified organisms (LMOs) 43,
159–62, 229, 230
low-carbon technologies 184–85, 187
Lula da Silva, Luiz Inácio *35*
LULUCF *see* Land Use, Land-Use
Change and Forestry (LULUCF)

MA 2005 (Millennium Ecosystem
Assessment) 62, 68–69, 201, 226, 258
Maastricht Treaty (1992) 1, 87

McAlpine, Jan 166, *166*
Major Economies Forum 22, 101
major groups 2, 140, 141, 261
Maldives: Cartagena Dialogue for
Progressive Action 101
Marglin, Stephen, A. 269
market access (agriculture) 187, 188, 189
market system 186, 257, 268
Marrakesh Accords 34, 163, 233, 234,
242–43; *see also* Kyoto Protocol
Marrakesh Agreement (WTO) 177
Mayr, Juan 43–45, 90–91, 102, 260
MBTOC (Methyl Bromide Technical
Options Committee) 68
MDGs (Millennium Development Goals)
48, 201
MEAs *see* multilateral environmental
agreements
media, and international negotiations 31,
33–34
meetings, proliferation of 21–23
Methyl Bromide Technical Options
Committee (MBTOC) 68
Mexico: *Tuna-Dolphin* dispute (1991) 175
Miami Group 43–44, 46, 90–91, 161
Micronesia Challenge 135
migratory species *see* Convention on
Migratory Species (CMS)
Millennium Development Goals (MDGs)
48, 201
Millennium Ecosystem Assessment (MA
2005) 62, 68–69, 201, 226, 258
ministers, greater involvement of 34–36,
35
mobile phones, impact on negotiations
29, 30–31
momentum building 68–69
Mongolia: Saiga antelope 118, *119*; Saker
falcon 237
Montreal Protocol on Substances
that Deplete the Ozone Layer:
bandwagoning 210–14, 216, 217;
expert advice 66, 68, 74; going
paperless 32, *32*; negotiation process 20,
24, 26; secretariat 108; *see also* United
Nations Environment Programme
(UNEP)
Morales, Evo *186*
Morgera, Elisa 13, 266
Müller, Benito 52, 53
multilateral environmental agreements
(MEAs): characteristics and role 7–9;
evolution of actors 12–13, 261–64;

evolution of issues 13, 264–67;
evolution of process 10–12, 259–61;
and globalization 253–58, 270; MEAS
and Protocols lists (1992-2012)
3–6, **11**; *see also* coalitions; lessons
learned; negotiations, intensification
of; scientific advice; secretariats;
technological revolution; treaties; trust
building
multi-stakeholder dialogues (MSD) 141,
142
Muñoz, Miquel 208

Nagoya CBD Meeting (COP 10, 2010):
geo-engineering 114, 206; negotiation
process 21, 25, 26, 28; REDD+ 208;
see also Nagoya Protocol on Access to
Genetic Resources and the Fair and
Equitable Sharing of Benefits (CBD);
Convention on Biological Diversity
(CBD)
Nagoya-Kuala Lumpur Supplementary
Protocol on Liability and Redress 21,
230, *230*
Nagoya Protocol on Access to Genetic
Resources and the Fair and Equitable
Sharing of Benefits (CBD): expert
advice 74–75; implementation and
compliance mechanisms 227, *227*,
230–31, 239–41, 244; and trade
182–83, *183*; *see also* genetically
modified organisms (GMOs); genetic
use-restriction technologies (GURTs);
International Treaty on Plant Genetic
Resources for Food and Agriculture
(ITPGR); Nagoya CBD Meeting
(COP 10, 2010); Convention on
Biological Diversity (CBD)
National Biodiversity Strategy and
Action Plans (NBSAPs) 228–29,
244, 266
national security, impact of environmental
degradation on 269
NDFs (non-detriment findings) 224, 225
negotiations, intensification of 19,
36–37; greater involvement of
ministers/heads of state 34–36, *35*;
impact of technological revolution
29–34; "negotiation by exhaustion"
27–29, *28*; proliferation of documents
25–26; proliferation of informal
groups 26–27; proliferation of issues
23–25; proliferation of meetings

21–23; proliferation of participants
25; proliferation of treaties 20; *see also*
multilateral environmental agreements
(MEAs)
Nelson, Gerald *190*
neoliberalism 41
NGOs *see* non-governmental
organizations (NGOs)
Nieto, Jimena *230*
NLBI (Non-Legally Binding
Instrument on Forests) 49, 50, 92,
93–95, 167, 170
Nobel Peace Prize 1, *63*, 71, 201, 261
non-detriment findings (NDFs) 224, 225
non-governmental organizations (NGOs):
forests and ITTO 136–39, *138*; forests
and REDD+ (UNFCCC) 142–44,
165, 167, 208–9, *209*; forests and
UNCED (Forest Principles) 139–40;
forests and UNFF 140–42; greenhouse
gases (UNFCCC COP 13) *235*;
involvement at negotiations 2, 26, 27,
29, 30, 263–64; and market system 268;
protected areas and CBD 130–36, **134**,
135, 141; roles of 8, 12–13, 127–30,
144–45; and scientific advice 65, 72,
77; trade and CBD 179–80
Non-Legally Binding Instrument on
Forests (NLBI) 49, 50, 92, 93–95,
167, 170
norm entrepreneurs 115–16, 122
North American Free Trade
Agreement 175
North-South divide: blurring of 262;
Cartagena Biosafety Protocol 91;
coalitions 12, 86, 102; desertification
154–55; expert identity issues 72;
forests 92–93, 94, 95–96; sustainable
development 2, 7; UNCED
negotiations 40; UNFCCC discussion
groups 101; UNFCCC negotiations 97,
186–87; *see also* developing countries

Obama, Barack 33–34
Oberthür, Sebastian 30
ODS *see* ozone depleting substances
(ODS)
Organization for Economic Cooperation
and Development (OECD) 87, 89, 97
Organization of Petroleum Exporting
Countries (OPEC) 97, 98
Osman, Nadia *96*
Ott, Hermann 30

overlap management *see* secretariats, and
overlap management
ozone depleting substances (ODS)
211–13; *see also* Montreal Protocol on
Substances that Deplete the Ozone
Layer

Pachauri, Rajendra K. *63*
Pacific Small Island Developing States 90;
see also Alliance of Small Island States
(AOSIS); small island developing
states (SIDS)
paperless conferences 31–32, *32*
participants, number of 25, 52–53
Persistent Organic Pollutants (POPs) *see*
Stockholm Convention on Persistent
Organic Pollutants (POPs)
Philippines: Tebtebba 133
PIC *see* prior informed consent (PIC)
POPs Review Committee (POPRC)
70, *71*, 77
poverty eradication 7, 155, 270
precautionary principle 91, 161, 178,
180, 224
prior informed consent (PIC) 159–62,
169, 231, 240; *see also* advance
informed agreement (AIA); Rotterdam
Convention on the Prior Informed
Consent Procedure For Certain
Hazardous Chemicals and Pesticides
in International Trade
process, evolution of 10–12, **11**, 259–61
Pronk, Jan 34
protected areas 131–36, **134**
protocols and amendments to
treaties (1992-2012) 3, 5–6; *see also*
treaties
public-private partnerships 7, 268

Ramsar Convention on Wetlands 20;
conservation status mechanism 131;
desertification 201; expert advice 60,
72, 77; invasive alien species 182;
overlap management 116; secretariat
108; *see also* Biodiversity Liaison
Group (BLG)
Ranshofen-Wertheimer, Egon F. 109
Rasmussen, Lars Løkke 31
REDD+ 55, 97, 98; bandwagoning
208–10, 215–16; issue definition
162–68, 169–70; and NGOs 142–44,
165; *see also* forests
REDD+ Partnership 143

Rio+20 *see* United Nations Conference
on Sustainable Development (UNCSD)
Rio Conventions 23–24, 25, 65, 108,
168; *see also* Convention on Biological
Diversity (CBD); United Nations
Convention to Combat Desertification
(UNCCD); United Nations
Framework Convention on Climate
Change (UNFCCC)
Rio Declaration on Environment and
Development 2, 175–76, 184
Rio Earth Summit (UNCED
1992): forests 166–67; NGOs
127–28; significance of 1–3, 7,
253; technological revolution
29–30; trade 175–76; *see also* United
Nations Conference on Sustainable
Development (UNCSD)
Rio Group 90
Rio Principles 40
Rotterdam Convention on the Prior
Informed Consent Procedure For
Certain Hazardous Chemicals and
Pesticides in International Trade 20,
21, 66, *88*, 160, 257; *see also* Ad Hoc
Joint Working Group on Enhancing
Cooperation and Coordination
(AHJWG); Russian Federation: Saiga
antelope conservation 117–18

Saiga antelope conservation 117–18, 120
Saker falcon conservation 237
Sandford, Rosemary 110
Sarawak forests 137
Sarkozy, Nicolas 269
SBI (Subsidiary Body for Implementation,
UNFCCC) 23, 25, 233
SBSTA (Subsidiary Body for Scientific
and Technological Advice, UNFCCC)
23, 25, 65
SBSTTA *see* Subsidiary Body on
Scientific, Technical and Technological
Advice (SBSTTA, CBD)
scientific advice 7, 8, 12, 59–61; expert
identity issues 69–72, 77; institutional
structures 61–66; key functions
66–69; lessons learned 76–78, 261;
limitations of expert advice 72–76;
from NGOs 129
secretariats, and overlap management 12,
108–11, 123–24; biodiversity 111–16,
112, 123; chemicals 120–22, **121**, 123;
Chief Executives Board (CEB) 120;

lessons learned 262–63; migratory species 117–20, 123
SFM (sustainable forest management) 92, 95, 139, 166–68, 170
Shaw, Sabrina 13, 257, 265
Shrimp-Turtle decision (2001) 178
SICA (Central American Integration System) 94–95
Singh, Manmohan *35*
sinks 162–63, 189–90, 210, 268; *see also* carbon trading; greenhouse gases
SinksWatch 77
Sjöstedt, Gunnar 8–9
small island developing states (SIDS) 97, 98; *see also* Alliance of Small Island States (AOSIS); Pacific Small Island Developing States
social constructivism 41
social-networking sites, impact on negotiations 30
specialization 24–25, 36
Spector, Bertram I. 8–9
Spence, Chris 12, 260
SPMs (Summaries for Policymakers) 64, 73
state coalitions *see* coalitions
Steiner, Achim 32
Stern Review on the Economics of Climate Change 68–69, 210
Stiglitz Commission 269
Stockholm Conference (1972) *see* United Nations Conference on the Human Environment (UNCHE)
Stockholm Convention on Persistent Organic Pollutants (POPs): expert advice 67, 70, 71, 77; financial resources 153–54; negotiation process 20, 21, 24, 32, 34; *see also* Ad Hoc Joint Working Group on Enhancing Cooperation and Coordination (AHJWG);Strong, Maurice 1–2, 127, 176, 264
subsidiary bodies 64–66;
Subsidiary Body for Implementation (SBI, UNFCCC) 23, 25, 233
Subsidiary Body for Scientific and Technological Advice (SBSTA, UNFCCC) 23, 25, 65
Subsidiary Body on Scientific, Technical and Technological Advice (SBSTTA, CBD): biodiversity-climate change linkage 114, 205; geo-engineering *206*; protected areas 132–33, 135; role of 65, 66, 73–74, 238–39

Summaries for Policymakers (SPMs) 64, 73
sustainable development 3, 6–7, 189, 255, 256–57; *see also* United Nations Commission on Sustainable Development (CSD); United Nations Conference on Sustainable Development (UNCSD)
sustainable forest management (SFM) 92, 95, 139, 166–68, 170

Tebtebba 133
technological revolution, impact on international negotiations 29–34, *32*, *33*
technology transfer 184–85, 228, 233
Tewolde Berhan Gebre Egzibher 46
text messages, impact on international negotiations 30–31
The Economics of Ecosystem Services and Biodiversity (TEEB) Study 69
The Nature Conservancy (TNC) 132, 133, 135, 136
Tolba, Mostafa 63
Töpfer, Klaus 87
"Track II-type" negotiation techniques 12, 40–41, 42–43, 45–46, 48, 55
"Track I" negotiations 42, 43
trade-environment debate 13, 174–79, 192–95; agriculture 187–92; biodiversity 179–83; climate change 183–87; lessons learned 265–66, 269; *see also* growth-environment debate
Trade-related Aspects of Intellectual Property Rights (TRIPS) 177–78, 184–85
TRAFFIC 137, 237
transparency: *Earth Negotiations Bulletin* (ENB) xix, xx, 193; negotiation process 25, 27, 36, 39; scientific advice 68, 77, 78; trade-environment debate 193; trust building 43, 45, 53, 55
treaties 5–6, 20, **112**; *see also* multilateral environmental agreements (MEAs)
Trittin, Jürgen *51*
trust building 12, 39–43; biosafety negotiations (Cartagena Protocol) 43–46, 54–55; climate change (UNFCCC) 50–54; forest negotiations (UNFF) 47–50, 54–55; lessons learned 54–55, 260–61; *see also* coalitions
Tsioumani, Elsa 13, 266
Tuna-Dolphin dispute (1991) 175

Turkmenistan, Saiga antelope conservation
118, *119*
Twitter, impact on international
negotiations 30, 31, 32
"two-meeting rule" 26, 27

Umbrella Group 97, 102
UNCCD *see* United Nations
Convention to Combat Desertification
(UNCCD)
UNCED *see* United Nations Conference
on Environment and Development
(UNCED)
UNCHE (United Nations Conference on
the Human Environment) 2, 6
UNCSD (United Nations Conference on
Sustainable Development) 6–7, 270
UNCTAD (United Nations Conference
on Trade and Development) 136
UNEP *see* United Nations Environment
Programme (UNEP)
UNFCCC *see* United Nations Framework
Convention on Climate Change
(UNFCCC)
UNGA *see* United Nations General
Assembly (UNGA)
United Nations (UN) 1, 120, 261;
see also Agenda 21 (United Nations);
governance, and globalization
United Nations Commission on
Sustainable Development (CSD) 2;
agriculture 188, 189, 191; coalitions
87–90; consumption-production
patterns 268; forests 93, 140;
negotiation process 19, 20, 34; NGOs
127; public-private partnerships 268;
trade-environment debate 195; and
TRIPS 177–78
United Nations Conference on
Environment and Development
(UNCED): agriculture 188; financial
resources 152–54, 169; forests 92,
139–40; NGOs 127–28; PrepCom
IV negotiations (1992) 40, 152, 153;
see also Rio Earth Summit (UNCED
1992); World Summit on Sustainable
Development (WSSD, UNCED)
United Nations Conference on
Sustainable Development (UNCSD)
6–7, 270
United Nations Conference on the
Human Environment (UNCHE) 2, 6
United Nations Conference on Trade and
Development (UNCTAD) 136

United Nations Convention to
Combat Desertification (UNCCD)
20; bandwagoning 200–203, 215;
Committee on Science and Technology
(CST) 65, 68; issue definition 154–59;
ministers' greater involvement 34;
negotiation process 21, 22, 25, 28, 30,
31; secretariat 108; strategic objectives
(2008-2018) *157*, **158**
United Nations Development
Programme 62
United Nations Economic and
Social Council (ECOSOC) 47, 127,
140–41
United Nations Environment Programme
(UNEP) 2, 6; Global Environmental
Outlook (2007) 258; negotiation
process 19, 20; overlap management
114; secretariat 108; technology transfer
228; WTO-UNEP report on trade
and climate change 187, 193; *see also*
Convention on Biological Diversity
(CBD); Intergovernmental Panel on
Climate Change (IPCC); Millennium
Ecosystem Assessment (MA 2005);
World Conservation Monitoring
Centre (WCMC)
United Nations Food and Agriculture
Organization (FAO) 231–32;
Committee on Forestry (COFO)
47, 143, 168, 207
United Nations Forum on Forests
(UNFF): and agriculture 189;
deforestation 207; and NGOs 140–42;
and REDD+ 165–66; trust building
47–50; UNFF 4 (2004) 47; UNFF
5 (2005) 47–50, 92, 93–95, 141–42;
UNFF 6 (2006) 49, 94, 95, 142;
UNFF 7 (2007) 28, *28*, 49, 92,
94–95, 142; UNFF 8 (2009) 92, 95–96,
96, 166, 167–68; *see also* forests;
Non-Legally Binding Instrument on
Forests (NLBI);
United Nations Framework Convention
on Climate Change (UNFCCC):
Ad Hoc Working Group on
Long-term Cooperative Action 201;
agriculture 189; bandwagoning and
CBD 205–6; bandwagoning and
UNCCD 201–3; coalitions 96–100;
COP 3 (Kyoto, 1997) 25, 30, 54;
COP 6 (The Hague, 2000) 34; COP
11 (Montreal, 2005) 142, 163–64,
208; COP 14 (Poznan, 2008) 143;

expert advice 73; forests 47 (*see also*
REDD+); HFCs 212; implementation
and compliance mechanism 233–36,
242–43, 244; ministers' greater
involvement 34; negotiation process
20, 21, 25, 26, 28, 30; origin of 2,
67, 93; secretariat 108; and trade
174, 175, 183–87, 194; trust building
50–53, 54–55; *see also* Bali Action
Plan (UNFCCC 2007); Bali Climate
Change Conference (UNFCCC
COP 13, 2007); Cancún Climate
Change Conference (UNFCCC
COP 16, 2010); Copenhagen Climate
Change Conference (UNFCCC
COP 15, 2009); Kyoto Protocol;
Marrakesh Accords; Subsidiary Body
for Implementation (SBI, UNFCCC);
Subsidiary Body for Scientific and
Technological Advice (SBSTA,
UNFCCC)
United Nations General Assembly
(UNGA): 38/161 resolution 2; 44/228
resolution 3, 152; 64/236 resolution
270; 65/276 resolution 89; negotiation
process 19, 22
United Nations World Meteorological
Organization (WMO) 63
United States: carbon trading
185; Department of Energy 64;
Environmental Protection Agency 64;
GMOs 182; LMOs and PIC/AIA 160;
National Wildlife Federation 137; and
Rio Declaration 176; *Shrimp-Turtle*
decision (2001) 178; *Tuna-Dolphin*
dispute (1991) 175; UNCED finance
negotiations 152–53, 169; *see also*
Major Economies Forum
UN-REDD 143
Uzbekistan: Saiga antelope conservation
118, *119*

Vienna Convention for the Protection of
the Ozone Layer 20, 66, 211–12; *see
also* Montreal Protocol on Substances
that Deplete the Ozone Layer
Vienna Setting 44, *44*, 45, 91, 260

Wagner, Lynn M. 12, 87, 260, 262
"Washington Consensus" 255
WCED (World Commission on
Environment and Development) 2–3

WCMC (World Conservation Monitoring
Centre) 124, 237
Wijnstekers, Willem 223
Wildlife Conservation Society 132
wildlife trade 224–25; *see also* Convention
on International Trade in Endangered
Species of Wild Fauna and Flora
(CITES)
Wilkins, Hugh 13, 266
Willis, Jim 122
Wood, Peter 12, 263
World Bank 62, 143, 268
World Commission on Environment
and Development (WCED) 2–3
World Conservation Monitoring
Centre (WCMC) 124, 237
World Food Security Conference
189, 191
World Heritage Convention 116;
see also Biodiversity Liaison Group
(BLG)
World Meteorological Organization
(WMO) 63
World Resources Institute 62, 131, 132
World Summit on Sustainable
Development (WSSD) 6, 34, *44*, 153,
267–68
World Trade Organization (WTO):
agriculture 187–88, 189, 191, 193;
Biosafety Protocol (Cartagena)
180–81, 182, 183; Cancún ministerial
conference (2003) 178, 182;
climate change 183–85, 187, 194;
desertification 201; Doha Round 178,
187; globalization 256, 257; GMOs
180; and NGOs 141, 179; Seattle
ministerial conference (1999) 178, 182;
trade-environment debate 13, 174–79,
192–93, 195, 265; Uruguay Round
175, 176–77, 187
World Wide Fund for Nature (WWF):
forests 137–38, 139, 142; protected
areas 130, 132, 133, 135, 136
WTO Agreement on Agriculture 187
WTO Committee on Trade and
Environment 177, 192, 193

Yamineva, Yulia 12, 261

Zartman, I. William 8–9
Zukang, Sha *166*
Zuma, Jacob *35*